Culturally Diverse Parent-Child and Family Relationships

A Guide for Social Workers and Other Practitioners

Edited by
NANCY BOYD WEBB

Foreword by
DOMAN LUM

COLUMBIA UNIVERSITY PRESS
New York

Columbia University Press Publishers
Since 1893
New York, Chichester, West Sussex

Copyright © 2001
Columbia University Press
All rights reserved

Library of Congress Cataloging-in-Publication Data

Culturally diverse parent-child and family relationships : a guide for
social workers and other practitioners / edited by Nancy Boyd Webb ;
foreword by Doman Lum
   p. cm.
   Includes bibliographical references and index.
   ISBN 0-231-11818-X (alk. paper)
   1. Cross-cultural counseling. 2. Social work with minorities. 3. Minorities—
Counseling of. 4. Parent and child. 5. Child rearing. I. Webb, Nancy Boyd, 1932– .
  BF637.C6 C776 2001
  361'.06—dc21
  2001017260

Printed in the United States of America
c 10 9 8 7 6 5 4 3 2 1

Culturally Diverse Parent-Child and Family Relationships

This book is lovingly dedicated to the memory of my parents, Angie and Earl Boyd; to my sisters, Charlotte and Barbara; to my husband, Kempton, my children and their spouses: Rachel and Bill, and Scott and Rosemary, and to my precious grandchildren, Katherine Scott, Sophia Webb, and Preston Webb. They each have taught me about the depth and breadth of family and of love.

CONTENTS

LIST OF CASE STUDIES

Nancy Boyd Webb, Fordham University Distinguished Professor of Social Work, has made a major contribution to culturally diverse social work practice with her *Culturally Diverse Parent-Child and Family Relationships: A Guide for Social Workers and Other Practitioners*. She is a seasoned scholar who has written *Play Therapy with Children in Crisis*, *Helping Bereaved Children*, and her major work, *Social Work Practice with Children*. This latest book follows in the footsteps of previous volumes: Ho, *Family Therapy with Ethnic Minorities* (1987); Gibbs and Huang, *Children of Color* (1989); and Ho, *Minority Children and Adolescents in Therapy* (1992). However, unlike these works, *Culturally Diverse Parent-Child and Family Relationships* closely covers the interaction between ethnic parents and children and, in this sense, offers a unique and singular emphasis for social work education and practice.

Focusing on the influence of cultural factors on parent-child and family relationships, Dr. Webb makes the case for the importance of the cultural and ethnic self-awareness of the practitioner; the different cultural value beliefs and child-rearing practices of ethnic parents; and the need for an ecological-cultural perspective on development.

Dr. Webb has assembled an outstanding group of contributors, each of whom has a particular message to impart about their topic and expertise area. Elaine P. Congress reviews the legal and ethical context and issues for children and presents the ETHIC model of decision making, which provides guidelines to measure and arrive at a basis for ethical practice. Brenda Williams-Gray offers a framework for culturally responsive practice that revolves around historical, cultural, and social-environmental factors on parent-child relationships.

The core of *Culturally Diverse Parent-Child and Family Relationships* is the five culture groups (African American, Latino, Native American, Asian American, and European American families), focusing on parent-child relationships and parenting patterns.

Harriette Pipes McAdoo provides essential family, parent, and child background on the dynamics of African American families. Of particular importance is her explanation of ethnic socialization, developmental stages of racial attitudes, and interactions with authority figures. Claudette P. J. Crawford-Brown and Melrose Rattray interpret the migration dilemmas of Caribbean families, especially a model of children's behavioral-emotional responses to migration, the effect of migration on the family upon reunification, and policy and practice recommendations for prevention and service.

Luis H. Zayas, Ian Canino, and Zulema E. Suárez emphasize the child-rearing and parenting strengths of mainland Puerto Rican families with a strong sense of familism, family roles, parenting and child-rearing values, and independence within an adolescent-parent familial relationship. Eunice C. Garcia identifies issues related to Mexican American child rearing: the barrio as a support system, religious traditions, family roles and systems, help-seeking and healing practices, and fifteen principles of culturally competent practice. Teresa Bevin discusses Cuban American parenting in families in terms of the waves of exodus from Cuba; child-rearing, parenting, and family issues (economics, values, and rites of passage); and practice approaches and attitudes.

Geri Glover, in discussing parenting in Native American families, identifies such parenting and family issues as interfacing with the dominant culture and keeping young people close to the tribe; parenting and family relationship involving acculturation levels; values; adolescent development; child abuse and neglect; and practice principles.

Concerning Asian American families, Shi-Jiuan Wu interprets parenting as a process of negotiation for Chinese American families (between mother and father, between parental and societal values, between children's experience in the world and at home, and between parents and children); she covers the spectrum from traditional to Western parenting practices hinging on the degree of family acculturation, Chinese value adherence, family diversity and evolving roles, the fit between parents' and teachers' values, and the children's adjustment; she presents a focus group pilot study of Chinese American parents; and she offers clinical guidelines for working with parents. Monit Cheung and Sabrina My Hang Nguyen focus on interpersonal barriers in parent-child relationship building, Vietnamese family values, three types of Vietnamese parents (traditional, bicultural, integrated), and practice principles for relating to Vietnamese parents and children. Tazuko Shibusawa writes about Japanese American parent-child relationships (developmental goals, education, child rearing, communication patterns), biracial and multiracial Japanese American children, and eight assumptions of clinical practice.

Peg McCartt Hess and Howard J. Hess discuss parenting in European American/white families and confront whiteness and racial identity, leading the reader through six statuses in a recognition and abandonment of white privilege (contact, disintegration, reintegration, pseudo-independence, immersion/emersion, and autonomy). They also identify seven norms and values characterizing the white culture, European American child development frameworks, and practice guidelines for working with white families.

Nancy Boyd Webb discloses her personal journey of understanding cultural diversity and emphasizes the need to tailor any guideline to the unique cultural situation of the individual client. She is an advocate of "culturally friendly" direct practice. She leads the reader through the critical practice process stages, and she covers such topics as the inclusion of the client's support network members and the use of the same or different ethnic group practitioners. She also discusses linear and relational worldviews.

Dr. Webb further focuses on culturally competent and responsive practice, professional program curriculum policies on multicultural content, curriculum models for delivering diversity, and practitioner education about culturally diverse practice.

Culturally Diverse Parent-Child and Family Relationships: A Guide for Social Workers and Other Practitioners is like a Chinese nine-course dinner. It provides such a variety of tasty food for thought, with each successive course offering surprising delicacies, that one is pleasantly filled with culinary joy over partaking the meal as an invited guest. There are so many sections of this book that I want to incorporate in my teaching as I begin my next semester in my university. Nancy Boyd Webb has covered all the bases in her topic of culturally diverse parent-child practice. I welcome this milestone text, which will be recognized as a cornerstone in the development of the social work diversity and populations-at-risk literature. It is a hallmark book that truly confirms that social work education and culturally diverse practice have turned a new corner as we begin the twenty-first century of reflecting, teaching, researching, and writing.

DOMAN LUM, PH.D, TH.D
Professor of Social Work
California State University, Sacramento

The questions from my social work students about how to work effectively with clients whose values and child-rearing practices diverged strongly from their own convinced me that we needed a book to help them and other counseling, psychology, and marriage and family students. Student internships in graduate programs in the metropolitan New York area increasingly include case assignments of clients from a variety of cultures, some of which use child-rearing methods that differ drastically from those of the mainstream white students who have been assigned to work with them. I am sure that these experiences are not unique to the New York area. Even social work students who have completed a mandatory course on oppression and social justice have trouble translating the principles of nonjudgmental practice in their firsthand work with clients whose values differ from their own.

My own interest in this topic has been lifelong, beginning in my school years in a working-class city near Boston, where I grew up as part of a WASP minority within a culturally diverse community populated by Italians, Irish, and Jews. Although I was a member of the "majority" culture in our current terminology, I felt almost like a foreigner in a white community with very few classmates who were Protestants. One of my memories related to cultural diversity was going to the movies on Saturday and being responsible for paying for my Jewish friends' admission because they were not allowed to handle money on their Sabbath. My Jewish friends were my peers in school, but on Sundays we went our separate ways, related to our different religious practices and youth activities.

Courses in cultural anthropology at Radcliffe/Harvard with Clyde Klukholm and others allowed me to read and fantasize about exotic people and think seriously about following Margaret Mead's example in conducting field work with families and children. In my junior year I obtained a summer job in France, teaching swimming at a French camp where almost no one spoke English. I was immersed in a different culture in which I witnessed young children given watered red wine, bread, and chocolate for lunch. Every day! There was also a main course, but given my teetotaling family background, I remember only the wine.

Three years later I married and began an extended period of residence in Brazil (three years) and travel in Latin America, related to my husband's profession as a cultural geographer. Since then we have traveled and lived for extended periods in Portugal, Mexico, Ecuador, Britain, Australia, China, northern and southern Africa, and Canada. I have had the experience of taking a black pregnant maid to a maternity hospital in Recife, Brazil, where the staff assumed I was "family" because I accompanied her, despite our obvious differences in skin color. Several years later, I had a different kind of cultural surprise when a New Zealander third-grade teacher in Lisbon thought that it was acceptable to rap my seven-year-old son on the knuckles with a ruler because he answered a math question incorrectly.

These experiences, and many others over the course of more than thirty years, have made me acutely aware of the role of cultural expectations in how people conduct their lives. Whenever I return "home" I see facets of middle-class white America of which I had been previously unaware. This comment may sound trite, but my reflections about my experiences in Latin and Asian cultures made me aware of the very pronounced differences between mainstream American family life and values and those of families in other continents with different histories and beliefs.

Because of my experiences in Brazil and other countries, I have always enjoyed relationships with people from different cultures. As a doctoral student at Columbia University in the 1970s, I joined a small study group to prepare for the comprehensive exams. The group consisted of two African Americans (Sadye Logan and Jim Pope), a Mexican American (Rudolpho Borrego), and myself. We would spend all day Saturdays studying together in one another's homes or apartments. As Sadye commented recently, "We were a working multicultural group, and we didn't even know it!"

The purpose of this book is to sensitize practitioners in a general way about the material presented. The chapters are not intended to present "one definitive profile" of any racial or ethnic group, because such a profile would be impossible and would negate the vast differences that exist within all groups. The purpose, instead, is to help practitioners develop awareness about the significant differences and similarities between their own views and those they are likely to encounter in their work with parents and children from diverse backgrounds. I hope that as a result of this book, counselors will understand more fully the importance of awareness of their own cultural identity as well as that of their clients. This recognition is essential to culturally friendly and responsive practice.

As a social work educator who also maintains a practice as a child and family therapist, I view this book as a bridge to help practitioners work more effectively with multicultural families. I have found that understanding other cultures is not easy, even after my several years of residence in different countries. However, I have always felt rewarded by the efforts I made, and I hope that this book, in its own way, proves equally rewarding to readers who are looking to expand their horizons and enter a new world of understanding and empathy as they carry out their work.

ACKNOWLEDGMENTS

Many people have helped to bring this book to publication. I deeply appreciate the contributions of the chapter authors, who worked steadily and patiently to write and rewrite their chapter drafts over the course of several months. Authors for whom English is a second language deserve special recognition. I am proud of the authors' diversity of backgrounds, and I know that they have brought insider knowledge and insights that illuminate the challenges of working with culturally diverse clients.

We all benefited from the suggestions of a group of readers who served as expert consultants, offering reactions and suggestions that were incorporated into the revised chapters. These professional colleagues, to whom I am most grateful, include (in alphabetical order): Dorcas Bowles, Douglas Davies, Laura Lee, Sadye Logan, Margarita Suarez, Zulema Suárez, William Tu, Suzanne Hall Vogel, and Shu-Chen Wu.

My doctoral assistant at Fordham, Roxia Bullock, helped track down many references, and my other student assistants, Stephanie McTigue and Kieran Delamere, handled photocoping, mailing, and other secretarial functions with efficiency and good spirit. As office manager, Marla Mendillo has consistently and calmly helped in numerous ways, including creating tables and figures for the book, obtaining permissions, and helping maintain the momentum of this project. Two librarians have located essential references: Mary Toor at Marymount College, and Christine Campbell at Fordham. All these people have helped me during various stages of preparing this book, and I am grateful to them.

Many of the chapter authors contributed photographs to portray children and families from diverse cultures. They knew that the people in the pictures would not be identified and that the photos would be inserted at the editor's and printer's discretion. I wish to thank the following people who contributed pictures for inclusion: Teresa Bevin, Monit Cheung, Eunice Garcia, Harriette McAdoo, Sabrina Nguyen, Zulema Suárez, Brenda Williams-Gray, Shu-Chen Wu, and Shi-Jiuan Wu.

Once again, my former dean, Mary Ann Quaranta, has appreciated and supported the time constraints involved with a project of this magnitude. Her commitment to the field of multicultural practice has been very evident in her efforts to hire culturally diverse faculty and to ensure that the standards of CSWE regarding diversity are reflected in Fordham's curriculum. As Dean Quaranta stepped down from the deanship in October 2000, she could feel proud that her leadership over the past twenty-five years has reflected and encouraged the faculty's commitment to social justice.

Finally, and primarily, I wish to thank and recognize my husband, Kempton, who has helped with this book in countless ways ranging from trivial to substantive. He read and coedited almost all the chapters, kept me stocked with priority mail envelopes, and worried along with me when a chapter was late or an author abruptly moved or left the country. I believe that the book has benefited from Kempton's astute comments based on his professional background as a cultural geographer and Latin American specialist. This book has been the most difficult one I have ever undertaken, and many times Kempton has commented, "You're *not* going to do another edited book again, are you?" It has been a lot of work, but his enthusiasm and spirit buoyed me up on a daily basis. It was his suggestion to include photos of each author and of children and families. He clips and marks related articles in the *New York Times* and has made a number of important contacts related to getting permission to use copyrighted photographs. I feel very fortunate and blessed to have a husband who is a collaborator and a friend in addition to being supportive, funny, and loving. I love him, and I am grateful to him and for our life together.

 Nancy Boyd Webb, D.S.W., B.C.D., R.P.T.-S., is a leading authority on child and family therapy. She has been on the faculty of the Fordham University Graduate School of Social Service since 1979 and was appointed in the fall of 1997 to the rank of University Distinguished Professor of Social Work. She established the Post-Master's Certificate Program in Child and Adolescent Therapy in 1985 at Fordham to meet the need in the metropolitan New York area for training in play therapy. She teaches courses in crisis intervention, death and dying, social work practice with children, and play therapy.

She has an international reputation as an educator and has given more than 100 invited presentations and staff trainings in the United States as well as in Australia, Britain, Ecuador, Taiwan, Hong Kong, and Canada. She is widely published in the field of social work and play therapy, especially on topics related to children and families, trauma, and bereavement. Her works include the books *Play Therapy with Children in Crisis, Helping Bereaved Children,* and *Social Work Practice with Children,* and an award-winning video, *Techniques of Play Therapy.* She also maintains a clinical practice as a child and family therapist and supervises and consults with schools and agencies.

Teresa Bevin, M.A., is Professor, Mental Health Program, Montgomery College, Takoma Park, Maryland. Born in Cuba, Teresa Bevin moved to Spain in 1969 and to the United States in 1972. For thirty years she has been dedicated to the welfare and mental health of culturally diverse children and families throughout the metropolitan Washington D.C. area.

Ian A. Canino, M.D., is Deputy Director of Training in Child and Adolescent Psychiatry and Clinical Professor of Psychiatry at Columbia University College of Physicians and Surgeons. Dr. Canino has authored books, articles, and chapters in the field of cross-cultural child psychiatry. He has been widely recognized for his dedication to children at risk for major psychiatric disorders, and is the cofounder of CARING, an organization that helps inner-city children-at-risk through the arts and literature. He has received several awards, including the Rafael A. Tavares Academic Award, the Lauretta Bender Award, and the Outstanding Mentor for the Presidential Scholar Award from the American Academy of Child and Adolescent Psychiatry.

Monit Chueng, Ph.D., LMSW-ACP, is Associate Professor, Chair of Children and Families Concentration, and Associate Director of the Child Welfare Education Project at the University of Houston Graduate School of Social Work. She is also Director of Clinical Service at the Asian American Family Counseling Center, specializing in counseling Asian families, child and adolescent counseling, and incest survivor treatment. In the 1970s, she worked at a UNHRC Vietnamese refugee camp in Hong Kong as Social Assistance Program Coordinator.

Elaine P. Congress, D.S.W., is Professor and Director of the Doctoral Program at Fordham University Graduate School of Social Service. She has published two books, *Multicultural Perspectives in Working with Families* and *Social Work Values and Ethics: Identifying and Resolving Professional Dilemmas,* as well as more than twenty journal articles and book chapters on cultural diversity and social work ethics. Dr. Congress is the President of the New York City chapter of the National Association of Social Workers.

Claudette P. J. Crawford-Brown, Ph.D., has been a lecturer in the Department of Sociology and Social Work at the University of the West Indies for the past twenty years. She is now an Associate Professor at the Springfield College School of Social Work in Massachusetts. Dr. Crawford-Brown is the founder and chairperson of The Children's Lobby of Jamaica and had been an advocate for the rights of children in Jamaica and the Caribbean for more than twenty years. Her most recent publications include a book, *Who Will Save Our Children: The Plight of the Jamaican Child in the Nineties,* and a chapter titled The Impact of Parent-Child Socialization on Conduct Disorder in Jamaican Male Adolescents in the book *Caribbean Families* (edited by Roopnarine and Brown).

Eunice C. Garcia, M.S.W., is an Adjunct Instructor, The University of Texas in Austin. Her thirty- year career has focused on teaching social work practice courses and the field practicum. She designed and regularly teaches an elective course on Social Work with Mexican American Families. She also works with a number of community agency boards and advisory groups. Eunice Garcia immigrated from Mexico with her parents and three sisters in 1950. She regularly celebrates holidays and attends cultural events as a way of updating her knowledge about Mexican people and their communities.

Geri Glover, Ph.D., has been working with children, their parents, and other adults for more than thirteen years in education, day treatment programs, and mental health clinics. She is a nonenrolled member of the Salish Tribe through her father, who was born and raised on the Flathead Reservation in northern Montana. Her dissertation research was on filial therapy with Native American families residing on the Flathead Reservation. She is coeditor of a book, *Play Therapy Interventions with Children's Problems,* and author of a chapter titled Multicultural Considerations in Group Play Therapy in *The Handbook of Group Play Therapy* (edited by Homeyer and Sweeney). She is a strong advocate of multicultural awareness and provides training workshops regarding its importance.

Howard J. Hess, D.S.W., is former Associate Dean and Professor, Fordham University Graduate School of Social Service in New York City. Dr. Hess has written extensively on the topics of social work practice in health and mental health, with an emphasis on families dealing with HIV/AIDS. He completed a Master's in Divinity at The Yale Divinity School and has a particular interest in the relationship between social work and spirituality. He is currently Assistant Rector at the St. Thaddeus Episcopal Church in Aiken, South Carolina.

Peg McCartt Hess, Ph.D., is Associate Dean and Professor, Columbia University School of Social Work. Dr. Hess has recently concluded a three-year study of the innovative programs of the Center for Family Life in Brooklyn, New York, and is working on a book reporting the study findings. Dr. Hess's practice experience has included clinical supervision and program development in services for children separated from their parents because of foster case placement or divorce. She has also consulted with agencies that provide intensive services to families at risk for breakup because of child neglect and abuse.

Harriette Pipes McAdoo, Ph.D., is a professor in the Department of Family and Child Ecology, College of Human Ecology, Michigan State University. She is editor of *Black Families, Family Ethnicity: Strengths in Diversity* and coedited with her late husband, John McAdoo, Ph.D., *Black Children: Social, Educational, and Parental Environments*. She has also published on upward mobility in black families, single mothers, values of parents, and parent-child interactions.

Sabrina My Hang Nguyen, M.Ed., is completing her Ed.D. degree at the University of Houston, specializing in multicultural education. Her focus is on Asian and, particularly, Vietnamese American students and parents. She is a Vietnamese-born American who has been an educator for the last thirteen years. She has lectured nationwide on cultural and educational topics to both American and Vietnamese audiences.

J. Melrose Rattray, M.S.W., is a graduate of McGill University and the University of the West Indies. She lectured at the University of the West Indies for fifteen years in the field of social work. She is the founder and director of Help for Parents, a private agency in Kingston, Jamaica, that provides counseling and training in parent education. She recently assumed a position with the Research Foundation (CUNY) as lecturer and program coordinator at Medgar Evers College in Brooklyn, New York.

Tazuko Shibusawa, Ph.D., is an Assistant Professor at the Columbia University School of Social Work. She has extensive experience as a clinical social worker specializing in individual, marital, and family therapy in both the United States and Japan. She has published many journal and chapter articles in both English and Japanese and has given numerous invited international and national presentations on topics related to cross-cultural perspectives in counseling Asians.

Zulema E. Suárez, Ph.D., is an Associate Professor in the Graduate School of Social Service of Fordham University. She is a Cuban-born Research Associate at Fordham University's Center for Hispanic Mental Health Research, where she is examining coping and resiliency among low-income African American and Latina women of childbearing age. Dr. Suárez teaches clinical practice and has written several chapters and articles about Cuban Americans, Hispanics' access to health care, and multicultural and feminist social work practice.

Brenda C. Williams-Gray, C.S.W., is Vice President for Community Youth Progams, Family Service of Westchester, White Plains, New York. She is an Adjunct Instructor at the Fordham University Graduate School of Social Service and is a Doctoral candidate in social work at Hunter College, City University of New York. Her interests and expertise are in the areas of trauma, resiliency, child and family treatment, and cultural diversity. She published a chapter on children in war in the second edition of *Play Therapy with Children in Crisis* (edited by Webb).

Shi-Jiuan Wu, Ph.D., is an Assistant Professor, Department of Counseling and School Psychology, University of Massachusetts, Boston, Massachusetts. She also is affiliated with the Marriage and Family Therapy Program of Saint Joseph College in West Hartford, Connecticut. Born in Taiwan, she received her advanced degrees in the United States, where she has been employed in family programs of several child welfare agencies over the past ten years. She has published several chapters on counseling Chinese families. Her research interests are in the area of multicultural counseling and family therapy with Chinese American families.

Luis H. Zayas, Ph.D., is a Professor at the Graduate School of Social Service of Fordham University in New York City and Director of the Center for Hispanic Research. Dr. Zayas's clinical and research interests are in the areas of child and adolescent mental health, parent-child relations, Hispanic and minority mental health, family functioning, and child rearing in different cultures. His research has been supported by the National Science Foundation,

National Institute of Mental Health, Ford Foundation, the National Research Council, and the Alcoholic Beverage Medical Research Foundation. Dr. Zayas received the 1993 Economic and Cultural Diversity Award from the American Family Therapy Academy in recognition of his work with AIDS orphans and their families.

PART 1

Parent-Child Relationships

A Culturally Responsive Strengths Perspective

CHAPTER 1

Working with Culturally Diverse Children and Families

NANCY BOYD WEBB

The social work profession has taught generations of students to "start where the client is," thereby emphasizing the importance of trying to understand all facets of a person and his or her situation in the process of making an assessment and setting goals for intervention. Some educators refer to this basic practice principle as "tuning in" (Shulman, 1999), a process that highlights the role of empathy as a starting point for helping. When a client comes from a background and culture similar to that of the practitioner, the tuning-in process may seem easy. However, it would be simplistic and inaccurate to assume that mere similarity of ethnicity, race, or culture will guarantee a meeting of the minds and feelings in contacts between a practitioner and a client. The tuning-in process is complex and depends on much more than commonalities of race and language to unite two individuals in a relationship of mutual respect and understanding.

This chapter, which serves as an introduction to the book, focuses on the influence of cultural factors on parent-child and family relationships. Because everybody's cultural identity inevitably affects his or her manner of communication with others, professionals must be aware of their *own* cultural persona and assumptions even as they attempt to understand the viewpoints and beliefs of their clients. Based on a strengths perspective (Cowger, 1994; DeJong & Miller, 1995; Hwang & Cowger, 1998; McQuaide & Ehrenreich, 1997; Saleebey, 1992; Weick, 1992), this chapter emphasizes the importance of a practitioner's self-awareness as the starting point for trying to understand others, whether they are of similar or different cultural backgrounds. Practitioners must realize that they, like their clients, reflect the values and beliefs of their respective culture and family and that it is unethical to "judge" the client who has beliefs about life and relationships that differ from those of the practitioner. Of course, there are limits to cultural relativism; in situations of violence or abuse, the practitioner must abide by legal mandates, as is discussed in chapter 2.

Families reveal their values in the way in which they socialize their children. However, many other influences in the community and school also affect children's development. Often children become confused when they encounter beliefs in the outside world that differ from those in their homes. Children whose cultural backgrounds are distinct from those of their classmates may become uncomfortable when they realize that they and their families are "different." Frequently, the child and family come into contact with school personnel who are unfamiliar with their family's language or their cultural values. The culturally based differences between the school's and family's expectations can have serious impact on a child's social and educational development, as various case studies in this book illustrate.

This chapter discusses the impact of cultural and family influences on child development in the context of the increasing numbers of culturally diverse people in the United States. The pivotal role of cultural values and beliefs regarding child rearing is emphasized using a nonjudgmental, strengths perspective rather than a "deficits" model focused on pathology. The chapter concludes with a discussion of methods to help practitioners review and assess their own values and beliefs as a basis for working with culturally diverse clients.

TERMINOLOGY

Definitions of the terms *culture, ethnicity,* and *race* come from the Council on Social Work Education's (CSWE) course outlines that contain content on racial, ethnic, and cultural diversity (Devore & Fletcher, 1997). It is important to recognize that there is a great deal of overlapping between these terms and that the concepts are complex, evolving, and not static (Laird, 1998).

Culture

The concept of culture includes learned knowledge, beliefs, arts, morals, laws, and customs of the members of a society. It encompasses the worldview, thoughts, behaviors, and communication patterns of persons affiliated with the culture (Chadiha, Miller-Cribbs, & Wilson-Klav, 1997). Another definition describes culture as the collective behavior patterns, communication styles, values, institutions, standards, and other factors unique to a community that are socially transmitted to individuals who are expected to conform (Banks, 1991).

Ethnicity

The concept of ethnicity refers to "the identification of people with a group on the basis of loyalty and consciousness for the group. Ethnicity includes national origin and cultural heritage" (Chadiha et al., 1997, p. 119). Another definition describes ethnicity as a sense of peoplehood and connectiveness based on commonalities of nationality, religion, region, ancestry, history, language, economics, and political interests; because specific aspects of cultural patterns are shared, their transmission over time creates a common history (Banks, 1991).

Race

The term *race* refers to a biological classification of people who have similar physical characteristics. Within a given racial group, there are considerable cultural differences according to ethnicity, geography, religion, class, and history (Banks, 1991).

The literature on cultural diversity points out that there are "literally hundreds of definitions of culture" in the fields of sociology and anthropology (Green, 1999, p. 13); it further maintains that the idea of race is not particularly helpful in understanding diversity and that culture is a preferable concept for understanding differences. However, I am including the concept of race in this book because it is basic to young children's early recognition of the physical differences between themselves and others. Preschoolers are aware of skin color and other physical features long before they have the ability to engage in the more mature abstract thinking that is necessary for identification with a culture.

THE CHANGING DEMOGRAPHIC FACE OF THE UNITED STATES

Demographic data attest to the rapid growth of "minority" populations in the United States (Miller, 1998; Shinagawa & Jang, 1998; U.S. Census Bureau, 1999). The term *minority* refers to people of various races and ethnicity who have historically comprised smaller proportions of the population and who collectively have been subjected to different treatment, including oppression (National Association of Social Workers [NASW], 1998). This term, *minority*, will soon become inaccurate and perhaps even obsolete, as the former minorities gradually increase to become the majority. In the 1990 census, individuals who classified themselves as African American, Hispanic American, Native American, and Asian Pacific American (America's "minority" populations) comprised 25 percent of the total population in the United States and 30.5 percent of children five to nineteen years of age (U.S. Census Bureau). These percentages have increased steadily, and in 1998, 35.4 percent of all children five to nineteen years old were minority. In 1998, the U.S. Census Bureau projected that, based on predicted birth and immigration rates, "minorities" would approach a *majority* population status by the middle of the twenty-first century (Shinagawa & Jang). We will have a clearer idea after the 2000 census whether the predicted drop in the non-Hispanic white population to 53 percent by 2050 is in fact occurring. Regardless of the precise numbers, however, it is evident that pronounced changes are taking place in the racial and ethnic composition of the United States population. Inevitably, these changes will affect future contacts with children and families from culturally and linguistically diverse groups by practitioners in the social service, mental health, and educational systems (Johnson-Powell, Yananotto, Wyatt, & Arroyo, 1997).

This book focuses on the five major ethnic, cultural, and racial groups that traditionally have been categorized according to the data collection practice of the U.S. Bureau of the Census, despite the great lack of clarity between the groups, as discussed here. The census attempts to count African Americans, Asian Americans, Latinos (Hispanics), Native Americans, and Caucasians. Notably, the 2000 census recognized many subcategories within the Asian and Hispanic groups and asked about specific tribal affiliation of American Indians and Alaska Natives. Possibly this recognition will lead toward a change or even elimination of racial categorizations in the future census collections, despite the argument that these categorizations, together with income data, help determine the need for basic programs and services such as schools, infrastructure, and hospitals. Because the census does not ask about the ethnicity of whites, persons with backgrounds as varied as Russians, Italians, and British are thereby grouped together. The attempt to document the increasing diversity of subgroups within each racial group may become unmanageable as people continue to intermarry between cultures and to share more than one heritage.

Understandably, it is difficult for individuals of mixed racial heritage to accurately designate their status. Furthermore, the mixture of racial and ethnic designations in the census form can be confusing, because, for example, Latinos or Hispanics may possess either white, black, or Native American racial characteristics. A letter to the *New York Times* stated the problem as follows: "My son is Nigerian (African, not African-American) and French Canadian (Quebec). He's multiracial, interracial and biracial. . . . The best response to these absurd racial boxes on the census is for all of us not to fill out that part of the form" (Belzile, 2000).

Despite these obvious problems with race as a descriptive category, the concepts of ethnicity and culture clearly have great significance for practitioners working with children and families. For this reason, this book emphasizes culturally based differences among people rather than differences of racial, physical characteristics. Practitioners need to know the beliefs and attitudes of culturally diverse parents toward their children, including their hopes and goals and their planned methods for achieving them.

This book divides the five major racial and ethnic groups into separate sections that discuss specific ethnic and cultural subgroups. There are three chapters within each of the sections on Latinos and Asian Americans because of the high growth rates and projected population increases in these groups. Figure 1.1 depicts these trends.

Practitioners must always be aware of the cultural values of the families with which they are working. They must also remember that there is great diversity among people who share the same skin color. The following case study illustrates the problems that can occur when the practitioner is oblivious to the clients' values.

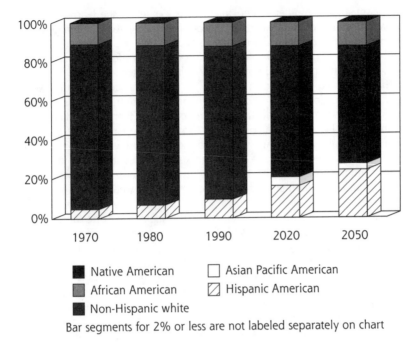

Native American
African American
Non-Hispanic white
Asian Pacific American
Hispanic American

Bar segments for 2% or less are not labeled separately on chart

Figure 1.1. Population trends 1970–2050

Adapted from Shinagawa and Jang (1998) *Atlas of American Diversity*, page 150. Copyright by Alta Mira Press. Used with permission.

CASE STUDY: THE PAPPAS FAMILY

A crisis situation occurred in a family counseling session in which the Anglo-American female therapist did not recognize the parent-child values of a European male father, who became incensed when his twelve-year old American-born daughter criticized him with the therapist's encouragement. (Note: Identifying data has been changed to preserve confidentiality.)

Many years ago, I received a referral to my private practice from a law guardian who wanted me to evaluate and counsel two girls, ages twelve and fifteen, whose parents were in the middle of a bitter divorce. Both parents wanted custody of the girls, who had remained living with their mother in the family home after the father moved out six months before. The father had visitation privileges every weekend, when he typically would take his daughters out for dinner and an occasional movie. Frequently they would stay overnight in his apartment.

This was a Greek family in which the parents had worked together in managing several successful restaurants. Both parents had been born in Greece and married there before coming to this country when they were young adults. The marriage was stormy, and the girls were accustomed to hearing loud arguments at night. Sometimes their father would throw furniture and break windows. The precipitant for the mother's filing for divorce was when she learned that her husband's girlfriend had a baby, and she became humiliated and enraged. During the ensuing argument, the mother locked the father out of the house and told him never to come back. He proceeded to destroy the front door, and the mother called the police and obtained an order of protection.

The parents agreed to bring the girls for counseling on alternating weeks. During these sessions I would typically see the girls with their parent for ten or fifteen minutes to discuss how things were going, and then, depending on the circumstances, I would see the girls either together or separately. The older girl, Tamara, was quite close to her father, and she was considering moving in with him. The twelve-year-old, Lucy, wanted to stay with her mother, and she was upset about the prospect of her sister moving out. She also viewed her father as being mean to her mother, and she sometimes didn't want to be with him on the weekends.

I had been seeing the family for about six weeks when the father left his apartment and moved in with his girlfriend and the baby daughter he had fathered. Mr. Pappas began to talk openly about planning to marry as soon as the divorce became final. Tamara said that she liked her father's twenty-four-year-old girlfriend, who was very nice to her, but Lucy did not. In a separate session with me, Lucy said that she really didn't want to spend time on the weekend with her father and this woman, and she felt very pressured by her father to accept someone who she felt had broken up her family. I asked Lucy if she had told her father how she felt, and she said, "I wouldn't dare."

As a child and adolescent therapist with twenty years of experience, I felt that I understood and agreed with Lucy's loyalty to her mother and resistance to accept a prospective stepmother and a child who was a rival for her father's attentions. I told Lucy that nobody could change her father's feelings and behavior and that she might have to learn to accept his decision even though she didn't like it. I also recognized that she might need some time to become accustomed to this very big change in her family. I asked her if she would like my help in telling her father these things. She eagerly accepted my offer, and I invited Mr. Pappas to join Lucy and me. Tamara also came in, with Lucy's permission, "because she already knows how I feel."

I took the initiative and began talking to Mr. Pappas as an advocate for Lucy. I said that I knew that teenage girls often have trouble accepting changes in their families and that some may even prefer to have their parents remain unhappily married rather than break up. I said that it is particularly difficult when one of the parents begins to date and talk about getting married. I mentioned that Lucy had told me that she has some of these feelings, and I turned to Lucy and suggested that she tell her father herself how she feels.

Lucy, feeling strengthened by my support, looked at her father and said, "I really don't like Mary, and I don't want to go out with her on Saturdays. I liked it before when you took just Tamara and me to a restaurant. You can be with Mary every day; I'm your daughter, and I just want to be with you one day!" I watched Mr. Pappas straighten up in his chair as Lucy spoke. His face was turning red as he began to shout at her: "You little shit! How dare you tell your father what to do! Don't you ever speak to me like that again!" Lucy dropped her head and began to cry. I stood up and looked directly at Mr. Pappas. "I apologize, Mr. Pappas," I said. "I take responsibility for encouraging Lucy to tell you how she feels. She did it because I told her that she should tell you. It never occurred to me that you would be insulted. That was certainly not my purpose. I hoped that the two of you could think of a way to be together, so that Lucy would feel comfortable. Your daughter loves you very much and wants to see you, and I still hope that we can work out some type of compromise. But I must tell you that I will not permit any parent to attack a child verbally in my office." I then turned to Lucy and said, "I'm very sorry your dad misunderstood what you were trying to say. I think he was very upset to hear you say that you don't like Mary. Maybe he overreacted because of this. You both need some time now to cool off, and I want you both to promise me not to discuss this matter further until our next appointment. Now let's settle the plans for next weekend."

This case study clearly demonstrates the clash of values between the therapist and the father based on opposing views about children's rights to have opinions that differ from those of their parents and about the parent's willingness to listen to a child's opinion when it differs from his own. The relationship between the therapist and the father was saved by the therapist's apology and because of the father's seeming deference to the therapist's role as a professional who was in a position to influence the forthcoming legal decision about custody. It took several weeks, however, before the relationship between Lucy and the therapist returned to its previous level of comfort. During this time the therapist did a lot of self-scrutiny about the danger of imposing her values about children's rights on a family with different views about parent-child roles.

IMPACT OF CULTURAL BELIEFS ON PROFESSIONAL PRACTICE

Because most practitioners are Caucasians of Anglo-European heritage (Gibelman & Schervish, 1997), they may be unfamiliar with the cultural beliefs and the expectations about parent-child roles in the culturally diverse families with which they work. The Pappas case study illustrates the potential problem when practitioners fail to anticipate the implications of applying their own value about the desirability of open expression of feelings in a family whose values do not permit children this type of expression.

Since 1992 the Council on Social Work Education has mandated curriculum content related to people of color and populations at risk ("distinguished by *age, ethnicity, culture* . . . ," Council on Social Work Education, Commission on Accreditation, 1992, my emphasis). Therefore, social work practitioners trained since the mid-1990s should have had some course work about people of color and about cultural differences. This course work may not have included content specifically about children, however, because children tend to be underrepresented in the social work curricula despite the fact that "social work practitioners are major providers of services for children and adolescents" (Thomas, 1993, p. 77). Inclusion of content about different family values and roles in different cultural groups depends on the specific curriculum of each school.

A growing number of textbooks (Congress, 1997; Devore & Schlesinger, 1991; Lum, 1992; Paniagua, 1998; Sue & Sue, 1990) address the topic of cultural sensitivity and suggest guidelines to increase the sensitivity and effectiveness of practitioners in their work with clients who are from diverse cultural backgrounds. There is increasing agreement, however, that comprehensive knowledge about *all* cultures is an impossible goal (Caple, Salcido, & diCecco, 1995; Lieberman, 1990; Webb, 1996). Therefore, instead of trying to learn everything about everybody, some general principles have been proposed to foster ethnically sensitive practice (Caple et al.; Lieberman). These principles include recognizing the great variability within the same culture (lest anyone believe that everyone in the same cultural group is the same) and emphasizing that cultures change and that acculturation is an ongoing, ever-evolving process. "There is no single American culture, nor is there a single profile that fits all members of any specific cultural group" (Caple et al., p. 167). The reality of diversity within diversity means that the practitioner must listen carefully and evaluate each person and family as unique within the framework of their culture. It does not mean that cultural factors are irrelevant but that culture affects different individuals differently, often due to the filtering effect of social class and education (Sue & Sue, 1977). The impact of culture on the individual is flexible and ever changing.

Amy Lee and Linda Tan are two Chinese American girls in the same fourth-grade classroom in a public school in San Francisco. Both have been invited to a classmate's tenth birthday party, which is to include a late afternoon trip to a beauty salon for makeup and manicures, followed by dinner in a popular restaurant, and then a sleep-over at the birthday girl's house. Six girls were invited, of which Amy and Linda are the only Chinese Americans. Amy is a vivacious and popular girl who does well in school and has many friends. Her parents were born in this country, but they try to maintain some Chinese practices by sending their children to Chinese school on Saturdays and cooking Chinese food on weekends and holidays. They don't particularly like the idea of the beauty salon, but Amy wants to go to the party to be with her friends, and they permitted her to accept the invitation.

On the other hand, Linda's parents, who are from a rural Taiwanese background and have been in this country only a year, have many objections to the party. They do not know the family of the birthday girl, and they worry about permitting Linda to stay overnight without knowing whether or by whom the girls would be supervised. They are afraid that Linda may start "getting ideas" about boys from the other girls. They do not feel comfortable talking with the teacher or with calling the girl's parents to find out more details. Linda, who is shy and embarrassed about her lack of friends, accepts without question her parents' decision that she should decline the invitation.

This example probably could be replicated with children from various other cultural backgrounds, including white European-American. The point is that *parents from the same ethnic group* have different beliefs about how to raise their children, and these beliefs may or may not reflect the traditional values of their own cultural background. In addition, parents' beliefs change over time and may be influenced by the prevailing values of the parents of their children's peers and by the media.

The practitioner's *own* beliefs also affect the manner in which he or she interacts with clients. The practitioner who shares values similar to those of the client may fail to see nuances in the clients' views (Pinderhughes, 1989). On the other hand, when the values of the client and practitioner are different, the practitioner must strive to maintain objectivity, to view the situation from the client's perspective, and let the client make his or her own decision. The topic of practitioner self-awareness is discussed more fully later in this chapter.

CULTURAL VALUES AND CHILD REARING

Values refer to the strongly held beliefs about life and about behavioral expectations that are heavily influenced by the culture. "Culture influences the goals parents have for their children and the methods they use to achieve those goals; cultural values are transmitted through child rearing practices from one generation to the next" (Keats, 1997, p. 1). Sometimes values are difficult to articulate. A family may have very firmly held beliefs that are not verbalized but that find expression in their actions. Values often become explicit when an expectation is breached. This is what happened in the Pappas family when twelve-year old Lucy criticized her father. Lucy had not dared to tell him her feelings earlier because she "knew" that, in *her* family, such communication would be unacceptable behavior. The cultural value in this family (unrecognized by the counselor) was that children should accept their father's behavior and wishes without question or criticism.

How do families transmit their cultural values through their child rearing? The following section presents some of the universal choices faced by parents of all cultural groups about their methods of raising their children. Parents' different child-rearing practices evolve from their own upbringing and advice from kin in addition to new ideas gained from seeing how other parents raise their children and hearing about recommended practices from experts and the media.

Many parents struggle with how strictly traditional or liberal they should be, and these choices become more difficult when their own cultural background and values are distinctly different from those of the dominant mainstream environment. Most parents know about the traditional expectations of their culture and use these expectations as the basis for making their decisions. When there is a major difference between the parents' culturally based norms and the norms of the child's peers and others in the family's current environment, then the child may become profoundly ambivalent and confused (Huang, 1997). For example, the case of the Chinese American girls and the birthday party might have turned out quite differently if Linda, who was from the "traditional" family, had wanted to go to the party and felt that her parents were being unreasonable and old-fashioned in forcing her to decline the invitation. She might have become quite miserable and depressed about her perceptions of her future social life at school; those depressed feelings, in turn, might have kept her from studying, which may have resulted in lower grades with subsequent disapproval and shaming responses from her parents.

Children in situations like Linda's have a foot in two cultures, and they have to learn to negotiate between the values of each culture even when the values are in opposition. Sometimes the school social worker, psychologist, or guidance counselor can assist the child and family to achieve a compromise that is acceptable within both sets of values. But in order for such an intervention to be effective, the practitioner must understand and respect the nature of the conflict and must respond in such a manner that the parents do not feel criticized or usurped. Chapter 14 presents suggestions for working effectively in situations of conflicting values. Harkness and Super (1996) state that all beliefs that parents have about the socialization of their children "are anchored in a cultural context" (p. 84). Practitioners, therefore, must understand this context in order for an effective helping relationship to occur.

AN ECOLOGICAL-CULTURAL PERSPECTIVE ON DEVELOPMENT

An ecological perspective on development recognizes the mutual interactive relationships between the child, the parents, and the social environment, which, of course, includes the culture. The concept of mutual interdependence of these systems was first proposed by Bronfenbrenner (1979) as a way of viewing the individual as a "dynamic and evolving being that interacts with, and thereby restructures, the many environments with which it comes into contact" (Gardiner, Mutter, & Kosmitzki, 1998, p. 9). Germain and Gitterman (1987) state with reference to the ecological perspective that "neither the people served, nor their environments, can be fully understood except in relationship to each other" (p. 493).

The idea of reciprocal influences between parent and child has been elaborated in the work of Stern (1985) with regard to the mother-infant interaction and in the publications of the Erikson Institute (Garbarino et al., 1989), which stress the mutual influences between children and their physical, social, and cultural contexts (Webb, 1996). The concept that even children can influence their cultures (Holloway & Minami, 1996) has replaced the anthropologist Caudill's (1973; Caudill & De Vos, 1956) highly respected earlier theory of one-way cultural transmission from parent to child.

In an earlier publication (Webb, 1996), I diagrammed the interactive influences of child, family, and environment for the purpose of illustrating an ecological perspective on children's development. The reciprocal influences of the child on the family and vice versa has now attained general acceptance, as has the influence of the culture on the individual. However, the ability of an individual to influence a culture is less frequently recognized apart from the well-publicized instances of heroic people such as Martin Luther King, Mahatma Gandhi, and even six-year-old Ruby Bridges, who was the first child to integrate the New Orleans school system.

Figure 1.2 presents my model of the interactive influences of culture, ethnicity, family, environment, and the child. This model expands on my earlier version (Webb, 1996) by providing more details and by specifying the numerous cultural and ethnic factors that can impact on the child in addition to the impact of the family and the physical and social environment.

Photo courtesy of The Norman Rockwell Museum at Stockbridge

STAGES OF CHILDREN'S DEVELOPMENT

All families guide their children's development in both direct and subtle ways. Babies are born helpless and depend on adults to feed, clothe, stimulate, and protect them; they also have an intrinsic need and capacity to form relationships with their caretakers (Bowlby, 1969). Whereas all children go through predictable developmental stages (sitting, walking, learning to feed themselves, learning to use the toilet, playing, and responding to people outside the family), there are many variations in when and how these achievements can occur. Furthermore, parental reactions to the child influence the nature of their child's response.

This section reviews the basic phases of child development, emphasizing how different cultural and familial reactions can shape the outcome for children at different stages. The intent is to reflect on how the parents' or caretakers' responses to the child's growth reflect their own beliefs, which in turn have been partly or strongly influenced by their specific cultural heritage.

Erikson's Psychosocial Theory Through a Cultural Lens

Erik Erikson's theory of psychosocial development (1950/1963) has particular relevance to understanding child development within a sociocultural context. Erikson's writings help us appreciate the impact of the cultural environment on how families raise their children. Erikson, himself a blonde Dane, reported feeling "different" in the southern German Jewish family and community of his stepfather, where he grew up after age three. These feelings, perhaps, contributed to his sensitivity to the issue of identity. As a child, Erikson did not know that his own Danish father had abandoned his mother, and he grew up thinking that Dr. Homburger was his father. Nonetheless, he felt that he was different and that he did not belong

RACE/ETHNICITY
Nationality
Ancestry
History
Language
Religion

CULTURE
Values and beliefs
Worldview
Customs
Communication style
Behaviors
Standards

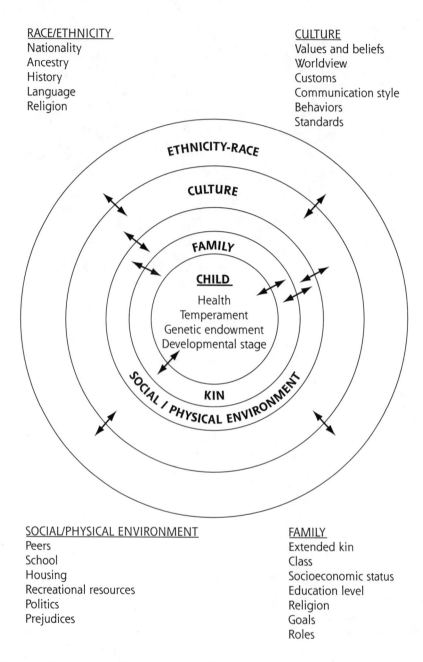

SOCIAL/PHYSICAL ENVIRONMENT
Peers
School
Housing
Recreational resources
Politics
Prejudices

FAMILY
Extended kin
Class
Socioeconomic status
Education level
Religion
Goals
Roles

Figure 1.2. Interactive influences of child, family, environment, culture, and ethnicity-race

Adapted from Webb, N. B. (1996).

(Erikson, 1975). Erikson came to the United States as an adult, and his studies of the Sioux Indians, Ghandi, and Martin Luther all conveyed his fascination with the reciprocal interaction among the individual and the family and the social, cultural, and historical environment.

I will condense Erikson's first five stages of development (from infancy to adolescence) into four stages (infancy, early childhood, middle childhood, and adolescence) and suggest some outcomes for children in each stage that can vary from Erikson's, depending on different child-rearing practices. This conceptualization intends to challenge the reader to consider how the malleability of children can result in very different behavioral and psychological outcomes, depending on whether the social and familial environment encourages or discourages them in certain directions. For example, all normal children learn to walk, but those who are kept in playpens and are restricted in their mobility and exploration may have a different feeling about the world at age two than do children whose parents allow them to explore the environment freely with few restrictions.

As I have already mentioned, practitioners must not assume that *all* parents from a particular group will socialize their children in the same way. Some writers even suggest that there may be as many differences in parental practices *within the same culture group* as there are between different cultures (Cole, 1990, quoted in Palacios & Moreno, 1996). Practitioners also must recognize that the parents' role in the transmission of cultural values to their children may be either supported, diminished, or even negated by the influences of grandparents, other kin, the school, peers, and the media (Keats, 1997).

Infancy

The infancy period is dominated by the infant's basic needs for food, sleep, stimulation, protection, and relationship (attachment). The baby begins to form an attachment relationship with his or her caretakers, and Erikson's psychosocial perspective recognizes the critical importance of the nature of the caretaker's interactions with the baby. When the parent meets the baby's needs consistently, the infant develops trust and a sense that the world is dependable, according to Erikson. On the other hand, when the caretakers are less attentive or even neglectful, the baby's response will reflect his or her insecurity, ambivalence, or disorganization (Bowlby, 1969). Some cultures (e.g., Japanese) emphasize very close contact between the child and the caretaker, in contrast to American culture, which tends to encourage the child's separation and independence.

Davies (1999) identifies three situations in which the caregiver may be unable to provide the child with a consistent positive interaction. These situations occur when (1) the caregiver lacks personal experience regarding appropriate parental responsiveness, (2) the caretaker is mentally ill or addicted, or (3) the caretaker lacks necessary outside support. Infants can have attachments reflecting different degrees of security with different caretakers (Davies). Therefore, the baby's degree of trust at this early stage of development depends both on the quality of his or her different caretaking experiences and on cultural child-rearing patterns.

There are many cultural variations in the way the child is fed and in his or her particular sleeping arrangements. Is the baby fed on demand, that is, whenever he or she cries, or do the adult caretakers prop up the bottle and let the child feed him- or herself? Is the baby expected to adapt to a timetable for feedings? How much of the time is the infant held close to an adult's body compared to the time the child spends lying alone in a cradle or crib with no other people nearby? Is the child typically rocked in someone's arms? How many different people take care of the child on a regular basis? What is the atmosphere around the child; are people happy when they look at him or her? Is the baby the "center of attention" in the family or taken for granted as "another mouth to be fed"? What happens when the infant cries? Does he or she receive attentive care, or is the baby left to "cry it out" until he or she falls asleep?

These questions are not meant to convey judgments of right or wrong or of better or worse. Rather, they are intended to help practitioners consider the particular experience of a baby in different caretaking environments and the possible effects these different experiences may have on the infant's psychological development. For example, the type of sleeping arrangements of babies may reflect the parents' culturally based views about whether they want to encourage their child's autonomy or dependence (Wolf, Lozoff, Latz & Pauladetto, 1996). Whereas middle-class American and Canadian parents frequently put their infants in a separate bed in their own room to sleep, many other cultures, such as Mexican and Japanese, would frown on this practice. Indeed, Japanese children may sleep in their parents' bed until age six or even later (LeVine, 1988). This sleeping arrangement may result in the child's continuing expectation to have a dependent relationship with the mother and the child's later ease with the cultural expectation for group interdependence and teamwork. A culture that does not expect autonomy or independence in young children may find ways to reward them for being quiet, cooperative, and "good" members of the family. This experience of togetherness can evolve into a cooperative work ethic in adulthood rather than into a philosophy of independent striving for individual personal goals.

Erikson's model of child development fits child-parent relationships in European-American families in the mid-twentieth century. Using a wider, culturally sensitive lens, practitioners will note that in different cultures a child might have varying degrees of trust with different caretakers. Erikson's polarity of trust versus mistrust can be converted today into a *range* of possible responses in the child toward different caretakers, from trust and confidence to uncertainty to apprehension to doubt and mistrust. Furthermore, in many cultures these feelings would be directed differentially to the child's entire network of relatives rather than only to a single caretaker (the mother, in Erikson's view).

Toddlerhood and Early Childhood

I am combining in this second category two of Erikson's developmental phases, from the period when the child begins to walk (or toddle) and gradually develops a sense of self through the time when the child is about five years old and enters kindergarten. The child's mobility and desire to explore at this age may be either encouraged, tolerated, or discouraged by the family, according to their particular beliefs about the child's growing independence and other factors related to the safety of the environment and the potential dangers awaiting the child explorer.

Erikson suggests that the outcome of these two phases determines if the child achieves a sense of autonomy and develops confidence because his or her initiatives have been accepted within the context of the family and society. A negative outcome for the child during this period would be the child's sense of shame, doubt, and guilt about his or her ineffectiveness.

Whereas Erikson's theory seems to apply to American children whose parents encourage their freedom of expression and whose goal is to raise self-confident, active, verbal, and independent youngsters, it may not relate at all to cultures that emphasize group interdependence rather than individual autonomy (e.g., cosleeping versus sleeping alone). Furthermore, some cultures (e.g., Chinese) deliberately instill the idea that an individual's behavior reflects on the entire family and that misbehavior results in "losing face" and in shame for the whole family (Keats, 1997). Therefore, in Chinese culture, instilling shame and guilt are typical and acceptable means of behavior control for parents who want to inculcate in their children a sense of duty and obligation to the family. The individual child's feelings do not matter because Chinese parents believe that it is more important for children to consider their obligation to their family than to be preoccupied with individual concerns. So the concept of autonomy can be considered to be very bound up in cultural expectations regarding early development.

Latino parents also use shaming as a method of controlling children's behavior. Falicov (1998) states that "active shaming, which includes teasing and mocking, humiliation, threats, ridicule, and punishment, including corporal punishment, appear to be more widespread and accepted in Latino as compared to Anglo-American families, even when social class differences are considered. Children are made to feel small, stupid, or clumsy when their parents use labels which signify essential character flaws rather than target specific, situational behaviors" (p. 221). This type of shaming seems different from that in Chinese families; the first is directed at the person (the individual), whereas the second stresses the impact of the child's behavior on others (the family).

All cultures use methods of controlling and shaping children's behavior. As various chapters in this book illustrate, the range of disciplinary methods varies from corporal punishment, to restrictions of privileges, to encouragement. Practitioners who work with families with young children must try to understand the values underneath the parents' behavior in order to assess the impact of the parents' expectations on the child.

Aggression and Gender Development

Additional areas of childhood socialization during the preschool years include the management of aggression and cultural expectations about gender roles. Cultures vary in their tolerance of aggression. One cross-cultural study showed that American parents were considered to be quite tolerant of aggression between children and that Mexican parents were less so (Lambert, Hammers, & Frasure-Smith, 1979). This study, based on the earlier work of the Whitings (Whiting, 1963; Whiting & Edwards, 1988; Whiting & Whiting, 1975) included families in India, Japan, Kenya, Mexico, and the Philippines. The authors explain these differences in terms of the cultural values of independence in American families and of interdependence (with greater levels of supervision) in Mexican families. In other words, the Mexican child is more apt to be observed, restrained, and punished for aggression, whereas the American child typically has more freedom to play without adult observation (and consequences for misbehavior; Gardiner et al., 1998).

Gender identity development is strongly influenced by cultural expectations. "From an early age, as part of the socialization process, children learn to conform to the roles that culture considers consistent with their biological sex. In general, girls are rewarded and praised for exhibiting behavior considered desirable for a woman in that culture, and discouraged from showing undesirable, or gender-inappropriate, behavior. In turn, boys are rewarded for male behavior, and ridiculed if they exhibit behaviors reserved for girls or women" (Gardiner et al., 1998, p. 139). Davies (1999) points out that by the age of two, toddlers have learned their own gender and are beginning to be aware of the characteristics associated with each gender.

Middle Childhood

Middle childhood is the period when the child begins school and comes under the influences of other adults and children who may or may not share the cultural beliefs of the child's family. According to Erikson, this phase is dominated by focused work, or industry, through which the child develops a sense of competence. In Erikson's view, children who do not succeed in this phase develop a sense of inferiority.

In many cultures, the outcome of this developmental stage has implications beyond those for the individual child. Academic success is considered the route to economic success, which is a desired goal in many families. Asian families emphasize the child's achievement and often insist that the school-age child spend many hours studying after school in order to succeed. Play and recreation do not have the same value in Asian families as in American families. Motivating the child occurs mainly through expectations and pressure to do well rather than through the use of rewards. Sometimes Asian parents do not understand or approve of American educational methods that employ rewards for academic success, because they consider the child's achievement to be a foregone conclusion. Practitioners can imagine the pressure and frustration of the Asian American child who has only "average" ability or who has a learning disability such as attention deficit disorder. The family simply may not comprehend that the child's poor school performance is beyond his or her control. When I was in China in 1998, I asked the tour guide about special education services for children who need extra help. She responded that these children would do better if the families gave them more discipline!

American children have many avenues to success other than academic, such as sports, music, and computer activities. It is possible for a child who is not gifted academically to perform well in a band or on the playing field, and the child's parents and classmates may focus on these achievements rather than on the child's weaknesses. For Chinese American children (and other Asian Americans) there often may be a tension between parental expectations, which are based on traditional values, and the expectations of mainstream American culture in which the children must function. This topic will be discussed further in chapters 10, 11, and 12.

Children's racial and ethnic awareness, which begins in early childhood, intensifies during the elementary school years (Katz, 1987; Rotheram & Phinney, 1987). During this period, race, ethnicity, and gender strongly influence peer relationships, and children tend to choose as friends the peers with whom they can identify (Davies, 1999; Rotheram & Phinney). This awareness can help the child strengthen his or her cultural identity, even as he or she begins to learn that there are differences in values even within the same ethnic group.

Adolescence

The adolescence stage of development encompasses the teenage years that Erikson characterized as the period of identity consolidation. This process has several facets, including resolutions of sexual identity, racial or ethnic identity, and career or occupational identity. "Identity is achieved through a complex process of judging oneself (1) as an individual, (2) in comparison with others' judgments, and (3) in comparison to social and cultural norms" (Gardiner et al., 1998, p. 124). The adolescent years have been characterized as times of turmoil for American teenagers and their parents (Hayman, 1986; Powell, 1986). However, critics of this view (Steinberg, 1990) point out that most adolescents actually embrace the values of their parents despite some conspicuous departures through their participation in the teen peer culture. Whether or not there is parent-child conflict in the teen years, the process of identity formation encourages young people to evaluate the ways in which their beliefs and goals are similar to or different from those of their parents, their peers, and others in their network. Notably, this evaluation can occur whether or not the teen lives with the parent until early adulthood or marriage. Clearly the European American expectation that adolescents should leave home and establish a separate residence as an indication that they have successfully completed their individuation from the family does not apply across cultures (especially in Hispanic families).

Many possible career choices present themselves to some American youth in their late adolescence. The young person from a European American background may struggle to decide on one of numerous alternatives, such as college or employment. Deciding what to do after high school can lead to sense of identity confusion not experienced by teenagers whose families clearly expect them to follow a particular path. Still other adolescents, because of unemployment or discrimination, may seem to have very few options. The lack of choices during this phase of life can sometimes lead to depression, to alcohol and substance abuse, and to an identity that mirrors mainstream society's negative views of that person's cultural identity. Thus, identity formation for minority children challenges them to integrate multiple cultural reference groups in the contexts of discrimination and the Euro-American world (Shapiro & Shapiro, 2001; Stevens, 1997). This process may be further complicated for biracial children who develop a negative identity because of their rejection of one part of their heritage (Gibbs et al., 1998).

Summary

A child's physical and psychosocial development takes place in the context of familial and cultural values that shape the child's behavior in culturally expected and acceptable ways. Although the family's values about child rearing may not be explicit, they are deeply felt and are communicated to the child in nonverbal ways that speak the spirit of the culture.

PRACTITIONERS' SELF-ASSESSMENT OF CHILD-REARING VALUES

In order to reduce personal bias and stereotyping, practitioners must identify and examine their own firmly held beliefs about families and children. Many practitioners assume that their beliefs about raising children are normative and preferable, because they are supported by the child development literature and courses in child psychology (Betancourt & Lopez, 1993; Koss-Chioino & Vargas, 1992). However, as I have discussed previously, the theoretical framework of some of this literature may not apply to culturally diverse families because of their different values and worldviews. It is essential, therefore, for practitioners to follow the numerous guidelines in the practice literature in order to avoid ethnocentrism and to work effectively with families and children from cultural backgrounds different from their own. Chapter 14 offers suggestions derived from this book's chapter authors for practice with clients from different cultural backgrounds. *These authors unanimously emphasize the importance of the self-awareness of the practitioner as a first step in working effectively with culturally diverse families.* I have selected two self-assessment tools to assist the practitioner in evaluating his or her own biases and prejudices.

The first self-assessment tool is Chadiha's questionnaire of "Similarities and Differences" (Chadiha et al., 1997) (see Table 1.1). This tool begins with a factual question about the different types of people with whom the student or practitioner has lived. Included among the possible choices are "other cultures, other classes, other ethnic backgrounds, other religious backgrounds, other races, and other sexual orientations." The questionnaire continues by asking for "one value of the culture that I grew up in" and "one thing my parents/family taught me about my gender, ethnicity, and race" and about "gay and lesbian people, black people, Jewish people, and white people." The questionnaire concludes by asking about "my biggest concern about working with people who are different from me."

Although this questionnaire was developed for class discussion purposes, it could also be used beneficially by a practitioner seeking to understand the roots of some

Table 1.1. Similarities and Differences

Complete each statement. There is no right or wrong way to complete the statement; it is just how you feel about it that is important.

1. I have lived among people of: (circle all that apply)

other cultures	other classes	other ethnic backgrounds
other religious backgrounds	other races	other sexual orientation

How many circles do you have? _____

2. One value of the culture that I grew up in is:

3. One thing my parents/family taught me about my:

Gender: _____

Ethnicity: _____

Race: _____

4. One thing my parents/family taught me about:

Gay and Lesbian People: _____

Black People: _____

Jewish People: _____

White People: _____

5. My biggest concern about working with people who are different from me is:

Source: Copyright 1997 Council on Social Work Education, Alexandria, VA. From L. Chadiha, J. Miller-Cribbs & D. Wilson-Klar, Human Diversity, *Human Diversity Content in Social Work Education: A Collection of Course Outlines with Content on Racial, Ethnic, and Cultural Diversity,* p. 116.

of his or her own beliefs. Completing the questionnaire would inevitably lead to more awareness about the important role of parents in the transmission of cultural values.

The second self-assessment tool is Paniagua's (1998) ten-item "Self-Evaluation of Biases and Prejudices Scale" (see Table 1.2). This tool permits a self-ranking and scoring of bias-prejudice toward the five major cultural groups. It begins by asking about training and knowledge about the different cultures, then moves into questions on attitudes about dating or marrying members of the different groups, and

Table 1.2. Self-Evaluation of Biases and Prejudices Scale

Question	1 (Very much)	2 (Somewhat)	3 (Not at all)
1. Have you had formal training with?			
African Americans	1	2	3
American Indians	1	2	3
Asians	1	2	3
Hispanics	1	2	3
Whites	1	2	3
2. Do you have cultural knowledge with?			
African Americans	1	2	3
American Indians	1	2	3
Asians	1	2	3
Hispanics	1	2	3
Whites	1	2	3
3. As a parent, would you approve of your son or daughter dating?			
African Americans	1	2	3
American Indians	1	2	3
Asians	1	2	3
Hispanics	1	2	3
Whites	1	2	3
4. Would you date or marry a member from the following group?			
African Americans	1	2	3
American Indians	1	2	3
Asians	1	2	3
Hispanics	1	2	3
Whites	1	2	3
5. Would you feel comfortable providing clinical services to?			
African Americans	1	2	3
American Indians	1	2	3
Asians	1	2	3
Hispanics	1	2	3
Whites	1	2	3
6. Have you been exposed to professional views of?			
African Americans	1	2	3
American Indians	1	2	3
Asians	1	2	3
Hispanics	1	2	3
Whites	1	2	3

Table 1.2. *(continued)*

Question	1 *(Very much)*	2 *(Somewhat)*	3 *(Not at all)*
7. Are you familiar with the current literature (journals, books, and periodicals) with?			
African Americans	1	2	3
American Indians	1	2	3
Asians	1	2	3
Hispanics	1	2	3
Whites	1	2	3
8. Would you feel comfortable if you have problems understanding?			
African Americans	1	2	3
American Indians	1	2	3
Asians	1	2	3
Hispanics	1	2	3
Whites	1	2	3
9. Would you expect favorable therapy outcome with?			
African Americans	1	2	3
American Indians	1	2	3
Asians	1	2	3
Hispanics	1	2	3
Whites	1	2	3
10. Would you expect a favorable therapeutic relationship with?			
African Americans	1	2	3
American Indians	1	2	3
Asians	1	2	3
Hispanics	1	2	3
Whites	1	2	3

	Total score	*Ratio*[a]
African Americans	_____	_____
American Indians	_____	_____
Asians	_____	_____
Hispanics	_____	_____
Whites	_____	_____

[a] For example, if 1 is circled for all questions involving African Americans, the total score is 10 and the ratio is 1.0 (or 10 ÷ 10). The maximum bias-prejudice ratio is 3.0, suggesting a high degree of bias and prejudice toward a given group.

Source: Paniagua, F. A. *Assessing and treating culturally diverse clients. A practical guide,* pp. 110–111, copyright © 1998 by Sage Publications. Reprinted by permission of publisher.

concludes with several questions concerning the practitioner's level of comfort with providing clinical services to members of various groups.

Either of these questionnaires would help counselors examine their biases and then modify their behavior accordingly. Paniagua (1998) suggests that in the event of a score indicating a high level of bias and prejudice, the practitioner "should either refer the client to another clinician or obtain consultation from other professionals" (p. 108). I would suggest, in addition, that the practitioner try to learn more about other cultures by reading both professional and popular literature about various ethnic groups, attending movies that focus on other groups, traveling to different countries, eating in restaurants that serve ethnic foods, and establishing professional and personal contacts with individuals from different groups. The point is to become as familiar as possible with different cultures. Of course, self-awareness about attitudes toward culturally diverse clients is only the first step toward the goal of putting that awareness into practice. Lum (1999) provides an excellent resource to help practitioners apply their greater cultural awareness in the various steps of engagement and intervention with clients.

An ability to work with all clients regardless of their culture may be an unrealistic goal, although anthropologist and social worker Goldberg (2000) quotes Goodenough (1981) as stating that "competence in multiple cultures is possible" (p. 15). Practitioners who have had contact and close interaction with another cultural group usually come to understand that culture's values sufficiently to be able to work effectively with members of the group. However, Canino and Spurlock (1994) state that "no therapist can claim to be aware of *all* the nuances of a culture that differs from her or his own or to be (completely) free of cultural bias" (p. 129).

Even when reasonably comfortable and culturally sensitive about working with clients from different cultures, the professional helper may still feel a strong allegiance for his or her own cultural values, and it is not necessary or expected for the practitioner to renounce that preference. Goldberg (2000) believes that through "consciously compartmentalizing" their personal biases, members of the helping professions can "bracket" (p. 15) their preferences for their own ethnic patterns and still work effectively with clients from other backgrounds. The essential first step, however, is to become culturally self-aware.

Discussion Questions

1. Think back to when you were eight or nine years old and in elementary school. How culturally diverse or homogeneous was your classroom? Did you have any contacts with children from other cultural backgrounds? Did you ever visit their homes or eat a meal that was different from what you usually had at home? What are some of the advantages and disadvantages of your early experience in view of your career as a human services professional?
2. If possible, visit a playground where children from different backgrounds are playing. Look for examples of disciplining used by different caretakers. Can you identify any distinctive methods used by caretakers from different cultural backgrounds? What is the nature of the child's affect when he or she is disciplined? Can you speculate about the child's relative degree of autonomy versus shame and doubt based on the caretaker's treatment of the child?

3. Look at one of the popular parenting magazines in terms of advice given by "experts." Try to identify the cultural or socioeconomic group for whom the magazine is written. What are some of the values you can identify from the articles and the advertising? Would a Native American or Asian American mother find values in this issue to support her child-rearing beliefs?
4. Speak to a classmate or to a coworker from a cultural background different from your own. Ask about child care roles and expectations in his or her family. Find out the extent of contact with the extended family. Think about contrasts between your family background and the culture of your friend or coworker. How would you each respond to a school social worker who told you that your child was having difficulties in school? How would you want the worker to treat you?

References

Banks, J. (1991). *Teaching strategies for ethnic studies* (5th ed.). Boston: Allyn & Bacon.

Belzile, R. (2000, March 18). Race can't fit in a box. *The New York Times*, p. A14.

Betancourt, H., & Lopez, S. R. (1993). The study of culture, ethnicity, and race in American psychology. *American Psychologist, 48*(6), 629–37.

Bowlby, J. (1969). *Attachment and loss: Vol. 1. Attachment.* New York: Basic Books.

Bronfenbrenner, U. (1979). *The ecology of human development.* Cambridge, MA: Harvard University Press.

Canino, I. A., & Spurlock, J. S. (1994). *Culturally diverse children and adolescents.* New York: Guilford Press.

Caple, F., Salcido, R. M., & diCecco, J. (1995). Engaging effectively with culturally diverse families and children. *Social Work in Education, 17*(3), 159–70.

Caudill, W. (1973). The influence of social structure and culture on humans in modern Japan. *Journal of Nursing and Mental Disease, 157,* 240–57.

Caudill, W., & De Vos, G. (1956). Achievement, culture, and personality: The case of the Japanese Americans. *American Anthropologist, 58*(6), 1022–1126.

Chadiha, L., Miller-Cribbs, J., & Wilson-Klar, D. (1997). Course syllabus on human diversity. George Warren Brown School of Social Work. In W. Devore & B. J. Fletcher (Eds.), *Human diversity content in social work education: A collection of course outlines with content on racial, ethnic, and cultural diversity* (pp. 103–29). Alexandria, VA: Council on Social Work Education.

Congress, E. P. (Ed.). (1997). *Multicultural perspectives in working with families.* New York: Springer.

Council on Social Work Education Commission on Accreditation. (1992). *Handbook of accreditation standards and procedures* (4th ed.). Alexandria, VA: Council on Social Work Education.

Cowger, C. (1994). Assessing client strengths: Clinical assessment for client empowerment. *Social Work, 39*(3), 262–68.

Davies, D. (1999). *Child development: A practitioners' guide.* New York: Guilford Press.

DeJong, P., & Miller, S. (1995). How to interview for client strengths. *Social Work, 40*(6), 729–36.

Devore, W., & Fletcher, B. J. (Eds.). (1997). *Human diversity content in social work education: A collection of course outlines with content on racial, ethnic, and cultural diversity.* Alexandria, VA: Council on Social Work Education.

Devore, W., & Schlesinger, E. G. (1991). *Ethnic-sensitive social work practice.* New York: Merrill/Macmillan.

Erikson, E. (1963). *Childhood and society* (rev. enlarged ed.). New York: Norton. (Original work published 1950)

Erikson, E. (1975). *Life history and the historical moment.* New York: Norton.

Falicov, C. (1998). *Latino families in therapy: A guide to multicultural practice.* New York: Guilford Press.

Garbarino, J., Stott, F. M., & Associates. (1989). *What children can tell us.* San Francisco: Jossey-Bass.

Gardiner, H. W., Mutter, J. D., & Kosmitzki, C. (1998). *Lives across cultures: Cross-cultural human development.* Boston: Allyn & Bacon.

Germain, C. B., & Gitterman, A. (1987). Ecological perspective. In A. Minahan (Ed.), *Encyclopedia of social work* (18th ed., pp. 488–99). Silver Spring, MD: National Association of Social Workers.

Gibbs, J. T., Huang, L. N., & Associates (Eds.). (1998). *Children of color: Psychological interventions with minority youth.* San Francisco: Jossey-Bass.

Gibelman, M., & Schervish, P. (1997). *Who we are: A second look.* Washington, DC: National Association of Social Workers.

Goldberg, M. (2000). Conflicting principles in multicultural social work. *Families in Society, 81*(1), 12–21.

Goodenough, W. (1981). *Culture, language, and society* (2nd ed.). Menlo Park, CA: Ben Cummings.

Green, J. W. (1999). *Cultural awareness in the human services. A multi-ethnic approach.* Boston: Allyn & Bacon.

Harkness, S., & Super, C. M. (Eds.). (1996). *Parents' cultural beliefs systems: Their origins, expressions, and consequences.* New York: Guilford Press.

Hayman, S. (1986). *Adolescence: A survival guide to the teenage years.* New York: Gower.

Holloway, S. D., & Minami, M. (1996). Production and reproduction of culture: The dynamic role of mothers and children in early socialization. In D. W. Shwalb & B. J. Shwalb, *Japanese childrearing: Two generations of scholarship* (pp. 164–76). New York: Guilford Press.

Huang, L. N. (1997). Asian American adolescents. In E. Lee (Ed.), *Working with Asian Americans: A guide for clinicians* (pp. 165–74). New York: Guilford Press.

Hwang, S. C., & Cowger, C. (1998). Utilizing strengths in assessment. *Families in Society. 79*(1), 25–31.

Johnson-Powell, G., Yananotto, J., Wyatt, G. E., & Arroyo, W. (Eds.). (1997). *Transcultural child development: Psychological assessment and treatment.* New York: Wiley.

Katz, P. A. (1987). Developmental and social processes in ethnic attitudes and self-identification. In J. S. Phinney & M. J. Rotheram (Eds.), *Children's ethnic socialization: Pluralism and development* (pp. 92–100). Newbury Park, CA: Sage.

Keats, D. M. (1997). *Culture and the child.* Chichester: Wiley.

Koss-Chioino, J. D., & Vargas, L. A. (1992). Through the cultural looking glass: A model for understanding culturally responsive psychotherapies. In L. A. Vargas & J. D. Koss-Chioino (Eds.), *Working with culture: Psychotherapeutic interventions with ethnic minority children and adolescents* (pp. 1–22). San Francisco: Jossey-Bass.

Laird, J. (1998). Theorizing culture: Narrative ideas and practice principles. In M. McGoldrick (Ed.), *Re-visioning family therapy: Race, culture, and gender in clinical practice* (pp. 20–30). New York: Guilford Press.

Lambert, W. E., Hammers, J. E., & Frasure-Smith, N. (1979). *Child-rearing values: A cross-national study.* New York: Praeger.

LeVine, R. A. (1988). Human parental care: Universal goals, cultural strategies, individual behavior. In R. A. LeVine, P. M. Miller, & M. M. West (Eds.), *Parental behavior in diverse societies: New directions for child development.* San Francisco: Jossey-Bass.

Lieberman, A. F. (1990). Culturally sensitive intervention with children and families. *Child and Adolescent Social Work, 7*(2), 101–20.

Lum, D. (1992). *Social work practice and people of color: A process-stage approach* (2nd ed.). Pacific Grove, CA: Brooks Cole.

Lum, D. (1999). *Culturally competent practice: A framework for growth and action.* Pacific Grove, CA: Brooks Cole.

McQuaide, S., & Ehrenreich, J. H. (1997). Assessing client strengths. *Families in Society, 78*(2), 201–12.

Miller, G. (1998). Foreword. *Children of color: Psychological interventions with culturally diverse youth.* San Francisco: Jossey-Bass. (Written in 1989)

National Association of Social Workers. (1998). *Information for authors.* Washington, DC: Author.

Palacios, J., & Moreno, M. C. (1996). Parents' and adolescents' ideas on children: Origins and transmission of intracultural diversity. In S. Harkness & C. M. Super (Eds.), *Parents' cultural beliefs systems: Their origins, expressions, and consequences* (pp. 215–53). New York: Guilford Press.

Paniagua, F. A. (1998). *Assessing and treating culturally diverse clients: A practical guide* (2nd ed.). Thousand Oaks, CA: Sage.

Pinderhughes, E. (1989). *Understanding race, ethnicity, and power: The key to efficacy in clinical practice.* New York: Free Press.

Powell, D. (1986). *Teenagers: When to worry, what to do.* New York: Doubleday.

Rotheram, M. J., & Phinney, J. S. (1987). Introduction: Definitions and perspectives in the study of children's ethnic socialization. In J. S. Phinney & M. J. Rotheram (Eds.), *Children's ethnic socialization: Pluralism and development* (pp. 10–28). Newbury Park, CA: Sage.

Saleebey, D. (Ed.). (1992). *The strengths perspective in social work practice.* New York: Longman.

Shapiro, V., & Shapiro, J. (2001). *Adoption and the new forms of parentage.* New York: Guilford.

Shinagawa, L. H., & Jang, M. (1998). *Atlas of American diversity.* Walnut Creek, CA: Altimira Press.

Shulman, L. (1999). *The skills of helping individuals, families, groups, and communities.* Itasca, IL: Peacock.

Steinberg, L. (1990). Autonomy, conflict, and harmony in the family relationship. In S. G. Feldman & G. R. Elliott (Eds.), *At the threshold: The developing adolescent* (pp. 255–76). Cambridge, MA: Harvard University Press.

Stern, D. (1985). *The interpersonal world of the infant.* New York: Basic Books.

Stevens, J. W. (1997). African-American female adolescent identity development: A three-dimensional perspective. *Child Welfare, 76*(1), 145–72.

Sue, D., & Sue, E. (1977). Barriers to effective cross-cultural counseling. *Journal of Counseling Psychology, 24,* 420–29.

Sue, D. W. & Sue, D. (1990). *Counseling the culturally different: Theory and practice* (2nd ed.). New York: Wiley.

Thomas, C. (1993). Psychosocial interventions. In H. C. Johnson (Ed.), *Child mental health in the 1990s: Curricula for graduate and undergraduate professional education* (pp. 77–85). Rockville, MD: U.S. Department of Health and Human Services.

U. S. Census Bureau (1999). *Statistical abstract of the U.S. The National Data Book* (119th ed.). Washington, DC: U.S. Census Bureau, U.S. Department of Commerce.

Webb, N. B. (1996). *Social work practice with children.* New York: Guilford Press.

Weick, A. (1992). Building a strengths perspective for social work. In D. Saleebey (Ed.), *The strengths perspective in social work practice.* New York: Longman.

Whiting, B. B. (1963). *Six cultures: Studies of child rearing.* Cambridge, MA: Harvard University Press.

Whiting, B. B., & Edwards, C. P. (1988). *Children of different worlds: The formation of social behavior.* Cambridge, MA: Harvard University Press.

Whiting, B. B., & Whiting, J. W. M. (1975). *Children of six cultures: A psycho-cultural analysis.* Cambridge, MA: Harvard University Press.

Wolf, A. W., Lozoff, B., Latz, S., & Pauladetto, R. (1996). Parental theories in the management of sleep routines in Japan, Italy, and the United States. In S. Harkness & C. M. Super (Eds.), *Parents' cultural belief systems.* New York: Guilford Press.

CHAPTER 2

Ethical Issues in Work with Culturally Diverse Children and Their Families

ELAINE P. CONGRESS

Ethical issues and dilemmas frequently occur when practitioners provide social and psychological services to culturally diverse children and their families. Working in interdisciplinary settings may prove especially challenging for practitioners, as the following case study indicates.

CASE STUDY: THE GARCIA FAMILY

A professional social worker with Legal Aid, an agency representing the birth mother, was involved in a pending court case to terminate parental rights for eight-year-old Antonio. When she interviewed the mother prior to the hearing, the social worker noted that Antonio's birth mother came to the agency with another child, five-year-old José, who was in the mother's care. This child had bruises on his arms, which the mother attributed to falling down the stairs. The social worker wanted to report this suspected abuse to the child abuse central registry but was told not to by the attorney because this report might be damaging for the impending court case. The social worker was very concerned because she is a mandated child abuse reporter and wanted to promote the best interests of all of her clients, including Antonio and José, whereas the lawyer seemed to be concerned only about the interests of Ms. Garcia, the birth mother. The social worker was also aware that her clients were from a culture that believed in "spare the rod and spoil the child" discipline. Antonio had been removed from the home because Ms. Garcia had disciplined Antonio with a severe strapping that she reported was the way she had been disciplined as a child.

The social worker faces two challenging ethical dilemmas:

1. The social worker is a mandated child abuse reporter and has a legal and ethical obligation to report suspicion of child abuse. Yet she knows that child welfare standards are based on American practices of child rearing and that she has an ethical responsibility to be culturally sensitive.
2. The social worker is employed by lawyers who have different beliefs about confidentiality and about who the client is. The lawyer believes that Ms. Garcia is the one client that Legal Aid is representing and that her confidentiality must be upheld above all. On the other hand, the social worker views the whole Garcia family as her clients and believes that she can not ethically maintain confidentiality if there is threat of harm to one of her clients.

As this case study demonstrates, culturally sensitive practice with children and their families requires an understanding of the legal and ethical context in which clients live. This chapter focuses first on legal issues involving children, with special attention to children's rights and child welfare laws. The implications of these issues for culturally diverse children and families is discussed. The second part of the chapter addresses ethical standards in regard to practice with diverse children as set forth in the social work code of ethics. Exploration of differences in professional, personal, and client values constitutes the third part of the chapter. Finally, ethical dilemmas and a model of ethical decision making in work with culturally diverse children and their families is presented and illustrated through a case study.

The difference between laws and ethics has been equated to Rambo versus Bambi (Kocher & Keith-Speigel, 1990). While laws and professional ethics often have similar goals and underlying value perspectives, laws are considered more enforceable. In contrast, ethical codes vary among professions and are primarily enforceable within each professional organization's system for imposing sanctions. In most situations laws and ethics coincide, yet there may be some instances where they differ (Dickson, 1998). One area of concern relates to culturally diverse families. Most professional codes mandate respect and nondiscrimination against individuals because of cultural and ethnic differences. Yet current anti-immigration laws that require the reporting of undocumented families seem to contradict the social work code of ethics (National Association of Social Workers [NASW], 1999). This contradiction certainly has implications for clinicians who work with culturally diverse children and their families, because undocumented children and their families may reject treatment or not fully participate because of their fear of being reported and deported (Congress & Lynn, 1994).

ISSUES AND LAWS

What laws should practitioners know about in working with culturally diverse children and their families? Although children were not named in the original

Constitution of the United States, the 1967 Gault decision recognized them as "persons" in constitutional law (Stein, 1991). Prior to this decision the courts had operated under the assumption that they were acting in the best interests of the child with a focus on rehabilitation, not punishment. In reality this approach meant that children were often denied due process procedures such as right to counsel and a jury trial. The lack of due process often led to a stiffer penalty than would have been incurred by an adult charged with the same crime. This situation happened in the case of Gerald Gault, a fifteen-year-old charged with making obscene calls to a neighbor. Under existing juvenile laws he would have been remanded to a state institution for six years, until he was twenty-one had he not appealed and had the U.S. Supreme Court not ruled in his favor. If he had been tried under due process procedures of adults, the maximum penalty could have been as little as five dollars. The U.S. Supreme Court decision in favor of Gault extended due process rights to children and adolescents as a protection to children from the arbitrary decisions of juvenile courts (Stein, 1991).

Subsequent to this decision children have been assumed to have the same constitutional rights as adults (Kocher & Keith-Spiegel, 1990). Yet these rights are limited because of parental rights. Much legislation has focused on issues related to the boundaries of children's rights, parents' rights, and the state's right (*parens patriae*) to intervene when children's rights are threatened (Dickson, 1995; Kocher & Keith-Spiegel; Stein, 1991). One well-known and acknowledged law that exists in every state is mandatory reporting of suspected child abuse and neglect (Videka-Sherman, 1991). Actually, this law requiring child abuse reporting may be contrary to professional values in regard to confidentiality and the best interests of the child (Crenshaw, Bartell, & Lichtenberg, 1994).

Although laws differ slightly from state to state, the general consensus is that child abuse should be reported when there is a suspicion of physical or emotional harm or neglect (Stein, 1991). However, great variability exists in the definition of what constitutes child abuse and neglect (Morrison, 1997). It has been pointed out that poor families of color are likely to be overrepresented in reported cases of child abuse and neglect (Lindsey, 1994). This point suggests that there may be ethnic and class factors operative in the determination of what constitutes child abuse and neglect and that differences in child-rearing practices may place families of color at risk for reports of child abuse (Collier, McClure, Collier, Otto, & Polloi, 1999; Lum, 1996). Middle-class white Americans emphasize nonphysical methods of disciplining children, such as talking to children and punishing them by withholding privileges. Most Americans favor discussion with children and withdrawal of privileges (staying in room, no television, no videotapes) as methods of control. Because our child welfare system is based on American child-rearing practices, culturally diverse families with different practices have often had conflicts with the child welfare system.

For many years the preferred child welfare intervention was to place an abused or neglected child in a foster home, where the foster parents were often from a different culture. This practice had serious implications for culturally diverse families, since the majority of children in the foster care system come from backgrounds other than white American (Tataram, 1993). For several decades long-term foster care has been viewed as deleterious to the child's welfare (Fanshel & Shinn, 1978). The Adoption Assistance and Child Welfare Act of 1980 (P.L. 96-972) focused on avoiding placement, placing children in the most familiar setting, and making a permanent plan for a child within eighteen months of placement (McGowan & Stutz, 1991). The use of kinship placements that maintain the child with relatives continues as a preferred practice among culturally diverse families to keep the children within their own family circle (Carten & Dumpson, 1997). The most recent child welfare law, the Safe Families and Adoption Act of 1997, has not been viewed as helpful to the culturally diverse child and family (D. Roberts, 1999), because focus is on rapid termination of parental rights in order to free children for adoption rather than attempting to strengthen birth homes through intensive family preservation and the use of kinship placements. This approach seems to contradict the importance of families as a source of strength and support to culturally diverse children and their families.

CHILDREN'S RIGHTS IN DECISION MAKING

Do children have rights to make decisions about where they live or about whether or not to enter counseling? It has been suggested that almost all children are involuntary clients, because they do not know about how counseling might help them and their families (Webb, 1996). When children experience emotional and behavioral problems, parents often follow the school's recommendation and seek professional treatment for their children. The focus of early sessions is frequently on developing the children's trust in order to engage them more fully in treatment. In the last twenty years there has been a growing trend to involve older children and adolescents in making decisions about their living arrangements (Schroeder, 1995) and health care (Beauchamp & Walters, 1994; Silber, 1982).

What can or should a counselor promise a child in terms of confidentiality? Federal and state laws protect the confidentiality of adult patients/clients, but how do these laws apply in work with children? There is a long tradition of protecting confidentiality for children involved with the juvenile courts, but more recently this tradition has been challenged, especially when a juvenile offender becomes an adult offender (Schroeder, 1995). The importance of protecting confidentiality has been emphasized within schools (Berman-Rossi & Rossi, 1990; Kopels, 1992). However, although social workers have a legal and ethical responsibility to maintain confidentiality within the school setting (Kopels, 1993), school personnel frequently request sensitive information from school social workers (Berman-Rossi & Rossi, 1990; Garrett, 1994). The school setting can be very challenging for social workers because of different professional beliefs about confidentiality (Congress, 1986).

Since 1974 parents have had the legal right to review their children's school and medical records (Family Educational Rights and Privacy Act, P.L. 93-380). Because parents must sign to have their children receive treatment and because parents have the right to see all pertinent treatment records, the social worker has no authority to promise children confidentiality. From the beginning, practitioners must be clear to children and their families about the limits of confidentiality to avoid possible confusion and feelings of betrayal later.

From a developmental perspective, preschool children, who typically view their parents as omniscient, may not have the same expectation or concerns about confidentiality that older children and adolescents have (Kocher & Keith-Spiegel, 1990; Wachtel, 1994). Confidentiality and a concern for privacy that is stressed in both our laws and ethical codes may be primarily an American middle-class phenomenon. In a 1994 study I learned that latency-age immigrant children did not have the expectation that what they shared with a social worker would remain confidential (Congress & Lynn, 1994). In fact, some child therapists (Wachtel, 1994; Webb, 1996) question the value of creating a situation of confidence with a young child in which the parent is excluded.

Confidentiality becomes especially challenging for clinicians in professional treatment of adolescents. Adolescence is usually characterized by attempts to be more independent of parents (Erickson, 1968; Newman & Newman, 1991), and adolescents who continue to share everything with their parents have been labeled as pathologically enmeshed (Minuchin, 1974). However, this expectation clearly does not apply to Hispanic and Asian adolescents.

While the development of trust is crucial in all therapeutic relationships, establishing trust with adolescents who are distrustful of adults may be particularly challenging. Younger children, especially those who have been the victims of repeated parental abuse, abandonment, or cultural dislocation, may also have difficulty trusting their therapists.

To build a trusting relationship, social workers can best work with child and adolescent clients by discussing what types of confidential information must be disclosed to others. Even though parents who consent to treatment for adolescents may have the legal right to know about the treatment of their children, adolescents need to be reassured that therapists will not routinely disclose specific details and verbatim accounts of their therapeutic sessions. From the very beginning, however, adolescents and children should know about the clinician's responsibility to report behavior that is either life threatening or dangerous to others.

The case of *Tarasoff v. the Regents of University of California* (No. S.F. 23042) established the duty to warn when a third party is at risk (Kagle & Kopels, 1994). This decision has been applied in several cases in which an adolescent has told a therapist about an intention to harm another person (Schroeder, 1995). While clinicians have usually been held nonliable in litigation based on the *Tarasoff* decision (Kagle & Kopels), counselors should always be aware of their responsibility to prevent possible harm to a third party.

The high rate of suicide attempts among adolescents, especially among Hispanic females and Native American males, concerns mental health professionals (Zayas, Kaplan, Turner, Romano, & Gonzalez-Ramos, 2000). Clinicians who work with adolescents know that if an adolescent threatens suicide in a therapy session, this situation constitutes an obligation to break confidentiality in order to protect the life of the adolescent. But what about less obvious self-destructive "suicidal" behavior? How should the clinician handle adolescent disclosures about fasting regimes, unprotected sex in the age of HIV/AIDS, or experimentation with high-risk drugs?

What impact do laws on confidentiality have in work with culturally diverse children and their families? First, as previously stated, there is some evidence that culturally diverse latency-age children may not have the same expectation about confidentiality as do American-born children (Congress & Lynn, 1994). Furthermore, this concept actually runs counter to therapeutic attempts to enlist the parents as partners in their children's treatment. Confidentiality with culturally diverse adolescents may be particularly challenging. Often, culturally diverse families experience conflict when children reach adolescence and begin to identify primarily with the values of their American peer culture. In contrast to the elongated American adolescence phase devoted to continuing education and the formation of peer relationships, culturally diverse parents may have experienced their own abbreviated adolescence cut short by the need to find employment, by early marriage, and/or by parenting. They do not understand the push for independence among American adolescents. Culturally diverse adolescents may want to pursue the activities of American youth despite knowing their parents would disapprove (Congress, 1990). Anglo therapists sometimes may collude with adolescents in keeping secrets from parents. For example, in working with culturally diverse families that discourage peer relationships in adolescence, the therapist may keep confidential the fact that a young adolescent has a boyfriend. Is it appropriate for practitioners to have different standards of confidentiality for culturally diverse adolescents than for their American adolescent clients?

PROFESSIONAL ETHICS

All professions have ethical codes that address important values and principles in work with clients (Corey, Corey, & Callanan, 1993). The NASW Code of Ethics (1996), similar to other professional codes, does not specifically mention children. The only code of ethics that does refer specifically to children is that of the Society for Research in Child Development (Kocher & Keith-Spiegel, 1990). This document was developed in 1973, however, and it is so outdated that some of its provisions conflict with current federal standards about protection of children in research projects. Another code that may be helpful to practitioners in work with culturally diverse families was developed by the American Association of Black Social Workers. The code of ethics for black social workers advocates working for the advancement of black people and also for same-race adoptions. This stand is controversial because interracial adoptions have become more commonplace within the last thirty years (Shireman, 1994).

Although children are not specifically mentioned in the current NASW Code of Ethics (in keeping with the general tone of the code that does not address specific populations), the code does look at the role of the social worker in advocating against oppression and age discrimination. This focus suggests that the ethical social worker consistently advocates for children's rights, especially for children from culturally diverse backgrounds who may be especially vulnerable.

CULTURAL DIVERSITY

For the first time, the 1996 NASW Code of Ethics includes a section on cultural diversity. Social workers are advised to "have a knowledge base of their clients' cultures and be able to demonstrate competence in the provision of services that are sensitive to clients' cultures and to differences among people and cultural groups" (NASW, 1996, p. 9). For two decades the American Association for Counseling and Development (AACD, 1981) and the American Psychological Association (APA, 1981) have also had ethical guidelines that require members to learn about cultural differences. Although the ethical code of the American Association of Marriage and Family Therapists does not specifically address education about cultural differences, the organization does include a provision that their members should not discriminate against clients based on their race or national origin. The ethical code of the American Nursing Association (ANA, 1985) does not have a specific provision on cultural competency, although nursing literature suggests that teaching about cultural competency is of concern to the nursing profession (Pope-Davis, Eliason, & Ottavi, 1994).

Professionals are increasingly aware that a growing number of children and families come from backgrounds other than western European. By 2050 the majority of Americans will be from other backgrounds (Congress, 1994), and already in New York City 65 percent of residents are of non-western European origin (Rose, 1999). Although earlier immigrants to the United States were primarily men, recent waves of immigration have been mostly women and children (Foner, 1987). By the early part of the twenty-first century one out of every four children will be children of color, and by 2030 the majority of children will be from backgrounds other than Caucasian western European (Ozawa, 1997). A quarter of our population will be under age eighteen, with Hispanics constituting the largest and fastest growing ethnic group (Ozawa).

Practitioners must be prepared to provide services to these culturally diverse children and families. Not only will the number of diverse children increase, but the diversity within the child population will increase as well. When clients come from so many diverse backgrounds, it is impossible to be knowledgeable about every culture (Lieberman, 1990). When a school has children from over thirty countries, a counselor would have to have "encyclopedia ethnographic and anthropological knowledge" (Lieberman, p. 104) to know about the culture of each of their diverse clients. While it may be an unrealistic expectation that practitioners will be knowledgeable about all aspects of their clients' culture, the social worker does have the responsibility to tune in to their clients, to try to understand their clients' past and present experience (Hepworth & Larsen, 1993). Although tuning in can be difficult in professional work with all clients, it may be especially challenging when clients come from backgrounds that are very different from the counselor's. Asking both child and adult clients about their cultures has been seen as helpful and empowering to clients, especially when the practitioners' ethnic backgrounds differ from their clients (Green, 1995). However, because children may not have the verbal skills to describe cultural values and beliefs, play therapy often helps diverse children communicate about typical family practices in their respective cultures.

Physical Contact with Children

Other sections of the code that relate to culturally sensitive practice with children involve physical contact and dual relationships. The current code addresses the responsibility of the social worker to "not engage in physical contact with clients when there is a possibility of psychological harm to the client as a result of the contact [such as cradling or caressing clients]" (NASW, 1996, p. 165). Clinicians who work with children, however, recognize the importance of physical contact with children in a crisis, especially children who may lack other sources of support. The responsibility rests with the practitioners to decide what physical contact is appropriate and when the contact may result in harm to children. Social workers should set "clear, appropriate, and culturally sensitive boundaries" (NASW, 1996, p. 60). Appropriate physical contact may be especially important for immigrant children who have experienced many losses and who may expect this form of comforting behavior from adults.

Dual Relationships

Another provision of the NASW code requires that social workers establish appropriate culturally sensitive boundaries in terms of dual relationships. Social workers are advised to avoid dual relationships with clients. Dual relationships are defined as occurring when social workers have other than one relationship with a client, including sexual, social, or business relationships. When this code provision was enacted by the Delegate Assembly in 1996, many practitioners from rural areas argued that it was impossible to avoid dual relationships. For example, the child of a practitioner might be in the same school as a client's child. One social worker who worked with children mentioned that her ten-year-old son came home from school with a new play friend who turned out to be a child she had been seeing for the last six months for play therapy sessions.

The issue of dual relationships may be especially challenging with culturally diverse families. I have written previously about the importance of *personalismo* with Hispanic families (Congress, 1990), and this issue is also emphasized in other chapters of this book. Making a personal connection with a culturally diverse family actually may be a prerequisite to establishing a therapeutic relationship. For example, a school social worker who visited a Puerto Rican family found that it was very important to have coffee with the family. Another social worker working with an adolescent pregnant teenager decided to attend a baby shower for her client. Are these social workers establishing inappropriate social relationships with their clients? The responsibility falls to each practitioner to decide the appropriate culturally sensitive boundaries with culturally diverse children and their families.

PROFESSIONAL VALUES

The NASW Code of Ethics sets forth the following professional values:service, social justice, dignity and worth of the person, importance of human relationships, integrity, and competence in working with clients. While ethics involves the application of values to actual practice, values have been defined as general beliefs about what is right and good. The practitioner must be cognizant of these values in professional work with all clients, but especially in regard to culturally diverse children and their families. Of particular importance is the concept of social justice, that is, the promotion of equable services for diverse children who may have incurred injustices both in their country of origin and in America. Demonstrating respect for the dignity and worth of each client is essential, especially when clients' values differ from those of the professional. Hendricks (1997) addresses the challenges for the school social worker in helping bridge differences between the values of the school, the client, and the social worker. For families who value education, discussion of placement of children in special education may represent a crisis for culturally diverse families (Congress, 1990). Also, the value of integrity, or that the clinician should act in an trustworthy manner, seems particularly important in working with diverse clients. Undocumented clients may not trust the practitioner who is perceived as an authority figure with possible connections to the Immigration and Naturalization Service.

Personal Values

Although the majority of children and families come from diverse backgrounds, only approximately 11 percent of professional social workers are nonwhite (Gibelman & Schervish, 1997). Social workers' values may differ significantly from their clients' values, especially if clinicians are American with a western European background. In any work with clients, but especially work with diverse clients, practitioners must begin by examining their own values, as discussed in chapter 1. Some excellent models to guide clinicians in this self-examination include those by Devore and Schlesinger (1996), Green (1995), Ho (1991), and Lum (1996). This process is essential if practitioners are to avoid imposing their own values on clients and thus detrimentally affecting treatment with culturally diverse children and their families.

Should practitioners be from the same cultural backgrounds as the children and families they see? In reality such cultural matching is often not feasible because of the diversity of clients' backgrounds, while the majority of social workers are from white European backgrounds (Frecknall, 1996). Although there has been some evidence that same ethnic group matching may enhance communication, a culturally sensitive worker can also provide effective treatment with children and families from a different race (Devore & Schlesinger, 1996). Sometimes class differences can override ethnic matching. Practitioners who come from educated backgrounds must also recognize a possible vast difference between their values and those of an uneducated client, regardless of ethnicity and race.

Client Values

In addition to learning about the NASW Code of Ethics and professional and personal values, practitioners must strive to learn about the values of their clients. Unfortunately, only 3 percent to 8 percent of social work literature focuses on cultural and ethnic issues (Lum, 1996). Furthermore, the schools, agencies, and governmental organizations where culturally diverse children and their families are seen frequently have services based on white western European values (Lum). Culturally diverse children and adolescents are frequently misdiagnosed and improperly treated because of a lack of understanding of cultural differences (Canino & Spurlock, 1994). For example, a child's failure to establish eye contact may be considered a cognitive or emotional failure despite the fact that this behavior is appropriate for children in many cultures (McNeely & Badan, 1984). Sometimes culturally diverse children are referred for special education because of the examiner's failure to understand cultural differences in their receptive and expressive language (Francis, 1999).

Sometimes the cultural respect for authority may prevent a culturally diverse family from even questioning educational decisions (Congress, 1990). Practitioners must guard against judging individuals or families as pathological because they do not follow "American" individual and family development patterns. The adolescent who chooses not to separate from his or her parents to attend a distant college is not "enmeshed," but perhaps heeds a cultural norm that maintaining family connection is more important than individual achievement (Congress, 1999).

Lum (1996) has identified the following three areas involving important values for clinicians to be aware of in working with families of color.

1. *Maintenance of ethnic identification and solidarity.* Related to this topic is *familism* that stresses the importance of the family as a source of strength and refuge (Alvirez, Bean, & Williams, 1981). This issue is especially important for clinicians to recognize in working with culturally diverse families. Sometimes the interrelationship and dependence of family members can seem very foreign to American practitioners more accustomed to the independence of individual clients, as this example illustrates: A ten-year-old child did not want to attend after-school social activities and instead preferred to hurry home to help her chronically ill mother in the care of her mentally retarded younger brother.

Connection with family can be a source of strength and pride for culturally diverse families, especially in a society in which oppression and discrimination exist. Although clinicians are increasingly alert to avoid bias and discrimination in contact with culturally diverse children and their families, many children have repeatedly experienced bias and prejudice in their communities and at school. The child must function within two worlds, a family rooted in cultural traditions and an outside world of American ways. Culturally sensitive practitioners recognize that home is where families celebrate their unique cultural and ethnic holidays. Clinicians who work with culturally diverse children and their families can recognize and encourage these celebrations as promoting strength and positive identity.

2. *Extended family and kinship networks.* A second characteristic that Lum describes as common among culturally diverse families involves extended family

and kinship networks. For example, culturally diverse parents may often look to relatives for help with child care. When a school social worker wanted to see a parent about problems that a child was experiencing in school, both the mother and godparent came to see the social worker. The social worker became aware that in this family the godparent was involved in any and all major issues around the raising of children. Grandparents also may be very involved in raising children. School-based counselors and social workers must be willing to include all relevant family members in conferences related to the child. The current child welfare policy of kinship placement is an effort to put legal sanction behind the common informal practice within the African American community that involves extended family members in the raising of children (Carten & Dumpson, 1997).

3. *Authority*. A third issue in regard to families of color relates to the vertical hierarchy of authority in most cultural diverse families. While many American families support an egalitarian family structure, in culturally diverse families fathers are clearly in charge. Practitioners in professional work with culturally diverse children and their families must respect the hierarchical structure of families. Clinicians must be careful not to diminish the authority of the parent in front of the child (Ho, 1987) in order to develop and maintain effective therapeutic relationships.

Culturally diverse families have a respect for older persons that may not be as apparent in practice with American families (McGoldrick, Pearce, & Giordano, 1997). For example, an Asian family may want to consult with an aged family member who might not even be present in the household before making a major decision about a child's schooling. In addition to the values already mentioned, the family's religious beliefs should be considered by practitioners.

Religious and Spiritual Values

Religious and spiritual values may be very important to culturally diverse families (Boyd-Franklin, 1989). Up until recently practitioners did not typically explore the religious values of their clients. Since many culturally diverse families are very influenced by their spiritual beliefs, the culturally sensitive therapist must explore the extent and impact of spiritual beliefs on culturally diverse children and their families.

USE OF THE CULTURAGRAM WITH CULTURALLY DIVERSE FAMILIES

When social workers are attempting to understand culturally diverse families, it is important that they assess the family within a cultural context. Considering a family only in terms of its cultural identity, however, may lead to overgeneralization and stereotyping (Congress, 1994). A Puerto Rican family who has lived in the United States for forty years is very different from a Mexican family that emigrated last month, although both families are Hispanic. Furthermore, it cannot be assumed that even within a particular cultural group all families are similar.

Culturagram

While the ecomap (Hartman & Laird, 1983) and genogram (McGoldrick & Gerson, 1985) are useful tools in assessing the family, they do not emphasize the important role of culture in understanding the family. I developed the culturagram to help clinicians understand the role of culture in families (Congress, 1994, 1997). This tool subsequently has been applied to work with people of color (Lum, 1996), battered women (Brownell & Congress, 1998), children (Webb, 1996), and older people (Brownell, 1998). (See figure 2.1.)

Revised in 1999, the culturagram examines the following ten areas:

- Reasons for relocating
- Legal status
- Time in community
- Language spoken at home and in the community
- Health beliefs
- Impact of crisis events
- Holidays and special events
- Contact with cultural and religious institutions
- Values about education and work
- Values about family—structure, power, myths, and rules

The use of the culturagram can help practitioners understand and work more effectively with culturally diverse children and their families (Congress, 1994).

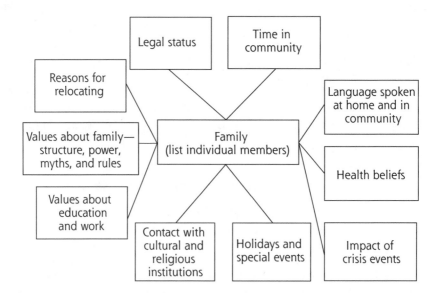

Figure 2.1. Culturagram

The ETHIC Model of Decision Making

While the NASW Code of Ethics sets forth social work ethical standards and values, it is less helpful in identifying and resolving ethical dilemmas. Cultural differences in child-rearing practices and definitions of child abuse have been identified (Dillion, 1994; Fong, 1994; Siegel, 1994; Tourigny & Bouchard, 1994). Ethical dilemmas may emerge when the practitioner tries to be respectful of a client's cultural background but still needs to respond to American institutional and societal beliefs and laws about child abuse. The code is silent about how to resolve ethical dilemmas of this type. Over a decade ago Pine (1987) developed a model of ethical decision making for the child welfare field but did not specifically refer to culturally diverse children and families. How can practitioners be culturally sensitive and respectful of differing values around child rearing without jeopardizing the health and safety of children?

Research suggests that most social workers do not rely on a model of ethical decision making but rather make decisions quickly based on their prior practice experience (Walden, Wolock, & Demone, 1990). Yet ethical dilemmas involving children are weighty, and the potential consequences of "wrong" decisions are formidable. I developed the ETHIC model (Congress, 1999) to help the social worker arrive at ethical decisions quickly and comprehensively. The next section presents this model and then applies it to work with culturally diverse children and families. Based on an acronym that is easy to remember and use ("ETHIC"), this model includes the five steps described in the following sections. (See figure 2.2.)

E *Examine* **relevant personal, societal, agency, client, and professional values** Personal, societal, agency, client, and professional values all influence ethical decision making. Practitioners who rely only on professional values are not likely to have a full understanding of all the important issues on which to base an ethical decision. For example, counselors need to recognize that a child's personal values may differ significantly from those of the parents. An example of this situation occurred when a parent wanted to move to a different city because of a new job opportunity, while his ten-year-old son was very depressed about the possibility of separation from his long-time elementary school friends. Sometimes value conflicts occur between the social worker and the client. While self-determination is a very important value, clients may subscribe to strong personal values of *family* responsibility. One social worker who strongly believed in higher education encountered a dilemma when her adolescent client did not want to attend college because of his need to care for his mother and younger siblings.

A discrepancy between agency and professional values can also produce dilemmas for practitioners. For example, the agency's value system may stress that every child must be adopted and placed in a permanent home, while the child client may prefer to stay with a grandparent in a kinship placement.

T *Think* **about what ethical standard of the NASW Code of Ethics or other professional code applies as well as about relevant laws and case decisions** Practitioners can begin to examine the ethical standards in the NASW Code of Ethics or in the code of their professions and see how these standards apply to work

- **E**   EXAMINE
    - Personal values
    - Societal values
    - Agency values
    - Client values
    - Professional values

- **T**   THINK ABOUT
    - Ethical standards (e.g.,NASW code)
    - Federal, state, and local laws
    - Case decisions

- **H**   HYPOTHESIZE
    - Different consequences

- **I**   IDENTIFY
    - Who will benefit
    - Who will be harmed
        - Social work's commitment to the most vulnerable

- **C**   CONSULT
    - Supervisors

Figure 2.2. The Ethic Model

with culturally diverse children and their families. The NASW code is divided into six sections:

- Social workers' ethical responsibilities to clients
- Social workers' ethical responsibilities to colleagues
- Social workers' ethical responsibilities in practice settings
- Social workers' ethical responsibilities as professionals
- Social workers' ethical responsibilities to the profession
- Social workers' ethical responsibilities to the broader society

While the code of ethics does not provide specific answers to ethical dilemmas, it does present specific areas that relate to social work practice with culturally diverse children and their families. Some of these topics, as already discussed, focus on confidentiality, family work, access to records, physical contact with clients, and dual relationships.

Practitioners also need to know about relevant federal, state, and local laws that may impact on the ethical dilemmas they encounter. Legal rights of children differ from state to state, and clinicians should become familiar with the laws and case decisions in their states that impact on their work with children (Kocher & Keith-Spiegel, 1990).

Social work ethics differ from but often parallel legal regulations. However, practitioners need to be aware of situations in which a law or regulation may support an unethical practice. Historical examples include Jim Crow laws in the South and discriminatory welfare regulations. Laws that deny undocumented children and their families needed social services can definitely impact on work with children (Lum, 1996).

For example, a social worker seeing an undocumented mother and ten-year-old child was reluctant to reveal to a child welfare agency attorney the illegal immigration status of the family, because she feared that this disclosure might lead to the child not receiving further mental health services or perhaps even to their deportation.

H *Hypothesize* **about possible consequences of different decisions** When the practitioner is undecided about a specific decision, he or she should analyze different consequences. For example, a clinician struggling about whether to place a child in foster care should think about two different scenarios, one in which the child is placed and the other in which the child remains with the birth family. The practitioner can list the pros and cons of these two alternatives. Analyzing possible results helps the social worker decide which is the preferred alternative.

I *Identify* **who will benefit and who will be harmed in view of the practitioner's commitment to the most vulnerable** Since practitioners must often decide between two bad alternatives rather than between one that is clearly right and another that is clearly wrong (Keith-Lucas, 1977), this step may elicit very convincing reasons for or against different courses of action.

Social work has had a lengthy tradition of concern for the most vulnerable in our society, and this concern distinguishes social work from other professions (Lewis, 1972). On a macro level, concern for the most vulnerable has been proposed as a principle to guide downsizing (Reisch & Taylor, 1983). The current code proposes that "social workers should act to expand choice and opportunity for all persons, with special regard for vulnerable, disadvantaged, oppressed, and exploited persons and groups" (NASW, 1996, p. 27). Since children have long been considered a vulnerable population, this step is most important for social workers in resolving an ethical dilemma involving a child.

C *Consult* **with supervisors and colleagues about the most ethical choice** Because making an ethical decision alone can be challenging, talking to others who can suggest alternatives or present new information is essential. A counselor who has a supervisor should use this person as a first resource in ethical decision making. However, due to current cutbacks, the more experienced practitioner and even beginning workers may have minimal supervision. These clinicians should bring their questions about ethical dilemmas to other colleagues for informal consultation. Furthermore, ethical dilemmas can be presented as part of a case conference.

Sometimes practitioners can help the agency develop an ethics committee. This step may be especially useful in a multidiscipline agency in which the social worker works with other professionals who may not share social work values and ethics. When social workers participate in ethics committees, their decisions about ethical dilemmas are often respected by other members (Joseph & Conrad, 1989). Often social workers working in multidiscipline settings struggle with ethical decision making (Congress, 1999). Some of the differences between social workers and doctors (C. Roberts, 1989) and social workers and public school educators (Congress & Lynn, 1994) in ethical decision making have been discussed previously.

CASE STUDY AND APPLICATION OF THE ETHIC MODEL

The ETHIC model can be helpful in resolving ethical dilemmas in child welfare with culturally diverse families, as this case study illustrates:

> Ms. Carmen Sanchez immigrated to this country three years ago from Mexico with hopes of a better life. Her husband had abandoned her shortly before her youngest child was born. Several months ago both of Ms. Sanchez's children (Juanita, age twelve, and Maria, age five) were placed after Juanita told her teacher that her mother had severely beaten her when she failed to come home from school. Three years ago the family had become known to child welfare when it was suspected that Juanita had been sexually abused by a visiting relative. This report had not been substantiated.
>
> Ms. Sanchez's sister Anna was interested in taking the children. She had not been considered for kinship placement when the children were initially placed because she was in the hospital recovering from surgery. The sister lived in a two-bedroom apartment in a housing project. She also cared for a fifteen-year-old severely retarded son, while another adult son who had an alcohol and heroin problem visited frequently to "borrow" money from his mother.

The practitioner applied the ETHIC model in the following way:

E *Examine* relevant personal, social, agency, client, and professional values

The worker began by reviewing her own beliefs and values about birth families. She herself had been raised by her grandmother after her own mother had died when she was two years old. She had fond memories of how caring her grandmother had been. In fact, her grandmother's influence had led her to major in social work. The social worker was aware that what had been a positive experience for her might not be the same for another person. In comparison with the Sanchez family, she noted that her grandmother did not have any health or other family problems that could have interfered with her care.

The social worker wondered if she was transferring her own values about child rearing to the Sanchez family. She herself had a twelve-year-old daughter, and she even encouraged her daughter to get together with friends after school. She had never physically disciplined her daughter, but instead would punish her daughter by reducing her allowance.

The social worker also considered societal and cultural values that related to the Sanchez family. She recognized the prevailing societal belief that families can and should provide children with a sense of security. This value could lead her to return the children either to the birth mother or their aunt. Also, the cultural values of the Sanchez family reflected their belief that a relative should care for the children. She realized that despite these beliefs the child welfare agency where she worked had removed the children from their family and separated them into two different foster home placements.

The precipitating incident for Ms. Sanchez's abuse of Juanita had involved Juanita's refusal to come home after school and care for her younger sibling. The social worker knew that Ms. Sanchez had never been independent during her adolescence because she had left school and was married at a young age. In addition, Ms. Sanchez was very fearful of Juanita's desire to associate with peers after school because of the possibility of bad influences from them. She chose to discipline Juanita the way she had been disciplined as a child.

The agency's values were rooted in permanency planning. The social worker had been given a deadline by which she must make a permanent plan for the children. She was concerned that the deadline seemed arbitrary and as much based on the agency's financial need to reduce the number of children in foster care as with the concern for the best psychological and social interests of the children. She also knew that her agency had recently entered a managed care contract that dictated that children could remain in foster care only a specific length of time and that her agency had financial problems.

What were her clients' values? The social worker realized that she felt very judgmental toward Ms. Sanchez. She was worried that Juanita could not have a "normal" adolescence, because Ms. Sanchez was insisting on raising her as she had been raised. The social worker was concerned that Juanita had been strapped so severely that she showed welts for weeks afterward. She wondered if Juanita's sister, who offered to provide a kinship placement, might share the same beliefs about discipline. The social worker also worried that Ms. Sanchez had not adequately protected Juanita three years ago when she allowed a potentially abusive relative to stay in her house. The social worker became increasingly aware that she really did not know much about her clients' values. Consequently, she had a long discussion with Ms. Sanchez and was pleasantly surprised to learn how important being a good mother was to Ms. Sanchez.

In exploring client values, the social worker looked at the children's values as well as those of Ms. Sanchez. The social worker had met individually with both children on a weekly basis since their placement. At first Juanita was very withdrawn and did not trust the worker. After several sessions Juanita shared with the social worker her belief that her mother did not want her to have any friends because she did not love her and only wanted to use her as a housekeeper and babysitter. It became very clear that she had a much better relationship with her aunt Anna and had often looked to her for support and guidance. The younger girl, Maria, seemed very sad, and whenever she saw the social worker she cried and refused to talk to her. The social worker learned through play therapy that Maria's placement had been very traumatic and that she blamed the agency for taking her away from her mother. It became clear that Maria wanted to return to live with her mother.

Finally, the social worker examined professional values that might be helpful in resolving this ethical dilemma. She knew she had a professional responsibility to provide service for the children as well as for Ms. Sanchez, her sister, and the foster mother. The social worker also knew that the professional value of social justice was relevant in this case. She had the responsibility to provide appropriate service to all the clients regardless of their ethnic background or legal status. She knew that the current charges against Ms. Sanchez had been dropped by Family Court, and therefore she could not consider Ms. Sanchez guilty of neglecting to provide for Juanita's safety. Furthermore, there never had been a concern about abuse of the younger daughter, Maria. The social worker was also aware that professional values stress that social workers must respect the inherent dignity and worth of the person. She should strive not to be judgmental of Ms. Sanchez, a twenty-six-year-old single mother of two with a history of child abuse. Also, she should avoid judgments about the aunt who had two adult children with special problems. The social work value of the importance of human relationships was particularly important in this situation. The social worker knew that she wanted to work on strengthening the family. She saw the oldest child's attempt to live with her aunt as a strength rather than a deficit.

H *Hypothesize* about different courses of action and possible consequences

The social worker believed that she had three possible courses of action:
  1. Return the children to Ms. Sanchez
  2. Continue the placement of the children in foster care and begin adoption procedures
  3. Place the children in a kinship placement

Return the children to Ms. Sanchez   The social worker could return the children to Ms. Sanchez. In the months the children had been in placement Ms. Sanchez had complied with the treatment plan by enrolling and keeping regular appointments for her parenting classes. The social worker also knew that these classes may not have been effective because of language differences. The social worker needed to follow up to determine if Ms. Sanchez had been helped by the parenting classes, which emphasized various approaches to child discipline.

If the children did return home, there would be need for additional services. The social worker was concerned that under the 1996 Personal Responsibility Act the family could continue on public assistance for only two years. Ms. Sanchez had left school in Mexico after the eighth grade. Prior to that she had attended school irregularly and could barely read. The social worker knew that with Ms. Sanchez's educational background she could pursue employment at only an unskilled minimal wage level. Could she support her family of three, especially with their need for medical and social service care? The social worker was concerned that Juanita seemed very depressed and could possibly benefit from ongoing therapy. Yet if she returned home, would the family be able to afford this care?

The social worker knew that Ms. Sanchez might need ongoing support through the agency. Yet a recent cutback in funds had brought an end to follow-up services. The social worker anticipated that there would be stress when the children returned home and that social work services might be helpful then.

The wishes of children, especially adolescents, are taken into account in making placement decisions (Stein, 1991). Juanita had run away to her aunt, whereas Maria had repeatedly asked when she could go home. The social worker knew that children often want to return home to their familiar environment, even when they have been neglected, because birth parents provide a sense of family that may be lacking in a foster home. Furthermore, family connections were very important for the Sanchez family because of their cultural background.

The social worker was also concerned about the risk of Ms. Sanchez becoming abusive again, especially with the stresses of raising two children on a limited income.

When the children were placed three months ago, they had both been severely ne-glected. In fact, the precipitating event had been the neighbors' report that they heard a child crying continually. When child welfare investigated, they learned that the chil-dren had only cereal to eat for an entire week because of a delayed welfare check. After interviewing Juanita there had been suspicion that she had been sexually abused, but there was no specific evidence to substantiate this concern. The social worker was worried about new abuse or neglect if the children were returned home.

Continue the placement of the children in foster care and begin adoption procedures If the social worker believed that Ms. Sanchez might be abusive again, then the best alternative might be to continue the out-of-home placement. However, a foster home might not be an ideal arrangement, because foster care does not provide a permanent plan for child care and the children remain in limbo. Furthermore, foster care is not always the best plan for children, since some children have been abused or even killed in foster care, especially children with special problems. Another focus might be to work toward adoption, but it seemed unlikely that an adoptive family would want to adopt both children. The current foster family was interested in adopting only Maria. It might be difficult to find an adoptive home for Juanita, who is older and may have emotional problems.

Place the children in a kinship placement Kinship placements make it possible for chil-dren to remain within their extended family network. Kinship placements formalize a placement method that has been used informally in African American families for many years when birth parents needed help in raising their children (Boyd-Franklin 1989; Carten & Dumpson, 1997). Children often prefer to remain in kinship placements, as Juanita's running away behavior suggests. Is a return to their birth parents or adoption appropriate goals for children in kinship placements when they are already "at home" (Gleeson, O'Donnell, & Bonecutter, 1997)? Sometimes there is also a concern that children in kinship placements continue to have unsupervised contact with their birth parents, which in certain circumstances may be problematic (Tonning, 1999).

The social worker viewed Ms. Sanchez's sister as a strong, positive parenting resource for the family. She knew that both the children were very fond of her and that Juanita especially would prefer to be placed with this aunt. Yet she also knew that the sister had had major surgery last year from which she was not fully recovered. She wondered if the sister had the strength to raise two children, especially with the ongoing care of her adult retarded son. The social worker was also concerned that the sister might share Ms. Sanchez's attitudes toward child discipline and thus would not provide a safe en-vironment for the children.

A homemaker could help in the care and supervision of the children. Yet the social worker knew that the agency had cut back in services, especially to kinship families. She could, however, recommend social services to help this family if the children were returned to the sister. If the sister, because of her deteriorating health, was not able to continue with the two children, then they could be returned to their mother or placed in a foster home.

I *Identify* who will benefit and who will be harmed in view of social work's commitment to the most vulnerable

Social work regards those with limited power as the most vulnerable. In the child welfare field *children* are frequently regarded as the least powerful, the most vulnerable, and therefore the most in need of social work intervention. A concern for the vulnerability of children led to adoption of child abuse laws and mandatory child abuse reporting in all fifty states. A belief of American society in general and child welfare practice in particular is that a home and family are in the best interests of every child. A permanent plan for each child in placement is considered the primary goal in child welfare.

Will the children benefit the most from return to their mother? Although Ms. Sanchez may want the children to be returned to her, there is some concern that they will be harmed by this decision to return them. Will the children benefit more by remaining in placement? This option would create uncertainty over their future, since foster homes are not considered permanent placements and children often have limited power over the length of time they remain in foster homes. Already Juanita's foster parents are questioning whether they can continue to keep her.

The social worker needed to decide if she should evaluate the benefits to the whole family as a unit or consider the welfare of individual members. The possibility that one of the children may be adopted might greatly benefit that child but not the other child or the birth mother, and finding a family to adopt both children might not be possible. It can also be argued that adoption will not benefit one child if she loses contact with her sibling. Also, the social worker questioned the effect of adoption on the children's connection with their birth mother and aunt.

The children might benefit the most by a return to their aunt, who will provide a family connection and also give the structure and nurturing so important to the children. Juanita wants this change and would probably benefit from this placement. The aunt also wanted it. Will Ms. Sanchez be harmed? She opposes the return of the children to her sister, but she would benefit if the children are placed there because she could have frequent contact with them.

C *Consult* **with supervisors and colleagues about the most ethical choice**

Before making the final decision, the social worker brought the case to her supervisor. She learned about the Ethics Review Committee that her agency had recently developed to resolve difficult child welfare decisions. Prior to meeting with this committee, the social worker gathered additional information about the family. She learned from the parenting group counselor that Ms. Sanchez's attendance had been erratic, possibly because of the fact that she could not understand English. The social worker was concerned that a significant part of the treatment plan had failed because of the lack of availability of Spanish-speaking parenting classes. She planned to make a referral to an outside parenting group. At the ethics committee meeting, some of the social worker's colleagues raised a concern that Ms. Sanchez might need continued support as the children became adolescents.

Placing Juanita with her aunt seemed like a good option. One member of the committee provided information about a homemaking service that could help the aunt in caring for Juanita and her retarded son. The agency had just been notified that a new public housing facility with large apartments recently opened. The aunt might be able to move into one of these apartments. With the support of her supervisor and the ethics committee, the social worker decided to recommend placement of Juanita with the maternal aunt. The younger child, Maria, would return to her mother. This decision was also consistent with the values and desires of the children, whom she had seen weekly throughout their placement. The social worker would offer continued counseling to Ms. Sanchez to help her work toward the goal of reuniting her family. The supervisor and the ethics committee supported the social worker in making this decision. The social worker, however, continued to feel uneasy that she was in effect punishing Ms. Sanchez by continuing to withhold her older child until she developed understanding and tolerance of her daughter's "Americanized" attitudes.

This case study demonstrates that there are no easy answers to ethical dilemmas that surround culturally sensitive practice with children and families. Use of the model, however, enables practitioners to address important issues and analyze various possibilities before arriving at a decision.

SUMMARY AND IMPLICATIONS FOR PRACTICE

This chapter has traced the relevant legal and ethical issues related to practice with culturally diverse children and families. The NASW Code of Ethics provisions about confidentiality and self-determination have received special attention.

As America becomes increasingly culturally diverse, practitioners must develop methods of culturally sensitive practice with children. An important first step is self-examination. Practitioners are urged to avoid generalizations and stereotyping in working with culturally diverse families. The use of a family assessment tool, the culturagram, to understand and empower culturally diverse families can deepen this understanding.

Ethical dilemmas often emerge when culturally diverse families encounter American institutions based on differing values and practices. A model of ethical decision making that focuses on work with culturally diverse families can assist in resolving ethical dilemmas in practice within the child welfare system.

As we begin the new millennium, we may wonder about the future direction of ethical practice with culturally diverse families. When the "minority" becomes the majority, the institutions and practices as well as our codes of ethics must reflect the diversity of our society. Our beliefs about confidentiality and self-determination are basic to our code of ethics. Yet we should always be mindful of how rooted they are in Anglo-American culture (Lum, 1996).

The rights of self-determination and confidentiality for children have never been clear. Yet there has been a trend to give children rights to self-determination at younger and younger ages (Kocher & Keith-Speigel, 1990). Culturally diverse children and adolescents may prefer to make decisions in the context of family, rather than individual, considerations. In a similar way, culturally diverse children and adolescents may not value confidentiality in the same manner as their American counterparts. Often the child and the families all want to be involved in the treatment process without concerns about confidential material. Ironically this greater openness is occurring simultaneously with an emerging societal trend that all information once thought private is no longer kept confidential. Social workers must become increasingly aware of emerging ethical issues and dilemmas in their work with culturally diverse children and their families.

Discussion Questions and Role-Play Exercises

1. Refer back to the study at the beginning of this chapter: The social worker for Legal Aid was participating in a team conference with legal staff regarding an impending court case that involved termination of parental rights. Remember that Legal Aid was representing the birth mother and at the last interview with the mother, the social worker observed that the mother's other child, who remained with the birth mother, looked neglected. Discuss how the ETHIC model could assist this social worker in determining how to proceed.

2. A client from a different culture indicates that she has not brought her child for regular health care examinations because "he is never sick." Role-play how you would handle this issue with the client.

3. If an adolescent discusses that she is having unprotected sexual activities with an older adolescent who has a substance abuse problem, what should the therapist say to the adolescent? Should this information be reported to the parents?

4. In a first interview, an eight-year-old girl refuses to communicate verbally. Finally, she draws a picture of a graveyard with tombstones. On one of the tombstones she writes her own name. How should this situation be handled?

5. A sixteen-year-old Puerto Rican girl discloses that she is two months pregnant. She asks for help in securing an abortion. She fears that her parents, who are very religious, will oppose her choice. What should the clinician do?

References

Alvirez, D., Bean, F., & Williams, D. (1981). The Mexican American family. In C. H. Mindel & R. W. Habenstein (Eds.), *Ethnic families in America: Patterns and variations* (pp. 269–92). New York: Elsevier.

American Association for Counseling and Development. (1981). *Ethical standards.* Alexandria, VA: Author.

American Nursing Association. (1985). *Code for nurses with interpretive statements.* Washington, DC: American Nursing Publishing.

American Psychological Association. (1981). Ethical principles of psychologists. *American Psychologist, 36,* 633–38.

Beauchamp, T., & Walters, L. (1994). *Contemporary issues in bioethics* (4th ed.). Belmont, CA: Wadsworth.

Berman-Rossi, T., & Rossi, P. (1990). Confidentiality and informed consent in school social work. *Social Work in Education, 12*(3), 195–207.

Boyd-Franklin, N. (1989). *Black families in therapy: A multisystems approach.* New York: Guilford Press.

Brownell, P. (1998). The application of the culturagram in cross cultural practice with elder abuse victims. *Journal of Elder Abuse and Neglect, 9*(2), 19–33.

Brownell, P., & Congress, E. (1998). Cross cultural issues in work with battered women. In A. Roberts, *Battered Women* (2nd ed., pp. 387–404). New York: Springer.

Canino, I., & Spurlock, J. (1994). *Culturally diverse children and adolescents: Assessment, diagnosis, and treatment.* New York: Guilford Press.

Carten, A., & Dumpson, J. (1997). *Removing risks from children: Shifting the paradigm.* Silver Springs, MD: Beckham House.

Collier, A., McClure, F., Collier, J., Otto, J., & Polloi, A. (1999). Culture specific views of childhood rearing and parenting styles in a Pacific Asian community. *Child Abuse and Neglect 23*(3), 229–44.

Congress, E. (1986). *Ethical decision making among social work supervisors.* Unpublished doctoral dissertation, City University of New York.

Congress, E. (1990). Crisis intervention with Hispanic clients in an urban mental health clinic. In A. Roberts (Ed.), *Crisis intervention handbook: Assessment, treatment, and research* (pp. 221–36). Belmont, CA: Wadsworth.

Congress, E. (1994). The use of culturagrams to assess and empower culturally diverse families. *Families in Society, 75*(9), 531–40.

Congress, E. (Ed.). (1997). *Multicultural perspectives in working with families.* New York: Springer.

Congress, E. (1999). *Social work ethics for the twenty-first century: Identifying and resolving ethical dilemmas.* Chicago: Nelson Hall.

Congress, E., & Lynn, M. (1994). Group work programs in public schools: Ethical dilemmas and cultural diversity. *Social Work in Education, 16*(2), 107–14.

Corey, G., Corey, M., & Callanan, P. (1993). *Issues and ethics in the helping professions.* Pacific Grove, CA: Brooks Cole.

Crenshaw, W., Bartell, P., & Lichtenberg, J. (1994). Proposed revisions to mandatory reporting laws: An exploratory survey of chid protective service agencies. *Child Welfare, 73*(1), 15–27.

Devore, W., & Schlesinger, E. (1996). *Ethnic sensitive social work practice.* Boston: Allyn & Bacon.

Dickson, D. (1995). *Law in the health and human services: A guide for social workers, psychologists, psychiatrists, and related professionals.* New York: Free Press.

Dickson, D. (1998). *Confidentiality and privacy in social work.* New York: Free Press.

Dillion, D. (1994). Understanding and assessment of intragroup dynamics in family foster care among African American families. *Child Welfare, 73*(2), 129–39.

Erickson, E. (1968). *Identity, youth, and crisis.* New York: Norton.

Fanshel, D., and Shinn, E. (1978). *Children in foster care: A longitudinal study.* New York: Columbia University Press.

Foner, N. (1987). Introduction: New immigrants and changing patterns in New York City. In N. Foner (Ed.), *New immigrants in New York* (pp. 1–33). New York: Columbia University Press.

Fong, R. (1994). Family preservation: Making it work for Asians. *Child Welfare, 73*(4), 331–41.

Francis, C. (1999). *Degree of parental acceptance of services and some of the factors related to their acceptance.* Unpublished doctoral dissertation, Fordham University Graduate School of Social Service, New York.

Frecknall, P. (1996, August 27). Big Brothers/Big Sisters of New York City: Cultural Matching/Parental Satisfaction Follow-Up Survey. Unpublished report.

Garrett, K. (1994). Caught in a bind: Ethical decision making in schools. *Social Work in Education, 16*(2), 97–105.

Gibelman, M., & Schervish, P. (1997). *Who we are: A second look.* Washington, DC: NASW.

Gleeson, J., O'Donnell, J., & Bonecutter, F. (1997). Understanding the complexity of practice in kinship foster care. *Child Welfare, 76*(6), 801–26.

Green, J. (1995). *Cultural awareness in the human services.* Englewood Cliffs, NJ: Prentice Hall.

Hartman, A., & Laird, J. (1983). *Family centered social work.* New York: Free Press.

Hendricks, C. O. (1997). The child, the family, and the school: A multicultural triangle. In E. Congress (Ed.), *Multicultural perspectives in working with families* (pp. 37–60). New York: Springer Press.

Hepworth, D., & Larsen, J. (1993). *Direct social work practice: Theory and skills.* Pacific Grove, CA: Brooks/Cole.

Ho, M. K. (1987). *Family therapy with ethnic minorities.* Newbury Park, CA: Sage.

Ho, M. K. (1991). The use of the ethnic sensitive inventory (ESI) to enhance practitioner skills with minorities. *Journal of Multicultural Social Work, 1*(1), 57–68.

Joseph, M. V., & Conrad, A. (1989). Social work influence on interdisciplinary ethical decision making in health care settings. *Health and Social Work, 14*(1), 22–30.

Kagle, J., & Kopels, S. (1994). Confidentiality after *Tarasoff. Health and Social Work, 19*(3), 217–22.

Keith-Lucas, A. (1977). Ethics in social work. In *Encyclopedia of Social Work* (17th ed., pp. 350–55). Washington, DC: NASW.

Kocher, G., & Keith-Speigel, P. (1990). *Children, ethics, and the law.* Lincoln: University of Nebraska Press.

Kopels, S. (1992). Confidentiality and the school social worker. *Social Work in Education, 14*(4), 203–5.

Kopels, S. (1993). Response to "Confidentiality: A different perspective." *Social Work in Education, 15*(4), 250–52.

Lewis, H. (1972). Morality and the politics of practice. *Social Casework, 5*(13), 404–17.

Lieberman, A. (1990). Culturally sensitive intervention with children and families. *Child and Adolescent Social Work, 7*(2), 101–20.

Lindsey. D. (1994). *The welfare of children.* New York: Oxford University Press.

Lum, D. (1996). *Social work practice and people of color: A process-stage approach* (3rd ed.). Belmont, CA: Wadsworth.

McGoldrick, M., & Gerson, R. (1985). *Genograms in family assessment.* New York: Norton.

McGoldrick, M., Pearce, J., & Giordano, J. (1997). *Ethnicity and family therapy* (2nd ed.). New York: Guilford.

McGowan, B., & Stutz, E. (1991). Children in foster care. In A. Gitterman, *Handbook of social work practice with vulnerable populations* (pp. 382–415). New York: Columbia University Press.

McNeely, R., & Badan, M. (1984). Interracial communication in school social work. *Social Work, 29,* 22–25.

Minuchin, S. (1974). *Families and family therapy.* Cambridge, MA: Harvard University Press.

Morrison, B. (1997). Reframing the research agenda. In A. Carten & J. Dumpson, *Removing risks from children* (pp. 49–61). Silver Springs, MD: Beckham House.

National Association of Social Workers. (1996). *Code of Ethics.* Washington, DC: Author.

National Association of Social Workers. (1999, October). *NASW News, 44*(9), 10.

Newman, B., & Newman, P. (1991). *Development through life: A psychosocial approach* (5th ed.). Pacific Grove, CA: Brooks Cole.

Ozawa, M. (1997). Demographic changes and their implications. In M. Reisch and E. Gambrill, *Social work in the twenty-first century* (pp. 8–27). Thousand Oaks, CA: Pine Forge Press.

Pine, B. (1987). Strategies for more ethical decision making in child welfare practice. *Child Welfare, 66*(4), 315–26.

Pope-Davis, D. B., Eliason, M. J. & Ottavi, T. M. (1994). Are nursing students multiculturally competent? An exploratory investigation. *Journal of Nursing Education, 33*(1), 31–33.

Reisch, M., & Taylor, C. (1983). Ethical guidelines for cutback management: A preliminary approach. *Administration in Social Work, 7*(3/4), 59–72.

Roberts, C. (1989). Conflicting professional values in social work and medicine. *Health and Social Work, 14*(3), 211–18.

Roberts, D. (1999). Access to justice: Poverty, race, and new directions in child welfare policy. *Washington University Journal of Law and Policy,* 1999, 63–76.

Rose, J. (1999). *The newest New Yorkers.* New York: Department of City Planning.

Schroeder, L. (1995). *Legal environment of social work.* Washington, DC: NASW.

Shireman. J. (1994). Should interracial adoptions be permitted? In E. Gambrill & T. Stein (Eds.), *Controversial issues in child welfare* (pp. 246–60). Boston: Allyn & Bacon.

Siegel, L. (1994). Cultural differences and their impact on practice in child welfare. *Journal of Multicultural Social Work, 3*(3), 87–96.

Silber, T. (1982). Ethical consideration in the medical care of adolescents who consult for treatment of gonorrhea. *Adolescence, 17*(66), 267–71.

Stein, T. (1991). *Child welfare and the law.* New York: Longman.

Tataram, T. (1993). *Characteristics of children in substitute and adoptive care.* Washington, DC: Voluntary Cooperative Information System: American Public Welfare Association.

Tonning, L. (1999). Persistent and chronic neglect in the context of poverty—When parents can't parent. Case of Ricky, age 3. In N. B. Webb (Ed.), *Play therapy with children in crisis: Individual, group, and family treatment* (2nd ed., pp. 203–24). New York: Guilford.

Tourigny, M., & Bouchard, C. (1994). Incidence and characteristics of signs of child abuse: An intercultural comparison. *Child Abuse and Neglect, 19*(10), 797–808.

Videka-Sherman, L. (1991). *Child abuse and neglect.* In A. Gitterman (Ed.), *Handbook of social work practice with vulnerable populations* (pp. 345–81). New York: Columbia University Press.

Wachtel, E. F. (1994). *Treating troubled children and their families.* New York: Guilford.

Walden, T., Wolock, I., & Demone, H. (1990). Ethical decision making in human services. *Families in Society, 71*(2), 67–75.

Webb, N. (1996). *Social work practice with children.* New York: Guilford.

Zayas, L., Kaplan, C., Turner, S., Romano, K., & Gonzalez-Ramos, G. (2000). Understanding suicide attempts by adolescent Hispanic females. *Social Work, 45*(1), 53–63.

A Framework
for Culturally
Responsive Practice

BRENDA WILLIAMS-GRAY

The beauty of a patchwork quilt is in the colors, textures, and patterns that individuate each square of the fabric. There is no symmetry or matching necessary among the pieces. The patches, like culture, are rich and attractive because of their diversity and uniqueness. However, the patches are not a quilt until they are joined together by a common thread that links each piece into a functional whole. The threads, like our shared "humanness," join the pieces of the quilt together. The quilt is a metaphor for both the richness and diversity of culture and the universality of humanity that connect individuals to one another.

Social workers and other mental health practitioners enter the helping relationship prepared with knowledge, skills, and resources to assist children and families in problem solving. The goal of our work is to enhance our clients' functioning within a psychosocial, person-in-environment fit. We understand the course of development and life cycle stages, and we are empathic to the stresses of the human condition. Our professional value system tells us to "start where the client is," to promote client self-determination and treat clients with respect and dignity.

Attention to culture and its dynamic interplay in families would seem to be a given for competent clinical practice. Yet practice philosophies and modalities of

Special thanks to Nancy Boyd Webb, Keidron Gray, and Dorothy Nelson. Dedicated to the special gifts that fathers and brothers bring to a family, especially Weldon "Sonny" Williams, Weldon "Guy" Williams, and Leon Gray treatment often do not specify how to include the cultural essence of the family and its worldview into the treatment process. Instead, the client's culture is sometimes presented as an add-on to the assessment process and filed as a comment in the client's records. Difficulties that emerge later in the relationship that are attributed to resistance or negative transference can actually result from cultural clashes and differing views on appropriate help-seeking behaviors and attitudes. Focusing attention on these dilemmas helps the practitioner understand the meanings that families attach to their life circumstances, behaviors, problems, and help-seeking attitudes.

The purpose of this chapter is to present and illustrate a framework for culturally sensitive practice that integrates a multicultural strengths perspective (Saleebey, 1992) into the practitioner's frame of reference as a normative means of working with families. This framework can guide social workers and other mental health professionals in becoming more culturally aware. This understanding will help practitioners recognize the cultural influences that impact on the presenting problem, treatment formulation, and intervention considerations. This framework does not provide a cookie cutter checklist of "do and don't" stereotype and responses for the worker. Instead, it proposes that practitioners expand their worldview and join with their clients, whose sense of self, life experiences, coping difficulties, and personal strengths, although unfamiliar, may be as valid as that of the practitioner. Engaging, validating, and working with clients within the contextual language of culture can facilitate the communication process and create more positive outcomes in the worker-family relationship.

The chapter first presents an operational definition of cultural competence. An ecological schema of the parent-child relationship, juxtaposed with an environmental, historical, and social context, is presented in terms of themes that are embedded within the family dynamics. Evolving family structures and cultural belief systems are discussed, and dilemmas associated with extrafamilial child care are addressed. Finally, challenging issues for practitioners—such as discipline, child abuse, domestic violence, and substance abuse—are discussed as these issues impact on relationships within the family and larger systems. Suggested guidelines are offered for culturally sensitive and responsive practice.

CULTURE, CULTURAL DIVERSITY, AND CULTURAL COMPETENCE

Operational definitions of culture, cultural diversity, and cultural competence are essential starting points for this discussion of culturally responsive practice.

Culture

The Child Welfare League of America (CWLA)[1] defines *culture* as "thoughts, ideas, behavior patterns, customs, belief, values, skills, arts, religions, and prejudices of a particular people at a given point in time" (CWLA, 1999).

Falicov (1998) views culture as multidimensional with "sets of shared worldviews, meanings, and adaptive behaviors derived from simultaneous membership and participation in a variety of contexts" (p. 14). Logan, Freeman, and McRoy

(1990) look at culture beyond its formal definition of a group's shared values and meanings. They note that culture is "the essence and ethos of a people as well as a way of life . . . culture is viewed also as the more subtle human orientation, to the problems of existence, as ways of being in the world" (p. 25). Greenfield (1997) states that culture "implies sharing or agreement or social convention. In symbolic culture . . . what is shared are values, knowledge, and communication" (p. 115).

These definitions of culture create a broad context that is inclusive of the ways in which "one is." These ways encompass the following:

- ways of personal identification (race, ethnicity, gender, class, nationality, religion, sexual orientation, age)
- ways of thinking (thoughts, ideas, prejudices)
- ways of acting (behavior patterns, coping skills, customs, rituals, traditions)
- ways of being (beliefs, values, political ideology)
- ways of expression (arts, music, dance, literature, and communication)
- ways of living (family role, social and economic status, employment, education)
- ways of interaction (intrafamily, extended family, local community, social organizations, and social institutions)

Culture simultaneously defines how families function and influences the way that families interact with their environment. McPhatter (1997) notes that "culture connotes world view, behavioral styles and inclinations and thinking patterns that present and can be anticipated in interpersonal interaction across social boundaries" (p. 261).

Cultures evolve and are influenced by time, history, and social conditions that alter worldviews and traditional values over time. A particular people or culturally defined group membership can be based on primary factors such as race, ethnicity, religion, and nationality, or on combinations of these factors. Additional cultural indices include gender and economic class. More importantly, some members of ethnic groups exist in a bicultural experience that requires the ability to function in, and between, more than one group simultaneously. The degree of ease and flexibility with which one is able to move within and out of the dominant culture, while being true to one's primary culture, influences choices and trade-offs.

Cultural Diversity

With the exception of its Native American inhabitants, the United States is a country that is populated by worldwide immigrants who immigrated here through voluntary and involuntary means, tinged by feelings of hope and desperation. Issues of force, slavery, ambitious dreams, and lost family bonds fill immigrants' emotional baggage. Ironically, four hundred years into this country's history, the richness of its cultural diversity is juxtaposed against the tensions, inequities, myths, fear, bias, oppression, and racism among people.

The CWLA views cultural diversity as the "rich mixture of ethnic, racial, religious, national and individual characteristics" (CWLA, 1999). To this list it is important to add gender, social and economic class, and sexual orientation. Subtleties based on primary and secondary cultural affiliation such as racial and national or religious and ethnic differences, family migration patterns, and bicultural identity also deepen the layers of cultural diversity among people who appear on the surface to have similar cultural backgrounds.

The concept of cultural diversity acknowledges that there are differences among persons based on the interplay of race, nationality, and so forth. "Cultural differences exist on many levels, including help-seeking behaviors, language and communications styles, symptom patterns and expression, and non-traditional healing practices" (Comas-Diaz & Griffith as quoted in National Technical Assistance Center for State Mental Health Planning, 1999).

While all people share a common humanity, the implicit message for this discussion is that these differences must be acknowledged, accepted, understood, and embraced in order to create "a safe house" (Fox, 1993), or an environment conducive to competent practice. Competent practice requires an understanding of cultural diversity as a necessary foundation of a practitioner's knowledge base, since cross-cultural influences permeate the worker-client relationship.

Cultural Competence

McPhatter (1997) defines cultural competence as "the ability to transform knowledge and cultural awareness into health and/or psychosocial interventions that support and sustain healthy client-system functioning within the appropriate cultural context" (p. 261).

The CWLA further describes the interactions of both professionals and systems as culturally competent when the response to "people of all cultures, classes, races, ethnic backgrounds and religions recognizes, affirms and values the worth of individuals, families and communities and protects and preserves the dignity of each" (CWLA, 1999). Atkinson, Morten, and Sue (1998) identify key variables that help the mental health community increase cultural competence. "Providers need:

- to develop an awareness of their own racial and cultural heritage
- to understand how that heritage influences their understanding and biases
- to understand the significant impact of differences both in language and in verbal and non-verbal styles on the process of communication" (p. 4–5)

Vargas and Koss-Chioino (1992) use the term *culturally responsive* as an active stance toward integrating culture into psychotherapy as opposed to the similar but subtly passive connotation associated with *culturally sensitive* (p. 2). They affirm the requirement that therapy be cultural *responsive,* because the failure to understand the client's contextual environment can derail the development of a therapeutic alliance.

For practitioners, the question often becomes how to translate these practice ideals into practice styles. Ask and listen. We must invite clients to tell their stories, in their own words. This process must unfold and not be confined to the boundaries of the standard psychosocial format. Congress's culturagram (1994; also see chapter 2) provides a model to assist practitioners who wish to include a cultural dimension to the assessment and treatment process.

INFLUENCES OF HISTORICAL, CULTURAL, AND SOCIAL-ENVIRONMENTAL FACTORS ON PARENT-CHILD RELATIONSHIPS

This section presents an ecological framework toward cultural assessment with an emphasis on key concepts that impact on the thinking, behaviors, needs, and strength of culturally diverse children and families. This wide-angle lens provides a means for increased awareness and understanding about variables that comprise the worldview of children and families with norms outside the mainstream culture.

This approach to understanding the needs of culturally diverse children and families underscores professional values of respect, client dignity, and self-determination. Therefore, examining parent-child relationships within a cultural competency framework fully utilizes the life model and person-environment fit (Gitterman, 1996), the ego-oriented assessment (Goldstein, 1995), the strengths perspective (Saleebey, 1992), the values of empowerment (Collins, 1998), and feminist perspectives (Hartman, 1992).

Figure 3.1 illustrates the interplay of factors for this discussion. The figures in the center of the diagram represent a three-generation family, because the role of grandparent(s) and extended family in a cultural context must be recognized. The family's interrelationships are defined by a variety of normative factors:

- Family life cycles
- Individual child and adult developmental stages
- Birth order and sibling group configuration
- Overall health of family members

None of these factors are static or linear. Families move back and forth between stages as their needs change and as the environment responds to their individual and collective needs. Layered with these dynamics is the juxtaposition of the historical, cultural, and social-environmental overlay that interacts with parent-child relationships in culturally diverse families.

Historical Factors

Immigration and Migration   In this discussion, *immigration* refers to the movement or relocation of persons or families from a country to the United States. Examples include migrations from Europe following persecutions and famine; Caribbean migrations; and the recent increase in Asian, East Indian, and South Amer-

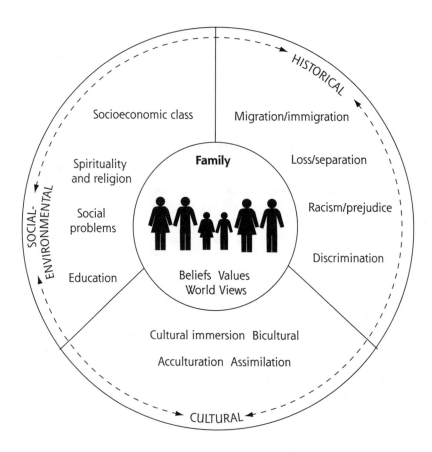

Figure 3.1. Influences of historical, cultural, and social-environmental factors on parent-child relationships

ican refugees to the United States. *Migration*, on the other hand, refers to those who move from one region to another within the United States. The 1940s post–World War II migration of black Americans from the rural south to northern industrial cities best illustrates migration. According to Satterwhite (n.d.) at the Academy for Child Welfare Training, people migrate because of:

- Political or religious persecution
- Poor economic conditions or educational opportunities
- Racism or prejudice
- Space (land and housing)

Hopes for a safe environment, a better life and opportunities for education, and prosperity for their family have often been achieved or dashed by what people find after they arrive. "The land of opportunity" does include economic and educational opportunities. However, changes of climate, pace, and language all affect immigrants and regional migrants. Losses of familial and familiar comforts can create isolation for those who have left family behind and charted their own course. Many cultures send for relatives once part of the family has established itself in the new land, a step that provides both emotional support and a cultural enclave or sub-community (see chapter 5). In these communities, traditional customs can openly exist without the scrutiny of the mainstream environment. These neighborhoods sometimes evolve into impoverished ghettos when access to broader opportunities and resources are curtailed. Historically, when large numbers of migrants settle in a given region the prior immigrants move up (economically, socially) and out. Satterwhite (n.d.) raises several questions about these families that impact on child-rearing and family conditions. These questions include:

- Can they and do they plan to return?
- What is their immigration status (documented or undocumented)?
- Did the family leave voluntarily or involuntarily?
- Did they leave family members behind?

Additionally, he cites other conditions that can impact on the health of the family and the parenting of the children:

- Parent-child role reversal
- Lower status or lower-paying job
- A lack of resources and information
- Unrealistic expectations

Loss/separation Typical cultural clashes and difficulties that arise for immigrant families include:

Depression—The loss of familiar surroundings, changes in weather, comfortable routines, work, and familial relationships are often not immediately resolved in the new location. In addition to negotiating new surroundings, the sadness related to isolation and loneliness can create depressed moods because of the loss of all that is familiar.

Abandonment versus survival—For many immigrants, leaving a child with relatives while in pursuit of the American Dream is a practical and safe way to venture into the unfamiliar. Sending for the children once the parent is established is a typical means of family reunification. Some practitioners consider this option to be abandonment. Consequently, difficulties that later arise between parents and children who have lived apart require special understanding by practitioners. The typical developmental intergenerational crises can become exacerbated depending on the timing of reunification and the nature of the pre-separation relationship. (See chapter 5.)

Racism, Prejudice, and Discrimination Racism is a condition that stems from an individual or group's belief that they are superior to others based specifically on race and skin color. This belief is translated into attitudes, behaviors, and stereotypes that permeate all aspects of daily functioning, creating oppressed conditions for those designated as racial minorities. In the United States, racism has traditionally been manifested by white versus black. Jacobs and Bowles (1988) note that Asian Indians experience degrees of racial discrimination because of their brown skin color. Likewise, darker-skinned Caribbean Hispanics also become victims because of their brown skin and African features. Those who have lighter skin and Spanish features are more likely to be exempt from bias.

While some people of color may have racially based beliefs toward the white majority, the power differential nullifies its impact. The power of racism is based on the ability to control economic and social opportunities and reduce access for people of color. Racism has its greatest impact when its values are both institutionalized and internalized.

Institutionalized racism occurs when the political, social, educational, and economic structures, either through omission or commission, sanction practices that legalize racism. Institutionalized racism enables social structures to allow racial minorities to have limited access to housing, resources, education, and prosperity and to be blamed for their difficulties as if those problems are individually caused, not socially driven. Jacobs and Bowles (1988) describe a history of federalism that institutionalized policies of racism against people of color. Some examples include:

- The Chinese Exclusion Act of 1882, which suspended Chinese immigration for ten years
- The Dawes Act of 1887, which resulted in the loss of ninety-one million acres of land by Native Americans during 1887–1914
- The War Relocation Authority, which supervised Japanese Americans placed under detention during World War II

The most noteworthy example of institutionalized racism in the United States is slavery, which created a legacy of family destruction, a disregard for humanity, and a denial of basic freedoms for black Americans. Even after its abolishment, the South held onto Jim Crow laws until the pressures of the Civil Rights movement prevailed. Since the Civil Rights movement, conditions regarding racism have shifted toward affirmative action setbacks, glass ceiling corporate politics, police brutality, and racial profiling.

The relevance of racism for practitioners working with people of color is that the degree and severity of overt racism and the subtlety of chronic racism may contribute to self-protective behaviors that can lead to difficulties in developing a therapeutic alliance. Nancy Boyd-Franklin (1989) discusses "healthy cultural paranoia" as a survival skill utilized by blacks when approaching persons and institutions that may hold discriminatory views and behaviors. The hypervigilance required to "check out" vibes and messages resembles Herman's (1992) description of trauma symptoms. The energy expended at trying to decipher *daily* whether experiences are based on racial bias is an additional stress to one's coping and living. Even when the guard of hypervigilance is dropped, there are daily reminders that others' judgments may not be based on who you are, but on what color you are.

Internalized racism exists when people of minority groups absorb the belief regarding their "inferiority." Low self-worth and self-esteem are perpetuated by media stereotypes that reinforce beauty as having light skin and less pronounced African features. Skin color and hair texture are pervasive themes of how people of color view and identify themselves, either embracing Afro-centric styles or distancing themselves from them.

Shorris (1992) notes that a child's color can influence his or her place and value in the family. "The darkest one may become the pet or the outsider, the success or the troublemaker . . . The darkest one will always be singled out" (p. 166). Likewise, the lightest family member may also be singled out. This theme is an important one for practitioners working with children and families. Issues about family alliances and scapegoats that are attached to color can be explored as part of the genogram or as an issue raised by a family member. Practitioners must be open to addressing the color–self-esteem relationship if it is apparent that family relationships are defined by color. When these negative values are internalized, a sense of rage often develops as well, which when acted upon is often against those in the same position or against oneself. The use of ethnic slurs as an "acceptable" term of endearment is a prime example of internalized racism.

CASE STUDY: BALANCE

With a colleague, I coled a parent support group for families with children in care. We thought the combination of a black female social work director and a white male psychologist provided a perfect gender, ethnic, professional balance. Many of the parents used the group to discuss their own trauma and losses and to gain mutual support. An interesting dynamic occurred. The male and female clients always deferred to Dr. T., even if I posed the initial inquiry. It became evident that I was made invisible once the pleasantries were dispensed with despite my active efforts to join with the group facilitation. I raised this issue during post-group processing, and we reflected on the cause and on appropriate strategies to shift the dynamic. It became clear to me that instead of creating a comfort zone for the women of color in the group, my presence created something else. Because I looked like them and because they were powerless as women, parents, and people of color, then I could be of no use to them because I represented the negativity they saw in themselves.

Racismo as described by Shorris (1992) reflects the pecking order among Latinos who have immigrated to the United States from Mexico, Cuba, South America, and Puerto Rico. The color and class hierarchy follows "the well-known rules of racism: rich/poor, light/dark, English/Spanish, educated/ignorant, citizen/newcomer . . . To illustrate the complexity of the hierarchy, one might ask whether, in the eyes of a Puerto Rican, a poor, black Cuban who completed high school stands higher or lower than a middle class, third generation Mexican-American who speaks no Spanish and attended a community college for one year?" (p. 160).

It is important to stress that people designated as oppressed often demonstrate cultural pride and a resiliency perspective despite the toll exacted by overt and subtle racism. Coping in the face of adversity is a strength that sustains the forward motion of people of color.

Cultural Factors

Assimilation, Acculturation, and Cultural Immersion English (1995) defines *assimilation* as "the adoption of another culture's values and way of life" (p. 32). It is important to note that total adaptation does not guarantee the absence of discrimination, since it is the dominant culture's acceptance that dictates the degree of access to its opportunities. Additionally, one's natural identity becomes submerged in the assimilation process. This situation is in contrast to English's (1995) view of *acculturation* as "the adaptation of one's own cultural values to existence within another cultural context" (p. 32). Logan et al. (1990) broaden the "cultural identity spectrum" to include *biculturalism,* a dual perspective that is the "increased ability to function effectively in the dominant society and in the Black culture, [this means] access to resources in *both* environments, and provision of cultural maintenance and a positive racial identity" (p. 61). These authors note the negative trade-off of biculturalism as the "emotional stress associated with adapting to two often conflicting sets of expectations" (p. 61).

Additionally, Logan et al. (1990) describe *cultural immersion* within the black culture as making lifestyle choices that limit interaction with the dominant culture. The benefits include high group support for cultural maintenance, a higher likelihood of positive racial identity formation, and less opportunity for racial discrimination and rejection (due to limited exposure to out-of-race experiences). The negative trade-off to cultural immersion, according to Logan et al., is limited access to resources and opportunities in the larger society and to the benefits of cultural diversity. Clearly this model can be applied to other ethnic groups whose members straddle different points in the cultural continuum. A metaphor that combines English's definition and Logan's continuum illustrates the complexity of norms that can coexist in a family.

Assimilation	Acculturation	Biculturation	Cultural immersion
↓	↓	↓	↓
When in Rome, eat Italian	When in Rome, eat Italian but bring your own seasoning	When in Rome, find Italian soul food	When in Rome, bring your own food

The choices made within families as to their cultural identity can be a function of several factors: what countries they immigrated from; how they immigrated; their ability to maintain or rise in social class; and their degree of comfort and fluidity in adapting to dominant cultural expectations. Additionally, family politics and hierarchical subsystems often dictate where family members fit culturally. The opportunity for conflict is great between the generations since history, economics, and political changes influence a family's cultural mind-set and their degree of cultural fluidity. These cultural positions are not static; they shift with age, time, family dynamics, or changing social needs.

Biculturalism Persons of color inevitably deal with some degree of biculturalism. The emotional tug-of-war of balancing acceptance by the mainstream without giving up "who you are" is a lifelong dilemma played out in many families. A person's choice and position on the cultural spectrum can even be unstated. Add to this dilemma those issues related to normative family and individual life cycles, and the potential complexity for conflict becomes evident.

Social-Environmental Factors

Ortega and Nunez (1997) describe the interrelationship among the historical, cultural, and social-environmental factors described in figure 3.1 among Latin Americans. "Latino families experience stress due to acculturation; poverty; exposure to violence, drugs, disease, and environmental hazards; and mobility. Many Latino families experience segregation, social marginalization, discrimination, and oppression—all of which are manifested in mental health breakdown, alcohol and substance abuse, and social withdrawal. Also, language and cultural differences often prevent them from accessing resources and services" (p. 8).

Socioeconomic Class Persons of the same ethnic group who are in a different socioeconomic class can have some over-arching ethnic value similarities, e.g., value of education, while having differing life experiences and priorities. Practitioners working with children and families need to keep in mind the following key concepts related to class:

- Don't assume that all ethnic minorities seeking or referred for help are poor, are not working, and are government dependent. Fletcher (1997) says, "A strong work ethic and an increase in the number of working women have fueled a broad expansion of the Latino middle class in recent years" (p. A8). The following case example illustrates the point: A thirty-five-year-old professional black woman completing her chemical dependency program began to complain to the counselor about the psychiatrist's refusal to give her a return-to-work letter. She was enraged because he suggested that she not return to work at this time. She informed him that she had a life and in order to move forward, she needed to resume work. He suggested that she apply for SSI and move into an SRO to see if she could handle stress. She continued to complain to the counselor—"Who does he think I am? I have never lived that way. He wouldn't suggest that to his own daughter. Just because I'm in recovery doesn't mean I'm poor. I have a standard of living, and I need to get back to work."

- Recognize that many families have multiple economic classes within the family subgroups. For example, the sibling who is a college graduate in corporate America can have a sibling who works at odd jobs off the book or at minimum wage. This dichotomy raises issues with extended families. The concept that the family members who have "made it" gave up a part of their ethnic identity is a refrain in minority communities that erroneously suggests that success is not normative for ethnic minorities unless they mirror the language and attitude of mainstream America. Concurrently, the successful family members can be embarrassed by their less financially stable counterparts. Often family members trade supports. According to Jarrett (1999), "When kin are better off economically, youngsters gain access to resources in rich communities that offer a wide array of institutional, informational, and economic assets, including well-functioning schools" (p. 47). He cites a case, noting that the child's "family and history are not contained in a single geographical area but rather in a kinship centered in two neighborhoods differentiated by social class and culture" (p. 48).

- Poverty as an economic condition is not the same as poverty as a state of mind. Many families of color go about raising children, working, and achieving financial and social success without fanfare. For the working poor, the effort may not net access and opportunity. However, the value system for wanting more for themselves and their children is not unlike the value system of those who are financially better off. "Inner-city neighborhoods with limited social, economic, and institutional resources demand that parents be 'super-parents' to ensure conventional development for their adolescents" (Jarrett, 1999, p. 48). The point for practitioners is not to assume that economic poverty is equal to poverty of the spirit; even when families struggle to attain the values they hope for their children, it doesn't mean they are without these values.

Spirituality and Religion Boyd-Franklin (1989) discusses spiritual reframing as a tool for families who believe in the power of faith and inner strength. Spirituality is an orientation and belief system in a higher power. Religion is an organized formal set of practices and rituals that communities of people share and practice generally within a church setting. Ethnic groups practice a range of religions including but not limited to Protestant sects, Catholicism, Judaism, Muslim, Hindu, Buddhism, and Jehovah's Witness. One's church family functions as a place of emotional support and camaraderie, physical and social resources, political action, and an opportunity for leadership (Boyd-Franklin), as illustrated in the following example.

CASE STUDY: CALVIN

Ms. Green, Calvin's social worker, looked at his sad face and said, "If God could forgive you, why can't you forgive yourself?" She handed him a Bible that his grandmother had left for him. Shortly thereafter, he was able to join the family session with his grandmother and disclose his inappropriate sexual behavior.

Nontraditional spiritual beliefs rooted in the Caribbean include voodoo and Santeria. These beliefs stem from African influences in the region. The spiritual supernatural is sometimes not understood by professionals who are not from these cultures. Practitioners should not assume pathology or paranoia when confronted with rituals and beliefs that are foreign to them. It is important to determine if the person can differentiate between the supernatural and reality. Practitioners should also encourage families involved in treatment to simultaneously engage in treatment and maintain respect for their spiritual beliefs (Norma Vega, personal communication, April 2000).

Education   The work of childhood is school; a child's success or failure in the educational system can create a pathway or a dead end for his or her future. School is often the first critical opportunity for people of color to interface with formal institutions on behalf of their children. Help-seeking, active participation in their child's education and advocacy for their child's needs are influenced by the fit between the family and the school environment. The following considerations reflect the complexity of educational factors impacting on culturally diverse families and children.

• *History.* The U.S. Supreme Court's 1896 decision in *Plessy v. Ferguson* gave states the right to "impose racial segregation via the formula, 'separate but equal' . . . the separate but equal doctrine relegated African-American children to inadequate and unsafe schools" (Appiah & Gates, 1999, pp. 1531–32). The Supreme Court reversed itself in 1954 when Thurgood Marshall argued the case of *Brown v. the Board of Education*. Racially segregated public schools were deemed "inherently unequal . . . and causing psychological damage to Black children" (Appiah & Gates, pp. 321–22). This legacy still has its influences, as desegregation was hard fought and de facto segregation has occurred because of white flight from urban locales. Thus minority children and new immigrants utilizing the public school system often have the least resources. Catholic schools have been an educational "window of opportunity" for minority children regardless of the family's religion. Poor and working class families make economic sacrifices since these schools are seen as successful in academics, discipline, and a future orientation.

• *Value of education.* Despite the noted historical difficulties, education is often viewed as the key to mobility in ethnic communities. Hill (1997) reaffirms this value of education as a strength for African American families. Traditionally black colleges emerged as a response to providing opportunity for academic achievement for those who were not welcomed in other institutions of higher learning.

• *Special education.* Special education designed for needy children has become the warehouse for children with a variety of behavioral, learning, and emotional needs (Cooper, Denner, & Lopez, 1999). Educators act as institutional gatekeepers when they assess students against standardized benchmarks of achievement that determine eligibility for college-prep classes or placement in vocational or remedial classes. Cooper et al. note that when elementary schools' Latino students are disproportionately placed in special education classes and in low reading and math ability groups, these students are then routed toward remedial tracts in middle and high school. Teachers from any ethnic background can also act as cultural brokers who help Latino children succeed in school and achieve their dreams. Some teachers review the assessments of Spanish-speaking students to ensure that the students are not wrongly placed in special education because of language differences (Cooper et al., p. 52).

FAMILY CONSIDERATIONS: CULTURAL BELIEFS, VALUES, AND WORLDVIEWS

The values and cultural belief systems of a people carry through the generations and mingle with the current social-environmental context of a family. The merging of the traditional and the current sociocultural elements can redefine the worldview of family members. The tug-of-war between adolescents and parents, particularly among new immigrants, can result in the normative teen-parent crises coupled with the differences between Old World traditions and New World modernism. As suggested previously, the family's life cycle is developed and compounded by biculturation as well as generational issues.

Cultural differences may produce perceptions, coping styles, or belief systems that appear strange or even irrational to practitioners (Harper & Lantz, 1996). As the faces of Americans change, workers must understand and respect the value systems and strengths of different cultures. Within each culture are usually many shared values, even if religious, social class, and regional differences exist. *However, there also are differences within each cultural group, and practitioners must avoid generalizing and must always listen for individual meaning.*

The worldviews of many minority groups share similarities and differ from Anglo-American value systems in a number of ways. These similarities support a worldview stance that Kunjufu (1984) describes as a "dichotomy of values":

Traditional	as compared to	Contemporary
African	as compared to	American
We	as compared to	I
Cooperation	as compared to	Competition
Internal	as compared to	External

CASE STUDY: THE MITCHELLS

An illustration of a shared value between two different minority cultures is esteem for the elders. The Mitchells, an African American family, were purchasing their first home. They were having an apartment added to the house so Ms. Mitchell's mother could move in with them and still have some private space. For Ms. Mitchell, this addition meant that she and the children could enjoy her mother. The builders were Korean immigrants. When they learned that the extra apartment was for a family elder, they found creative ways to increase the space without changing the design.

McGee (1997) cites Vasquez's (1994) delineation of the differences between the Latino and majority cultures:

Majority		Latino
Rugged individualism	vs.	Group achievement
Protestant work ethic	vs.	Work for community
Nuclear family structure	vs.	Extended family structure
Assertiveness	vs.	Less assertiveness
Rigid time orientation	vs.	Present focused

Furthermore, Ho (1990) describes significant worldview differences between white American mainstream views and ethnic minorities in the spheres of time frame, relationality, and family as follows:

In contrast with middle-class White American cultural values, which emphasized man's control of nature and the environment, most ethnic minority groups emphasize man's harmony with the environment. While the mainstream society is future-oriented, worshipping youth and making sacrifices for a better tomorrow, ethnic groups reminisce about the past and take pleasure in the present. In the relational dimension, while middle-class White Americans prefer individual autonomy, ethnic minorities prefer collectivity. Because the "doing orientation" is basic to the middle-class White Americans' life-style, competitiveness and upward mobility characterize their mode of activity. Asian/Pacific Americans prefer self-discipline, Black Americans adopt endurance of suffering, and both American Indians and Hispanic Americans may prefer a being-in-becoming mode of activity. Finally, the sociological structure of the mainstream society addresses itself basically to the nuclear family, which contrasts to the extended family common to minority groups. (p. 15)

Given this dichotomy of worldviews, a culturally based conflict between workers and clients is inevitable if workers do not:

1. Understand their own worldview
2. Appreciate that their view is only one of many possible views
3. Try to understand the client's view in order to offer help in a culturally sensitive manner (N. B. Webb, personal communication, February 2000)

A cultural awareness and conflict management exercise that I have adapted from Giordano and Levine's (1994) ethnic sharing curriculum attempts to help professionals look at the influence of their family's culture on their worldview and consider how it defines what they see as "normal." After selecting a diverse group of volunteers, I pose the following activities:

- Describe a family funeral.
- Explain your family's view of the elderly and the use of nursing homes.
- Describe the expectations in your family regarding education; explain whether these expectations differ for girls and boys.
- Describe what is considered "on time" or "late" in your family.
- Name an important family value.

Inevitably the commonalities and differences provide interesting dilemmas for consideration. How does the clinician who comes from a culture where nursing homes are taboo assist a family in locating an appropriate home for an elderly family member? How does the therapist who comes from an emotionally reserved stance comfort a client whose emotionality is overwhelming? How can a practitioner differentiate healthy family boundaries from enmeshed boundaries when the client's family dynamics and membership differ drastically from the workers' nuclear norm?

EXTRAFAMILIAL CHILD CARE

Informal Adoption

CASE STUDY: MS. DANE

There was not a prouder parent at the high school graduation than Ms. Dane. Her daughter, Cheryl, would begin college in the fall, and Ms. Dane could not remember a time when Cheryl was not underfoot. Ms. Dane and her grandmother raised Cheryl since she was three years old, when Cheryl's biological mother, Ms. Dane's cousin, brought Cheryl to them. As her grandmother's

health declined, Ms. Dane became one of her grandmother's caretakers and took full responsibility for Cheryl. Cheryl is very clear about who her mother is—Ms. Dane.

The role of positive kinship networks and extended families exemplify the we-versus-I value system among people of color. Raising children among family members and as a shared family responsibility can be framed as part of the collective family's responsibility to take care of the family's business—the child rearing of its members. Nuclear boundaries are less significant in this task than are extended family boundaries. Multiple developmental and family life cycle issues can emerge for the child, the relatives, and the biological parents, depending on the circumstances, perceptions, secrecy, rationale, and the quality of care given to the child. Informal adoption has been a practice since slavery and continues because:

- It meets the needs of black families that are not addressed by agencies, since minority children are not the focus of the formal adoption and child welfare institutions. (The original intention of formal adoption agencies was to place white babies.)
- When unwed teens become pregnant, older (generally female) relatives step in as primary caregivers.
- Family crises such as divorce, hard times. or relocation created the need for a short-term plan (Boyd-Franklin, 1989, p. 53).

Informal adoptions also extend beyond the boundaries of the biological extended family. It is not uncommon for the extended family to include lifelong friends, neighbors, distant relatives, and members of one's church. Children are raised to show respect for all elders. Aunt and uncle status may be bestowed on those persons designated by the family as "emotionally close enough" to be treated as relatives. In the Hispanic culture *Comandrazos* (coparents) or *Padrinos* (godparents) are persons traditionally designated as surrogate supports to the child.

A practitioner not familiar with the roles of extended family members, nonrelated family members, and informal family networks with regard to surrogate parenting may have difficulty evaluating the normative family dynamics compared to the existence of difficulties within the family. Secrecy about these informal nonbiological parent-child relationships occurs in order to "protect" the family from outside social systems that may not legitimize the extrafamilial relationships. It may be difficult for a child to describe his or her complex family, and the resulting confusion and secretiveness sometimes is viewed by professionals as "resistance."

For this reason, genograms may be useful only after the child and family have established trust with the worker. The simple task of signing consent forms can be difficult when there is a difference between the culturally normative family structure and the expectations of formal social organizations.

Workers must assess how child and family issues are imbedded in the family configuration and must sift out a family's strengths and the source of the current dilemma. These two factors can be one and the same. Problems occur when:

- A short-term plan becomes long term.
- The child is bonding to the caretaker, doesn't view the biological parent as a parent, and doesn't want to "go back home." This situation sometimes occurs when the child thinks that the biological parent is a sibling.
- The child experiences the parent as abandoning him or her.
- The care by the surrogate has been inadequate.
- Parental authority still resides with the nonresidential parent.
- The parent and the surrogate have different parenting styles.
- The parent and child are attempting to develop a bond late in the child's childhood without a sense of mutual history.

Child Welfare Institutions

An extended case study helps demonstrate the impact of an out-of-home placement from a family's perspective.

CASE STUDY: MIKE

It's been a long day. I had to work a double shift and I missed my train. Thank goodness my eleven-year-old is so responsible. She got the little ones doing their homework, and there are enough leftovers for dinner tonight. My husband has to work late tonight but that's okay. Things are so much better since he found a new job. It was crazy when he was home, unemployed and drinking.

That's when all the difficulties began with the little one, nine-year-old Mike. The school was calling every minute complaining that he was hyper, aggressive, and distracted. Going to his school all the time cut into my work schedule, and God knows the extra cash would have been helpful. Things are almost settled down except for the one fight Mike had in school. Now they are talking about this medication again. I'm not going to do it. He can get addicted, like it's a drug; he's too young for this. Besides, my mother would have a fit if she found out we couldn't control our child and had to put him on a drug. That counselor doesn't know anything about our family. Besides, Mike's allergic to penicillin and God knows what this medication would do. A little bit more discipline in that school and he'd be fine. That "time out" they use doesn't teach respect.

There's a knock at the door. It's half past nine; who could be coming to our house now? You're from where? ACS? CPS? What's this about? You're investigating a report about my son for neglect? Are you crazy? What do you mean, if I don't sign him into care you'll file a neglect petition? What is this about? Medication!!! I'm his parent, I decide if he goes on medication. Yes, he has a bruise on his elbow; he fell off his bicycle over the weekend. Of course he was supervised, and I have the emergency room forms right here. We're a hard-working family, we take care of our children; I resent you butting into our lives.

Two weeks have passed. The court decided that Mike needed residential treatment. They didn't care what my husband or I said. Everyone was crying. I didn't even get to go with him to make sure he was safe. Finally, I received a call from a social worker. She would have called sooner, she said, but my son was placed on a Friday and Monday was a holiday, so this was her first chance to contact me. She could not schedule a meeting for another two weeks, but when it was time, our whole family went. God knows, Mom's pressure's been up since Mike's been at this place for children who don't have families. The social worker was friendly and chirpy; she doesn't look a day over twenty-two. She's white and she assumed it was okay to call my husband by his first name even though she introduced herself as Ms. Smith. If she refers to my family as being dysfunctional one more time I may get up and hit her. She thinks we have poor boundaries, an enmeshed family, she called it, because my mother, sister, nephew, and minister all came for the meeting. I tried to be polite as I explained my concerns. My son tells me that he's the smallest kid in his cottage. He is afraid and doesn't understand why he can't come home. Of course he cries every night. I didn't have a chance to pack his night-light or his teddy bear. I wish this woman wouldn't act like she knows my child better than I do. That person who answers the phone in the cottage times my phone call. I understand that they only have one phone, but they supervise me on the phone with my child and want me off in five minutes! I've been up every Sunday to see him. He looks like a ragamuffin, and they won't let him have any of the food that I bring for him. They don't season the rice like we do at home. I can't stand the look in his eyes when I have to leave.

First he was begging, now it's just silent rage. I'm afraid that when I get my son back he won't still be in there. And these people say I'm not cooperative because I can't rearrange my schedule for all their meetings and support groups. Do they know what they can do with their support groups?

"The passage of the Adoption Assistance and Child Welfare Act of 1980 (P.L. 96-272) provided federal support for permanency planning as a guiding principle in child welfare. It established a national policy affecting permanency initiatives for children in out-of-home care" (Brown & Bailey-Etta, 1997, p. 67). These authors further note that although African American children were initially excluded from the child welfare system, they now constitute 42 percent of children in care (p. 74–75).

Entry into the child welfare system has had dramatic shifts in the last twenty years. The child voluntarily placed or the family in need of temporary foster care no longer represents mainstream admissions into the spectrum of child welfare services. Out-of-home placements within the child welfare system currently include: guardianship with a relative; kinship, traditional, or therapeutic foster family; group home; and residential treatment centers. The Division for Youth serves children who have engaged in criminal activity. The Office of Mental Health serves children with psychiatric impairments.

The 1980s brought with it crises of epic proportion. The crack and other substance abuse epidemics brought about the border baby crisis, when urban hospitals became temporary nurseries for babies born with positive toxicology. The HIV/AIDS crisis in its earliest stages was considered a death sentence. Poverty and homelessness continued to impact on the quality of care and safety for children. Exposure to violence and the inconsistencies of life in a shelter influenced the emotional and behavioral development of children. Horrific and highly publicized cases of abuse and neglect shifted public policy toward child removal.

Instead of the "problem child" being removed from the family, *all* the children were being put into foster care. These children were faced with the trauma of separation, loss, and a system that was often not user friendly. The need for permanency planning often competed with the need for trauma treatment.

Practitioners face a myriad of problems when assessing the alternatives of family reunification, adoption, and child-specific treatment needs. Culturally competent practice can be especially challenging for practitioners who are dealing with the complexities of out-of-home placement. Family members may view the practitioner as part of the system that disrupted their home. It is difficult to function effectively when the family is confused about the worker's role, both as treatment provider and the agent of social control. Language barriers often leave the child-client as the interpreter for the parent and worker, which generally creates role conflicts within the family.

It is helpful for practitioners to be up front about their dual roles because it sets clear parameters regarding the nature of their mutual work. Being judgmental about activities and behaviors is different from judging the client. Practitioners must assess their own feelings when dealing with emotionally toxic issues such as sexual abuse. It is critical that practitioners understand their own family of origin issues so as to manage their countertransference reactions. Setting goals with the clients so that they can be involved in the problem solving is both empowering and creates a shared ownership for the process. Practitioners will find that it is not necessary to like all of their clients, but courtesy and respect can pave the way toward a productive working relationship. Empathy can occur only when the practitioner listens to the client's story. Listening will facilitate differentiating between pathology and culture and finding the client's strengths, which can be used toward problem solving.

If the extended family, church, or others play a critical role in the family, the practitioner should be open to including them in the process as illustrated by the following case study.

CASE STUDY: MS. JONES AND HER SISTERS

Ms. Smith, a social worker at a residential treatment center, had some concerns regarding Anthony's mom, Ms. Jones. She found the mother to be passive during individual meetings and deferential to her four sisters when they joined the family sessions. Ms. Smith thought it was ridiculous that Ms. Jones relied on her sisters to make family decisions when Anthony was her child. Ms. Smith's family functioned very differently, and she viewed Anthony's mom as being overly enmeshed with her sisters. When Ms. Smith explored the difference in her meetings with Ms. Jones alone compared to when she was with her sisters, the family dynamic became apparent. The family disapproved of Anthony's out-of-home placement. Anthony's mom was the youngest of her sisters, and family approval came through the hierarchy. Their presence meant that decisions could be made during the meeting instead of in consultation later. The sisters also provided Ms. Jones with support in the family meetings.

CHALLENGING ISSUES FOR PRACTITIONERS

This section focuses specifically on social-environmental factors as they interface with culture. Social problems such as domestic violence, child abuse, and substance abuse do not discriminate: all cultures, classes, religions, races, and nationalities experience these problems. The issue for practitioners is how each culture frames, understands, and copes with these difficulties. What is normative and what is unacceptable may vary. Practitioners must attempt to understand the unacceptable as a means of gaining empathy and in order to facilitate change. However, culture must not be used as an excuse for the unacceptable or as an avoidance for corrective action. In fact, practitioners insult the value of cultural beliefs when they assume that those people who are different from them do not have parameters for acceptable behavior.

Domestic Violence

Domestic or family violence includes the use of physical, emotional, financial, and sexual aggression to cause harm or injury to a partner or family member. This aggression includes but is not limited to hitting with hands or objects, assault, isolation, withholding or control of money or food, and forced sex.

Ironically, the cultural family values and norms that support family health also have imbedded idiosyncrasies that create a climate conducive to domestic violence. McGee (1997) eloquently describes how roles, values, and rules merge with culturally specific strengths to create a balance between the family's internal functioning and its relationship with the outside world. He employs this dynamic to uncover the contextual environment that contributes to domestic violence.

> For African Americans, racial and economic inequities negatively impact men who sometimes translate this frustration into violence towards their partners. This violent act, then, is further complicated when African American women internalize and tolerate such behavior.
>
> In the Asian American community, the power differential created by the Confucian-based social rules dictate male dominance. Many men abuse this power with their wives, who are considered subservient, and who become a target for male anger.
>
> The Latino American concept of family, embedded in the patriarchal assumptions of Catholic dogma, helps structure gender roles such that a power differential between men and women is rationalized. When men are frustrated, they may take their anger out on their wives who often endure this abuse as part of their subordinate role. Latino women often exhibit insufficient self-esteem to believe they don't deserve this action. (p. 138)

Consistent with McGee's dynamic is understanding that the rationale does not diminish each person's responsibility for his or her actions, since domestic family violence is a "dysfunctional and destructive approach to problem-solving" (p. 138).

Interventions that take a culturally competent approach must look at both the individual players and the macrosystem dynamics. This approach includes attention to safety, intergenerational patterns, and psycho-education about internalized oppression, anger management, and role re-socialization.

Child Abuse and Discipline

> One fish, two fish, red fish, blue fish . . . Yes. Some are red. And some are blue. Some are old. And some are new. Some are sad. And some are glad. And some are very, very bad. Why are they sad and glad and bad? I do not know. Go ask your dad.
>
> (Dr. Seuss, 1960, 1988)

The picture accompanying the very, very bad fish is the large red "parent" fish slapping the two smaller yellow and blue "children" fish. Dr. Seuss is an American institution; mainstream values have been instilled in generations of children through *Green Eggs and Ham* and *The Cat in the Hat*. Dr. Seuss's depiction of spanking implies that it is a normative consequence for bad behavior by good parents.

Baby boomers in the black community will often discuss how all parents in the neighborhood used to be considered responsible for disciplining all the neighborhood's children. It was an unwritten code of ethics that guaranteed community parenting. Comics and clergy alike lament that many parents would have been arrested for child abuse if parents in the 1970s were held to the standard of the 1990s. These comments are usually attached to a nostalgic sense that 1970s children turned out okay or maybe even better due to spankings.

Since the 1960s American society has slowly shifted its mainstream view of discipline versus abuse. This shift is attributed to the feminist movement; increased public awareness of domestic violence and family violence; children's rights advocacy and child welfare laws; the aging baby boomers who value understanding rather than fear as a parenting strategy; and societal permissiveness. Continuous debate and controversy have taken place about appropriate ways of discipline and punishment, including initiating time-outs, withholding privileges, and disconnecting Nintendos.

The disdain held by professionals toward families of culturally diverse backgrounds who still use physical punishment as a primary source of discipline seems to disregard the accepted attitudes of not long ago. Consequently, efforts must be made to understand the cultural context of the client's behavior.

Context for Hitting Several factors provide the context for parental use of hitting as discipline. These factors include respect/embarrassment, intergenerational modeling, and power/fear.

Respect/embarrassment. Families who are "looked down on" by the mainstream have a heightened desire to be seen as in control and respected by their children. This need is particularly true of those people who feel that they have no control in other venues of their life. Obedience and respect are linked in many cultures. Consequently, disobedience is viewed as disrespecting the family authority.

Some families consider spanking to be an appropriate but not exclusive method of discipline. If a child's behavior is particularly frightening to a parent (running into the street, touching a hot iron), the parent may react to the fear related to the danger of the child's behavior.

Intergenerational modeling. Parenting is often taught by modeling. Many people parent the way they or those around them were parented. For some people, modeling is their only frame of reference.

Power/fear. Current parenting models advocate understanding and communication as a means of enhancing the parent-child relationship. Previous models used parental power and fear as a means of ensuring that children were safe. When parents were fearful that their child could be harmed in threatening neighborhoods or wanted their child to blend in without being noticed, instilling fear accomplished this purpose.

When Discipline Becomes Abuse Abuse occurs when a child is injured physically, emotionally, or psychologically. Injury can be intentional, chronic, or acute. Accidental injury, when violence or force is used under the guise of discipline, can also be problematic. Sexually inappropriate behaviors toward or in view of children can create traumatic results. Additionally, withholding education, medical attention, and emotional nurturance is generally considered neglect.

Strategies for Change   There is a good case to be made against hitting and spanking for a host of reasons besides the unpopularity of such actions in mainstream culture. Hitting as a means of problem solving models for children the use of aggression when they are in other situations, such as in school or in the playground. Children aren't taught reasoning techniques. Instead, hitting reaffirms compliance through fear; it is painful and humiliating, and it often may not be effective. More importantly, some adults are unaware of when they cross the line between discipline and abuse, and they act out their anger on the child.

Working with families around this sensitive issues requires, first, an assessment of safety issues. There is a difference between a slap on the behind and a beating. Practitioners should differentiate so that their interventions are targeted appropriately. Families should know clearly what is unacceptable. It is not okay for practitioners or families to blame culture for inappropriate parenting. It is appropriate to look within the cultural and intergenerational norms to find alternative solutions. Time-out and other age-appropriate consequences are effective methods that are gaining popularity with parents from many diverse backgrounds.

Substance Abuse

Nearly every poor community contains a proliferation of both storefront and traditional churches as well as liquor stores—bootleg or licensed distributors. The juxtaposition of religion and liquor is not farfetched. The church provides hope and faith that a higher power will show the way and lighten one's pain. Liquor provides a temporary dulling of one's misery until "one's load is lightened."

Culture should not be used as a rationale for dealing with use, abuse, or addiction to alcohol or drugs. There is, however, a cultural context that influences how alcohol and other drug abuse impacts the family.

Migration. The experience of migration as discussed earlier in this chapter includes stress and losses that can exacerbate a sense of despair that is often associated with depression and substance abuse.

Poverty. Systemic oppression and lack of resources (jobs, housing) are linked to substance abuse.

Upward mobility. Movement up and down the class hierarchy has inherent stresses and social norms. As women move into "the corporate world, drinking is often expected . . . sexual discrimination and occupational stress contributed to increased and problematic drinking" (Amodeo & Jones, 1998, p. 391).

In-group norms. Native Americans were introduced to drinking in a purposeful effort by Europeans to influence trade conditions. Initially drinking was not normative for this group, but eventually this substance has become a social problem in this community.

Health, Well-Being, and Medication

CASE STUDY: MS. BROWN

Ms. Brown listened intently as Dr. Miles, the school psychologist, described her seven-year-old son's attention deficit disorder. Dr. Miles sensitively talked about the limited opportunities that the classroom could provide to Richard if he did not receive any medication. The doctor expressed her concern for Richard's improved academic function, and she highlighted his strengths. Ms. Brown spoke of Richard's previous hospitalizations and the horrible side effects she saw when he was put on a combination of psychotropic medications. Not only was he zombielike and bloated, she pointed out, but he didn't get better. Dr. Miles supported Ms. Brown's belief that the wrong choices were made and asked her to consider a different alternative in a smaller dose. Ms. Brown said that she would look for a school that could deal with her son, because she was not experimenting or letting anybody "drug" her son ever again. It was not healthy for him. She said she would consider a homeopathic approach or something natural instead.

For patients of diverse cultures, illness may be seen as a "weakness, punishment, irreparable loss, or relief from responsibilities" (Amodeo & Jones, 1998, p. 389). Likewise, healing practices may include nontraditional approaches such as natural base remedies, herbal treatment, folk medicine, or spiritual rituals as a primary course of action (English, 1995).

The popularity of such remedies does not suggest that the medical establishment is shunned by people of color, but that they reserve an exclusive reliance or trust in it. Western cultures have begun to look more favorably at Eastern methods of pain reduction such as acupuncture, meditation, and yoga. Practitioners working with families who explore nontraditional coping strategies may open a dialogue that incorporates the family's culture into treatment.

Medication issues for children remain a sore spot between mental health professionals and families of color. The following considerations may provide practitioners with the cultural context around this discord:

- *Cultural paranoia*. There is a historical context that creates distrust regarding medication as experimentation. The infamous Tuskegee syphilis trials in the mid-1900s add a reality base to this fear. Black men, without their permission, were used to test the effects of untreated syphilis. These victims were intentionally denied the available treatment, and they suffered the disease's horrible symptoms and death. When new pharmaceuticals are made available to the public and are presented as symptom-free, people of color often feel a sense of distrust and fear that the symptoms will become apparent only after it is too late to protect the patient.

- *Drug abuse/addiction.* The fear that psychotropic medications will become addictive and will cause the child to become dependent or a drug addict is a fear close to the heart of many ethnic minority families. Regardless of social class, many families can cite an example of a family member or friend who was destroyed by substance abuse. For some families there is a thin line between medication and drugs. Practitioners can offer a helpful perspective by making a comparison between a child's psychotropic medication and the prescription that a family member may take for high blood pressure or a heart ailment as a nonaddictive aid to well-being.
- *Illness.* Well children are not viewed as needing medication. Psychotropic drugs infer illness at best, and craziness at worst.
- *The Ritalin debate.* The current crisis in the mental health community over dispensing Ritalin to preschoolers or to older children in variable doses has hampered the public's trust in general and, in particular, the trust of minorities who approach attention-deficit hyperactivity disorder with skepticism.

SUGGESTED GUIDELINES FOR CULTURALLY SENSITIVE AND RESPONSIVE PRACTICE

The literature, according to English (1995, p. 31), identifies the following four consistent themes as important for ethnically competent practitioners:

- Acknowledge and accept differences.
- Be familiar with your own values and orientation.
- Understand the dynamics of differences and how these differences affect the helping relationship.
- Be able to adapt these principles in practice.

English (p. 32) further notes Brown and Miller's following transcultural interaction principles:

1. Approach family members as individuals first and then seek to understand their heritage.
2. Don't assume that a particular ethnic appearance means that individuals adopt specific practices.
3. Understand that all minority groups are bicultural.
4. Learn cultural strengths as well as weakness.
5. Make decisions with, not for, clients.
6. Understand the differences between individual family practices and broader cultural traditions.

To this list, it is essential to add the importance of fathers and significant male relatives. Practitioners often assume that these family members don't exist or are not interested in treatment, so they are left out without ever being invited in. The literature (McAdoo, 1998; Comer & Poussaint, 1992; Boyd-Franklin, 1989) as well as my personal experience validates that a major piece of the puzzle is missing when the male family members are omitted.

Taking a stance of color blindness in a society that has an ingrained color consciousness is a naive position that negates the practitioner's conscious values and unconscious biases; this approach ultimately is a disservice to clients. Amodeo and Jones (1998) note that clinicians who have discomfort or limited experience with other ethnic groups sometimes become "hyper-professional . . . cultural romantics" or they over- or misdiagnose (p. 389).

Likewise, the assumption that ethnically matched practitioner-client scenarios will maximize sensitive and responsive practice also ignores subtle differences within cultures that shift the worker's or client's perspective. Many "same group" issues arise, such as high expectations about sameness; anger or disapproval that the worker is on the "other side"; efforts to merge the worker as another family member; and transferring the client's own negative racial esteem onto the worker. Certainly a shared common heritage, especially when language is an issue, provides optimal opportunity for cultural clarity. However, a healthy therapeutic alliance requires that the practitioner does the work of knowing through empathy, asking, and listening. Lakoff and Johnson (1980) in Amodeo & Jones (1998) describe a culturally competent therapist as one who can "recognize the metaphors that have power within the client's world, or construct metaphors powerful enough to help clients with self-transformation" (p. 389). Whether the practitioner is from the same or a different culture, the first essential step is to listen and respond to the client as an *individual,* not as a member of a particular group. Once this connection has been made, the practitioner must acknowledge cultural identity issues and invite the client to express whether and how these issues impact on the presenting situation.

Discussion Questions and Role-Play Exercises

1. Discuss how a school social worker could approach an African American divorced mother about her seven-year-old son's behavioral and learning problems. Role-play the telephone call and the first session with the mother at school.
2. Discuss how a young female social worker should approach an older Hispanic father about his son's aggressive behavior toward girls in school. The social worker believes the son is acting out the domestic violence in the home.
3. The Asian parents of a teenaged daughter are distressed because she is rebuffing their wishes about dating. They have selected an appropriate future husband for her, and she wants to date boys who are outside her nationality and religion. How does a therapist reframe this dynamic?
4. The practitioner is frustrated about a family's secretiveness and suspects the family is fearful about disclosing their illegal immigration status. How should the worker proceed?

Note

1. The Child Welfare League of America is a national coalition of agencies servicing children and families, with a mission of "guarding children's rights and serving children's needs."

References

Amodeo, M., & Jones, K. (1998). Using the AOD cultural framework to view alcohol and drug issues through various cultural lenses. *Journal of Social Work Education, 34*(3), 387–98.

Appiah, K., & Gates, H., Jr. (Eds.). (1999). *Africana. The encyclopedia of the African and African American experience*. New York: Basic Civitas Books.

Atkinson, D. R., Morten, G., & Sue, D. W. (1998). Racial/ethnic minorities and cross-cultural counseling. In D. R. Atkinson et al. (Eds.), *Counseling American minorities*. New York: McGraw Hill.

Boyd-Franklin, N. (1989). *Black families in therapy: A multisystems approach*. New York: Guilford Press.

Brown, A., & Bailey-Etta, B. (1997). An out-of-home care system in crisis: Implications for African American children in the child welfare system. *Journal of Policy, Practice, and Program, 76*(1), 65–84.

Child Welfare League of America Cultural Competence Fact Sheet. (1999). Washington, DC: Author.

Collins, P. A. (1998). *Fighting words, Black women and the search for justice*. Minneapolis: University of Minnesota Press.

Comer, J., & Poussaint, A. (1992). *Raising black children*. New York: Penguin Group.

Congress, E. P. (1994). The use of culturagrams to assess and empower culturally diverse families. *Families in Society, 75*(9), 531–39.

Cooper, C. R., Denner, J., & Lopez, E. (1999). Cultural brokers: Helping Latino children on pathways toward success. *The Future of Children When School Is Out, 9*(2), 51–57.

English, D. (1995). Cultural issues related to the assessment of child abuse and neglect. *Contemporary Group Care Practice, Research, and Evaluation, 5*(1), 31–35.

Falicov, C. (1998). *Latino families in therapy*. New York: Guilford Press.

Fletcher, M. (1997). Latinos see signs of hope as middle class expands. *The Washington Post*, p. A8.

Fox, R. (1993). *Elements of the helping process: A guide for clinicians*. New York: Hawthorne Press.

Giordano, J., & Levine, J. (1994). *Train the trainer workshop on diversity* (workbook), p. 8. New York: Ethnicity and Mental Health Associates.

Gitterman, A. (1996). Life model theory and social work treatment. In F. J. Turner (Ed.), *Social work treatment: Interlocking theoretical approaches* (pp. 389–408). New York: Free Press.

Goldstein, E. G. (1995). *Ego psychology and social work practice* (2nd ed.). New York: Free Press.

Greenfield, P. (1997). You can't take it with you: Why ability assessments don't cross cultures. *American Psychologist, 52*(10), 115–24.

Harper, K., & Lantz, J. (1996). *Cross-cultural practice—Social work with diverse populations*. Chicago: Lyceum Books.

Hartman, A. (1992). In search of subjugated knowledge. *Social Work, 37*(6), 483–84.

Herman, J. L. (1992). *Trauma and recovery*. New York: Basic Books.

Hill, R. (1997). Supporting African American families: Dispelling myths, building on strengths. *Children's Voice (Child Welfare League of America), 6*(3), 4–7.

Ho, M. (1990). Theoretical framework for therapy with ethnic minority families. In M. K. Ho (Ed.), *Family therapy with ethnic minorities* (pp. 11–26). Newbury Park, CA: Sage.

Jacobs, C., & Bowles, D. (Eds.). (1988). *Ethnicity and race: Critical concepts in social work*. Washington, DC: National Association of Social Workers.

Jarrett, R. (1999). Successful parenting in high-risk neighborhoods. *The Future of Children When School is Out, 9*(2), 45–50.

Kunjufu, J. (1984). *Developing positive self-images and discipline in black children*. Chicago: African American Images.

Lakoff, G., & Johnson, M. (1980). *Metaphors we live by*. Chicago: University of Chicago Press.

Logan, S., Freeman, E., & McRoy, R. (1990). *Social work practice with black families*. New York: Longman.

McAdoo, H. (1998). African-American families: Strengths and realities. In H. I. McCubbin, E. A. Thompson, A. I. Thompson, & J. A. Futrell (Eds.), *Resiliency in African-American families* (pp. 17–30). Thousand Oaks, CA: Sage.

McGee, M. (1997). Cultural values and domestic violence. In P. M. Brown & J. S. Shalett (Eds.), *Cross-cultural practice with couples and families* (pp. 129–40). New York: Hawthorne Press.

McPhatter, A. (1997). Cultural competence in child welfare: What is it? How do we achieve it? What happens without it? *Journal of Policy, Practice, and Program, 86*(1), 255–78.

National Technical Assistance Center for State Mental Health Planning. (1999). *Cultural diversity series: Meeting the mental health needs of African Americans*. Alexandria, VA: Author.

Ortega, R., & Nunez, E. (1997). Latino families and child welfare. *Family Resource Coalition of America Report, 16*(1 & 2), 8.

Saleebey, D. (1992). *The strengths perspective in social work practice*. New York: Longman.

Satterwhite, J. (n.d.). *Why people leave* [fact sheet]. Academy for Child Welfare Training.

Seuss, Dr. (1960, 1988). *One fish, two fish, red fish, blue fish*. New York: Random House.

Shorris, E. (1992). *Latino*. New York: Norton.

Vargas, L., & Koss-Chioino, J. (Eds.). (1992). *Working with culture. Psychotherapeutic interventions with ethnic minority children and adolescents*. San Francisco: Jossey-Bass.

Vasquez, M. (1994). Latinas. In L. Diaz & B. Greene (Eds.), *Women of color: A portrait of heterogeneity* (pp. 114–38). New York: Guilford Press.

PART 2

Parent-Child Relationships and Parenting Patterns in Selected Culture Groups

African American Families

CHAPTER 4

Parent and Child Relationships in African American Families

HARRIETTE PIPES MCADOO

In this chapter are heard the voices of parents themselves as they respond to some of the issues of parent and child relationships in African American families. This chapter, written for both the parent population and the professional community, provides grounds for discussion that will grow out of the end-of-chapter questions.

CASE STUDY: THE BROWNS

The Browns are a three-generation family consisting of the parents, their three children, and the father's mother. Their presenting problems are the behavior of their sons, Bill, thirteen years, and Andre, fifteen years, who are rapidly moving into manhood. There is one daughter, Clare, twelve, who has been an ideal child. The parents have high educational expectations for their children.

Both parents work full time. The father is a teacher in the local high school and directs the band. The mother is an administrative assistant in a lawyer's office. Both are first-generation middle class. The grandmother takes care of the children after school and has a warm relationship with them. The grand-

This chapter was prepared with the assistance of the College of Human Ecology and Radcliffe Research Grant No. 61-6164.

mother helps with the cooking and laundry through the week, whereas the mother has full responsibility of the housework, shopping, and cooking on the weekends.

Bill and Andre have started skipping school and have been in fights, and the parents are concerned that the boys are smoking marijuana. The parents suspect that petty larceny has had a role in the extra money that is required for the boys' pot and other expenses. The boys' friends have changed during the past year to children who are marginal compared to their earlier friends. Clare is quiet, friendly, and a good student. However, she too has shown signs of rebellion that has the parents worried. The parents feel that they are losing control at a key point in their children's lives.

Both parents were raised Baptist, and the grandmother goes to church every Sunday. The parents usually go, but carry their religion more lightly than the grandmother does. The children went to church and Sunday school every week as young children, but getting them to go now has turned into a big issue. The parents have been inconsistent about their children's attendance, sometimes insisting that they go and other times giving in to the children. The grandmother lets it be known that they are raising a group of sinners if God is not in their lives. The minister speaks a lot about Biblical times, but is no help with the younger generation.

The family has not dealt with the cultural background of their ethnic group. Similar to many African American families, they have never discussed civil rights nor have they prepared their children to face racism. The parents have the attitude that good grades will lead to a good education and a secure future. However, the children have continually run into subtle discrimination and outright racism in their schools and in the playground. Their parents have not been approachable by the children on these issues.

The parents have been worried about the children for more than a year. They talk about it constantly, and the grandmother chips in with her bits of advice. The parents have had discussions with each child separately, but have not seen the problem as a systemwide one in their family.

This situation with their children has caused tension between the parents. The mother has wanted to seek help from somewhere. The father is adamantly against letting someone outside the family into their family "secrets." He feels that they have never, as a family, gone outside to seek help and he'd be damned if he was going to talk to a social worker or a psychiatrist. They were at an impasse.

Finally, the boys' trouble led the school to suspend them and require counseling for the entire family. The social worker was female, middle class, White, and a graduate of an eastern MSW program. She was thrust into this family situation for which she was almost unprepared. The social worker had had only limited experience with African Americans and never with those of status similar to her own. She had been led in her training to expect most African American families to be dependent welfare mothers. She had no experience of working with a family that did not fit that stereotype. She was aware of hostility but did not realize the source of it. She assumed that it was due to the family being in a new situation. She was unaware of the centuries-old antagonism toward Whites in general, and of resistance to outsiders in dealing with family issues in specific.

HISTORICAL AND SOCIOECONOMIC BACKGROUND
OF AFRICAN AMERICANS

The historical heritage that is shared by many African American families is substantially different from that of all other immigrant groups that have come to the United States. Earlier groups of people coming to this country were free. These groups were escaping oppression or were seeking new freedoms and economic possibilities. In contrast, Africans were brought against their wills. As enslaved Africans, they built the foundations of many American cities. Major pools of family wealth exist today because of the hundreds of years of free African labor. The enslaved were freed in the 1860s but were devalued as a group, whether they came from Africa, the Caribbean, or other countries. The cultural and racial diversity that now exists among blacks is because of the masses of groups who came to America, either under enslavement or as immigrants who were hoping for a better life. The economic diversity is shown in the case study of the Browns.

African Americans at the present time are no longer as essential to the economic survival of the United States as they were during enslavement. Nor are they as essential as they were during the period of industrial growth or during the two world wars. As the nation has moved into a global economy with greater emphasis on technology and offshore production, there is less need for large numbers of low-skilled and less-educated people in the workforce (H. P. McAdoo, 1997).

Schools previously segregated are now legally integrated because of the Civil Rights movement, but racial isolation continues because of white flight to the supposedly safer suburbs. Quality education has been kept from blacks for many years, first under a segregated system and then under a separate-but-equal period. Even now the schools in the inner city are inferior to those in the suburban areas. The blame for inferior schools, and thus inferior education, is placed on the negligence of parents and on poverty rather than on an unjust educational system. School systems have not succeeded in the promise of equal education for all.

We need to understand the economic situations, the cultural patterns, and the socialization practices of African American families. Over the years, significant changes have occurred in the lives of African Americans. Major policy changes at the federal and local levels in the late 1990s have truncated government programs, which has contributed to the vulnerability of these families. Some African Americans have benefited from earlier government programs and have been upwardly mobile. Many others have fallen deeper into despair.

Poverty is a reality of life for 65 percent of single mother–child units but only 18 percent of families with two parents (Despeignes, 1999, quoting Center on Budget and Priority Policies). Marriage is losing its key role in African American families, and African American children have only one chance in five of reaching the age of sixteen in a home that has two parents (Ingrassia, 1993, quoting L. Bumpass). Black mothers have more children out of wedlock than do their white counterparts. Only 22 percent of well-off African American women (those who make more than $75,000 per year) have children outside of marriage, but 65 percent of low-income African American women do (Ingrassia). Incarceration of black men is greater than for the population as a whole. The situations are apparently not getting better. When African Americans were asked if things were better or worse now than they were five years ago, 32 percent said that things are better today and 52 percent said things are the same (Witt, 1999).

African American parents have had to overcome adversity, develop mobility paths for their families, and socialize their children for devalued positions in our society. Some of these parents over the generations have been extremely successful, but others have barely managed to hold on, while still others have fallen by the wayside.

Assessments of the need for economic self-sufficiency have run parallel to policy decisions that have limited the opportunities of families to remove themselves from dependency. The African American patterns of mutual support and the coping strategies that were so effective in the past are even more important today but are becoming more strained (H. P. McAdoo, 1997).

As families cope with adversities, African derivations and accommodations to the American experiences have resulted in many of the strengths that have facilitated coping in families (Dodson, 1997; Sudarkasa, 1993, 1999). Among the cultural legacies that are African derived, and have been altered with the U.S. experiences, are the oral traditions, spirituality, rhythmic movement expressions, and communalism between groups (Boykin, 1997; Jones, 1991). Parents have had to draw strength from all these legacies, because their experiences have been stressful.

OVERVIEW OF EXTENDED FAMILY AND RELIGION OR SPIRITUALITY

Extended Family

The cultural patterns that are most common to African American parents include the following:

- extended family structures
- extensive use of extended family helping arrangements
- supportive social networks, including family and close friends
- flexible relationships within the family structure (Billingsley, 1968; Boyd-Franklin, 1989; H. P. McAdoo, 1995a; Wilkinson, 1997).

Although many other groups have similar patterns, parents of color are more likely to have a greater concentration of these patterns. Many of these patterns have existed for hundreds of years. Parents at all economic classes have continued these patterns, and most African American families feel close to their relatives (Hatchett & Jackson, 1999). Grandparents may live with their children and grandchildren and share child care, as in the Brown family. Families interact frequently with their kin, and they exchange many forms of aid with their extended families. Some exchanges are now being eroded because of financial difficulties.

The support network continues to be a very important coping mechanism. The size of the support network is important, because parents need to have many people who can give them assistance when it is called for (H. P. McAdoo, 1999; Stack, 1974). When more kin and friends are involved in the family networks, there are more people to give financial support and alleviate stress; a larger network results in a greater sense of mastery over the everyday events of the family's lives.

Religion or Spirituality

African American churches often serve as the organizational hub of community life. Spirituality is the most recognized dimension of African American culture (Boykin & Toms, 1985). Churches have been one of the special strengths of families (Hill, 1978, 1997). In addition to religious reinforcement, members of the church community obtain solace, relief, and support from one another. Families have found that religion is one of the most important coping strategies to help them deal with stress (H. P. McAdoo, 1995b). Churches also provide spiritual sustenance and even temporary refuge from discrimination and racism of the broader society (Taylor & Chatters, 1991).

The family values that are reinforced within churches and supported by parents have been found to be related to values of self-sufficiency, strong work orientation, positive racial attitudes, perseverance, and respect for the mother's role within families (H. P. McAdoo & Crawford, 1991). These values are extensions of the broader extended-family concepts that encompass the church community.

In Christian denominations, most African Americans are Baptists, followed by Methodists and Roman Catholics, while 10 percent have no religious affiliation. Islam is growing in African American communities. About one in four Muslim Americans are black (Billingsley, 1999). However, church membership is not as reflective of religiosity as is spirituality. Spirituality and the values that form the basis for our ways of life continue to be important, but the involvement in the institutional church appears to be undergoing changes.

The role that churches play appears to be changing, especially as teens grow up to become parents themselves. Despite the importance of religion for African Americans, many black people are "unchurched." These people have not attended church in the past six months other than for special religious holidays, weddings, or funerals. A Gallup poll found that 32 percent of African Americans fit this category (Gardyn, 2000). Religion and churches may be even less important in the future, because many teens currently use the Internet for religious or spiritual experiences. It is predicted that the Internet will be a substitute for current church-based religious experiences for 31 percent of African Americans in the next five years (Gardyn). They will access the Internet rather than go into a church building.

This finding may reflect the changes that were evident in the Brown family. The grandmother was very religious and the church was paramount in her life; the parents were less involved, and the grandchildren could take it or leave it. Even if the parents were insistent on church attendance, it is questionable whether the children would be able to overcome peer pressure and the appeal of the growing technology found on the Internet. Children's values are being influenced by many sources that are often beyond the parents' control.

SIGNIFICANT PARENTING ISSUES RELATED TO CHILD REARING

Ethnic Socialization

One very important parenting task that African Americans must handle, which is common with other parents of color, is to help their children understand their own places in terms of the racial and ethnic groups' history within our multicultural society. This task is of foremost importance to parents; they must attend to it at the same time they attend to routine parental tasks that are common to all parents.

Parents must provide their children with a historical summary, on an appropriate level for the children's understanding, of how they belong to a devalued group. Although insufficient attention is paid to this lesson in the practice or clinical literature or by writers in the field, it is probably the most important task that parents have. African American families and children can be fully understood only in relation to the interaction of social class, culture, ethnicity, and race (Garcia Coll et al., 1996).

Parents must protect their children, and at the same time they must prepare them for racial and discriminatory actions that are their fate in life. Racial socialization requires that children learn to cope effectively with their racial position in life, so children can make appropriate responses and, at the same time, develop into functional adults (Boykin & Toms, 1985; Harrison, 1985; Tatum, 1987). Overprotecting the children will underprepare them for the harsh realities of life. To underprotect them is to expose them to grief that could turn into hostility toward those who are not of color. This balance is a very delicate one for parents to maintain.

Color or Race and Identity

One hypothesis about racial development and self-esteem is the "racial self-hate hypothesis" (H. P. McAdoo, 1985). This hypothesis proposes that children of color actually desire to be another color and therefore have a core of self-hatred or ambivalence about being of color. Although this hypothesis is almost universally believed and taken for granted, it has, no empirical support.

Measures of self-esteem and racial attitude have been compared repeatedly in the past thirty years, and no relationship has been found between these two variables. In spite of this empirical evidence, many social scientists have continued to maintain that self-esteem and racial identity are connected, especially among young children. For an extensive review of many studies, see Cross (1991) and H. P. McAdoo (2000).

A close look at the literature reveals that many authors measure self-esteem and then make references to ethnic identities or vice versa. Even the Clarks (1939) measured only racial identification of children with their dolls and then proceeded to discuss self-esteem. The children in the Clarks' study were enrolled in an upper-middle-class, predominantly white nursery school in the 1930s in New York City. Many of these children were light-skinned offspring of the traditional black upper-middle class. The children who answered "yes" when asked if the white doll resembled them as a baby or even now as a preschooler were in fact correct. Lighter-skinned children do have more ambivalence than darker-skinned children. However, the Clarks' study was so phenomenal that decades of researchers went on to repeat their findings without question. The Clarks' major contribution was to present and publish an empirical study of an important issue within the community using African American children as the sole model group. Their research was also a major contributor to the Brown decision in the Supreme Court, which led to the end of segregated schools.

Our growing knowledge has led to even more sophisticated studies over the years (Banks, 1976; Bowles, 1988; Peters, 1997; Semaj, 1985). It was not until the 1960s and 1970s that actual measurements were made of both variables. No relationship was found between racial attitudes and self-esteem (H. P. McAdoo, 1970). What was found was that young African American and white children have similar but different developmental tasks that they have to master to establish their identities. Children of color are more reactive to color because it is a more salient issue in their lives, even when parents do not verbalize to them about race. This recognition of skin color, a process that all children have to go through, is accomplished earlier for children of color than most social scientists believe.

Stages of Development of Racial Attitudes

At ages three to four, all children become aware of differences in gender and race (Davies, 1999). They do not understand the significance, but they simply know that people come in different colors and different genders. At ages four to five, children become aware that they belong to one of the groups, but still they do not understand the significance of such membership. At ages five or six, they begin to make accurate self-identities related to race and gender and begin to understand the concepts related to white and Black (Bowles, 1988; H. P. McAdoo, 1985).

Children of color at age six reach the conclusion that society prefers white over black (Cross, 1985; H. P. McAdoo, 1985). When psychological testing is done in the preschool years, children of all races respond with similar answers. All groups either are or indicate that they prefer to be white. They align themselves with the predominant societal view. This racial preference for whiteness over blackness has caused many problems with the development of racial attitudes and preferences of African American children and adults. African American preschool and school-age children have consistently shown a preference for whiteness over blackness (Cross, 1985).

Although originally researchers believed that this preference was a rejection of the children's own selves, research has shown that children *are* able to discriminate between their racial preference (white oriented) and their self-esteem (black oriented). Thus, their racial attitudes can be modified (J. McAdoo, 1985). They maintain a preference for being white over black for about three additional years (until age nine). Young white children reach similar conclusions of racial self-preference at about seven years of age and they continue to prefer to be white for the rest of their lives. They are continually reinforced by the media, by books, and by significant others in their lives. Only when blacks reach the age of about nine, or in approximately the third grade, do they show a strong preference for being black (Cross, 1985; H. P. McAdoo, 1985). They reach the appropriate racial self-preference two years later than white children. This difference in timing between blacks and whites is rarely mentioned in the literature.

Racial Socialization Approaches

Many parents of color, like the Browns in the case study, do not deal effectively with racial issues with their children. Only about one-fourth of African American parents talk to their children about race (Bowman & Howard, 1985). Parents are often undecided as to what approach they should take or about whether the approach that they have taken has been the appropriate one. Parents use different methods to socialize their children about race.

The first approach is to simply say nothing to their children but to emphasize achievement and education as the panacea for getting ahead. This belief is that we are all dependant on our own efforts. Race is not important. The children are made to believe that they are empowered to achieve on a flat playing field. Often this approach is taken to extremes, and assimilation becomes the ultimate goal of children brought up this way. They may live in predominately white neighborhoods and go to mostly white schools. They may seek careers that do not touch the wider African American community, and they are often cut off from the African American community. They may end up dating persons of another race and eventually marry outside their race. However, African Americans intermarry at a lower rate than do other ethnic groups. Only 8 percent of blacks marry non-blacks. Asians marry out at a higher rate, 36 percent to 45 percent, as do Hispanics, 31 percent (Holmes, 2000). Blacks who assimilate within the wider culture often become alienated from other African Americans.

The problem with this approach is that children from families such as these are not prepared to cope with the slights and the outright discriminatory acts that they encounter. These children often feel that with a little more effort or better training or better grades they will be able to succeed. They assume the entire burden of achievement on themselves, and they experience high stress levels.

Other parents talk about race to a lesser extent and are careful not to overdo it. This caution may be related to deep feelings that they have due to injustices or devaluation, or because they do not want to make their children bitter. But without the awareness of adults' responses to injustice, it becomes difficult for the children to make appropriate choices and decisions. They are often also confused when they do encounter racism.

Still other parents talk about race and white attitudes with their children. They balance their talk about the racist events in their lives and their expectation that the child will also encounter these events with the child's reaction to these events. One of the most powerful statements parents can say is, "Bad events that occur are not due to actions on your (the child's) part. They are the responsibility of the people who have put them in a different light. It is not your fault, but whites' own racial attitudes." This statement is powerful because of the release from attribution that it affords children. The children are freed from the responsibility of proving that they are just as good as others. They are provided with an explanation and a way to understand bad situations. They are able to maintain distance from the negative events and can move on to the next subject. This response dissipates anger and gives the young person something to say to themselves and to others.

A study undertaken by Jackson, McCullough, Gurin, and Broman (1991) found that 61 percent of African American adults received some messages from their parents about what it is to be black and about getting along with whites. But those African American adults who did not receive messages were less identified with African Americans and were significantly less likely to have white friends. The socialization messages that parents pass on are important for children when they encounter police in tense neighborhood environments, when they interact with teachers and social workers in multicultural situations, and when they play with other children.

Relations with Authorities

The voices of parents appear in studies about children and racial socialization among black parents. Parents were given free rein to respond about the elements that they felt were important for their children (H. P. McAdoo, 1995a). This process is usually not followed in empirical studies. The comments that were made tie in to the Brown case study.

When parents were asked questions about racial socialization—"Do you feel black children need any special preparation for getting along in the world?"—they gave very strong responses (H. P. McAdoo, 2000).

FRANCIS: I feel that they should be more strongly advised and be told about racism in a positive manner. I'm writing a book about that to explain for my daughter. I explain to her the different situations of life in a reality basis.

MARIE: I feel that black culture is very unique. The artifacts are real and they should come out.

JANE: We try to give her a lot of love. We try to talk to her a lot. We're trying to give her a cultural background.

OTIS: I feel that they raise their children in a more defensive protective type manner. Black parents are stricter with their kids because they have experienced hurt and pain that white parents haven't been subjected to. So whites are less strict. Regardless of the fact that there have been changes, we are still not equal to hites.

Another question was asked about race attitudes within the African American community: "Some people say that skin color and hair type no longer can affect a person's status in the black community. What do you think?" Similar responses were frequently heard.

FRANCIS: I think it [racial attitude] is still very prominent in the black community. Based on my own personal involvement with people who have lighter complexion and "better" hair (more white-like or straighter), their job opportunities are better than when compared with a darker one. The lighter one will get the job. I speak from experience. But I accept a person as they present themselves to me. I'm not worrying about the hair, but how they are with me.

These responses demonstrate the multiple tasks of racial socialization. Preparations for coping with racism and discrimination are needed both in the wider community and within the black community. If parents are able to master the developmental tasks of helping their children establish appropriate stances in relation to others and to their race and ethnicity, parents have mastered one of their most crucial challenges. Pressures both from inside their own racial group and from outside sources must be recognized with appropriate responses.

Interactions with Authority Figures

Parents in all socioeconomic levels must prepare their African American children to interact with police officers and survive. Whether the children are in an inner city and driving a beat-up Chevy or in an upper-middle-class neighborhood and driving their father's Mercedes, they will be stopped and hassled. These police stops are almost universal for youth, who call the experience DWB, or "driving while black." African American children have to know how to respond—how to not get arrested or shot—and be able to continue on their way.

Drummond (2000) has collected clear, concise rules that can be communicated to youth. He states definite rules of etiquette for encounter situations. Here is his list of what youth should do when they are stopped, especially at night:

- Turn on the interior lights.
- Put your hands on the steering wheel.
- Don't be loud. Answer the officer in a calm, clear voice.
- Don't reach for an ID. Ask the officer first before pulling it out.
- Don't volunteer. If in doubt, you have a right to remain silent.
- Don't antagonize.
- Be personal. Check out the badges and use the officers' names.
- Do not ask for a badge number or threaten to file a complaint. (Do it later, if warranted.)

Parents can save themselves and their children much grief if they teach these procedures to their children. However, if the parents do not talk to their children, the children will learn over time from their own sad experiences and from the messages of their peers.

MENTAL HEALTH CONCERNS RELATED TO PARENTING

When parents are under a great deal of stress, they tend to have lower estimations of their self-worth. Health affects parents' ability to parent and to maintain their employment while caring for children. As expected, parents who are under the greatest amount of stress report more dissatisfaction with their physical health.

Loneliness and stress impact on the ability of a parent to fulfill the parental role. In one study of parenting, stress was found to be much lower for parents who had never felt lonely (H. P. McAdoo, 1999). Among the various types of stress related to expressive concerns of the parents are family stress, emotional stress, and interpersonal stress. Stress is connected with family relations and personal habits and with all the usual mental health measures.

All parents' feelings of usefulness or uselessness depend on whether they feel that they possess a number of good qualities and on their levels of self-respect (Depner, 1980). When the parents feel that they are persons of worth and that they possess a number of positive traits, then they respect themselves. In turn, the best predictors of self-worth in Depner's study were parents' perceptions of lower levels of stress, their feelings of mastery over the events in their lives, and their role as passive recipients of help from members of their support networks. The sense of control over their environments did depend on whether the parents had sufficient resources for their families.

Parents who have positive self-esteem are low in acute and chronic stress, they feel powerful in controlling the lives around them, they have more satisfying lives, and they have stronger feelings of well-being. Parents of color have expectations and hopes that are typical of parents in all other groups. Their lives are different only because of the continued devaluation of their families.

Parents are under stress from their jobs, from the expectations of their children's schools, and from the children themselves. The area of discipline is important to them and to all the people who are placing demands on the parents. *Essence* (Gault-Caviness, 2000) compiled a collection of short quotes from African American child development experts. "The parent must from the beginning love and nurture their children, so the children will feel connected to others" (Comer & Poussaint, 1992). "Every child should sense that they are the gleam in their parents' eyes; that they are loved and admired" (Gault-Caviness, quoting M. Benoit, president, American Academy of Child/Adolescent Psychiatry). "The child must be respected as a person and he will learn to respect his elders. Discipline must occur without belittling the child" (Beal, Villaros, & Abner, 1999). Children should be told not to be afraid of failing, that what matters is the way they do things. As Edelman (1992) said, "It does not matter how many times you fall down. What matters is how many times you get up." Parents will be more positive about discipline and will have less stress if they are able to keep these statements in mind.

PREPARATION FOR WORKING WITH AFRICAN AMERICAN PARENTS

There are problems related to race and ethnicity in the overall ecological atmosphere of our nation. The usual way of including people of color into the "American way" masks the fact that the "problems" are not the black people themselves (West, 1993, quoting W. E. B. Du Bois in his 1903 book *The Souls of Black Folk*). Responsibilities for the cultural and moral work necessary for healthy race relations should not be left to the people of color alone, apart from the entire society (West).

We live in a society that is unfamiliar with the realities of parents who are not in dominant groups. Even therapists from similar racial groups may have lost some of their awareness of home cultures because of their training. This book and others (Lum, 1986; Green, 1999) attempt to prepare practitioners by increasing their cultural competence. Excellent books related specifically to black socialization include *Black Family Therapy* by Boyd-Franklin (1989) and *Boys into Men: Raising our African American Teenage Sons* by Boyd-Franklin, Franklin, and Toussaint (2000). Therapists who are familiar with the content of these books will be better able to understand and work effectively with African American parents. Social workers and other practitioners will have to openly examine their attitudes of racism and prejudice toward different ethnic groups as discussed in chapter 1 and throughout this book. The race of the therapist is not as important as the therapist's knowledge about families' situations. Blacks, in talking about non-black counselors, have often said that they do not want to pay to see a professional and then have to educate that person "on their own nickel." This need to educate leads to hostility and missed opportunities within ethnic social work practice. One essential goal for any counselor or therapist is to avoid the stereotyping that we all tend to do. This goal calls for hard self-examination.

The race of the therapist should of course be taken into consideration. Some parents have strongly held positions for or against a therapist of another race. One of the first exchanges must acknowledge the racial factor, and the client's feelings should be explored. Often reassignment is impossible because of staff limitations, but attempts should be made to respect or accommodate the client's wishes whenever possible.

ATTITUDES OF BLACKS TOWARD COUNSELING

The attitude of not wanting to go outside the family to gain assistance is characteristic of many African American families (Boyd-Franklin, 1989). Many such families have a tendency to want to look first within the family for help and then to go outside. Even then, fictive kin and the resources in the community are preferred (H. P. McAdoo, 1997). Therefore, a family who seeks outside counseling usually feels forced to do so or feels that they are at their hopes' limits (Boyd-Franklin, 1989). A classic example of interracial misunderstanding and difficulty in successful engagement occurs when clients are labeled "resistant." Suspicion, former negative experiences, and anxiety about entering in a new situation impact the counseling experience (Lum, 1986). These feelings should be addressed to avoid further alienation. Parental attitudes toward counseling done by outsiders will be less marked if the counselors are culturally responsive to the family and are careful to be culturally sensitive to the family's issues of importance (Green, 1999; Stevenson & Renard, 1993).

In H. P. McAdoo (2000), parents responded to the question, "What would you do if things get too stressful?" These responses came after the parents had already shared their distrust of going outside to seek help.

FRANCIS: I want to go see a counselor or a professional.

MARTHA: I would have to go to somebody, a counselor, to try to help me. Somebody to make me see the bright side of things and have faith in God.

JANE: Sometimes I just go in the bedroom if my daughter is yelling and just lock the door. Or take the dog for a walk. If I tried to talk to her and have not been successful with her or my husband, I wash my hair or take a bath.

MARY: But sometimes I just scream.

FLORENCE: I simply go to my great-grandmother. She's my rock in time of dire need. Then I usually try to sort it out by myself. If the going gets rough, I go outside. But then I have to go to a professional.

The use of genograms has been suggested by Pearlmutter (1996) to help reframe some of the issues that families bring into therapy. Genograms have been useful in therapy and in classes in which black graduate students approach their families and delve into their family histories. I have used this approach for more than twenty-five years. However, genograms are areas in which "family secrets" play a big part. These issues should be addressed carefully and are especially important when a therapist is not of color or is not from the same cultural group as the parents. A large number of adolescent single mothers may bring out embarrassing data for parents. Miscegenation, dating from enslavement times through the present, is another sensitive issue that the parent may not wish to discuss. In spite of these cautions, much data and family patterning may be gathered through the use of multigenerational genograms.

In the same study (H. P. McAdoo, 2000), parents were asked what services they would consider the most supportive for other parents who faced the same situations as theirs.

> JOHN: Counseling services helped my son to feel better, because he couldn't read, was poor in sports, and his best friend moved. It helped him look at himself better.
>
> JANE: I have taken medication, and gone to counseling sessions.
>
> MARY: Social workers have helped with decent housing, with food and emergency relief. I like when they go to homes and help parents with their children and parenting skills.
>
> FLORENCE: Health care for blacks; social activities; low-income housing; senior citizen programs; and for the little children, food programs.

Parents were asked, "To deal with your everyday problems and emergency crises, what services would you like to see provided?"

> ANGEL: More financial help for parents to plan their money. If a family is on social services the mother may need assistance as far as how to stretch that money.
>
> MARTHA: I'd like to see services provided for young girls out there having babies. You should tell them that just because they have babies, they're not going to get that check.
>
> FRANCIS: Better child care; more direct involvement with the agency and the parent, if there has to be an agency.

The perception of how satisfied parents are with their overall life depends on the differences that exist between the parents' aspirations and their actual attainment. Three of the standard satisfaction survey items were used to measure the level of global life satisfaction of middle-class parents (H. P. McAdoo, 1997) and also with single mothers (H. P. McAdoo, 1995b) on several dimensions: life in general, their family life, and their anticipated life in ten years. Happier and more satisfied parents felt much more in control of their situations and were more satisfied with their abilities to play all the life roles that were expected of them. The happy parents were significantly lower on all the stress measures: intensity, frequency, and perceived intensity (H. P. McAdoo, 2000). Parents who were lower in stress were more effective in parenting ability and in the socialization of their children.

THE FUTURE FOR PARENTING CHILDREN

Parents continue to rely on their relatives and fictive kin in order to raise their children. Programs that provide assistance to families who are urban, of color, or poor should follow the motto, "First, do no harm; Second, make no mistakes." Some guidelines are very important in this work. First, we must rid ourselves of stereotypes and negative images of parents and their children. Second, we must present a more realistic picture of African American parents to the media, the general public, and the professional community. We must recognize how the kin and nonkin support systems, the community social services, and the families themselves have developed networks of resiliency and coping. Only then will we be able to implement social, medical, and educational programs that will further strengthen these families.

Discussion Questions and Role-Play Exercises

1. How much background information about an African American family should be gathered in the initial interview? Discuss the methods of obtaining this information, including the pros and cons of using a genogram to obtain family history.
2. In the Brown case, what interpretation do you make of the therapist's lack of knowledge about this middle-class family? How can the therapist approach this family in a helpful way?
3. Do you think the Brown parents can address the crux of the issues that are confronting them? Should the therapist offer to set separate appointments with the couple or focus on work with the entire family as a unit?
4. Discuss the racial socialization messages that may have been given to Amadou Diallo, the young West African man killed by New York City police officers, and those given to the sons of the Brown family in relation to their survival when confronting police in urban centers.
5. Act out the initial meeting between the social worker and the Brown family, being consistent with the race of the individuals. Now, reverse the race of the respective individuals and replay the initial interview.
6. As the Brown family, eat a meal and spend time discussing your family situation with all members.

References

Banks, W. C. (1976). White preference in blacks: A paradigm in search of a phenomenon. *Psychological Bulletin, 83,* 1179–86.

Beal, A. C., Villaros, L., & Abner, A. (1999). *The black parenting book: Caring for our children in the first five years.* New York: Broadway Books.

Billingsley, A. (1968). *Black families in White America.* Englewood Cliffs, NJ: Prentice Hall.

Billingsley, A. (1999). *Mighty like a river: The black church and social reform.* New York: Oxford University Press.

Bowles, D. D. (1988). Development of an ethnic self-concept among blacks. In C. Jacobs & D. D. Bowles (Eds.), *Ethnicity and race: Critical concepts in social work* (pp. 103–13). Washington, DC: National Association of Social Workers.

Bowman, P. J., & Howard, C. (1985). Race related socialization, motivation, and academic achievement: A study of black youths in three-generation families. *Journal of the American Academy of Child Psychiatry, 24,* 134–41.

Boyd-Franklin, N. (1989). *Black families in therapy: A multisystem approach.* New York: Guilford Press.

Boyd-Franklin, N., Franklin, A. J., & Toussaint, A. (2000). *Boys into men: Raising our African American teenage sons.* New York: Dutton.

Boykin, A. W. (1997). Communalism: Conceptualization and measurement of a Afrocultural social orientation. *Journal of Black Studies, 17*(3), 409–18.

Boykin, A. W., & Toms, F. (1985). Black child socialization: A conceptual framework. In H. McAdoo & J. McAdoo (Eds.), *Black children: Social, educational, and parental environment* (pp. 35–51). Newbury Park, CA: Sage.

Clark, K., & Clark, M. (1939). The development of consciousness of self and the emergence of racial identification in negro preschool children. *Journal of Social Psychology 10,* 591–99.

Comer, J. P., & Poussaint, A. F. (1992). *Raising black children: Two leading psychiatrists confront the educational, social, and emotional problems facing black children.* New York: Plume.

Cross, W. E. (1985). Black identity: Rediscovering the distinction between personal identity and reference group orientation. In M. B. Spencer, G. K. Brookins, & W. R. Allen (Eds.), *Beginnings: The social and affective development of black children* (pp. 152–72). Hillsdale, NJ: Lawrence Erlbaum.

Cross, W. E. (1991). *Shades of black: Diversity in African-American identity.* Philadelphia: Temple University Press.

Davies, D. (1999). *Child development.* New York: Guilford Press.

Depner, C. (1980). *Multiple roles and individual functioning.* Paper presented at Groves Family Conference, Gatlinburg, TN.

Despeignes, P. (1999, February 1). Blacks see wealth shrink amid national boom. *Detroit News,* pp. A1, A6.

Dodson, J. (1997). Conceptualization of African American families. In H. P. McAdoo (Ed.), *Black families* (3rd ed., pp. 67–82). Thousand Oaks, CA: Sage.

Drummond, T. (2000, April 3). Coping with cops: For minorities, growing up now means learning how to survive the police. *Time,* 72–73.

Edelman, M. W. (1992). *The measure of our success: A letter to my children and yours.* Boston: Beacon Press.

Garcia Coll, C., Lamberty, G., Jenkins, R., McAdoo, H. P., Crnic, K., Wasik, B. H., and Vasquez Garcia, H. (1996). An integrative model for the study of developmental competencies in minority children. *Child Development, 67*(5), 1891–1914.

Gardyn, R. (2000, April). Somebody say amen! *American Demographics, 22*(4), 72.

Gault-Caviness, Y. (2000, May). Wise words. *Essence,* 242–44.

Green, J. W. (1999). *Cultural awareness in the human services: A multi-ethnic approach* (3rd ed.). Boston: Allyn & Bacon.

Harrison, A. O. (1985). The black family's socializing environment: Self-esteem and ethnic attitude among black children. In H. P. McAdoo & H. McAdoo, (Eds.), *Black children: Social, educational, and parental environment* (pp. 174–93). Newbury Park, CA: Sage.

Hatchett, S. J., & Jackson, J. S. (1999). African American extended kin systems: An empirical assessment in the national survey of black Americans. In H. P. McAdoo (Ed.), *Family ethnicity: Strength in diversity* (2nd ed., pp. 171–90). Thousand Oaks, CA: Sage.

Hill, R. B. (1978). *The strengths of black families.* New York: Emerson Hall.

Hill, R. B. (1997). *The strengths of African American families: Twenty-five years later.* Washington, DC: R & B Publishing.

Holmes, S. A. (2000, March 19). The politics of race and the census. *The New York Times*, p. WK3.

Ingrassia, M. (1993, August 30). A world without fathers: The struggle to save the black family [special report]. *Newsweek*, 16–29.

Jackson, J. S., McCullough, W. R., Gurin, G., & Broman, C. L. (1991). Race identity. In J. S. Jackson (Ed.), *Life in black America*. Newbury Park, CA: Sage.

Jones, J. (1991). Racism: A cultural analysis of the problem. In R. L. Jones (Ed.), *Black psychology* (3rd ed., pp. 609–35). Berkeley, CA: Cobb & Henry.

Lum, D. (1986). *Social work practice and people of color: A process-stage approach*. Belmont, CA: Wadsworth.

McAdoo, H. P. (1970). *Racial attitudes and self-concept of black preschool children*. Unpublished doctoral dissertation, University of Michigan, Ann Arbor.

McAdoo, H. P. (1985). Racial attitude and self-concept of young black children over time. In H. P. McAdoo & J. L. McAdoo (Eds.), *Black children: Social, educational, and parental environments* (pp. 213–42). Newbury Park, CA: Sage.

McAdoo, H. P. (1995a). *Family ethnicity: Strength in diversity*. Newbury Park, CA: Sage.

McAdoo, H. P. (1995b). Stress levels, family help patterns, and religiosity in middle- and working-class African American single mothers. *Journal of Black Psychology, 21*, 424–49.

McAdoo, H. P. (1997). *Black families* (3rd ed.). Thousand Oaks, CA: Sage.

McAdoo, H. P. (Ed.). (1999). *Family ethnicity: Strength in diversity* (2nd ed.). Thousand Oaks, CA: Sage.

McAdoo, H. P. (2000). *Black children: Social, educational, and parental environments*. Thousand Oaks, CA: Sage.

McAdoo, H. P., & Crawford, V. (1991). The black church and family support programs. In D. Unger & D. Powell (Eds.), *Families as nurturing systems: Support across the life span* (pp. 193–222). New York: Haworth Press.

McAdoo, J. (1985). Modification of racial attitudes and preferences in young black children. In H. P. McAdoo & J. L. McAdoo (Eds.), *Black children: Social, educational, and parental environments* (pp. 243–56). Newbury Park, CA: Sage.

Pearlmutter, L. (1996). Using culture and the intersubjective perspective as a resource: A case study of an African-American couple. *Clinical Social Work Journal, 24*(4), 389–402.

Peters, M. F. (1997). Parenting of young children in black families. In H. P. McAdoo (Ed.), *Black families* (3rd ed., pp. 167–82). Thousand Oaks, CA: Sage.

Semaj, L. T. (1985). Afrikanity, cognition, and extended self-identity. In M. B. Spencer, G. K. Brookins, & W. R. Allen (Eds.), *Beginnings: The social and affective development of black children* (pp. 173–84). Hillsdale, NJ: Lawrence Erlbaum.

Stack, C. B. (1974). *All our kin: Strategies for survival in a black community*. New York: Harper & Row.

Stevenson, H. C., & Renard, G. (1993). Trusting ole' wise owls: Therapeutic use of cultural strengths in African American families. *Professional Psychology: Research and Practice, 24*(4), 433–42.

Sudarkasa, N. (1993). Female-headed African American households. In H. P. McAdoo (Ed.), *Family ethnicity: Strength in diversity* (pp. 81–89). Newbury Park, CA: Sage.

Sudarkasa, N. (1999). African American females as primary parents. In H. P. McAdoo (Ed.), *Family ethnicity: Strength in diversity* (2nd ed., pp. 191–200). Thousand Oaks, CA: Sage.

Tatum, B. (1987). *Assimilation blues*. Westport, CT: Greenwood.

Taylor, R., & Chatters, L. (1991). Religious life. In J. Jackson (Ed.), *Life in black America* (pp. 105–23). Newbury Park, CA: Sage.

West, C. (1993). *Race matters*. Boston: Beacon Press.

Wilkinson, D. (1997). American families of African descent. In M. K. DeGenova (Ed.), *Families in cultural context: Strengths and challenges in diversity*. Mountain View, CA: Mayfield.

Witt, G. E. (1999, October). In the eye of the beholder. *American Demographics, 21*(10), 24.

CHAPTER 5

Parent-Child Relationships in Caribbean Families

CLAUDETTE P. J. CRAWFORD-BROWN
J. MELROSE RATTRAY

A knowledge of the lifestyles and special problems of the different ethnic groups in the American cultural mosaic is essential for contemporary mental health practitioners in America. This necessity is in part due to specific global socioeconomic and political realities that have forced large numbers of new immigrants to become an integral part of metropolitan and suburban America since the 1970s. Some social analysts have suggested that the sociocultural profile of contemporary American society is similar, in terms of the rapid changes occurring in the demographic landscape of American families and its communities, to the now-famous period of mass migration from Europe that occurred in the late nineteenth and early twentieth centuries. During that period many indexes suggest that tremendous energy was funneled into American society as its members responded to the different immigrant groups (Devore & Schlesinger, 1999). The wave of migration in the post-1970s consists of a very different blend of migrant peoples (particularly those of African, Asian, and Hispanic origins) who bring with them rich sociocultural histories, distinctive and unique premigration experiences, and different social and geopolitical histories. As a consequence, these groups have a wide variety of needs that have an impact on the members of the host society. As a result of the dynamic interaction between the culture of the host society and that of the different ethnic groups that make up contemporary American society, the twin topics of "diversity and ethnicity" have become the new cutting-edge issues in social work practice.

McGoldrick, Pearce, and Giordano (1982) refer to ethnicity as "a concept of peoplehood based on a combination of race, religion, geographic origin and cultural history" (p. 4) and suggest that it involves conscious as well unconscious processes that fulfill a deep psychological need for identity and historical continuity. One definition of the term *diversity* suggests that it expresses the concept of difference as it exists among different ethnic groups based on such variables as race, culture, religion, and gender (McGoldrick et al., p. 4). Many of these elements of American society are shaped by patterns of migration.

One ethnic group that has been part of this migration pattern over the past three decades is the West Indian or Caribbean immigrant.[1] Because the majority of Caribbean peoples migrating to the United States are of African origin, these peoples were initially assumed to share lifestyles and cultures similar to the African American population of the host country (Gopaul-McNichol, 1993, p. 12). However, although there are some similarities between the two groups, there are also important differences, some of which are directly related to the nature of the Caribbean migratory experience.

The purpose of this chapter is to identify and discuss the stresses on families caused by various migration experiences of Caribbean parents and children and to help practitioners work more effectively with this population.

THE SOCIOCULTURAL CONTEXT OF CARIBBEAN MIGRATION

The position of Caribbean people within the context of the international division of labor is determined to a large extent by the social and economic structure of Caribbean society (Thomas-Hope, 1992). This, in turn, has historically dictated the social circumstances and the migrating behavior of the families who have gone to North America and the United Kingdom from the Caribbean.

Thomas-Hope (1992) makes the point that class is a very significant aspect of migratory behavior in the Caribbean, and it is important that the Caribbean immigrant *not* be seen as part of a socially *homogenous* group. The movement of upper-class families to the more economically developed countries, for example, usually occurs with entire family units immigrating together. Working-class Caribbean families, however, tend to migrate serially, with one family member going first and others following later. This difference is an important sociocultural pattern of Caribbean migration. Historically, migration from the Caribbean has been closely tied to employment patterns as well as to the labor demands of the metropolitan societies to which these people have migrated, namely the United Kingdom and North America. Initially, during the first wave of migration in the post–World War II era, as shown in table 5.1, the men migrated in large numbers, leaving the women and children in the country of origin. These women and children would migrate and rejoin their men in the host countries at a later date. During that era, children were left behind with their mothers or grandmothers, and the men would go ahead, first finding employment until the migration process was completed and their families could join them (Smith, 1981, p. 21).

Table 5.1. Jamaican Migration to Britain 1953–1962 (number of men, women, and children)

Year	Men	Women	Children	Total
1953	1,284	875	51	2,210
1954	5,178	2,861	110	8,149
1955	11,515	6,718	331	18,564
1956	9,144	7,577	581	17,302
1957	6,257	6,097	733	13,087
1958	4,425	4,509	1,059	9,993
1959	6,410	4,955	1,431	12,796
1960	18,372	11,258	2,430	32,060
1961	19,181	16,276	3,746	39,203
1962	8,434	10,207	4,138	22,779
Total	90,200	71,333	14,610	176,143

Source: Social and Economic Survey of Jamaica (1953–1962).

When the "doors" of migration to Britain closed as a result of changes in immigration laws in the United Kingdom in the 1960s, the doors to North America were utilized by employment-hungry and opportunity-hungry working-class Caribbean peoples. Thus, a different migratory pattern emerged for working-class Caribbean families, one in which the women in the household migrated first and then sent for their husbands and children at a later date. Though the serial pattern continued, the gender of the first immigrant shifted from being predominantly male to being predominantly female. The migratory process could take from two to ten years. Smith reported in 1981 that, in Canada, the result was that "a smaller proportion of Caribbean immigrants than all immigrants arrive in Canada, under the age of five years." A similar pattern existed in the United Kingdom and still exists today.

It is important to note that these migratory patterns refer to working-class Caribbean families. Middle- and upper-class Caribbean immigrants traditionally will immigrate with their entire families intact and will not therefore have the same problems as families from the lower socioeconomic classes of Caribbean society.

To understand the reasons for the patterns and flow of the Caribbean migration process, it is necessary to understand the sociocultural context of the process. Elizabeth Thomas-Hope (1992, p. 21) suggests that a number of social and cultural factors impact on the migration process. *Long-term child-minding arrangements* between kin or strangers are common in Caribbean cultures. Kinfolk who care for the children of migrating family members are compensated by the migrant family members through different levels of economic support, such as housing accommodation, access to land, or remittances or gifts that were traditionally sent in corrugated cardboard barrels for the purposes of international shipping. The concept of barrel children is a phenomenon that has emerged from this particular cultural practice. The term "barrel children" was coined in the 1980s by Jamaican social work practitioners to describe children waiting in the Caribbean and who meanwhile receive material resources in the form of food and clothing from their parents, who have migrated to the metropolitan centers of North America and the United Kingdom. The children are cared for by surrogate parents and receive material goods, but they often do not receive the emotional support and nurturance that they so desperately need (Crawford-Brown, 1999).

Inheritance-related land-tenure patterns and a *strong familial kinship network* are other factors that allow important family members, such as a mother or father, to leave their young children for prolonged periods, according to Thomas-Hope. These children are then expected to join the parents several years later. This migrating pattern is one of the most significant single factors affecting the household organization and structure of the working-class Caribbean family. This chapter discusses the effects of these factors on the family and on parent-child relationships.

THE EFFECT OF MIGRATION ON THE FAMILY LEFT BEHIND

The effect of migration on the family left behind in the Caribbean revolves around the issues of attachment, separation, and loss. Many families try to maintain contact through letters, telephone calls, and when possible, brief visits during vacation periods. Sometimes, however, all communication is discontinued, as in the case of an illegal immigrant parent who is afraid of being discovered. As new technologies emerge and as telephones become more readily available in the Caribbean, letter writing has become less frequent. Its unifying function for the separated family, however, makes it invaluable.

> The fact that my mother wrote directly to me, made all the difference in our relationship when we were reunited . . . the bond was maintained, because my grandmother used to sit down and force me to reply. (Jordan, 1983)

When Caribbean families do not immigrate together, the period of separation between parent and child can vary by as much as three to ten years. Some children are left as soon as they are but a few months old, others at somewhat older, more critical stages when separation is known to cause psychological damage (Freud, 1977). An interview with a Jamaican mother sums up the acute sense of loss very well. In response to the question of how she coped with leaving her baby, she said, "I left him when he was 2 years old. I bottled and brought the 'navel string' (the umbilical cord) with me. Every time I feel lonely, discouraged, or discriminated against, I take it out and cry over it, knowing that this is the only reason I am here, to give him a better opportunity" (Rattray, 1983).

Separation is difficult for both mother and child. For the child who is left at a very early age, the memory of the parent fades. The child who is left at a later stage experiences fear, anger, resentment, and rejection. The results of the separation manifest themselves later through the absence of bonding between parent and child, the "strangeness" of reunification, and the antisocial tendencies acted out. This acting out could be described on the one hand as a search for something the child once had and then lost, and on the other hand, as a search for something that never existed (i.e., a relationship). According to Bowlby (1961), who emphasizes the importance of the mother-child relationship, the anxiety and loneliness experienced by the child, at the first loss, (that is, when the relationship is first broken) evokes an ancient instinctive response in the child. This response can range from depression and withdrawal to anger and hostility.

Bowlby (1961) identifies the various stages through which the loss and bereavement experiences will move, although all the stages overlap as part of a single process. Stages of anger, weeping, and despair are seen as the child's expressions of the urge to recover the lost object. The final phase is the development of a new interactive structure through which the individual can relate to his or her environment. This structure can include acting out behavior and sometimes depression. According to Bowlby (1960), when loss cannot be articulated, its suppressed tensions in the end prove more profoundly disruptive than the social conflicts which precipitated them. Many of the problems experienced by Caribbean children and their parents at home, school, and society can be considered the result of unresolved grief. In the child, this grief is manifested in terms of withdrawal or anger, whereas in the parent, it is manifested as guilt.

A Model of Children's Behavioral-Emotional Responses to Migration

The specific effects of the migratory pattern on the Caribbean family, and on children and their relationships, will be discussed in terms of a model that describes the social and cultural context of the migratory process. As shown in the model, the process of migration affects two groups of family members: the family left behind in the Caribbean and the family in the host country.

The model of children's behavioral-emotional responses to migration (figure 5.1) describes some of the major responses experienced by the immigrant child. (This figure is an adaptation of a model developed originally by Lonner, 1986, to explain migrating behavior generally.) The adapted model in figure 5.1 describes five of the major theoretical concepts that contribute to adverse reactions in the child left in the Caribbean. These concepts are: spatial factors, control factors, organismic factors, intrapersonal factors, and interpersonal factors. *Control factors* relate to the fact that the migration process is usually beyond the child's control. *Spatial factors* relate to the disorientation the child feels when the parent migrates and there is spatial movement to an alternative parenting environment. *Organismic factors* refer to physical and biological changes the child may experience; and *intrapersonal* and *interpersonal factors* relate to the difficulties experienced by the child in adjusting to new household members and rules in his or her alternative family situation as well as to internal personality factors that may create a specific predisposition in terms of the child's ability to cope. These factors result in certain reactions on the part of the child that affect his or her behavior in the country of origin. These reactions can take a variety of forms, which are described in the following sections.

Deviant or Acting Out Behavior Sometimes acting out behavior is manifested in terms of delinquent behavior. In a comparative study of factors associated with

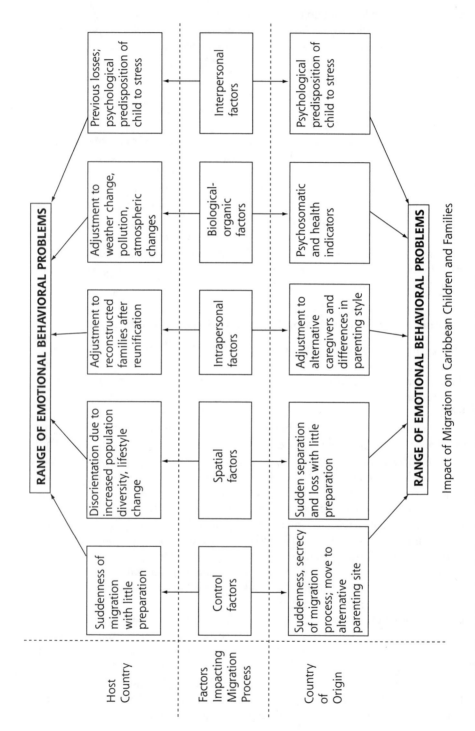

Figure 5.1. Model Showing Sociocultural Context of Caribbean Migration (adapted from Lonner, 1986)

conduct disorders in adolescence, 70 delinquent and 69 nondelinquent male adolescents in Jamaica were investigated to determine what family factors may have been associated with their behavior (Crawford-Brown, 1997). The results showed that there was a preponderance of absent mothers (86 percent) in the delinquent group compared to 13 percent in the comparison group. The biggest factor causing mothers' absence in the delinquent group was migration (see figure 5.2).

Withdrawal and Depressive Reactions   Some children act out their anger at being separated from parents through withdrawal and depressive reactions. These reactions relate to the fact that the child often feels helpless and unable to control the situation. Most decisions are made without the child, and the "immigration process" is perceived as preordained. Once it is set in motion, the child has no choice.

Defensive and Runaway Behavior   Another type of reaction, defensive and runaway behavior, is usually associated with feeling helpless and unable to control one's life. This behavior may or may not lead to drug abuse or other deviant behavior.

Alternative Parental Arrangements

The degree of withdrawal or depressive reactions or degree of acting out or aggressive behavior depends to a large extent on the type of alternative parenting arrangements put in place for the child by the migrated parent. The following four basic arrangements are typical: child is placed into the extended family; child is boarded with strangers or friends; child is placed in an institution; or child is placed in the natural family. Each of these arrangements is explained in more detail in the sections that follow.

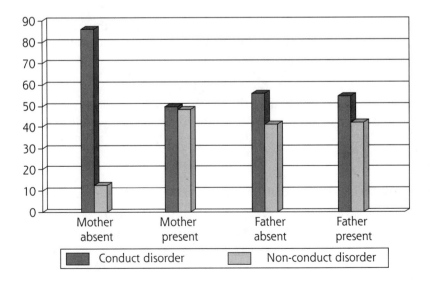

Figure 5.2. Presence of Parents During Childhood for Population Studied

Extended Family Placing the child into the extended family is the traditional alternative parenting arrangement for many Caribbean families. Extended family members such as grandparents or uncles and aunts look after the child or children in the parents' absence. However, as grandparents become busier, other caretaking options are increasingly used.

Strangers or Friends Sometimes children are placed in the home of strangers or friends of their parents. This placement may be with someone who lives in the same community, but frequently rural children, because of the availability of "better" schools, are placed in boarding arrangements with individuals who live in urban areas. Such changes in parental arrangements require that the child adjust to care by strangers or friends, and sometimes personality conflicts occur. When these clashes are coupled with the child's need to adjust to the absence of the parents and, in some cases, little or no communication with migrated parents, the child reacts to these multiple pressures, which can lead to a breakdown in these living situations. Such a breakdown in the alternative parental arrangement may result in institutionalization of the child. Frequent changes in parental arrangements was one significant variable found in Crawford-Brown's (1997) study of conduct disorders in Jamaican adolescent males.

Institutions Children may be boarded in educational institutions or in child care institutions for children in need of care and protection. These child welfare institutions, although ill-equipped, fill the need for alternative care when there is a breakdown in the extended familial situations or in the alternative parenting situations.

Natural Family In the natural family arrangement, children may be left with a spouse (usually the father or stepfather of the child), or in some cases, the children are left alone to care for each other, with the older child, usually a female adolescent, in charge of younger siblings.

This pattern is part of a relatively recent migratory pattern that has been occurring in Jamaican society, one in which family members participate in short-term migration. This type of migration typically involves the mother, who leaves for the host country and remains there for a period of time. During that time, she works assiduously, sending home remittances for school fees, mortgage payments, and so forth. She then comes home for a few months or weeks, usually at the beginning of the school year to send the children off to school, remains until her household is settled, then returns to the host country. Such a migrant lives with one foot in the host country and one foot in the Caribbean.

Adaptive Social and Economic Responses to Migration

These migratory patterns, which are discussed in the vignette presented later in this chapter, seem to be a result of economic pressures affecting Caribbean families, pressures caused by socioeconomic policies such as government and international structural adjustment programs being used as economic incentives in many Caribbean countries. It appears, therefore, that Caribbean families have developed these various migratory patterns as adaptive mechanisms to ensure their family's survival at some cost to the emotional well-being of the family. Following are some of the social implications of these phenomena.

Sexual Abuse Anecdotal reports from schools, family clinics, and social service agencies document the fact that children left unprotected and unsupervised in the Caribbean by parents often become the victims of sexual abuse. Because the children are unprotected, they are easy targets for sexually abusive relatives, neighbors, or others. Given the lack of legal and policy consequences in many Caribbean societies for management of the sexual abuse of children, many of these cases go unreported and untreated, and many of these children carry burdens and scars from these experiences into adulthood.

The Parentified Child Parentified children are given the responsibilities of rearing themselves as well as, sometimes, their entire households, including their father and their siblings. Social work practitioners in the Caribbean are very concerned about the increasing numbers of parents following this pattern of family migration and child care. Often these children cannot attend adequately to their schoolwork, and they become overwhelmed and sometimes develop depression or even become promiscuous. Many of these children are given awesome responsibilities inappropriate for their adolescent years. For example, parents may send barrels of consumer items to children, who are expected to sell the contents to provide for their own welfare, which places tremendous responsibility on the child. Such activity goes far beyond the normal expectations of the child's role as daughter or son.

THE EFFECT OF MIGRATION ON THE FAMILY UPON REUNIFICATION

Another factor that must be considered is the second phase of the migratory experience, that is, when the family unifies. Many children experience additional trauma and pain when the family reunites. Figure 5.1 identifies five major factors affecting the migration process that impact on the family upon reunification. Four of those factors—spatial factors, control factors, organismic-biological factors, and interpersonal factors—are described here.

Spatial Factors

Children migrating from the Caribbean come, for the most part, from a life spent in the open air in a warm, sunny, and generally friendly climate where the warmth of the atmosphere often translates into human relationships. They come from a setting where people live together in closely knit kinship groups and communities; where people share one another's hopes, fears, joys, sorrows, and troubles; where there is a sense of community involvement in family occasions.

When the decision is made to reunite with parents who have migrated, the children are informed usually only a few weeks before departure. Age and educational and emotional development will influence the child's response, but most children consider migration only in terms of joining mom or dad and in terms of the "new pretty things" they will get. The immigrant child is totally unprepared for the changes that he or she will encounter in the United States or other host country. These changes include not only climatic and culture shock, but also what Morrish (1971, p. 86) calls "color shock." Children find themselves to be black individuals in a predominantly white society, where for the first time they are in the minority, where they do not in any way belong to the mainstream, and where members of their own race are viewed as inferior.

Intolerance for oppression is characteristic of Caribbean people. This coping mechanism can have both positive and negative consequences. Caribbean children may have the tendency to challenge systems more overtly (a positive coping mechanism), but this challenging nature also can be seen as aggressive (a negative label). In fact, Caribbean children possess values and concepts that have originated in a milieu with a strong cultural history and background. The children then find themselves transplanted to a milieu that is resistant and hostile to their presence. These children soon discover that their own values and cultural concepts are virtually without positive reinforcement.

Morrish (1971, p. 85) says about the Caribbean child immigrant, "his own thought forms are not easily communicated in the sort of English that he speaks and in which he thinks. He is caught up in cultural tests and selection procedures which are not sensitive to him, and these invariably leave him at a disadvantage compared with white children of his own age and ability."

Delroy Louden (1993, p. 29) further reflects on such situations and suggests that "the net result is that children, already confused, are thrust into a school environment which is very different from home. Accustomed to strict discipline and the provision of 'correct' answers, they hesitate to enter classroom discussions or to interpret issues for themselves. As a consequence, many teachers conclude that the children are 'backward' and they may be held back from promotion or otherwise receive negative school reports."

The following quote conveys the challenges and the understandable response of the Caribbean child:

> The West Indian finds himself in the new world of different sounds in which he must acclimatize his hearing, his understanding and his expression of different accents at a variety of special levels. These psycho-linguistic problems can make him feel a total stranger, insecure, inferior and unadjusted. (Morrish, 1971, p. 86)

Control Factors

The model in figure 5.1 suggests that the average child coming from the Caribbean has little control over the migration process and absolutely no choice. The child joins the parents because the migration papers have been processed after years of waiting, permission has been finally granted, and a date has been set, all with no consultation with the child. The child is not aware of the major reasons for delays in joining parents: immigration setbacks, and the necessity that parents be settled in the host country before they can send for the child.

The majority of children migrate between the ages of five and nineteen. Many have never before experienced international travel. The majority also lack language skills; although English is spoken and understood in the Caribbean, most rural children speak in the local dialect of their particular region. The culture from which they come fosters interdependence, perseverance, and fortitude. Other important traits include survival skills, both positive and negative. The children's capacity to tolerate ambiguities and frustrations, which has already been tested by the long separation from their parents, is often tested again as they journey through the strange and unfamiliar landscape of a different school and community environment. Because of their appearance, these children form part of the visible minority and therefore are not acknowledged as possessing unique personal characteristics.

Organismic-Biological Factors

Children who migrate from the Caribbean are usually healthy because immigration requires a medical fitness report. Their ability to tolerate the climatic conditions sometimes poses initial problems, because the drastic change in climate can be very traumatic for children who are suddenly introduced to cold weather with very little preparation. Dietary needs for home cooking are usually satisfied at home, but when they enroll in school and eat in large cafeterias with conveyer belt services, children may feel shy and disoriented. One eight-year-old male child reported feeling extremely frightened by the cafeteria. He suffered school phobia that was based on a fear of the cafeteria. The numbers, the scale, and the seeming impersonality of the way in which food was served was disconcerting to this child and was also a manifestation of everything that was strange and alien. These differences in customs could be easily addressed through orientation programs for new arrivals in the school system.

Interpersonal Factors

Usually the support group that surrounds the child is strong both at home and in the host country. Sometimes, however, the nature of the support group in the host country is weakened by a number of factors: reconstituted families, a mother or father who is a stranger, or siblings who are strangers. Expectations of gratitude from child to parent may not be forthcoming. Parents and children may discover that their expectations are not mutual and that both sides harbor resentments over the way contacts had been maintained before, during, and after migration.

PRACTICE IMPLICATIONS OF THE MIGRATION EXPERIENCE

Practitioners must realize that the difficulties of transition do not end when parents and children are reunited. On the contrary, the participants are frequently unaware of the extent of the stressful nature of the experience and of its cumulative impact. Following what might be a period of initial relative calm, major relationship crises frequently develop for which the family is totally unprepared.

Family Conflict

Crises often erupt in the family through the newly arrived child, who must adjust to a different society and culture. Sometimes the child meets a reconstituted family in which the child may have a new parent as well as new siblings. Very often the child will find it difficult to adjust to these new family situations; the child may feel like the "odd child out." In many instances, the relationships between child and mother or child and stepfather or stepmother become strained and conflictual. These conflicts can cause parental friction that sometimes leads to separation of child and parent and even divorce of the parents.

Very often the parent of the newcomer is caught between the dynamics of his or her life and the child's life. When this conflict happens, the newcomer immigrant child is blamed for causing the disruption in the family. The blaming and nagging often become one of the push factors that result in the child distancing himself or herself from the family and possibly taking to the streets. The parent or parents may have forgotten their own earlier discomfort in adjusting to a new culture and may fail to reassure and support their child during this vulnerable adjustment period.

Child Abuse and Children's Rights

Abusive behavior toward children who have reunited with families usually takes the form of verbal attacks and expressed disappointment by the parents, who have sacrificed so much to send for that child. The child who has trouble adjusting is viewed as ungrateful for the years of sacrifice the parents have made. The child in this situation is made to feel guilty and once again rejected, while the parent feels disappointed and hurt, believing that the child of their dreams has turned out just like other children from the host country—rebellious, defiant, and even acting out. In addition, the immigrant child may have discovered that children in the host country have rights and that the host country has different views regarding child abuse. The child's newfound confidence creates situations in which parents cannot use the old ways of discipline; perhaps the parents just give up and let go of the child completely, which leaves the child to wander without direction.

Sibling Conflicts

At times, this one child's distress causes conflicts between siblings who may be strangers to each other. Siblings sometimes have different cultural outlooks and view the newcomer's ways and accent as strange and funny. The newcomer to this already established family may even be viewed as an intruder. It is easy to see how the newcomer could begin to feel that there is really no space in the new family for him or her.

Parents as Strangers

It is often difficult for practitioners to understand that neither the parent nor the child know each other. This situation is particularly difficult for the parents, because the admission that they do not know their own child constitutes failure and reinforces their feelings of not being a good enough parent. Children are sometimes unsure of how to address their new parent figures and uncertain about how to adjust to parental authority. Conflict around this issue can arise when, for example, a mother may insist on being called "mom" or "mama," when from the child's perspective the grandmother who was left behind is the only mama the child has known and no one seems to understand how much the child misses that mama. Oftentimes, after the migration not much contact is kept with that psychological parent (e.g., grandmother) because parents desire to cut the child off from his or her "backward" past that the parents consider not helpful to the child's advancement in the new environment.

Confusion Regarding Differences in Sociocultural Practices

Using titles (such as ma'am and sir) is standard practice in the Caribbean, where formality between children and adults is considered mandatory and commonplace. The titles used to address adults in the Caribbean are a symbol of respect and deference. In the host country, one observer reported, there have been instances where teenage sons, much to the chagrin of the mother, will approach her or the stepfather and start talking without using any title. It is surprising, but true, that these small things can put a strain on relationships. This kind of behavior is often interpreted as insubordinate and rude and is not understood from the point of view of the child, who may be confused by the many changes in customs. Practitioners can prepare parents for this awkward transition and help them find ways to deal with it. Practitioners also should be sensitive to such sociocultural practices when working with families and children from the Caribbean. More formality is expected than with mainstream North American parents.

Parental Expectations

Another source of tension in the family dynamics has to do with parental aspirations and expectations for their children. Parents who bring their children to the host country truly believe that they are offering the best possible opportunity to their children. Unfortunately, major tensions arise when the children, particularly adolescents, do not share these expectations. Parents, wanting desperately to live out their hopes through their children, pressure the children by telling them "in no uncertain terms" what they are to become. Parents are not wrong in dreaming for the best for their children, but the way in which parents articulate these dreams can seem to be threatening and authoritarian to the children.

Teenage pregnancy often brings intense reactions from parents, who may be so upset with their teenage daughters that they literally abandon them. The burden of the immigrant is that he or she *must succeed* at all costs. Teenage pregnancy destroys that dream and is not accommodated at all in many families.

Differences in Child-Rearing Practices

Child rearing constitutes another crucial area of family life for which both parents and children are ill-prepared because of the differing expectations and standards in the host country. Many Caribbean parents have been accustomed to an authoritarian and directive style of parenting as well as to the availability of extended family support systems. When these parents move to a culture where negotiation skills are preferred, where the state exercises oversight of family matters, and where there is an absence of extended family or community support, the Caribbean family is often left confused and without its normal resources. As one parent observed following her encounter with the Department of Social Services: "They put the parents down in front of the child, they give the child telephone numbers to call if the parents discipline them in any way. They are basically telling the child, 'do as you like until you are eighteen.' The only thing is, after the child reaches eighteen, they cannot do as they like any more, or they will be put in jail. Then they blame us, the parents, when they never allowed us to be parents the way we have always been taught to bring up children."

Summary

The process of separation and then reunification presents difficulties for all family members. Parents are often unaware of the psychological and emotional trauma that the dual experiences of separation and reunification can cause for their children. Parents, therefore, tend to place more emphasis on the *instrumental* aspect of reunification, leaving the affective components connected to the separation buried and unattended. Practitioners need to be aware of this essential component and its relationship to the child's experiences in the country of origin as well as in the host country.

Figure 5.3 illustrates the numerous psychosocial factors that impact on the immigrant child and family in the host country. These factors include physical changes, psychological and behavioral changes, and a complex pattern of new relationships. The result is possible identity confusion, feelings of disconnectedness, feelings of hopelessness and alienation, and a range of symptoms that may include mild feelings of depression as well as more serious deviant and dysfunctional behavior.

The tasks of the reunited family are multifaceted. These facets sometimes overlap and require compromise for their accomplishment. These tasks include reshaping the family's new reality and maximizing the family's continuity in terms of both its identity and its adaptation to the environment.

Reunification, as it relates to the uniqueness of the Caribbean situation, requires further research by social workers and other practitioners. Preparation of children and their parents for migration and reunification demands careful attention and skill. This process should be facilitated at both the original and host sources.

The normal migration processes are made more difficult for Caribbean children because of their many (sometimes sequential) experiences of separation. For children, the phenomenon of separation takes place several times—initially the separation from biological parent, followed by the separation from the grandparent or

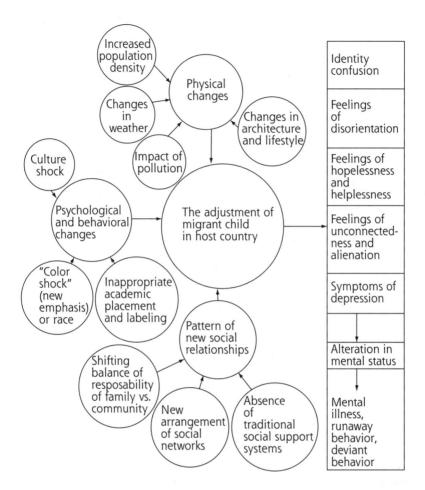

Figure 5.3. Model Showing Psychosocial Factors Impacting on the Migrant Child and Family (New Arrivals) in the Host Country

other caregiver prior to reunification, and in some instances, again when they are removed from home and placed in state care once they are in the host country. The fear of going through the pain of repeated separation may seriously impede the Caribbean child's ability to achieve successful adaptation.

Not only do children from the Caribbean encounter many changes in climate, relationships, routine, skin color, and language, but they also bring with them false pictures that help to create false expectations. The children gain these false expectations from the media, from their family in the country of origin, and from their parents in the host country. When Caribbean children confront reality and their expectations are dashed, practitioners in the host country must pick up the pieces of a complex situation about which they may know little.

POLICY AND PRACTICE RECOMMENDATIONS FOR INTERVENTION

The sociocultural context of the Caribbean migration experience—both in the country of origin and in the host country—highlights numerous interrelated problems that confront immigrant children and their families upon reunification (see figure 5.1). These problems and some possible intervention modalities are presented in table 5.2. Potential obstacles and the rationale for each intervention are also presented in this table.

The sociocultural factors discussed in this chapter help clarify the reasons for the emergence of conduct and behavioral problems in children who become victims of the migration process. It is in the interest of the Caribbean "sending" countries to institute some kind of preventive intervention at the premigration phase. Similarly, it is in the interest of the host country to provide intervention services for children during the reunification process. The following recommendations are presented at the level of macro and micro policy and practice as depicted in figure 5.4.

Premigration Phase

• It is recommended that the Children Services division of the relevant government ministry in the country of origin include premigration counseling as part of a preventive program. Such a program must interface with the national embassies of the receiving countries, such as the United States and Canada, to ensure that all migrating families with children are referred for mandatory counseling. Such families could be provided with educational material via videotapes in waiting rooms as well as with handouts and other written material on practical strategies for maintaining contact with children. In addition, these parents could be offered basic information about normal development of children and about the impact of separation on children at the different stages of their development.

• The government children's agency in the country of origin (e.g., Children Services division) should also be informed of the location of children left behind and should include these families in their preventive programs. Children most at risk for emotional and behavioral problems as a result of the migration process could be identified via systematic assessment and screening processes through the school and social service systems (Crawford-Brown, 1999), and these families could be identified for special attention.

• Another macro level recommendation is that government policy should expand existing parenting education programs to sensitize the populace generally about the importance of continuous parenting for the healthy psychological development of the child and about the implications of leaving children without parents for extended periods of time.

• As part of the premigration counseling phase, children who are due to rejoin their parents should be specially targeted and provided with basic information about (a) what to expect during the migration from the country of origin to the host country, (b) the changes in temperature and the implications of climate differences (e.g., What is snow? How does it form? How do you dress for cold weather?), and

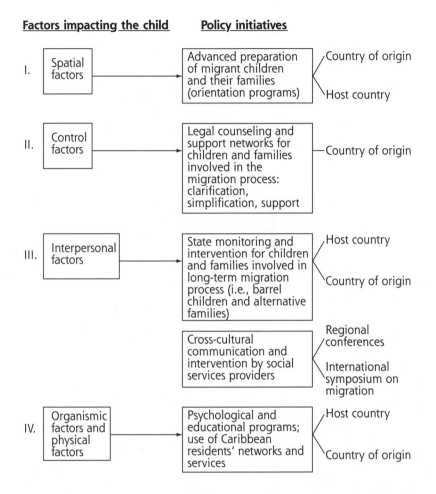

Figure 5.4. Policy Implications that Will Ensure Maintenance of the Rights of the Migrant Caribbean Child

(c) problems they might encounter in adjusting to their new family. This material should be presented in age appropriate formats in manuals, books, and videotapes and preferably should be written and produced by practitioners with some cross-cultural experience.

Reunification Phase

It is in the interest of the host country to also provide intervention services in the form of orientation programs targeted at new arrivals, especially children and families. In developing these programs, Caribbean organizations such as the West Indian social organizations and churches should be involved in the planning and

Table 5.2. Intervention Modalities for Migrant Caribbean Families

Areas of Potential Family Difficulties	Sociological or Cultural Basis for Difficulties	Intervention	Potential Obstacles
Altered patterns of social relationships	Unstructured communal interdependent lifestyle to a more individualized formal independent existence Lack of information, knowledge about the resources in the new environment	Support groups for new arrivals, psychological and educational groups, referrals to relevant resources: health, housing; educational policies and placement; community and recreational resources for children and families; legal support regarding immigration policies	Inability to trust service providers Belief that asking for help from outside family scene is culturally inappropriate
Social, psychological, and behavioral reactions to emotional sessions	Children, adolescents, and families experience feelings of disconnection and alienation due to the drastic changes in living environment, quality of life, and lifestyle	Support groups for new arrivals Journaling for individual family members, within or outside of group setting Individual therapeutic counseling Socializing relating to West Indian social activities and groups	Inability to trust service providers Belief that asking for help from outside family scene is culturally inappropriate

| Physical changes in environment | Drastic changes in weather and population density may lead to feelings of alienation and depression
Many Caribbean peoples unaccustomed to cold weather and a drier atmosphere suffer minor or major problems such as allergies, dermatological reactions, and other health problems | Referral to agencies to assist with communication with loved ones in country of origin
Educational information sessions on topics such as phone cards and computer-based communication systems
Referral to health providers or specialists, especially for sickle-cell anemia, diabetes, and hypertension | Caribbean peoples often do not want to bring any attention to themselves and will try to cope without outside help
Asking for help is often seen as failure
Succeeding in the immigration experience is very important, as is feeling that they must not let down those at home who are depending on them |

implementation of maintenance and orientation exercises, using positive Caribbean role models from the local communities. Here are some suggestions for these programs:

- Family contact can be maintained through new technologies, for example, videotape recorders and computers at community-based facilities where families can use e-mail and the video contact for communication.
- Programs should focus particularly on language differences and difficulties and on dealing with differences in educational requirements.
- Direct service to families should be provided to help immigrant children adjust to "new" parents and siblings and to help ease some of the stresses of the adjustment process. These special services should include family therapy for reconstituted families.
- Direct service (possibly school-based) individual and group counseling must be accessible to the children to help with special difficulties related to feelings of rejection, abandonment, and the repeated losses these children have experienced. Many public schools offer "newcomers" groups for children who are new to the school. Some issues raised in such groups could be shared by newly arrived immigrant children, but the history of parental separation is quite different for the Caribbean child and needs to be addressed separately.
- Parenting workshops can be held in collaboration with the West Indian community for public educational purposes so that parents can be involved in discussions of the issues and offer solutions to the problems affecting themselves and their children. Workshops must be organized through local organizations or by other professionals who are culturally sensitive to this population.

These policies will help children and their families cope better with the adjustment process. Children would be allowed, in a therapeutic environment, to grieve their losses and would be helped to accept their new situation at their own pace. Through these strategies, parents can also be helped in a nonthreatening and safe atmosphere to understand the nature of the adjustment process and what it means for their children.

West Indian parents who leave their children should not be seen as willfully neglectful and uncaring. Practitioners should view these parents not in negative terms but as parents, like other immigrant parents, trying to escape social and economic difficulties and provide for their children as best as they can. The following case study, which describes the experiences of a Caribbean child in the country of origin as well as in the host country, illustrates some of the issues discussed in this chapter.

CASE STUDY: ANDREA

Andrea is a fifteen-year-old adolescent girl whose mother left her in Jamaica with neighbors ten years ago to migrate to the United States. These neighbors, who were lifelong friends of Andrea's mother, live in a small but well-kept working class dwelling in a stable community in urban Jamaica. They had taken good care of Andrea for the past ten years.

Social Life and School in the Country of Origin

Andrea did well in school in Jamaica and won a coveted place in one of the country's best high schools at age twelve. While there, Andrea was reported as being well-adjusted by her teachers and guidance counselors in school, and she was involved in many extracurricular activities, which included netball (the English version of basketball) and junior service clubs. She had a wide range of male and female friends from school, from her church, and to a lesser extent, from her community. She was reported as being well-behaved by her surrogate parents and returned home promptly every day to complete homework assignments and to do her chores.

Contact with Her Mother

Andrea had maintained some contact with her mother over the past ten years, mainly by writing letters since her surrogate family did not have a telephone. Because of the mother's work situation in the United States, where she had few benefits or opportunities for vacations, she could not visit very often, and consequently Andrea had infrequent personal contact with her mother. Though Andrea tried on many occasions to obtain a visa to visit her mother in the United States, she was always denied this opportunity by the U.S. immigration authorities.

Andrea's mother, however, provided her with numerous material goods in the form of clothing, shoes and toys; things that many of her peers were never able to afford in Jamaica. Andrea's mother also paid Andrea's school fees regularly and sent remittances to Andrea's surrogate parents, who were able to provide adequately for Andrea's basic needs.

Despite all the material items sent by her mother, Andrea pined after her mother and missed her terribly. She would sometimes cry when she saw other children having fun with their mothers. She dreamed constantly of the day she would live with her mother again.

Family Reunification

When Andrea came to the United States, she reported experiencing overwhelming feelings of loss. She said she felt as if she had lost the only true parents she ever had. For a second time, therefore, Andrea was experiencing separation from a parental figure. She also reported feelings of disconnectedness and a sense of alienation from her biological mother about whom she had dreamed for so long. She now saw this mother as a stranger. Andrea arrived in her mother's household to find a ready-made family of two boys, ages twelve and seven, as well as a stepfather whom she had never met.

Her mother and stepfather used Andrea as a virtual maid who did all the family's chores. Andrea was not allowed to go out with the family when they were enjoying recreational activities and was often left at home to wash the dishes, do the laundry, and clean the house. Her brothers made fun of her Jamaican accent, and Andrea reported that her mother made her feel as though her brothers were special and somehow better than she was because they were U.S. citizens. Her mother, she stated, did little to intervene when she was teased, and actively encouraged her to change her accent. This behavior created tremendous feelings of resentment in Andrea, who had always had strong feelings of pride in her country of origin and had never been taught to see herself as inferior to anyone. She cried continuously for the first three weeks of her arrival in the United States and appeared to be in a depressed mood for prolonged periods of time.

School in the Host Country

On arrival in her new high school, Andrea was placed in a class she considered to be below her academic level. She was automatically put in a class for students needing remedial English or who spoke English as a second language. This placement was done without testing, although she had spoken and understood only English all her life. Andrea was told that this placement policy, based on the school's prior experience, applied to all Jamaican students. Andrea felt that she received no support from her mother in approaching the school officials about this matter, which she considered to be a grave injustice and an insult to her intelligence. Using her school transcripts, she tried by herself to explain to the school officials the complexities and the different levels of the Jamaican educational system, but none of the school personnel would listen to her. Her mother felt that Andrea was being too persistent and warned her that the U.S. officials would deport her back to Jamaica if she appeared too assertive and rebellious.

At this point, Andrea started presenting with symptoms of depression; she seemed unmotivated and appeared withdrawn, particularly at school. Her grades started falling, and on one occasion, she exhibited aggressive behavior at school when she was reported to the principal for fighting a classmate who had teased her about her accent. Andrea was referred for counseling, and her parents were called in. Her parents' reaction was one of extreme hostility to the school social worker, and at home Andrea was berated for bringing shame to the family and for being ungrateful.

Andrea felt that her dreams were shattered and that she had no one to turn to. She wanted to communicate with her surrogate parents in Jamaica but was not allowed to write to them about the issue, because her mother felt that Andrea would be taking the family's business out of the house. Her mother explained that it was important to maintain a semblance of success and prosperity to friends and relatives "back home," and so no complaints could be mentioned in her letters, which her mother read prior to mailing.

Suicidal Ideation

After six months in the United States, Andrea had the experience of having her stepfather fondle her inappropriately in the kitchen at home. At this point Andrea wrote a suicide note and showed it to one of her friends at school, who reported it to the social worker. The suicide note contained a detailed plan and a desire for her body to be shipped back to Jamaica for burial.

Andrea was again referred to the school social worker, but she refused to disclose any information about her home situation or about herself that might have led her to write the suicide note. At this point the school social worker referred the case to another social worker, who was a cultural consultant on issues relating to this population.

Discussion Questions and Role-Play Exercises

1. If you were the cultural consultant in Andrea's case, what would you identify as the major issues in Andrea's environment that are impacting on her at this time?
2. Why has Andrea's behavior changed so radically, as exhibited by her aggressive outbursts and symptoms of depression and withdrawal, by the drop in her academic grades, and by the suicidal ideation and gestures?
3. How would you intervene with Andrea and her family in a manner that would (a) obtain the family's cooperation, and (b) be sensitive to the cultural context of the child and the family? Role-play your telephone call to Andrea's mother and the first session with the family. Which family members should be included in the first session?
4. Discuss the special challenges presented by Andrea's case if the social worker was white, African American, Hispanic, or Jamaican. Role-play the worker's opening comments to the family members, based on each of these different racial identities.
5. How can Andrea's mother be helped to become more sensitive and responsive to her daughter?
6. At what point, and how, can the sexual abuse in Andrea's situation be confronted?
7. Do you think that sexual abuse can ever be considered a cultural phenomenon? Why or why not?

Note

1. The terms "West Indian" and "Caribbean" will be used interchangeably; however, the term "West Indian" normally refers to people from the English-speaking Caribbean islands such as Jamaica, Trinidad and Tobago, Barbados, Antigua, St. Kitts and Nevis, St. Lucia, Monsterrat, the Bahamas, Bermuda, and other smaller islands. The Spanish-speaking islands of the Caribbean include Cuba, Puerto Rico, the Dominican Republic, and other islands. The French-speaking islands include Haiti and Martinique, and the Dutch-speaking islands include Curacao and Bonaire. The different languages spoken in these islands reflect the language of their European colonizers. It is to be noted, however, that despite the language differences there are numerous sociocultural similarities among the different people of the Caribbean.

References

Bowlby, J. (1960). Grief and mourning in infancy and early childhood. *Psychoanalytic Study of the Child, 15,* 9–52.

Bowlby J. (1961). Process of mourning. *International Journal of Psychoanalysis, 42,* 317–40.

Crawford-Brown, C. (1997). The impact of parent-child socialization on conduct disorder in Jamaican male adolescents. In J. R. Roopnarine & J. Brown (Eds.), *Caribbean families.* Norwood, NJ: Ablex.

Crawford-Brown, C. (1999). *Who will save our children: The plight of the Jamaican child in the nineties.* Kingston: University of the West Indies Canoe Press.

Devore, W., & Schlesinger, E. (1999). *Ethnic-sensitive social work practice* (5th ed.). Needham Heights, MA: Allyn & Bacon.

Freud, A. (1977). *In the best interest of the child.* London: Dorsey Press.

Gopaul-McNichol, S. (1993). *Working with West Indian families.* New York: Guilford Press.

Jordan, C. (1983). *The case of the West Indian migration: Effect on families.* Unpublished casebook. Department of Sociology–Social Work, University of the West Indies, Kingston, Jamaica.

Lonner, W. J. (Ed.). (1986). *Culture shock.* Bellingham, WA: Western Washington University.

Louden, D. (1993). *Charting a new course: African-Canadians in Metro-Toronto in the 21st century—Strategies for change* [unpublished report]. Toronto: Metro-Toronto African-Canadian Community Retreat.

McGoldrick, M., Pearce, J., & Giordano, J. (Eds.). (1982). *Ethnicity and family therapy.* New York: Guilford Press.

Morrish, I. (1971). *The background of immigrant children: Cultural contact with host Society* (pp. 85–86). London: Allen & Unwin.

Rattray, M. (1983). *The families left behind: An analysis of factors affecting the Caribbean migrant family in the Caribbean.* Unpublished paper, McGill University School of Social Work, Montreal, Canada.

Smith, T. E. (1981). *Commonwealth migration: Flows and policies.* Macmillan: London.

Thomas-Hope, E. (1992). *Explanations in Caribbean.* Warwick, UK: Warwick University Press.

Latino Families

CHAPTER 6

Parenting in Mainland Puerto Rican Families

LUIS H. ZAYAS
IAN CANINO
ZULEMA E. SUÁREZ

Raising children in contemporary life is a complex and demanding challenge. The context of family life differs dramatically from that of family life during the first half of the twentieth century, or from the context of families living in today's simpler agrarian societies. Many families in the past lived in small villages and towns, were engaged in specialized subsistence work, and were backed up by abundant supports from the extended family. In today's large cities, the ever-present needs of paid employment plus the financial demands of families require a mobility that removes workers from their family home and roots. Immigration and the inexorable process of acculturation in many ethnic and racial minority groups in the U.S. mainland have intensified these demands on families. Among these groups, Puerto Ricans are unique because of the circumstances under which most of their fathers and mothers migrated.

This chapter emphasizes the impact of positive changes in child rearing and parenting practices that have occurred in this group. Although this chapter focuses on the strengths of child rearing in mainland Puerto Rican families, it does not deny the presence of families with multiple problems in psychosocial functioning. The purpose of this chapter is to sensitize practitioners to the child-rearing values and practices of Puerto Ricans and to provide some ideas for effective interventions with Puerto Rican families.

Support for this chapter was provided, in part, by NIMH grant R24 MH60002, to Luis H. Zayas, Ph.D.

MAINLAND PUERTO RICAN DEMOGRAPHICS

Puerto Ricans are the second largest Hispanic group in the mainland United States. People of Mexican descent constitute the largest Hispanic group. During the 1980s, virtually a third of all Puerto Ricans lived on the mainland (the other two-thirds remaining on the island of Puerto Rico); by 1990 about 44 percent of all Puerto Ricans resided on the mainland (Duany, 1996; Rodriguez, 1994). Puerto Ricans are a diverse group in terms of area of residence, unemployment rates, level of acculturation, and language utilization. Indeed, both Spanish and English are spoken equally, and many mainland Puerto Rican children speak primarily English. Although they may be less fluent in speaking Spanish than the island-residing child is, they usually understand spoken Spanish. Primarily concentrated in the Northeast, Puerto Ricans have also established communities in the Midwest, Texas, and increasingly in the Southeast, especially in Florida. These geographic dispersals have usually occurred because of economic opportunities in those areas. For example, when manufacturing centers developed in the Northeast, Puerto Ricans moved to the region. Pennsylvania and Ohio saw large migrations of Puerto Ricans when steel mills of those states needed infusions of laborers.

Puerto Rican migration is different from that of other Hispanic migrations. Because Puerto Ricans are U.S. citizens at birth, they have not immigrated but rather *migrated* to the mainland. No passports or visas are needed, and relatively inexpensive airfares between the island and the mainland have always existed. Many Puerto Ricans have therefore benefited from easy accessibility between the island and the U.S. mainland. Many have lived for extended periods of time in both the island and the mainland (Ortiz, 1996). Between 1950 and 1970, Puerto Ricans migrated to the U.S. mainland in large numbers, the majority to New York City. Most of the persons who migrated to the mainland originally came from impoverished rural areas of Puerto Rico and had limited education and skills. Indeed, the reason frequently given for the massive influx of Puerto Ricans is economic, although political and social factors have also been reported (Ortiz; Rodriguez, 1994). Recent waves of migration have brought more skilled workers and professionals. Despite these changes in migration demographics, the Puerto Rican population remains younger, has a lower educational attainment, earns less, and is more likely to be unemployed when compared to the U.S. population in general (Rodriguez).

PORTRAYAL OF PUERTO RICANS IN THE BEHAVIORAL SCIENCES AND MENTAL HEALTH LITERATURE

Despite the persistent socioeconomic disadvantage that exists among Puerto Ricans on the mainland, the focus of this chapter will be on the child rearing and parenting *strengths* of families, not on their deficits. Unfortunately, the mental health literature of the past portrayed Puerto Rican parenting, like that of other Hispanic Americans, with negative stereotypes.

One reason for this negative stereotyping has been the Euro-American orientation of the psychoanalytic literature on child-rearing practices, with its emphasis on separation, individuation, and autonomy. Another reason has been the considerable tradition in psychology that uses theories drawn from Euro-American samples and applies them to persons of color and to persons of non-European immigrant groups. According to Betancourt and Lopez (1993), this tradition reflects American psychology's long-held tendency to draw on "universal" theories of development and functioning for understanding human behavior and individual differences. The major problem with this approach—brought about by what Betancourt and Lopez term a "top-down" perspective—is that it treats culture as irrelevant and applies theories based on one group to other groups on which the theories were not developed. Further, this approach creates the fallacy that populations that do not fit the universal model may appear deviant. Betancourt and Lopez propose that American psychology must instead operate from what they term a "bottom-up" approach to viewing human functioning that encompasses culture. In the so-called bottom-up approach, researchers and clinicians take ground-level observations from a variety of ethno-cultural groups and adjust theories of human behavior accordingly. Ground-level, ethnographic observations study normality and deviance from the context of a specific group and then draw conclusions.

These issues as well as the paucity of cross-cultural research findings based on sound research methodology have caused problems with diagnostic manuals and instruments that purport to identify mental health disorders (I. A. Canino, Canino, & Arroyo, 1998; G. Canino, Canino, & Bravo, 1994). Cultural context frequently affects the idiomatic expressions of distress, the definition of normality and psychopathology, disorder phenomenology, and the number and duration of symptoms required for a formal DSM-IV diagnosis of impairment (Guarnaccia & Rodriguez, 1996; Kleinman, 1988; Mezzich et al., 1997). Errors by clinicians and researchers who are not competent in the contextual aspects of behavior and who, in addition, do not carefully assess levels of functional impairment and individuals' strengths may overdiagnose or misdiagnose this population.

Another possible reason for the negative stereotypes is that descriptions of the Puerto Rican family for a long time have been written by clinicians whose only exposure to Puerto Rican families were those who came to their consulting rooms with psychiatric and psychosocial problems. Clinicians thus viewed patients who sought services as the "norm" rather than the exception. This approach overlooked the reality of many mainland Puerto Rican families who raised healthy and successful children against numerous odds, as illustrated in the following case study.

CASE STUDY: MRS. SANCHEZ

Mrs. Sanchez, a fifty-four-year-old Puerto Rican woman seen for ongoing medical care in a community health center in the South Bronx, spoke proudly of her two adult sons, both of whom had graduated from high school, had some college, and were now police officers in a large city. Mrs. Sanchez was asked how she managed to raise two successful young men as a single mother in a dangerous neighborhood. Many of her children's peers were unemployed, underemployed, in jail, or active in crime, or had simply lost the desire to succeed. Mrs. Sanchez recounted how she managed her public assistance benefits and augmented them by sewing at home for neighbors, long after being abandoned by the boys' father. She frequently bought her sons the games that were in vogue at the time they were growing up, set clear limits on their behavior from early on, and walked them to and picked them up from school until the early adolescent years when the boys started to complain. When asked how she managed to keep her children away from the negative influences of the neighborhood, she answered that she kept them at home as much as possible and always kept them busy with activities. When they needed to go out, she said, "I would get on the subway and go to Central Park, where they didn't know any of the kids. I kept them away from the boys in the neighborhood that way. We would spend entire days in Central Park, while they played, and though I was dead tired from being on my feet all day, my sons would also come home too tired to want to hang out."

FAMILY STRUCTURE AND FUNCTIONING

Familism

To provide a context for mainland Puerto Rican parenting, practitioners need to understand the core elements in the family that are influenced by both the traditional culture and the process of acculturation. For example, an intergenerational study of Puerto Rican families in New York found that the greatest changes among participants was in their socioeconomic status, language used at home, values and self-concept, and bicultural preferences (Rogler & Cooney, 1984). As education in the next generation increased, so did the knowledge of English and Spanish, even though the use of Spanish decreased. Respondents with more education were less fatalistic, less family oriented, and less traditional.

The importance of family ties and family obligations reflect Puerto Rican family solidarity and closeness. Family-centered values remain strong even among highly acculturated, mainland-born Puerto Ricans. Often referred to as "familism" (Rogler & Cooney, 1984; Sabogal, Marín, Otero-Sabogal, VanOss Marín, & Perez-Stable, 1987; Zayas & Palleja, 1988), this orientation emphasizes the bonds and obligations toward one's relatives, including the need to help each other during periods of distress.

One obvious element of familism is its emphasis on closeness among family members. It is not unusual for family members to seek social contact primarily with each other and for extended families to live together or near each other. Blank and Torrecilha (1998) suggest that familial interdependence, such as extended family living arrangements, reflects life-cycle stages more than it does culture or economic standing. Extended living arrangements among Puerto Rican and other Hispanic immigrants serve as a resource-generating strategy for providing care to young children and older adults. For the different Hispanic groups, the presence of children and family members who are age fifty-five or older is a significant determinant of extended living arrangements. Although Mexican and Cuban immigrants with young children are twice as likely as other Hispanics to live in extended families, Puerto Ricans are *seven* times more likely to do so. One reason given by Blank and Torrecilha is the greater ease of Puerto Ricans in bringing relatives to the United States to help with child care.

For many years, this closeness among Puerto Rican families was viewed in stereotypically negative ways as being overinvolved and pathologically enmeshed. I. A. Canino and Canino (1980) challenged this view of Puerto Rican families by proposing that the Puerto Rican family was "normally enmeshed" when viewed through the prism of structural family theory (Minuchin, 1974). In this theoretical model, families are conceived as falling on a spectrum from disengaged (i.e., thick internal boundaries that give members a great deal of autonomy and separation) to enmeshed (i.e., thick external boundaries with porous internal boundaries resulting in overinvolvement of family members, interdependence, and decreased differentiation). Rather than view the traditional Puerto Rican family as lying at the enmeshed end, implying pathology, Canino and Canino conclude that the typical Puerto Rican family can be located on the normal span of the spectrum but toward the enmeshed side. These authors support this view by noting that the traditional Puerto Rican family has a "tendency to fall on the enmeshed end of the spectrum. [This is based] on several characteristics: frequent and prolonged mother-child interaction, as exemplified by the extended time the young adult remains at home before leaving to get married; discouragement of autonomous and independent behavior in adolescent girls; frequent overlapping of the extended family system into the Puerto Rican nuclear family; and the perception of illness as a family rather than an individual problem. These cultural patterns of transaction *have often been misinterpreted as dysfunctional enmeshed patterns by culturally insensitive therapists*" (pp. 536–37, original emphasis).

Written in 1980, this conceptualization is still valid for the typical Puerto Rican family on the mainland today. With the influence of acculturation and the number of generations of Puerto Ricans who now call the United States mainland their home, this basic pattern may be altered toward the middle of the spectrum. However, proximity and ease of travel to the island helps many families maintain their ties to their culture of origin. At the same time, cultural changes have occurred that have reduced the differences between island life and mainland life.

Within the context of permeable family boundaries, the inclusiveness of blood-related kin and nonblood kin allows for a strong influence of the extended family. In fact, in the traditional culture of the island of Puerto Rico, the lineal system known as *hijos de crianza* is one example of this inclusiveness. *Hijos de crianza* refers to an informal system of adoption in which families take in children of less fortunate friends and neighbors and raise them as their own. In most such arrangements, the children became integral parts of the family raising them. Often these children grow up recognizing the love of both their biological parents, whether alive or deceased, and the parents who rear them, but not without some possible adverse psychological consequences, such as a sense of abandonment. Another example of this pattern of familial inclusiveness is the informal system of coparenting (*compadrazgo*), in which an adult who by being a baptismal godmother or godfather (*madrina* or *padrino*) holds an important position in the family system, with some rights to discipline the child and offer counsel to parents. *Padrinos* and *madrinas* are not perceived as interfering in internal family matters when offering advice and guidance; however, there exists a tacit understanding of boundaries. In some instances in which formal baptismal arrangements have not occurred, beloved friends and in-laws may be referred to as *compadres,* denoting their respectful and affectionate stature in the families of friends. In contemporary times the system of *compadrazgo* remains as an idealized tradition around which affection for others is expressed. Although *compadrazgo* may have served a function in the history of Puerto Rican communities when concrete help was provided to families, today it may be simply an honorific relationship rather than a real source of support in child rearing.

The immediate and extended Puerto Rican family is typically the first line of support for individual members. The extended family is important in a wide variety of activities, from repairing something in the home to enlisting help in correcting a misbehaving adolescent. This assistance is expected from both the person requesting help and the person called on to help. At times of crisis the extended family expects that the parents experiencing the crisis will ask for help first from them. It is not uncommon for a family experiencing behavioral or emotional difficulties with a latency-age or adolescent child to have a significant member of the family, such as a grandmother, uncle, or aunt, take the child into their home to help correct the child's problems and give some respite to the beleaguered parents. Indeed, parents may "threaten" the child with being sent back to Puerto Rico to the home of a family member to either correct the child's behavior or to remove them from a dangerous situation, such as the negative influences of the peer environment or an unwelcomed suitor of an adolescent female. While the wish that such environmental changes will work is often greater than the actual reality, this possibility remains a prominent source of comfort to parents. Likewise, there is a clear preference and tacit trust that the best child care is provided by a family member.

CASE STUDY: TITO AND SANDRA

Tito and Sandra, a highly acculturated young Puerto Rican couple, have a five-month-old son, Joaquin. Both parents are white-collar workers living in a suburban community. They typify the traditionally structured Puerto Rican family in which grandparents assume a revered position and whose home becomes the children and grandchildren's meeting place and central venue for family meals and activities. Tito and Sandra have arranged for child care on an alternating arrangement with both grandmothers despite the availability of an excellent day care facility near their home. These parents drive twenty to thirty minutes out of their way to deliver Joaquin to the grandmothers. Tito and Sandra are motivated to this action not only because of the implicit trust in the quality of care Joaquin will receive from his grandmothers but also because the parents prefer to have Joaquin grow up within the extended family environment that can provide him with the stimulation and abundant affection of aunts, uncles, cousins, and family friends. They want Joaquin to grow in an ambience in which the centrality of the family is paramount so that they can inculcate in him the traditional sense of loyalty and obligation to the extended family.

———

Family Roles

One traditional structural characteristic of Puerto Rican families has been that of the patriarchy. In this hierarchy, fathers are the designated heads of families and thus govern their children firmly. Traditionally, patriarchy has meant that the father is the disciplinarian and principal breadwinner. The other less-recognized but equally important structural component has been the matri-centric nature of traditional Puerto Rican families. In family systems terms, the authority of the father in the patriarchal hierarchy is balanced by the powerful influence of the mother in child rearing and other household matters. In matri-centric families, members are drawn to the center of the family by a strong concern for the mother's physical and emotional health. This systemic balance helps operationalize the emphasis on the family being at the center of one's life and identity, since much of the child care has been the responsibility of women, as in other traditional societies. (In an unpublished study of Puerto Rican, Dominican, and Colombian men in their twenties, Zayas, 2000, found virtually no variation among the men in response to the question of whose emotional well-being concerned them most in their homes during adolescence. Ninety-eight percent of the men identified their mother as the person whose emotions they most considered.)

While the traditional position of the father in the Puerto Rican family has been that of head of the family, exposure to the dominant mainland culture and the subsequent process of acculturation as well as multiple socioeconomic influences have produced significant changes in this once-powerful patriarchal structure. Young Puerto Rican men and women have made important adaptations in their spousal and marital roles. For example, among the second generation's working class and middle class, men have moved beyond the narrow role of the past as principally that of breadwinner and disciplinarian. Current generation men are more likely than their fathers were to be involved in child care activities such as diapering and feeding their children (Hossain, Field, Pickens, Malphurs, & Del Valle, 1997). Consonant with the child care change has been the shift in men's roles within marriages. In addition to changes in jobs and careers that mirror current patterns of two-income families, there is more acceptance of female career choices and earnings. Contemporary Puerto Rican men have begun to adapt themselves to defining their roles within their marriages differently than did their fathers. The two couples described in the following vignettes exemplify these differences.

CASE STUDY: NILDA AND JOSE

Nilda and Jose, a young couple in their late twenties, have three young daughters, one of whom is a preadolescent. Nilda and Jose grew up in a small rural

Puerto Rican Day Parade. © Associated Press.

town in Puerto Rico, married after high school, and moved to the mainland less than ten years ago. Their marital roles are very distinct. Jose is an achievement-oriented blue-collar worker. Nilda is a homemaker. Jose displays behavior more typical of traditional roles: he is active in his work and community, provides well for his family, makes plans with family and friends with relatively little consultation from Nilda, and spends much time outside the home. Nilda remains at home with the girls, manages the home, and retains close ties to her family in Puerto Rico. She returns to the island regularly with her daughters while Jose remains on the mainland. Nilda delayed learning English and was slow about venturing into the English-speaking community. She is encouraged by Jose to take a part-time job in a small store in their community. There is no ostensible conflict in this couple about their defined marital roles. Likewise, they agree on the manner in which their daughters will be raised: namely, that the girls will appreciate the importance of maintaining strong relations with their extended family and that they will be raised with the greater freedom assigned to women in their new culture.

CASE STUDY: ELIZABETH AND CARLOS

Elizabeth and Carlos are a middle-class professional couple in their forties with two adolescent children. They are a highly acculturated Puerto Rican family who speak English at home but preserve many of the Puerto Rican customs taught to them by their parents. They clearly define themselves as Puerto Ricans and inculcate this attitude in their English-speaking children. Elizabeth was born on the mainland; Carlos was born in Puerto Rico but then raised on the mainland. Their spousal roles reflect an adaptation based on their education and level of acculturation. Carlos participates in many household chores and, when the children were younger, in child care. At that time Carlos worked and supported Elizabeth while she remained at home. Elizabeth returned to school for a professional degree when the children were older. The parents confer with each other regarding their respective plans. Both enjoy personal and professional relationships and activities outside the home and are not strictly defined by traditional beliefs.

Both of these well-functioning couples hold firmly to values of family unity, affectionate contact with extended families, the preservation of Puerto Rican culture, and the role of parental authority in relation to their children. In other areas, the couples have made adaptations based on their backgrounds and levels of acculturation. Differing in social class and education as well as in level of acculturation, these two Puerto Rican couples have adopted different bicultural orientations according to their distinct needs.

PARENTING AND CHILD-REARING VALUES

Values that have endured over decades, and even centuries, are deemed important to transmit to children in order to guarantee the child's accommodation and survival within the family and its society (Harrison, Wilson, Pine, Chan, & Buriel, 1990; LeVine, 1977; Rogoff, Mistry, Goncu, & Mosier, 1993). Some cultural characteristics based on traditional island culture have been emphasized among mainland Puerto Ricans as well. The available literature on child rearing among Puerto Rican and other Hispanics provides evidence of an emphasis on the following values:

- parental control
- importance of children's affection toward parents and family members
- proximity seeking
- deference to parental authority
- obedience
- family loyalty
- personal honor

With respect to the close interaction between parents and their children, research has shown that there are cultural differences in the physical contact of mother-infant dyads. Franco, Fogel, Messinger, and Frazier (1996) found that in videotaped interactions Hispanic mothers showed closer and more affectionate touching than did non-Hispanic white mothers.

Teaching children the personal values of dignity and respect also characterize Puerto Ricans (Lucca-Irizarry, 1988; Quirk et al., 1986). Lucca-Irizarry and Pacheco (1989) report that island Puerto Rican mothers place primary emphasis on teaching preschool children sociocultural values (e.g., respect, obedience, generosity), followed by ethical-religious values (e.g., belief in God, honesty) and educational values. The transmission of sociocultural and ethical values effectively to their children connotes "good" mothering to Puerto Ricans.

Gonzalez-Ramos, Zayas, and Cohen (1998) studied the child-rearing values of a group of eighty low-income mainland Puerto Rican mothers. The mothers' ranking of the values is shown in table 6.1.

These researchers found that less acculturated Puerto Rican mothers gave more importance to the values of humility and respectfulness in their child rearing, affirming the significance of these two values in traditional Puerto Rican culture. More acculturated mothers gave more importance to the values of independence and creativity than did the less acculturated mothers. Both groups of Puerto Rican mothers, nevertheless, ranked the two values associated with Anglo culture—assertiveness and creativity—as being *of least importance* in the ranking of child-rearing values. Humility, loyalty to family, respectfulness, and dignity (values related to traditional Puerto Rican culture) clustered together, creating a familial factor and supporting the Puerto Rican emphasis on the centrality of the family (Gonzalez-Ramos et al., 1998; Zayas & Palleja, 1988).

An interesting finding in this study (Gonzalez-Ramos et al., 1998) was the placement of independence in the very middle of the ranking. The investigators had anticipated that these Puerto Rican mothers would rank independence as much less important, in keeping with the clinical, theoretical, and empirical literature on Puerto Rican and other Hispanic child rearing. The researchers, in seeking to understand this ranking, conducted follow-up interviews with the mothers and found that the mothers appeared to hold a different definition of a child's independence than that present in the literature. The mothers viewed independence in instrumental terms rather than in psychological terms. Therefore, a young child's capacity to entertain herself or himself while mother does household chores or the child's ability to put on shoes or a coat in readiness to go out was considered "independence." The psychological independence as defined by psychoanalytic theories of psychological and emotional autonomy and individuation was *not* recognized as important by these mothers.

Table 6.1. Ranking of Child-Rearing Values by Eighty Puerto Rican Mothers

1. Honesty	8. Getting along with others
2. Respectfulness	9. Dignity
3. Responsibility	10. Valuing older persons
4. Loyalty to family	11. Humility
5. Affection	12. Assertiveness
6. Sharing with others	13. Creativity
7. Independence	

Field and Widmayer (1981) studied a group of low-socioeconomic-status mothers and their four-month-old infants from four cultural groups—Puerto Rican, Cuban, South American immigrant, and African American—in free play with their children. Puerto Rican mothers demonstrated more positive interactive behavior (contingent on responsivity and game playing) than did the other three groups. Cuban mothers interacted with their infants in tones that were more educational than playful. In feeding behavior, Puerto Rican mothers showed greater alertness and attention to their infants and better overall feeding behavior than did the other groups.

Religious Influences

The influence of Christian religions in Puerto Rican culture remains relatively strong today, although probably less so than thirty years ago. Whereas Roman Catholicism was the predominant religion, other fundamental Protestant denominations have made strong inroads among Puerto Ricans. Still evident today in the small towns of Puerto Rico are the plazas that were the centers of the communities. The centerpiece of these plazas are the Catholic churches, some dating back to the 1600s and 1700s. The influence of religion generally has been a strong presence in traditional Puerto Rican life. Religion is of particular relevance to this chapter because religiousness is often associated with positive developmental outcomes in children and adolescents (Bensen, Masters, & Larson, 1997; Varon & Riley, 1999).

One aspect of the influence of religion on the interaction between children and adults is evident in the tradition of a child's requesting *la bendición* of parents and adult kin. *La bendición* is a request from the child to the adult for his or her blessing

or benediction. When a child enters a room and greets his or her parent or a respected family member or other significant adult, the child is expected to request the person's blessing. Often stated by the child as simply "*Bendición*," it implies a request of "please give me your blessing." In addition to following a religious prescription, the child is reminded of the superior role of the adult and the importance of behaving deferentially to adult family members. This custom is seen less frequently in more acculturated mainland families and those in the middle and upper social classes.

Another key factor that religion plays is that religious affiliation and church attendance comprise part of the extended family network in reducing stress and offering support. Priests, ministers, nuns, and fellow congregation members often supply families and individuals with much-needed spiritual, emotional, and instrumental support, as illustrated in the case of Julian.

CASE STUDY: JULIAN

Julian, age fifteen, had emigrated from Puerto Rico to the United States as a young child. His mother, a recent widow, was very supportive and had raised three other children, now adults. Julian began to drink habitually after the death of his father and his school grades dropped as a result. His family discussed this problem with his godfather, who after some unsuccessful conversations with him realized Julian needed professional help and told his mother to discuss this issue with Julian's school counselor. The school counselor referred Julian to an adolescent AA group. Julian did not want to cooperate and stopped going to the meetings. His family sought multiple treatments for him with no success. Julian was taken to his school guidance counselor but there was little change. He was then referred to a child and adolescent clinic, but after two sessions Julian refused to go. His family got him involved in a peer support group at a local community center, but Julian felt ill at ease in the group and discontinued his participation. In short, Julian did not want to cooperate. His drinking problem worsened, he became depressed, and the combination of alcohol abuse, depression, and school failure seriously affected the interaction with his family. His mother, who had been raised in a religious family, finally approached the parish priest. Julian was initially resistant to discussing his problems with alcohol and family matters with the priest because going to church "was for women." However, he finally agreed to see the priest, knowing that the priest was known to play the *cuatro,* a four-string instrument Julian had heard as a child when his father played it during the Christmas holidays in the island.

Julian met with the priest, who involved him as a student in a music program for community youth. Julian's resistance receded, and he later talked to the priest about the loss of his father. Through religious counseling, his drinking decreased, his self-confidence was raised, and he was able to find an after-school job in the community. The job distanced him from his drinking buddies. Julian volunteered time in the church as a big brother during the weekends. His family relations improved, and he was able to graduate with honors from high school.

Self-Worth, *Dignidad,* and *Respeto*

Self-worth in traditional and contemporary Puerto Rican culture encompasses values governing how people treat themselves and others. *Dignidad,* or dignity, is one such value that has endured in Puerto Rican culture and child rearing. *Dignidad* is the belief in the innate worth of the individual regardless of that person's societal status (Ghali, 1982). Parents teach children to guard both their own *dignidad* and that of others. Part of displaying *dignidad* is in the manner in which the child presents herself or himself, an attitude that conveys a sense of personal dignity and self-worth. In the focus groups conducted by Gonzalez-Ramos et al. (1998), dignity was one of the values that Puerto Rican mothers and grandmothers thought were important for a child to demonstrate. The definition of dignity derived from the mothers and grandmothers was "to be gracious and behave with good manners in public . . . that the child know how to behave with dignity in public and earn the respect of others even if at times it is difficult" (p. 379).

Carrying oneself with *dignidad* also encompasses the opposite feeling, known as *vergüenza,* or shame (Harwood, Miller, & Lucca-Irizarry, 1995). That is, the child who is well-mannered is conscious of the potential loss of face that can occur in interpersonal situations and has been taught to avoid bringing shame on self and the family. The influence of familism and family obligation is evident in the concept of *vergüenza:* Not only is it something the child feels as a result of misbehaving, but it is something felt by other family members as a result of the child's misdeeds. Harwood et al. point out also that children who misbehave not only shame themselves but also expose the poor child rearing of their parents.

Another key rule of behavior is that of *respeto* (respect), which involves respecting self as well as others; *respeto* could be considered the interpersonal quality that accompanies having *dignidad* (I. A. Canino & Spurlock, 1994; Koss-Chioino & Vargas, 1999; de la Garza, Newcomb, & Myers, 1995). In their research with Puerto Rican mothers, Harwood et al. (1995) created a category of child behavior preferred by the mothers. They call this behavior "Proper Demeanor," referring to the mothers' preference that their children be "well mannered, well behaved, cooperative, and accepted by the larger community" (p. 55). *Respeto* is the key rule that dictates Proper Demeanor, an intrinsically social-contextual category (p. 99). *Respeto,* like *dignidad,* is a *public* matter in that it defines the child as a person and influences how others will respond to the child (and, by extension, it involves the public's perception of the parent). Proper Demeanor includes the child's capacity to be *obediente* (obedient), *tranquilo* (calm), *amable* (polite, gentle, kind), and *educado* (well-raised). More than one Puerto Rican elder has been heard to say *"No es lo mismo ser una persona educada que ser una persona instruida"* ("To be a well-educated person is not the same as being a well-instructed person"), implying that school instruction does not necessarily make a person well educated (i.e., well-bred and polite).

CASE STUDY: MANUEL

Manuel, a five-year-old boy who recently migrated from a small town in Puerto Rico to Philadelphia, came to the child psychiatry clinic because his parents were dismayed by his behavior. He could not sit quietly, was not well behaved, and had become more oppositional, impulsive, and disrespectful to his parents and his teachers since arriving. He was unable to listen to his parents' requests and certainly was not obedient, calm, polite, or well mannered. On closer inspection, this behavior had been present for a while but the parents and the family felt that as Manuel grew, his behavior would improve. What initially had been seen as childish and cute had become an embarrassment to the family. The school felt that Manuel was a "problem child in a problem family," and the family's community believed they were not raising their son appropriately. The parents knew otherwise since they had successfully raised two other children. The mother called the child's godmother, who had worked in a community center in Philadelphia and who recommended that Manuel receive a full psychological and psychiatric evaluation. The godmother reassured the somewhat alarmed mother that such an evaluation did not mean that her son was "crazy." After a careful assessment to rule out the impact of migration, a new school, a new language, a possible learning disability, and the role of cultural expectations, the clinician diagnosed an attention deficit disorder. Manuel's parents were educated about this disorder, were assured that there was no concomitant learning disability, and were given suggestions concerning the appropriate medication and therapeutic interventions. The parents were initially hesitant to give their child the psycho-stimulant medication, but the social worker and child psychiatrist sat with them and informed them carefully about the possible side effects as well as the significant therapeutic effects. The clinicians discussed the need to involve the school and offered a program for parenting children with ADHD. The community had a chapter of Children with Hyperactive Attention Deficit Disorder (CHADD) for parents, and some of the members spoke Spanish. After the parents felt sufficiently informed and talked with some of the other parents, they acceded to the treatment plan. After the treatment plan was instituted, Manuel's symptoms dramatically improved. Manuel was not as fidgety, he was able to concentrate well, and his oppositional behavior dramatically improved.

The family's belief in their own good child-rearing methods and their extended and acculturated network (the godmother) allowed them to seek an early evaluation. In this case, the child's behavior was so dissonant to the behavioral expectations in the family that it allowed early identification and treatment.

As cultural mores change in both the mainland United States and Puerto Rico, so too have the interactions between children and adults. Whereas in traditional Puerto Rican culture the interpersonal relations between children and adults require children to use the formal address toward adults, that is, the *usted* rather than the informal *tu* (and the adult could address the younger person with the *tu* form), changing social conventions have led to greater informality between children and adults, evident in the growing frequency with which the informal *tu* is used by young persons toward their elders. The formal addresses used for adults, such as *señor, señora, don,* or *doña* as a way of conveying *respeto* to their elders (I. A. Canino

& Spurlock, 1994; Rendon, 1974) have also given way to less formality and the use of first names. Parents who held on to more traditional conventions in the interactions between children and adults have had to accommodate these changes into their child rearing. While some people believe that such change represents an erosion of the principle of *respeto,* it is a reality parents must face in view of changing mores.

Like families on the island, mainland Puerto Rican families have made parenting adaptations to meet the demands of the contexts in which they live. Adaptations to their environments have required adjustments in the ways in which they raise their children. The following vignette shows parents' struggle with the issue of children's interactions with adults.

CASE STUDY: PACO AND JOSEFINA

Paco, a first-generation Puerto Rican, and Josefina, a second-generation mainland Puerto Rican, resolved early in their marriage to raise their three children using core beliefs from Puerto Rican culture about how children should interact with adults. Both are highly educated parents with professional and graduate degrees (Josefina in early childhood development) who also wanted their children to grow with a sense of self-assurance and an appropriate sense of assertiveness. In their experience, they felt that traditional Puerto Rican child rearing gave too much emphasis to the deferential behavior to adults, behavior that Paco and Josefina felt sometimes diminished a child's self-confidence. The challenge they reported was in teaching their children *respeto* while also being appropriately assertive. Their efforts to have their children use the formal titles of *señor* or *señora* and the formal address of *usted* was made more difficult by adult friends and acquaintances, both Hispanic and non-Hispanic, who asked their children to refer to them by first names. Paco and Josefina finally acceded but asked their children to continue to use the formal titles and address of *respeto* with other adults. It was a compromise the parents felt was necessary in deference to their awareness of changing values within their community.

INDEPENDENCE AND ADOLESCENT-PARENT RELATIONS

Independence and Familism

Independence among Puerto Rican families must be understood within the context of the cultural value of familism. Unlike European-American families' adherence to the values of independence and autonomy, Puerto Ricans, like other Hispanic groups, are raised according to a more collectivist orientation (Fuligni, Tseng, & Lam, 1999). Hence, Puerto Rican young adolescents, instead of being encouraged to develop increasing separation from the family and greater interactions with peers, are raised with greater expectations to assist, respect, and support their families than their European counterparts are, as illustrated by the following vignette.

CASE STUDY: LISA

At age nineteen, Lisa is the pride of her working-class Puerto Rican parents. The first one in her family to attend college, Lisa is a sophomore at a major New England university. She is studying journalism and is doing very well in school. Her mother attributes Lisa's success to her single-mindedness and focus when it comes to her studies. This determination became compromised, however, when her father developed financial problems. Mr. Ortiz, who has not lived with the family since Lisa was two but has kept close ties with his children, was at risk of being evicted from his apartment despite being gainfully employed. Financial obligations to his extended family and children had eventually caught up with him. In desperation, he turned to his older daughter for financial assistance, but she was unable to help him. When Lisa found out about her father's predicament, she seriously contemplated leaving school in order to work to help her father. Her determination to succeed was balanced by her commitment and loyalty to her family. Knowing that she was in danger of leaving school rather than see her father homeless, Lisa's mother implored her current husband to lend Mr. Ortiz the money so that Lisa could remain in school. Having grown up biculturally, Lisa was independent and autonomous enough to go away to school and to pursue a career. Yet, she still maintained an unyielding sense of familial loyalty and responsibility.

Independence and Gender

Children's independence in traditional Puerto Rican culture has typically been determined by age and gender. As in other ethnic groups, Puerto Rican older adolescents are given more independence than younger children are, in accord with their higher level cognitive skills, capacity for judgment, responsibility, and decision making as well as societal age norms that prescribe greater rights inside and outside the home (Bulcroft, Carmody, & Bulcroft, 1996). In a study that contrasted patterns of parental independence given to adolescents among African American, non-Hispanic white, and Hispanic families (with the Hispanic sample including Puerto Ricans), Bulcroft et al. found that as Hispanic girls grew older they were less likely than boys were to be given freedom to stay at home alone. Part of this increased restriction is seen by the researchers as parents' perceptions regarding the vulnerability of their daughters if left alone at home. For all age adolescents, Hispanic parents held earlier curfews for their children than did parents from the other two groups. There was also a significant reduction in the household rules on later adolescent boys' behavior, whereas *higher* expectations were placed on girls.

Bulcroft et al. (1996) found that, across all measures of independence given to adolescents by parents, Hispanic girls in middle and late adolescence were among the most restricted groups both inside and outside the home. As boys entered late adolescence, however, there were more constraints placed on their behaviors *outside* the home. There are two possible explanations: (a) the importance of keeping the adolescent male close to the family's center (influence of familism) and (b) the greater risks of adolescent males toward involvement in negative activities (e.g., alcohol and drugs, delinquency). Yet, as older male adolescents are given more independence inside the home and more restriction outside the home, older adolescent girls were provided more freedom outside the home. Bulcroft et al. note that the combination of strong norms of patriarchy in Puerto Rican and other Hispanic families and the emphasis on familism appear to shape the parents' differential willingness to give their younger sons more independence than their daughters. The greater freedom given to older Hispanic adolescent females outside the home may be considered legitimate by parents in the context of their daughters' movement toward marriage (Bulcroft et al., p. 879). Many Puerto Rican parents feel that their daughters will bring their husbands closer to their families of origin, thereby lessening the threat to familism. Sons, on the other hand, will marry and may possibly drift toward their spouses' families. This attitude may explain the importance of keeping sons close to the family for an extended period to guard against the drift away from their family of origin.

A description of mainland Puerto Rican families' adaptation of their adolescent-rearing approaches is well documented by G. Canino's (1982) study on transactional family patterns in Puerto Rican parent-daughter relationships. Canino found that well-functioning Puerto Rican families allow daughters to express ideas different from their parents, allow them to have friends outside the home, and permit them a modicum of privacy. Despite the fact that traditional sex-roles existed, flexible accommodation characterized the parents' interaction with each other, their daughters, and their environment.

CASE STUDY: MIRABEL

Mirabel decided to start dating seriously at the age of fifteen. Raised in New York of Puerto Rican–born parents, she was uncertain about her parents' reaction to her boyfriend, a young man of mixed heritage whose family had been in the United States for many generations. The parents had raised Mirabel with the ideal of selecting a partner who came from an intact family with good mores. The boy's family was a "good" family, but Mirabel's parents felt it was somewhat distant and disengaged. Mirabel's parents welcomed the young man and, in their characteristic hospitable manner, made the young man feel comfortable and accepted. They eventually called the young man's parents and established an amiable and consistent communication with them by phone as the relationship developed between the two adolescents. Soon the boy felt so at ease with Mirabel's parents that he enjoyed spending time with his newly discovered family and joined them in all family activities. Mirabel had mixed feelings about her boyfriend's attitude because she felt she wanted to move *out* of her family and not further into it. However, she also realized the importance of family unity and support. Mirabel, as a consequence, joined her boyfriend's family more frequently and learned about other family styles. She then became more autonomous, but interdependent when necessary; feminine and assertive; and resourceful but willing to ask for help. She became what she considered to be a "true Latina."

CHILDREN AND DISABILITIES

Because cultural context often drives the definitions of normalcy, psychopathology, and help-seeking behavior, it is important to examine how Puerto Rican parents make sense of their children's disabilities. A study (Harry, 1992) found that with regard to their children's development, Puerto Rican parents have much broader parameters of "normalcy" than those used by the educational system. The study also found that "different designations for disability led to parents' confusion of terms like handicapped and retarded with more extreme forms of deviance" (p. 31). For example, most parents had difficulty accepting the label "mentally retarded" unless the child was "severely impaired" or was considered "mentally deranged." Puerto Rican parents, according to Harry, preferred the word "slow" to describe their mentally retarded children, thereby differentiating the word "retarded" from the term *loco,* or crazy.

Parents attributed their children's problems to three distinct environmental sources. First, they were likely to understand their children's problems according to family identity, as for example attributing a child's behavior to being an idiosyncratic family trait ("he's just like his father") that is not considered to be outside the range of normalcy. Problems were often attributed, second, to "the detrimental effects of second-language acquisition on school learning" and, finally, "to the detrimental effects of educational practices such as frequent changes in placement, out-of-neighborhood placement, an un-challenging curriculum, and inflexible reading instruction" (Harry, 1992, p. 32).

Despite parents' disagreement with the educational system's labeling of their children, parents were able to accept that their children could be having difficulty and did not object to their receiving special assistance. A more recent study explores Latino parents' awareness, use, and satisfaction with services for young children with disabilities (Bailey, Skinner, Rodriguez, & Correa, 1999). Bailey et al. found that 61 percent of 100 Puerto Rican and Mexican couples with young children with disabilities reported extensive use of biomedical, educational, or psychological treatments. Another 37 percent reported using these treatments in conjunction with only occasional use of religious rites, folk medicines (herbs, special teas, ointments), and traditional healers such as *sobadores* (masseurs) and herbalists. Parents sought to improve, not necessarily cure, their children's conditions in any way they could.

CASE STUDY: THE CONTRERAS FAMILY

Carmen is a young, single mother of two children, a boy, age six, and a girl, age five. Since Carmen does not work outside the home, she chose not to send her children to preschool or day care. On the rare occasions when she needs to go somewhere, she leaves her children with her older sister Isabel. Isabel, who has three grown children of her own, noticed that her niece and nephew were "different." The little boy would talk at length about his violent fantasies and of the voices he heard that told him to do "mean things." The little girl, on the other hand, was very quiet and seemed unusually withdrawn. Isabel struggled with sharing her observations with Carmen because she did not want to alienate her sister, but she also wanted to alert her so that she could seek appropriate help for the children. When Isabel spoke about her concerns, Carmen was unable to hear them. Carmen felt that her children were not experiencing any difficulties that they would not outgrow or that would not clear up once they started school. When the children began attending school, however, they were soon tested for developmental delays and emotional disabilities. Although Carmen initially denied that anything was wrong with her children, she cooperated with the special education team at the school and eventually accepted the special services that were recommended.

IMPLICATIONS FOR PRACTICE

This chapter has described some core background issues that pertain to child rearing and family functioning of mainland Puerto Rican families. Our emphasis has been on describing typical child rearing and parent-child interactions in well-functioning families. We have emphasized the cultural strengths of this group and the adaptability and malleability of these patterns as these families undergo the stresses of migration, acculturation, and other life changes.

When the stresses become overwhelming and other factors are involved, these vulnerable families seek help in the mental health clinics. Clinicians must employ cultural sensitivity and competence in their assessment strategies in dealing with both situational and developmental crises as well as the manifestation of severe and chronic disorders. Always aware of the strengths as well as the vulnerabilities of each family and its beliefs, the effective clinician can then implement the appropriate treatment intervention.

A series of fundamental factors (applicable to other Hispanic groups as well) must be addressed by therapists working with Puerto Rican parents and children. First, therapists must consider the importance of *dignidad* and *respeto*, particularly when addressing parents. Whether the work to be done is play therapy with the child, parental counseling, or family therapy, therapists need to keep in mind that their interaction with parents must follow these two cultural values. This factor can be operationalized through the use of formal addresses until some familiarity has been achieved. Thus, parents and adults should be addressed with conventional titles of Mr., Mrs., Ms., and so on. Therapists who establish a use of first names too early, intending to reduce the distance between themselves and parents, may inadvertently convey disrespect, particularly when substantial social class differences exist between therapist and family.

Second, therapists can show respect for Puerto Rican cultural values by inter-acting in a manner that employs *personalismo,* that is, that sets a tone of trust and authenticity. *Personalismo* implies the use of a personal connection in the interaction among people. Therefore, therapists can further this connection by avoiding a dis-tant, neutral stance with Puerto Rican clients. Rather, part of *personalismo* is assum-ing a stance of interest and engaging in talk about the family without focusing immediately on the problem. Therapists might ask about the family and reach for some connection with the family by discussing things the therapist and family might have in common, such as places they know. For example, a therapist might express familiarity with shops in the family's neighborhood. Therapists will find that a mo-dicum of appropriate self-disclosure with Puerto Rican parents and children assists in the engagement process. *Personalismo* should not be misunderstood by therapists going to the extreme of becoming too informal with families and children. *Dignidad* and *respeto* can be maintained within the framework of *personalismo.*

CASE STUDY: THERAPIST, PARENTS, AND CHILD

In a case supervised by the first author, a young Anglo-American female psy-chologist raised concern that the mother and grandmother of a boy she was initiating work with appeared to act in a surly manner toward her. The child had been referred for some behavioral problems in his class. In supervision, the psy-chologist talked about her efforts to be culturally sensitive in the treatment and interaction with the family but felt it was to no avail. When she tried to initiate parent counseling sessions, the mother and grandmother participated but seemed not to accept recommendations about managing the child's behavior at home. After some discussions in supervision, the psychologist agreed to invite the mother alone to a meeting in which she might bring up the issue. At the next parent counseling session, only the child's mother appeared. As planned in supervision, the psychologist sensitively pointed out that she thought that the mother and grandmother had some concerns about her that had not been ex-pressed. The mother denied anything, but the psychologist persisted gently. Finally, the mother pointed out that she and her mother could not understand how the psychologist could help the boy behave and be more respectful in class if he was allowed to call the therapist by her first name. The mother indicated that she felt the boy needed to be more respectful to adults and that being on a first name basis would not help. The psychologist did not disagree with the mother and accepted the criticism well. She engaged the mother in more dis-cussion about what the issue of the first name meant. The mother was able to state that she and her mother were trying to protect the son from the influence of his peers and that they were rather strict in their demands on his behavior. The child was expected to use the formal *usted* in the home with both mother and grandmother. The mother noted also that the child's father was not in the home and his grandfather had died many years ago; thus, no men were there to help in disciplining the boy. The mother made compelling points about why she and her mother preferred more formality between the psychologist and child. The two women saw it as an important way in which the psychologist could help the boy and support what they were doing at home. Mother and therapist (and later, supervisor) agreed that, because it was early in the treatment, switching to a more formal approach would accommodate their request. The child was asked by mother, grandmother, and therapist to call the therapist "Doctor Julie."

Third, in situations in which the therapist does not speak Spanish and the family does not speak English, the therapist must be aware of the importance of competent translators. In community treatment settings, translators are frequently used with parents. It is not enough to enlist the help of a Spanish-speaking clerical worker to translate when parents are being informed about the results of assessments or are being given parent counseling. Agencies and clinics must develop a cadre of translators who can convey accurately the emotional content of the clients' worries and understand the idioms of distress that are commonly used by Puerto Rican and other immigrant groups.

Fourth, for families that require it and if there are sufficient resources in the clinic, home- and community-based interventions that involve parents in helping their children improve are most effective. This type of intervention conveys respect for the family and its ecology, enhances the closeness between therapist and family, and demonstrates the clinician's care and interest in the child and family. In a study of Spanish-dominant Puerto Ricans in eastern Pennsylvania, a home-based intervention promoted parental involvement by allowing parents to provide their children with helpful instructional content. As a result of this intervention, parents gained a greater perception of their children's physical, social, self-help, academic, and communication abilities (Sung, Kim, & Yawkey, 1997). Involving parents as coparticipants in the education of their children helps both parents and children, whether they be Puerto Rican or some other racial or ethnic minority group. Although Sung et al.'s study emphasizes educational skills enhancement, similar effects can be gained in parenting education, parent counseling, and family therapy.

CONCLUSION

Effective practice with mainland Puerto Rican families necessitates that clinicians try to understand as much as possible the cultural background and beliefs of the parents with whom they are working. Professionals working with Puerto Rican or any other family system must emphasize and keep in mind the uniqueness of each individual and each family. In particular, clinicians must be aware that acculturation disparities occur between parents and their children and between different families, depending on the length of time they have lived in the mainland United States. Practitioners cannot assume a homogeneity in the acculturation of mainland Puerto Ricans because, after all, some have been on the mainland for decades while others are newcomers. The key challenge for clinicians is to identify the parents' and family's reality and to use the cultural context as the basis for understanding and for achieving change.

Discussion Questions and Role-Play Exercises

1. Imagine that you are a school social worker assigned to a high school with a high concentration of Puerto Rican students. The mother of fifteen-year-old Julían calls and asks for help with her son, who has begun drinking. What factors would you consider prior to approaching the boy? Role-play your initial contact with him.

2. Identify five values that are characteristic of Puerto Rican culture. How have you seen them manifested by your clients? How might these values clash with your own personal and professional values?

3. What strengths of Puerto Rican families have helped them cope with the challenges of migrating to the United States? As a clinician, what factors do you need to be cognizant of to avoid stereotyping and pathologizing Puerto Rican families?

4. Jackie and Junior, a young Puerto Rican couple in their early twenties, come to see you for counseling because they are struggling with several life transitions. Within the past year and a half, they have married, become parents, reentered civilian life after completing a tour of duty in the army, started new jobs, and moved to another state. Because they are struggling financially and are attending school while working full-time, they twice have sent their eighteen-month-old daughter, Alyssa, to stay with Junior's mother, who lives in another part of the country. At a year old, Alyssa was separated from her parents for two months. She was then sent away again at seventeen months for about a month. As a clinician, you are concerned about these separations and how they might affect Alyssa's development. How would you handle this situation? What cultural factors must you consider before making a culturally informed clinical decision?

5. You have an appointment with Enrique and his mother, Mrs. Carrasquillo, because Enrique has missed several days of school to stay with his younger sister, Noemi. Because Noemi suffers from spina bifida, Mrs. Carrasquillo has difficulty finding a babysitter if her regular babysitter is unavailable. Mrs. Carrasquillo is a single mother who must work to support her children. You are surprised to find that Mrs. Carrasquillo has come to the appointment with her fictive kin Mercedes, and both enter your office. Why would Mrs. Carrasquillo keep her son from school, and what thoughts and feelings are evoked in you? How can you inquire about her decision and convey your concern about his school absence? How do you feel about having Mercedes present during the interview, and what are the implications of her presence on your work with Mrs. Carrasquillo? How would you handle this situation in a culturally respectful manner? Role-play your interventions.

References

Bailey, D. B., Skinner, D., Rodriguez, D., & Correa, V. (1999). Awareness, use, and satisfaction with services for Latino parents of young children with disabilities. *Exceptional Children, 65,* 367–81.

Bensen, P. L., Masters, K. S., & Larson, D. B. (1997). Religious influences in child and adolescent development. In J. D. Noshpitz & N. E. Alessi (Eds.), *Handbook of child and adolescent psychiatry* (Vol. 4, pp. 206–19). New York: Wiley & Sons.

Betancourt, H., & Lopez, S. R. (1993). The study of culture, ethnicity, and race in American psychology. *American Psychologist, 48*(6), 629–37.

Blank, S., & Torrecilha, R. S. (1998). Understanding living arrangements of Latino immigrants: A life course approach. *International Migration Review, 32,* 3–20.

Bulcroft, R. A., Carmody, D. C., & Bulcroft, K. A. (1996). Patterns of parental independence giving to adolescents: Variations by race, age, and gender of child. *Journal of Marriage and the Family, 58,* 866–83.

Canino, G. (1982). Transactional family patterns: A preliminary exploration of Puerto Rican female adolescents. In R. E. Zambrana (Ed.), *Work, family, and health: Latina women in transition* (pp. 27–36). New York: Hispanic Research Center, Fordham University (Monograph No. 7).

Canino, G., Canino, I. A., & Bravo, M. (1994). Diagnostic assessment with Hispanic children. In S. K. Hoppe & W. H. Hotzman (Eds.), *In search for a common language in psychiatric assessment* (pp. 36–47). Austin, TX: Hogg Foundation for Mental Health, University of Texas.

Canino, I. A., & Canino, G. (1980). Impact of stress on the Puerto Rican family: Treatment considerations. *American Journal of Orthopsychiatry, 50*(3), 535–41.

Canino I. A., Canino, G., & Arroyo, W. (1998). Cultural considerations for childhood disorders: How much was included in DSM-IV? *Transcultural Psychiatry, 35*(3), 343–55.

Canino, I. A., & Spurlock, J. (1994). *Culturally diverse children and adolescents: Assessment, diagnosis, and treatment.* New York: Guilford.

de la Garza, M. F. O., Newcomb, M. D., & Myers, H. F. (1995). A multidimensional measure of cultural identity for Latino and Latina adolescents. In A. M. Padilla (Ed.), *Hispanic psychology: Critical issues in theory and research* (pp. 26–42). Thousand Oaks, CA: Sage.

Duany, J. (1996). The commuter nation: Perspectives on Puerto Rican migration. *Revista de Ciencias Sociales, 1,* 225–30.

Field, T. M., & Widmayer, S. M. (1981). Mother-infant interaction among low SES black, Cuban, Puerto Rican, and South American immigrants. In T. M. Field, A. M. Sostek, P. Vietze, & P. H. Liederman (Eds.), *Culture and early interaction* (pp. 41–62). Hillsdale, NJ: Lawrence Erlbaum.

Franco, F., Fogel, A., Messinger, D. S., & Frazier, C. A. (1996). Cultural differences in physical contact between Hispanic and Anglo mother-infant dyads living in the United States. *Early Development and Parenting, 5,* 119–27.

Fuligni, A. J., Tseng, V., & Lam, M. (1999). Attitudes toward family obligations among American adolescents with Asian, Latin American, and European backgrounds. *Child Development, 70*(4), 1030–44.

Ghali, S. B. (1982). Understanding Puerto Rican traditions. *Social Work, 30,* 323–30.

Gonzalez-Ramos, G., Zayas, L. H., & Cohen, E. V. (1998). Child-rearing values of low income, urban Puerto Rican mothers of preschool children. *Professional Psychology: Practice and Research, 29*(4), 377–82.

Guarnaccia, P. J., & Rodriguez, O. (1996). Concepts of culture and their role in the development of culturally competent mental health services. *Hispanic Journal of Behavioral Sciences, 18*(4), 419–43.

Harrison, A. O., Wilson, M. N., Pine, C. J., Chan, S. Q., & Buriel, R. (1990). Family ecologies of ethnic minority children. *Child Development, 61,* 347–62.

Harry, B. (1992). Making sense of disability: Low income, Puerto Rican parents' theories of the problem. *Exceptional Children, 59*(1), 27–41.

Harwood, R. L., Miller, J. G., & Lucca-Irizarry, N. (1995). *Culture and attachment: Perceptions of the child in context.* New York: Guilford.

Hossain, Z., Field, T., Pickens, J., Malphurs, J., & Del Valle, C. (1997). Fathers' caregiving in low-income African-American and Hispanic-American families. *Early Development and Parenting, 6,* 73–82.

Kleinman, A. (1988). *Rethinking psychiatry: From cultural category to personal experience*. New York: Free Press.

Koss-Chioino, J. D., & Vargas, L. A. (1999). *Working with Latino youth: Culture, development, and context*. San Francisco: Jossey-Bass.

LeVine, R. A. (1977). Child-rearing as cultural adaptation. In P. H. Leiderman, S. R. Tulkin, & A. Rosenfeld (Eds.), *Culture and infancy* (p. 15–27). San Diego, CA: Academic Press.

Lucca-Irizarry, N. (1988). Self-understanding in a Puerto Rican fishing village. In W. Damon & D. Hart (Eds.), *Self-understanding in childhood and adolescence* (pp. 158–98). Cambridge, England: Cambridge University Press.

Lucca-Irizarry, N., & Pacheco, A. (1989). Metas para crianza en dos generaciones de madres puertoriqueñas: Implicaciones para la terapia familiar [Child-rearing goals of two generations of Puerto Rican mothers: Implications for family therapy]. *Revista Interamericana de Psicologia, 23*, 83–102.

Mezzich, J. E., Kleinman, A., Fabrega, H., Parron, D. L., Good, B. J., Lin, K. M., & Manson, S. M. (1997). Cultural issues for DSM-IV. In T. Widiger, A. J. Frances, H. A. Pincus, R. Ross, M. B. First, & W. Davis (Eds.), *DSM-IV Sourcebook* (Vol. 3, pp. 861–66). Washington, DC: American Psychiatric Association.

Minuchin, S. (1974). *Families and family therapy*. Cambridge, MA: Harvard University Press.

Ortiz, V. (1996). Migration and marriage among Puerto Rican women. *International Migration Review, 30*, 460–85.

Quirk, M., Ciottone, R., Minami, H., Wapner, S., Yamamoto, T., Ishii, S., Lucca-Irizarry, N., & Pacheco, A. (1986). Values mothers hold for handicapped and nonhandicapped children in Japan, Puerto Rico, and the United States mainland. *International Journal of Psychology, 21*, 463–85.

Rendon, M. (1974). Transcultural aspects of Puerto Rican mental illness in New York. *International Journal of Social Psychiatry, 20*, 18–24.

Rodriguez, C. E. (1994). A summary of Puerto Rican migration to the United States. In G. Lamberty & C. Garcia Coll (Eds.), *Puerto Rican women and children: Issues in health, growth, and development* (pp. 11–28). New York: Plenum Press.

Rogler, L. H., & Cooney, R. S. (1984). *Puerto Rican families in New York City: Intergenerational processes*. Maplewood, NJ: Waterfront Press.

Rogoff, B., Mistry, J., Goncu, A., & Mosier, C. (1993). Guided participation in cultural activity by toddlers and caregivers. *Monographs of the Society for Research in Child Development, 58* (8, Serial No. 236).

Sabogal, F., Marín, G., Otero-Sabogal, R., VanOss Marín, B., & Perez-Stable, E. J. (1987). Hispanic familism and acculturation: What changes and what doesn't? *Hispanic Journal of Behavioral Sciences, 9*, 397–412.

Sung, K., Kim, J., & Yawkey, T. D. (1997). Puerto Rican parents' understanding of their young children's development: P.I.A.G.E.T. program impacts on family involvement in culturally and linguistically diverse populations. *Psychology in the Schools, 34*(4), 347–53.

Varon, S. R., & Riley, A. W. (1999). Relationship between maternal church attendance and adolescent mental health and social functioning. *Psychiatric Services, 50*(6), 799–805.

Zayas, L. H. (2000). [Alcohol use among young Colombian, Dominican, and Puerto Rican men.] Unpublished raw data.

Zayas, L. H., & Palleja, J. (1988). Puerto Rican familism: Considerations for family therapy. *Family Relations, 37*, 260–64.

7

Parenting in
Mexican American
Families

EUNICE C. GARCIA

INTRODUCTION AND HISTORICAL OVERVIEW

This chapter focuses on the parent-child and family relationships among the twelve million Mexican Americans in the United States. Twelve million is a conservative number; there continues to be strong evidence of many more uncounted people because of various factors, including ongoing illegal immigration and the continuous pattern of extended family arrangements on both sides of the United States/ Mexico border. The 1990 census, nevertheless, indicated that 68.7 percent of Mexican Americans were born in the United States and that 25.8 percent more were born in Mexico and were not citizens. Furthermore, half of the first-generation persons of Mexican origin immigrated between 1980 and 1990 (Shimaguawa & Jang, 1998). Population estimates prior to the report from Census 2000 indicate that between mid-1990 and mid-1999 "the Hispanic population grew 38.8 percent to 31.1 million" ("Minorities," 2000). According to these estimates, the proportion of the United States population that is Hispanic has increased steadily by approximate annual increments of .3 percent throughout the 1990s to reach 11.5 percent by 1999 (U.S. Census Bureau, 2000). These figures begin to explain the diversity that exists among the Mexican American population. A brief historical review of this population and its current status explains the unique historical and current challenges of this segment of the population.

According to McLemore and Romo (1985, p. 8), the historical circumstances of Mexican Americans in the United States designate them as a conquered population

157

at the end of the war between the United States and Mexico that culminated in the signing of the Treaty of Guadalupe Hidalgo in 1848. Thus, Mexico agreed to give up Texas and to sell the rest of the Southwest (currently Arizona, California, New Mexico, Utah, Nevada, and part of Colorado) to the United States for $15 million. Although the treaty assured the 100,000 Mexican citizens of ownership of their lands and offered U.S. citizenship if they desired to remain, history demonstrates that much of the land was soon taken away by often violent and illegal methods and that many citizens were deported to Mexico (Tijerina, 1978). One and a half centuries later, the treaty-set boundary and its buffer zone, now known as *la frontera*, is still a barrier posing legal challenges but no permanent separation of kinship, cultural, and linguistic ties among the many families linked by Mexican ancestry. Nevertheless, the collective experience of being conquered and dispossessed, the experience of being recruited for labor and repeatedly deported and rejected by U.S. immigration policies, and the experience of being subjected to ongoing racial discrimination as an ethnic minority in the United States have left their mark on this population (McLemore & Romo, p. 15).

Although some Mexican American families have maintained their European bloodlines and some have African ancestry because of intermarriage with slaves freed at the end the Mexican Revolution of 1810, a majority of Americans of Mexican heritage are of mixed race (mestizo)—thus reflecting the miscegenation of indigenous people with the Spanish conquistadores and subsequent European settlers. This origin is particularly important to acknowledge because it explains many of the traditional aspects of life in the Mexican American family and its community. Yet, it is that indigenous origin that also makes Mexican Americans vulnerable to policies and practices that discriminate against people of color in the United States. A strengths perspective on the mestizo experience promotes understanding about the ties that bind that population as well as about the traditional resources that have helped its survival. A socioeconomic perspective on the mestizo experience also explains the reasons why this population is one of the most vulnerable in American society (McLemore & Romo, 1985, pp. 23–26). Because of the high growth rate of the Mexican American population and, consequently, its importance to the stability of the American economy in the decades to come, it is important to review how the Mexican American family operates and how it can be sustained and developed as an effective system for launching successful generations. Therefore, a multigeneration perspective acknowledges the distinct experiences faced by the first, second, third, and subsequent generations in the Mexican American family network.

McLemore and Romo (1985) explain the trajectory of the Mexican American population in terms of labor, culture, and assimilation trends. Because the acquisition of the Southwest was prompted by expansionist goals of the United States, laborers in Mexico continued to be sought by agricultural and industrial enterprises in America (p. 12). Thus, when cheaper labor was needed, immigration policies allowed for immigration of Mexican workers, and when labor was not as needed or politics so dictated, immigration policies changed to discourage Mexican immigration. Likewise, when politics in Mexico caused political unrest and pointed to a safer haven to the north, both countries allowed for a permeable boundary and binational coexistence. Meanwhile, during the two world wars, the Korean conflict, and the Vietnam War, many Mexican Americans joined the U.S. armed forces and subsequently sought opportunities for greater integration in American society. Some veterans successfully joined mainstream American culture through acculturation and greater assimilation.

By the 1960s, when people of color joined African Americans in the fight for equal rights, Mexican Americans voiced a desire for equal rights and integration. However, their stance included the acknowledgment and ongoing pride in Mexican-origin cultural, kinship, and linguistic heritage. To express pride in their identity and commitment to further development of economic, cultural, linguistic, and educational spheres, the Mexican Americans called themselves *Chicanos*—a term used by those who wished to show solidarity with the more sociopolitically committed participants in the quest for social justice (McLemore & Romo, 1985, p. 4). A young Chicano poet expressed that identity in "Yo Soy Joaquin," the epic poem that stirred people to action during the late 1960s and 1970s.

> I am the masses of my people and
> I refuse to be absorbed.
> I am Joaquin.
> The odds are great
> but my spirit is strong. . . .
> I am Aztec Prince and Christian Christ
> I SHALL ENDURE!
> I WILL ENDURE!
>   (Gonzáles, 1972, pp. 89–90)

Ramsey Muñiz, a candidate for governor of Texas during the 1970s under La Raza Unida Party and now a political prisoner in the opinion of many Mexican Americans, has proposed the use of a term that more explicitly acknowledges the indigenous origin of Mexican Americans—Mexikas (Me-shee-käs). In a poem that reflects his personal experience in prison and the collective history of La Raza, he says,

> All my days are counted and checked by others
> Yet none know my heart.
> All my world is caged and confined,
> Yet my soul runs free. . . .
> I am free when all others feel caged.
> I am strong when others feel weak. . . .
> I am the Warrior Mexicano of the Sixth Sun awakened
> From the slumber of 500 years of enslavement.
> I am all that I will, I am all that was, I am all
> That will be.
> Yo Soy Mexika!
>   (Muñiz, 1998)

Because the original Mexican Americans were conquered and dispossessed, be-cause many of the subsequent waves of immigrants from Mexico emigrated north seeking jobs, and because many Mexican Americans encountered racial barriers dur-ing their search for survival and social and economic mobility, their socioeconomic stability was, and is, a continuous challenge. Various studies and texts about the Mexican American family ultimately sought to understand these difficulties through analysis and classification of the first, second, third, and subsequent generations. The results shed light on how the family survives and thrives in the midst of nu-merous challenges. These studies differentiate between the *first generation* (foreign born), the *second generation* (children of foreign born), and the *third + generation* (subsequent generations) to point out how the immigration experience begins to shape roles and functions of the initial immigrants and their offspring (Musolf, 1996, p. 311; Oropesa & Landale, 1997, p. 404). Numerous studies on Mexican American children and their parents also differentiate findings according to gener-ations within the family system. This observation is helpful as long as there is ac-knowledgment that many families *never immigrated*. They and their ancestors have simply always lived in what is now part of the United States. Another way by which to understand Mexican American familial patterns is by social class (Williams, 1990). Class differences and behaviors must be understood in the context of how families follow set patterns of *role making* and traditions.

Most of this chapter is exclusively about Mexican Americans, but some data is available only for "Hispanics" in the United States, including data on the Mexican

Americans. According to the 1990 census, Hispanics resided in all parts of the country, but most of the population was concentrated in the southwestern part of the United States, specifically in California (34.4 percent), Texas (19.4 percent), New Mexico (2.6 percent), Colorado (1.9 percent), and Arizona (3.1 percent). The Hispanic population in Florida was 7.0 percent; in Illinois it was 4.0 percent; and in Massachusetts it was 1.3 percent (Shimaguawa & Jang, 1998, p. 93). However, after 1990, Hispanics spread in greater numbers throughout states other than those in the Southwest, and the increased efforts to control illegal immigration through the southern border of the United States proved to be ineffectual (Harmon & Park, 1999). Data drawn from the census of 2000 will determine who currently lives where and the economic circumstances of the respective ethnic groups within the Hispanic population.

CASE STUDY: MRS. JUÁREZ

Mrs. Juárez (twenty-three years of age) took her three children (Marisa, eight; José, seven; and Janie, two) to a private, nonprofit health clinic for immunizations. The staff addressed Marisa's and José's needs but became concerned when they learned that Janie was running a temperature of 101 degrees and the mother could not identify what steps she had taken to reduce the fever. According to the nurse, Mrs. Juárez seemed unaware that Janie appeared to be undernourished. Mrs. Juárez responded by saying that Janie was born small, that she was doing better, and that a señora who lived close to her mother's home provided advice and special teas to help Mrs. Juárez and the baby. Mrs. Juárez changed the subject when asked the name of the woman she had been consulting for care of the baby.

The clinic staff noted positive interaction between Mrs. Juárez and the children. Marisa and José appeared to be typical kids who checked on Janie's well-being. The staff also learned that Mrs. Juárez recently left an abusive husband and filed for divorce. Mrs. Juárez shared that she and the children lived in transitional housing provided by a battered women's center and could stay there for another six months, or as long as Mrs. Juárez was looking for a job or had only part-time work. The older children would soon ride a bus to a new school. Mrs. Juárez seemed to be relatively sure of finding a job because she previously worked at a dry cleaners and at a restaurant. She shared that her plans included getting a job and leaving Janie at her mother's home for child care. Therefore, she had recently applied for public housing in her mother's neighborhood. Her primary concern, other than obtaining immunizations for the children so they could enroll in the new school, was to avoid further abuse from her husband, who was unemployed and was about to learn that she had filed for divorce.

ISSUES RELATED TO CHILD REARING AMONG MEXICAN AMERICANS

Numerous factors can affect parent-child relationships in Mexican American families. Some risk factors that can have a negative impact are low-class status, family poverty, the family's surrounding environment, membership in female-headed households, and the stresses associated with the immigration process including actual or threatened separation from the nuclear and/or extended family. Nevertheless, there often are also some protective factors that enhance parenting. These factors include the extended family and its resources, the context of barrio (neighborhood) as a buffer zone for all those who must continuously negotiate life between two cultures, the interdependence of neighbors within the barrio as found in *mutualista* groups (mutual aid societies), and the *compadrazgo* (coparenting) system.

Geographic location and the socioeconomic status of the Mexican American family can have significant implications for its offspring. A comparative study of the impact of immigration found that, in terms of family structure and poverty, Latinos who come from blue-collar and urban family backgrounds are at a disadvantage (Oropesa & Landale, 1997). Furthermore, children from Mexico had "relatively high rates of poverty, moderate rates of public assistance utilization, and low rates of single parenthood" (p. 415). Another significant finding was that the initial separation of family members in the first generation is a risk factor for the family's economic well-being, while the third and subsequent generations' risk increases because of poverty and single parenthood.

In addition to risk factors within the family, the politics that guide immigration policies create additional stress. Children have no say on their immigrant status, legal or illegal, yet immigration policies often are as harsh on them as they are intended to be on adults—that is, their parents. Children of Mexican parents can witness immigration officers' raids in their homes and witness arrest and detention of relatives. Thus, when Mexican parents are detained and deported, their children may be deported with them or left in the care of relatives or in the care of the state. A more recent threat is that of deportation of legal immigrants who have not obtained U.S. citizenship but have broken some law. The care of children by relatives must be prearranged by the parents, for it is not the responsibility of the immigration authorities to address that need. A chant often heard in protest marches is, "We didn't cross the border; the border crossed us"—a reminder that national borders are modern legal boundaries that mean less than the traditional worldview of Mexicans who continue to see "El Norte" (The North) as part of Aztlan (the geographic area now known as the Southwest of the United States).

The Barrio as a Support System

The geographic location of Mexican American families also determines their access to the cultural buffers and resources that are more likely to exist in traditional communities. Williams (1990), who distinguishes between the working-class and the middle-class Mexican American families in selected communities in Texas, points out that the middle class is less traditional in some respects, such as in the adoption of traditional coparenting (*compadrazgo*) responsibilities with the children's *padrinos* (godparents). However, within more traditional barrios, the middle-class families may uphold those traditions more firmly. In fact, this economic cooperation between families has existed since the time of the Aztecs more than five hundred years ago. Such collaboration benefits the less economically well off in terms of role modeling, brokering with the larger society, and shared resources (Valle, 1982). *Mutualistas* (mutual aid societies), groups that existed to foster sharing of resources and collaboration in the face of family and community hardship, developed and still exist within some of the most traditional Mexican American communities in the United States.

Thus, the role of the barrio as a support system is compatible with the role of *la familia,* the family, for the protection and development of children. In contrast to individualism, which characterizes American mainstream society, la familia supports and requires that the individual remain committed to the welfare of the family system. Collective goals can be supported by individual successes, but la familia becomes the center and focus of all endeavors. This approach may be related to survival during the many centuries of conquest, displacement, and discrimination. However, la familia has been well documented as a concept of life and governance among the already established indigenous cultures in ancient Mexico long before the arrival of the Spanish conquistadores.

Religious Traditions

Ancient Mexican traditions survived, even when citizens adopted the religion of the conquering Spaniards. The most obvious example is belief in the apparition and the adoption of *La Virgen de Guadalupe,* the patron saint who appeared at the site of the ancient goddess Tonantzin with skin coloring to match that of the population. The survival of the old beliefs and the aggressive Christianization efforts of the Catholic Church in Mexico has resulted in a blended pattern of Catholic and ancient traditions.

The more contemporary revival of Mexican traditions within Mexican American communities includes the celebration of *El Día de los Muertos* (The Day of the Dead), during which the traditional Mexican American family remembers its ancestors in a variety of ways. Although the celebration is not ancestor worship, it is a very individualized, respectful, and joyful community-wide remembrance of those who came before (Aguilar-Moreno, 1998). On November 1, the celebration focuses on the children who have died—*los angelitos*—the little angels who have left the family. On November 2, especially in traditional families, la familia prepares the favorite foods of the family members being honored, visits the cemetery, and celebrates the joining of the spirits of the living with the spirits of those who have passed on (Jacobs, 1999). In general, this tradition serves to emphasize that death is part of life and that life is to be celebrated in all its aspects. One of the celebration's characteristics is that it fully involves young and old—a pattern consistent with the level of involvement of all family members when a loved one dies. Although wakes are seldom possible now because of the use of modern funeral home services, the *novena,* a series of rosaries led in the family's home during nine consecutive evenings following the death, gathers together all family members, close friends, and neighbors. That period of shared experience (in which children are included) can further solidify the family network and reinforce the collective and supportive aspects of the culture in the community.

Language

Such events and traditions as *El Día de los Muertos* are part of a culture that has been passed from generation to generation through its oral linguistic heritage. Thus, the Spanish language, in its many variations throughout the Mexican American community, is critical to the communication of cultural beliefs and values. It is in *Spanish* that one generation passes its heritage—in the form of oral history, prayers, songs, and everyday stories—to its offspring. In contrast, the offspring learn English as the instrumental language with which to access mainstream systems and resources. That instrumental language, as taught in American public schools, presents a different history, different traditions, and the fostering of individualism and independence as central values. Thus, Mexican American children must learn to communicate within the two worlds, must struggle to learn and select values that often conflict, and must ultimately decide how to integrate the two.

OVERVIEW OF PARENT-CHILD AND EXTENDED FAMILY RELATIONSHIPS

Gender Roles

Children in pre-Columbian Mexico were socialized to assume gender-specific roles and functions. Although there is reason to believe that some groups had matriarchal family systems, historical documents show that most groups historically subscribed to a patriarchal system. *Machismo,* although much maligned today, required and still requires that the male head of household provide for and protect his family. The protection included both the physical protection against aggressors and the protection of the family honor. The woman, on the other hand, was the nurturer and caregiver for the family (Vélez-Ibáñez, 1997). Little has changed in more than five centuries! In families headed by women (as is common in third and subsequent generations), the members must find new ways to fulfill the provider and protector roles that are missing when the male is gone. Therefore, attention must be paid to how the children, both boys and girls, cope without a father and how the male children will learn how to play that role in their own future families. Absence of the father may be due not only to separation and divorce, but also to incarceration.

Female-Headed Households

A higher risk of poverty presents an additional stressor with which the third and subsequent generations must struggle (Oropesa & Landale, 1997). How do the Mexican American women left to raise children alone manage to provide, protect, nurture, care for, and teach the next generation? Although anecdotal accounts of Mexican American writers attest to the great strength demonstrated by their mothers, more recent studies of women's health demonstrate that the job incurs great sacrifice to the mother's personal well-being. These studies also show that, compared to their white counterparts, the Mexican American women of the first generation tend to have fewer low-weight babies, lower infant mortality rates, and better mental health status. These advantages may be due to dietary patterns and to reduced numbers of female heads of households among first generation Mexican Americans. In contrast, by the third and subsequent generations, the women are *more* at risk of heading households and having low-weight babies (Sherraden & Barrera, 1997). Although the families of Mexican American children show relatively low levels of single parenthood and public assistance utilization, their percentages below the poverty level are still significant: first generation is 44 percent; second generation is 32 percent; and third and subsequent generations are 28 percent. Overall, Mexican American children are likely to have poverty as a risk factor in their development and personal well-being (Oropesa & Landale, 1997, p. 404).

Martínez (1988) observed Mexican American mother-child dyads and confirmed the use of a variety of guidance practices by Mexican American mothers. Martínez concluded that child-rearing practices may range from permissive responses (including reasoning and positive reinforcement) to authoritarian responses (including more directive communications and punishment) regardless of socioeconomic status. Parent education programs can help Mexican American parents learn effective child-rearing methods.

The Extended Family

Few studies exist on the buffering role of grandparents in female-headed family systems or on their role in the socialization of their grandchildren. A recent news article pointed out an initiative to use the 2000 census to determine the number of children of all races who are currently living with grandparents (Sylvester, 1999). The article mentioned a general estimate of as many as 5.5 million children (nationwide); some of those children had lost one or both parents because of incarceration for drug abuse or other charges. Advocates for Hispanics and other minorities encouraged fuller community participation in the census because many grandparents appear to be struggling to meet the basic needs of children under their care (Sylvester). Moreover, use of the new census data may document how the extended family continues to protect and guide the younger generations. The extended family network is particularly important when the immigrant family needs some haven or additional resource for the protection or guidance of adolescents (Sherraden & Barrera, 1997). Family members may even come from Mexico or travel from the United States to Mexico to extend the family's caregiving resources (p. 626).

CASE STUDY: JESÚS TREVIÑO

Jesús Treviño (age twelve) was referred to a neighborhood recreation center for martial arts instruction. This referral followed several in-school detentions for verbal and physical aggression against peers in school. Jesús, known as "Chuy" within the family and "Jesse" in school and among peers, brought written approval from his grandmother, who had become his guardian approximately three years ago. According to the counselor who made this referral, several of Jesse's teachers expressed concern about his inability to manage his anger. They had underlined their belief that Jesse could succeed in school if he could improve his interactional skills. Occasionally, they caught a glimpse of Jesse's curiosity and optimism, but his most recent pattern included more confrontations and a beginning trend to show disrespect for his teachers and other school personnel. Consequently, Jesse was frequently referred to "in-school suspension" programs where he was further isolated from his peers.

When the recreation center staff interviewed Jesse for possible membership in martial arts training, Jesse appeared to be sufficiently motivated to engage in martial arts instruction but did not acknowledge its connection to his aggressive behavior. He said that several "bullies" at school and the neighborhood recently made him angry when they started saying bad things about his parents. Jesse said these comments were unfair. He added that he doesn't even know his father. (His mother and grandmother never talk about him.)

The recreation center staff also learned that Jesse has other concerns. His mother is in prison for possession and intent to distribute illegal substances; she is not eligible for parole for another six years. Recently, she wrote to him and advised him to do well in school. The grandmother, Mrs. Treviño, a first-generation immigrant whose husband had died ten years earlier, sent word with Chuy that she was willing to do whatever his teachers and counselors suggest as a way of improving his chances to do well in school. She obtained custody of Chuy in order to be authorized to act on his behalf.

Jesse was baptized in the Catholic church and completed confirmation rituals at the age of ten. He says, however, that he participated in the church mostly to please his grandmother. Another challenge for him is trying to communicate with his grandmother in Spanish. His godparents, his mother's second cousins, distanced themselves since his childhood.

This case illustrates how an adolescent's family is impacted by the incarceration of a parent. It also illustrates a female-headed household, absence of the father, and the surrogate parenting that grandparents offer to children who need extended family resources to survive and thrive. In this case, the grandmother is a first-generation immigrant, the mother is second generation, and Jesse is a third-generation Mexican American teen who is beginning to show signs of social alienation. Fortunately, school personnel note his aggressive behavior and seek a constructive way for him to channel his frustrations and his energy. Furthermore, in spite of his current problems, both the mother and grandmother are offering emotional and social support. His neighborhood offers training that is age appropriate and relevant to a developing young man. Above all, his life still has some measure of stability because of the continuing support of the extended family, as demonstrated by the grandmother's presence and caring. With continuing support from school personnel and the recreation center staff, Jesse and his grandmother may be able to successfully confront this developmental phase.

CHALLENGES FOR CURRENT IMMIGRANTS

The optimistic portrayal of extended family resources is not the reality faced by many of the young immigrant families. According to Partida (1996), the current wave of Mexican immigrants includes very young parents (under age twenty-five) who tend to be poor, to be unskilled, and to have little formal education. Although there are some middle-class Mexicans who arrive with more means, professions, and a higher level of formal education, most immigrants have few resources. By the time the family unites in the United States, they have typically experienced a year of separation, which represents the time it usually takes for the father to precede the family, find a job, and save enough money to send for the rest of the family members. During that year, however, the family has adapted to living without the father and has become a female-headed household; the roles of the mother and children have shifted to accommodate the new family arrangement. Consequently, when the family reunites, the father has lost some of his authority and the entire family system has to readapt to new expectations and challenges. The immigration process continues as each member of the family struggles with the dilemma of living in two cultures (p. 252). Moreover, if the family lacks legal entry to the United States, the constant threat of deportation and the effort to find or maintain employment cause stress and diminish the stability of the entire family system. Yet, the first-generation parents show remarkable strength and commitment to their children.

The instruction of the young has seldom been studied in terms of the potential within the mother-child and the older-younger-sibling subsystems. The question of how children are taught even prior to entry into the public school system led Pérez-Granados and Callahan (1997) to conduct a study in which they found that first-generation mothers were encouraging inquiry and giving explanations to their children in ways that were very similar to those that the children would encounter later within the mainstream science classroom settings. In fact, the first-generation mothers' patterns of teaching were similar to those of mainstream middle-class mothers in that they encouraged their children to search for alternative explanations and acknowledged their children's efforts to reach tentative conclusions. A distinct difference was found among mothers in the third and subsequent generations; their interaction seemed to be more task focused, that is, children were not encouraged to think through the learning process but were simply told what to do and how to complete the task. The study, however, does not clarify the rationale for such differences. The older children who were studied appeared to be task focused when instructing their younger siblings. However, the two approaches taken by the first-generation mothers and the older siblings were complementary rather than conflictual, which probably helped the younger children mediate the two perspectives on learning.

The acquisition of communication skills in English continues to challenge first-generation parents. Elena is a mother who fondly remembers understanding her children during their childhood in Mexico and who recounts her frustration as she tries to learn English to understand them when they reach adolescence in the United States:

> I remember how I'd smile listening to my little ones, . . .
> But that was in México. . . . I'm forty,

embarrassed at mispronouncing words,
embarrassed at the laughter of my children, . . .
Sometimes I take my English book
and lock myself in the bathroom,
say the thick words softly,
for if I stop trying, I will be deaf
when my children need my help.

(Mora, 1994, p. 369)

RITUALS AND VALUES

Life-cycle transitions often require the use of values in decision making and behaviors of the family. Thus, birth, marriage, and death cause la familia to define its values and play them out in the form of rituals. For instance, when the family is Catholic, the birth of a child requires infant baptism. The parents, whether in working and middle-class families, select godparents in conjunction with the baptismal ritual. However, traditional working-class parents select godparents who will be *padrinos* (godparents) to the child and *compadres* (coparents) with them, thus establishing a partnership that will last well beyond the child's childhood and adolescence and often through their own old age. While collaborating for the benefit of the child, compadres work with the natural parents to secure the religious, cultural, and familial supports for the duration of the child's development. Furthermore, the compadres, with their resources and moral support, remain accessible for the child and his or her parents. Middle-class parents, who may be less traditional, may merely acquire godparents for the baptismal ritual. Thus, life-cycle rituals are interwoven with religious beliefs (Williams, 1990). Of course, diversity exists within each class in terms of role expectations and maintenance of traditions associated with various life-cycle transitions.

Generational differences require the interplay of collective memory and ongoing negotiation among the members of la familia when observing life-cycle transitions. In addition to the transitions of birth, marriage, and death, the Mexican American community celebrates another life-cycle transition. This transition is known as *la quinciañera*, the social and religious event that introduces to the community a fifteen-year-old girl as a young woman. There is no similar ritual for the young man, whose transition is silently acknowledged at approximately thirteen years of age and is shown by granting him more freedom. However, the young woman, one who is expected to be a virgin and an honor to the family, is groomed and celebrated as much as if she were preparing for her wedding. Her parents, her padrinos, and the extended family network's community connections are all potentially involved in the religious ritual and follow-up celebration of her coming of age. This ritual is as important for the young woman as it is for the family and the community, because it helps solidify the status of the family in the community and, in turn, reinforces this life passage as part of the community's traditional heritage. Because the quinciañera can be a very expensive undertaking, the sponsors of this event contribute goods, labor, and/or money and, in turn, also help to reinforce the mutualist (collaborative) tradition in the community. In recent years, some families have staged multiple quinciañeras—perhaps as a way of maintaining tradition while keeping costs more affordable for the participants. First-generation parents, however, may be at odds with their more acculturated daughters who insist on sweet sixteen parties without the religious or social aspects of the quinciañera.

Socialization

Play and peer groups serve as laboratories in which children develop their self-concept, test roles, integrate peer group perspectives and expectations, and ultimately, adopt gender identity and behaviors. Thus, Mexican American school-age children may be better understood in terms of their peer culture. Musolf states as follows:

> Without the acquisition of language, one cannot view or act toward one's self as an object. And until the self becomes an object to itself through language, it cannot develop. Role-taking and language acquisition are inseparable, . . . processes of self-objectification and self-development. (1996, p. 305)

Furthermore, "Children transform culture even as they are socialized by it" (p. 315). Thus, through play and peer interaction, children simulate their multiple cultural contexts and test behaviors for more successful integration.

Contemporary Chicano literature utilizes childhood experiences in novels and anecdotes that illustrate a young Mexican American boy's or girl's experiences when, for example, leaving the haven of the family and entering the school system. In *Bless Me, Ultima,* Antonio (age seven) prepares for his first day of school and gets blessed by his mother and the folk healer, Ultima, who is living in their home because of her old age. When Antonio enters the classroom, his fascination grows as the teacher writes on the blackboard. By lunchtime, however, he feels "pain and sadness spread[ing] to [his] soul . . . I wanted to run away, to hide, to run and never come back" (Anaya, 1972, p. 55). In just a short period of time, Antonio had experienced discrimination and alienation in the school environment. This experience is repeated over and over by countless Mexican Americans who have succeeded in mainstream America but never forget these initial humiliating and alienating experiences in school. They speak of having their names changed to English names for the convenience of the teachers. They recall the daily inspections for dirt under their fingernails, lice on their heads, wax in their ears, inspections that the mainstream students were not required to endure. They still recall the corporal punishment and other stigmas received because they spoke Spanish or had trouble pronouncing some words in English. Children whose attire did not match that of mainstream students also felt conspicuous and inferior (García, 2000; Guajardo, Fineman, Colón, Sánchez, & Scheurich, 1999). In Antonio's experience, he and his friends found refuge among peers. Thus, the anecdote shows how parents can buffer some of the pain but they cannot change the discriminatory dynamics that characterize prejudice and racism in the larger society. Peers, therefore, develop special forms of language and offer friendships within which the young person develops gender identity and learns how to interact and confront problems. Parents do not play a major role in these important aspects of child development and socialization.

At times, there are significant problems in the interactions of the parents and their children.

> As children internalize a different cultural reality, where child and adult re-lationships are less formal, where the individual is stressed over the unit, and where everyone is expected to inquire about every element of their environ-ment, previously taught values are often experienced as incompatible and therefore useless and antiquated. (Partida 1996, p. 250)

That situation may cause conflict and pain in the family system, particularly if the parents react by trying to enforce their own cultural expectations, thereby further alienating their children. Certainly, there are as many variations of this dynamic as there are families. Those who can access and accept the support of extended family do so with full endorsement of the ethnic culture. The next level of support may come from the ethnic community's own resources. Only when the family and cul-tural community resources have been exhausted will the family go outside to access the resources of mainstream society. Delgado-Gaitan and Trueba (1991) stress that when an outside resource has to be accessed, such as when a child has a disability, parents "often seek institutions in which they can develop personal relationships" (p. 35). The parents must trust the service provider before they will risk sharing intimate information. They must feel respected in their interactions with societal institutions, and they must feel the freedom to make decisions on the basis of family priorities. That level of choice assumes, of course, that various institutions with that potential personal level of collaboration are available (p. 35). The family network, nevertheless, remains the primary resource at the time of need.

CASE STUDY: THE MARTÍNEZ FAMILY

Mr. and Mrs. Martínez (ages twenty-five and twenty-four, respectively) became anxious when the teacher of their oldest child, Tony (age five), sent a note in-dicating that Tony was experiencing serious problems in the classroom. Accord-ing to the note she attached to his second report card, Tony was not paying attention, did not finish his class work, could seldom sit still for more than five or six minutes, and did not ask for assistance if he did not understand her in-structions. Furthermore, she indicated on the note that a visiting teacher would soon call on them to discuss special testing that might help school personnel understand how best to work with Tony.

Mr. and Mrs. Martínez immediately called their compadres, Mr. and Mrs. Jiménez, to come and review the teacher's note and advise them on the most appropriate steps they should take concerning Tony's schooling. The parents had noticed no such problems at home. Tony appeared to them to be a very energetic child, curious and outgoing. They also thought he was especially smart.

In addition to Tony, Mr. and Mrs. Martínez had a daughter (age two and a half) and were expecting a third child shortly. Mr. Martínez worked as a chef and sometimes helped his brother with landscaping jobs during the weekends. He liked to work at least six days a week so that Mrs. Martínez could stay home to care for the children.

As they discussed the teacher's note with their compadres, Mr. Martínez expressed his suspicion that special testing would only lead to special education, something he remembered as a bad experience for his own younger brother, who took medication for many years and never regained entry in regular classes. According to Mr. Martínez, there are simply too many Mexican American children in special education classes. He did not want Tony to have the same problems as his brother. Mrs. Martínez and Mrs. Jiménez wondered if the nearby curandero (folk healer) could prescribe some teas to help Tony calm down so that his level of energy would be more acceptable to his teacher. Also, Mr. and Mrs. Jiménez offered to talk to their neighbor, a schoolteacher, to get other ideas on how to approach the school.

When the visiting teacher called to set an appointment at the school or in their home, Mr. Martínez very politely responded that his work precluded a visit during the next couple of weeks—a ploy for time during which they could continue to work with the compadres to learn what options they should consider.

This case study illustrates the reaction of a traditional Mexican American family to the possible learning problems of a child. Tony's school problems, as described by his teacher, may be alleviated by the use of medication, but Mr. and Mrs. Martínez's initial reaction was to seek the help of their compadres for problem solving. The women also wanted to consult the curandero for a more traditional approach to alleviate the hyperactivity—another attempt to utilize cultural resources prior to seeking help from mainstream resources. Mr. Martínez had a worldview, based on the experience of his brother, in which he questioned the adequacy of modern interventions.

The most significant factor in this initial reaction of parents to the special needs of a child is that they were not alone in facing this problem. They had compadres, who had other connections to additional resources. The parents needed to exhaust all these connections before they could fully engage in the school's own service system. However, if their own connections led them to a particular person within the school's service system, Mr. and Mrs. Martínez could proceed to work with that person, knowing that they would be more likely to obtain the assistance they needed.

In general, Mexican American traditions represent a source of strength for members of la familia. Cultural traditions often serve to define the individual within the family group (Partida, 1996, p. 250). Traditions in the form of events and rituals bring family members together, and they can reinforce "their identity, pride, and sense of belonging" (p. 248). Some families, however, may be so focused on survival that they no longer have the collective memory or traditions and values that can help them solve problems as they encounter life transitions. Some families also have dysfunctional dynamics that foster patterns of family violence, substance abuse, child neglect, or child abuse. To the extent that their extended families can buffer those hardships, children may still have access to the nurturing and guidance they need.

Extended family resources are often needed to support or substitute for the efforts of the parents. Nevertheless, the adjustments required by changes in the parenting system can cause unexpected dynamics because of differences in the level of acculturation among the family members. For instance, although acculturation is expected to be greater among grandchildren, some grandparents may find themselves rearing grandchildren whose parents are less traditional in their cultural preferences, or vice versa. Such a situation potentially places the middle generation—the parents—as the brokers. Language differences can create remoteness in relationships and lack of access when support is needed (Silverstein & Chen, 1999). What happens, for instance, when the parents are absent (because of deportation, incarceration, or death) and the grandparents become the *parents* to the young children or adolescents? What role do grandparents play in the socialization of young children?

Parents are usually held accountable for the manner in which their children are socialized. In traditional Mexican American families, education is viewed as consisting of both *home education* and *formal education*. Home education teaches norms for interacting with others in and out of the family and can be taught by any person older than the child, including older siblings, grandparents, padrinos, or older neighbors. Ultimately, however, it is the parents who must teach and require children to obey and collaborate (Delgado-Gaitan & Trueba, 1991, p. 63). In fact, all Mexican Americans, young or old, are expected to demonstrate *buena educación*

(good manners) learned at home to develop and maintain personal relationships (p. 35). Accordingly, *respeto*, respect, at its highest level must be demonstrated toward parents, even by adult children. In traditional families, individual behavior continues to reflect honor or dishonor on the family of origin, including the extended family. Perhaps, as Villanueva (1996) noted, the grandparents can be most influential on the upbringing of their grandchildren by supporting the parenting efforts of their adult children. She quotes one grandparent as saying the role of the parents is "to help them grow straight" (p. 13), meaning to instill a work ethic and the desire for a better life. Parents of educationally and culturally successful Chicanos spoke of the manner in which their parents had sacrificed and given them opportunities to become responsible and contributing participants in the life of the family (p. 19).

Formal education, on the other hand, refers to public or private education in which the child is socialized without parental participation because of language differences or the parents' limited education. Romo and Falbo (1996), focusing on Latino school dropouts, developed a list of strategies parents used to keep adolescents in school—a formidable challenge among Mexican Americans. The researchers stressed the importance of parents remaining in charge and setting limits and high expectations, openly communicating, constantly encouraging and supporting the children, and staying involved in school. Romo and Falbo also stressed the importance of the school's meeting the basic needs of the children, particularly when families cannot do so, by focusing on student learning, making education relevant, making expectations clear, making it easier to stay in school than to drop out, and mobilizing resources to link the school with parents and community.

Incarcerated Parents

No information is available on the number of Mexican American children and youth whose fathers or mothers or both are incarcerated. This lack of information is a critical gap in knowledge about Mexican American families. Children suffer emotional, social, and economic loss and stress when their parent is incarcerated and taken to a prison that may be inaccessible for visitation. Many children try to hide this situation from school authorities and their peers because of the stigma associated with imprisonment. Some children share their stories, only to be shunned by their peers. Others appear to express their frustration and their anger in self-defeating patterns of underachievement and belligerent behaviors. The spouses left behind as single parents, and the grandparents left in charge when both parents are incarcerated, give many accounts of their frustration and loss of hope because of having to fight a prison system that shows little or no concern for the families involved (Baagen, 1995).

A service project in San Antonio, Texas, identifies prisoners and their children and coordinates visitations, correspondence and other activities aimed at closing the gap created by the removal of one or both parents from the family. Similarly, parents of incarcerated adult children in Houston, Texas, have organized themselves as *Madres y Familias* in order to become more knowledgeable about prisoner rights and options for community advocacy and self-advocacy on behalf of prisoners and their families (García, 2000). Their stories indicate that the incarceration of youths and adults is very much a family issue. Thus, as the prison-industrial complex grows, so does the aftermath of separation and alienation for many Mexican Americans and their children. This pattern is expected to grow since prisons have become a privatized industry that offers jobs to communities at risk because of unemployment caused by downsizing of the military and other industries (Schlosser, 1998).

Child Abuse

Because most data on abused children is categorized by race, information is not available about the number of Mexican American children who are physically or sexually abused. A cross-cultural study examining the issue established that Latino children who are sexually abused within the family system are more likely to be abused by members of the extended family. The findings further showed that the depression level that resulted from the abuse was similar to the level in situations in which the abuser was a member of the immediate family (Moisan, Sanders-Phillips, & Moisan, 1997). Possible explanations that were cited were poverty and related circumstances such as overcrowding and the traditional cultural pattern of children having more contacts with extended family members. Further study needs to focus on the variation in responses between parents who are more traditional in family orientation and parents who are more acculturated. More pertinent, perhaps, is the question of how to educate Mexican American parents so that they can act to prevent such abuse in the first place. Prevention is crucial. Moreover, societal resources must relate to the cultural reality of each person involved.

HELP SEEKING AND HEALING PRACTICES

Traditional culture employs some special healing methods. *Curanderismo* (folk healing) is still used by many traditional families, regardless of socioeconomic status (Krajewski-Jaime, 1991). The healing process includes spiritual components, such as prayers, patron saints, herbs, and other articles often found in the family's immediate environment. Parents are often encouraged by their elders to consult a curandera or curandero when a child is not developing as expected, when a child has suffered some trauma, or when a child shows symptoms of illness, such as loss of appetite or excessive crying. Understanding this resource system in the barrio reveals some of the reasons why such help is sought even when a parent can afford to use conventional medicine. For example, a curandera is usually well known and respected by traditional families and their communities. Thus, many parents opt for curanderismo instead of updated medicinal methods used in a foreign environment (and often using a second language). Some parents, particularly those without health insurance coverage, may see curanderismo as their only option prior to taking a child directly to an emergency room in a hospital. Other middle-class, traditional, and bicultural parents consider curanderismo to be the *preferred* mental health and physical health alternative, to be used instead of conventional medicine, which involves separation of body, mind, and spirit. In traditional culture and in curanderismo, there is no such separation. Body, mind, spirit, God, Mother Earth, and la familia are interrelated. When a cure is achieved, many Catholic families in the states or in Mexico plan and carry out a pilgrimage of thanks to a shrine.

A quick review of the Juárez case presented at the beginning of this chapter clarifies, in light of curanderismo, that Mrs. Juárez was using a culturally encouraged practice of consulting a curandera (the señora she mentioned) and that the use of teas (herbs) for herself and the child was neither child neglect nor self-neglect. Without knowledge of this cultural preference, a practitioner could prematurely report the mother for child neglect and threaten the last shreds of stability of this single-parent family in transition from an abusive marital situation.

The case study also illustrates that traditional Mexican American parents may not only use but even protect traditional resources. Mrs. Juárez "changed the subject" when asked to identify the señora. Curanderos are at risk, if identified to health authorities, of being accused of providing treatment without a license. A culturally sensitive worker would, therefore, not ask for a name but would focus on finding out the type of teas being used. That way the worker could check for possible interactions with prescribed medications or the immunizations. Furthermore, knowing the types of teas Mrs. Juárez is taking would provide the worker with additional information about her symptoms, such as lack of appetite or insomnia. Finally, more in-depth discussion about advice received from the señora could shed light on the role of religion or other culturally related beliefs that operate within the family system.

CURRENT STATUS OF MEXICAN AMERICAN YOUTH

This chapter would be incomplete without a brief look at what is happening among Mexican American youth at the beginning of the twenty-first century. In reality, the Chicano movement of the 1960s never ended. It still exists. Ironically, Proposition 187 in California and ongoing anti-immigration efforts by the federal and some state governments helped support efforts for self-advocacy within Mexican American communities across the country. Some of the former leaders of the movement and a growing number of Chicano social scientists and educators continue to work to document and teach the collective memory of Mexican American history, culture, and sociopolitical and economic issues. They provide more systematic documentation of phenomena previously presented in terms of individual experience. They also share some priceless anecdotes of their experiences growing up (López, 1993, pp. 5–10). There is growing awareness regarding the potential political empowerment of Mexican Americans. Increasingly, men and women who are parents and grandparents of present-day Mexican American youth meet to address parenting and community issues such as education and incarceration (R. G. García, personal communication, August 13, 2000).

Moreover, many youths in high schools and colleges are eagerly asking for cultural education and training about their mestizo heritage as it relates to the

historical and spiritual foundation of their personal development. Some young people are adopting Aztec and other indigenous names, studying pre-Columbian mythology, and learning about their traditional musical heritage. Some who have not learned or mastered Spanish are realizing that a knowledge of Spanish can improve their opportunities for using their older relatives or barrio residents as cultural teachers. Other youths are joining their parents in the search for their genealogy. Moreover, some college youths are seriously considering their responsibility to the ethnic community and want to join their parents in the launching of Mexican American children who will be better prepared to succeed and contribute in American society.

PRACTICE IMPLICATIONS

One thing is clear: Mexican American parents care about their children and want them to succeed. History and tradition help parents instill and support values conducive to family solidarity, the work ethic, and success. However, although there is a growing number of studies by which to understand the parent-child relationship in la familia, current knowledge is challenged by the diversity that exists among and within Mexican American families.

Given the historical trajectory and current needs of Mexican American parents and their children, cultural competence for practice requires the following qualifications:

- Knowledge of the historical context in which the Mexican American community has evolved and the impact of that context on the community's current economic and social well-being
- Knowledge of the dynamics of the first, second, and subsequent generations in the Mexican American family and the varying ways in which these generations influence personal identities and acculturation patterns in a multicultural society
- Acceptance of different worldviews and each client's experience
- Willingness to acknowledge one's personal biases and the assumptions and values influenced by the larger society
- Willingness to learn Spanish or skills for use of interpreter services, for more effective communication with monolingual Mexican and Mexican American clients
- Skill in recognizing and using cultural nuances for effective communication with the more traditional Mexicans and Mexican Americans
- Recognition of needs and issues affecting Mexican and Mexican American parents and their children
- Respect for and skill in using cultural resources in the Mexican American community
- Commitment to surrogate parenting and other support for children and youths whose parents are incarcerated or otherwise inaccessible
- Skill in the planning and provision of family and group services for Mexicans and Mexican Americans who request training for effective communication with their more acculturated children
- Commitment to social and economic justice for the Mexican American community
- Readiness to build alliances with community individuals and groups who are ready to serve as advocates for the Mexican and Mexican American community
- Readiness and skill for work with formal service systems to encourage outreach and innovative responses to the many needs of Mexican Americans
- Commitment to continuing efforts to develop and apply new strategies for work with Mexicans and Mexican Americans
- Development of a philosophy of personal and professional values that support La Raza as a people in search of its own place in American society and the global community

Discussion Questions and Role-Play Exercises

1. How could the school social worker approach the Martínez family about arranging a meeting to discuss the need for testing of their son? Who should be invited to attend the meeting? Role-play the telephone contact and the first meeting.
2. Discuss the issues for different family members when a parent is incarcerated. What services should be provided by forensic social workers?

3. How can schools, churches, and other community resources respond to the needs of Mexican and Mexican American children in single-parent families? Simulate a task group of professionals and community leaders discussing the needs and alternative ways to offer support for these children and for the parents and other relatives who serve as caregivers.

4. How can social service agencies and mental health programs adapt their approaches to offer more culturally relevant services? Visit an agency or health institution to observe how the location, décor, and staff encourage service utilization by Mexican and Mexican American clients.

5. Review the recommendations for cultural competence and conduct a self-evaluation. Create a personal list of learning goals for further professional development for effective practice with Mexican American families.

References

Aguilar-Moreno, M. (1998). *The cult of the dead in Mexico: Continuity of a millennial tradition.* Austin, TX: Mexic-Arte.

Anaya, R. A. (1972). *Bless me, Ultima.* Berkeley, CA: Tonatiuh International.

Baagen, A. T. (1995). *Children and families of prison inmates: A challenge to the research and services communities.* Paper presented at the 42nd semiannual conference of the Association of Criminal Justice Research (California), Claremont, CA.

Delgado-Gaitan, C., & Trueba, H. (1991). *Cross cultural borders: Education for immigrant families in America* (pp. 26–86). New York: Falmer Press.

García, R. G. (2000, March). Presentation to community group at Narciso Martínez Cultural Center, San Benito, TX.

Gonzáles, R. (1972). Yo soy Joaquin. In A. C. Schular, T. Ybarra-Frausto, & J. Sommers (Eds.), *Chicano literature: Text and context* (pp. 89–90). Englewood Cliffs, NJ: Prentice-Hall.

Guajardo, M., Fineman, E., Colón, C., Sánchez, P. & Scheurich, J. (Primary contributors). (1999). *Labors of Life (Labores de la Vida)* [Video]. (Available from Texas Education Agency, Division of Migrant Education, 1701 N. Congress, Austin, TX 78701-1494)

Harmon, D., & Park, S. (1999, November 28). Billions for buildup don't stem the tide. *Austin American-Statesman,* pp. A1, A10, A11.

Jacobs, A. (1999, November 3). As joyous as it is macabre: Mexican holiday ensures the dead have their day. *The New York Times,* p. B1.

Krajewski-Jaime, E. R. (1991). Folk-healing among Mexican American families as a consideration in the delivery of child welfare and child health care services. *Child Welfare, 70,* 157–67.

López, T. A. (Ed.). (1993). *Growing up Chicana/o* (pp. 5–10). New York: Avon Books.

Martínez, E. A. (1988). Child behavior in Mexican American/Chicano families: Maternal teaching and child-rearing practices. *Family Relations, 37*(3), 275–80.

McLemore, S. D., & Romo, R. (1985). The origins and development of the Mexican American people. In R. De la Garza et al. (Eds.), *The Mexican American experience: An interdisciplinary anthology* (pp. 3–32). Austin: University of Texas Press.

Minorities become the majority. (2000, August 31). *The Daily Texan,* p. 3.

Moisan, P. A., Sanders-Phillips, K. S., & Moisan, P. M. (1997). Ethnic differences in circumstances of abuse and symptoms of depression and anger among sexually abused black and Latino boys. *Child Abuse and Neglect 21*(5), 473–88.

Mora, P. (1994). Elena. In D. L. D. Heyck, *Barrios and borderlands: Cultures of Latinos and Latinas in the United States* (p. 369). New York: Rutledge.

Muñiz, R. (1998). Yo soy Mexika. Unpublished poem.

Musolf, G. R. (1996). Interactionism and the child: Cahill, Corsaro, and Denzin on childhood socialization. *Symbolic Interaction, 19*(4), 303–21.

Oropesa, R. S., & Landale, N. S. (1997). Immigrant legacies: Ethnicity, generation, and children's familial and economic lives. *Social Science Quarterly, 78*(2), 399–416.

Partida, J. (1996). The effects of immigration on children in the Mexican American community. *Child and Adolescent Social Work Journal, 13*(3), 241–54.

Pérez-Granados, D. R., & Callahan, M. A. (1997). Parents and siblings as early resources for young children's learning in Mexican descent families. *Hispanic Journal of Behavioral Science, 19*(1), 3–33.

Romo, H. D., & Falbo, T. (1996). *Latino high school graduation: Defying the odds* (pp. 164–89). Austin: University of Texas Press.

Schlosser, E. (1998, December). The prison-industrial complex. *Atlantic Monthly,* pp. 50–77.

Sherraden, M. S., & Barrera, R. E. (1997). Family support and birth outcomes among second-generation Mexican immigrants. *Social Service Review, 17*(4), 607–33.

Shinagawa, L. H., & Jang, M. (1998). *Atlas of American diversity* (93, 151). Walnut Creek, CA: Alta Mira Press.

Silverstein, M., & Chen, X. (1999, February). The impact of acculturation in Mexican American families on the quality of adult grandchild-grandparent relationships. *Journal of Marriage and the Family, 61,* 188–98.

Sylvester, S. (1999, December 30). Census to focus on kids: Youths living with grandparents targeted. *San Antonio Express News,* pp. 1B, 3B.

Tijerina, R. L. (1978). *Mi lucha for la tierra* (pp. 7–26). Mexico D. F., Mexico: Fondo de Cultura Economica.

U.S. Census Bureau. (2000). Resident population estimates of the United States by sex, race, and Hispanic origin [on-line]. Available: http://www.census.gov/population/estimates/nation/intfile3-1.txt

Valle, R. (1982). Hispanic social networks and prevention. In R. L. Hough, P. A. Gongla, V. B. Brown, & S. E. Golston, *Psychiatric epidemiology and prevention: The possibilities* (pp. 131–57). Los Angeles: Neuropsychiatric Institute.

Vélez-Ibañez, C. G. (1997). *Border visions* (pp. 137–48). Tucson: University of Arizona Press.

Villanueva, I. (1996). Change in the educational life of Chicano families across three generations. *Education and Urban Society, 29*(1), 13–34.

Williams, N. (1990). *The Mexican American family: Tradition and change.* Dix Hills, NY: General Hall.

Parenting in Cuban American Families

TERESA BEVIN

I sensed the momentary flicker of my mother's presence, and I
thanked her in silence. I thanked her for her strength, because
she had wanted a different destiny for my siblings and me
than was being dished out for us. But she forgot herself.
Wanting the world for us, she sent us where we could find it,
but she didn't live long enough to enjoy her triumph.

—Bevin, 1998, p. 160

The trauma of exile, whether experienced firsthand or passed down through generations, resides deep within the psyche of most Cuban Americans. Those who live with the pain of forced, sometimes final, separations may take many years to recover, and some never do. Uprooting produces its own form of grief, one endured away from familiar environments and support systems and thus resistant to resolution. With rare exceptions, children born in the United States of Cuban parents live within their elders' longing for what was once lost. Some may be able to distance themselves from familial nostalgia, but Cuba is an inescapable aspect of the atmosphere in which they grow. The feelings of longing, however, are not unique to the older Cuban populations. Middle-aged Cubans brought to the United States as children, "with memories framed in English, not Spanish, share their parents' and grandparents' passion for Cuba to a surprising degree" (Rieff, 1993, p. 31).

But not all the dynamics of Cuban American families resonate in harmony. The hardships of having to start all over again in a new country, combined with culture shock, intergenerational conflict, and division between the first immigrants and subsequent waves of refugees, may have contributed adversely to the integrity of today's Cuban American family. The link to Cuba remains strong, nevertheless, perhaps because of a need to preserve a sense of dignity and pride in spite of the loss of family members, friends, property, and homeland. Because the basic social unit for Cubans is the extended family, regardless of how fragmented by distance this network might be, kinship among its members may reach far and wide, granting support and a sense of belonging even in exile. In addition, the drive for recovery and adaptation typical of Cuban Americans has contributed to the preservation of their familial unity and their overall success as an immigrant group.

In this chapter I hope to highlight, not only specific points relating to Cuban American families, but also the diversity within these families as far as the timing and circumstances of their migration. In sharing some of my own experiences as a Cuban American in combination with my observations as a psychotherapist, I hope to aid practitioners in their work with members of a relatively small but distinct ethnic group.

HISTORICAL AND SOCIOECONOMIC BACKGROUND: THE DIFFERENT WAVES OF CUBAN EXILES INTO THE UNITED STATES

The various waves of Cuban exiles have spanned over forty years, since 1959. The timing and circumstances of each wave are important to the socioeconomic, educational, racial, and religious dimensions, family dynamics, and parenting styles of different Cuban American groups. Also, the expectation for a productive life in the United States is sometimes influenced by the amount of time individuals have been exposed to the Castro regime. Lack of stimuli and the stress born of constant surveillance and widespread shortages of basic necessities within Cuba can dampen an exile's ambition, even in a new environment.

This discussion of the impact of migration on Cuban American family dynamics focuses on the period between 1959 and the year 2000, although Cuban American history dates back to the mid-nineteenth century, when many fled the Spanish regime that had taken over the island (Jiménez-Vásquez, 1995). After the 1869 declaration of independence, Cubans seemed to have very few reasons to leave their native country and settle elsewhere. "Migration to the United States was so sparse that there were only 50,000 Cubans living in the United States prior to the Cuban revolution in 1959" (Suárez, 1998, p. 173). But because of close economic ties between the United States and well-to-do Cubans, many sought to protect themselves against political instability in the island by strengthening their link with the United States. Working for American companies, making frequent trips to the United States, and sending their children to American schools made many Cubans feel more secure. Upper- and middle-class Cubans were very familiar with the American way of life, and many became naturalized Americans while still preserving their Cuban residence. Nevertheless, few abandoned the island completely until Castro's revolution. Since then, more than one million Cubans have crossed the Florida

Strait one way or another. Thousands have risked or lost their lives in flimsy rafts, while tens of thousands have left the island through a third country, hoping to eventually reach the United States.

Between 1959 and 1999 there have been several distinct waves of migration from Cuba, and different responses on both sides of the aisle, depending on the changing political and economic conditions in Cuba and the United States. The various waves and responses are described in the following section.

The First Wave of Exiles (1959)

"Between 1 January and 30 June 1959, a total of 26,527 Cubans emigrated to the United States, the vast majority settling in Miami" (Olson & Olson, 1995, p. 53). But that first wave was a small exodus compared to what was to come later, because the first truly large wave did not start until the time of the Cuban missile crisis, between January 1961 and October 1962 (p. 54). That wave brought more than 150,000 refugees to Florida. The trip was easy then, and Cubans were welcome because they were fleeing the ravages of Communism.

Believing that the United States would not allow a Communist government to take hold on an island ninety miles from its soil, Cuban refugees did not expect their exile to last long. But in 1961, a chain of events dashed their hopes for a quick return home. The United States broke diplomatic relations with Cuba in January, the Bay of Pigs invasion was defeated in April, and in December Castro declared: "I am a Marxist-Leninist and I shall be one to the end of my life" (Brenner, LeoGrande, Rich, & Siegel, 1989, p. 529).

The Second Wave of Refugees (1961)

A sense of doom filled the hearts of millions of Cubans, and a second wave of refugees fled the island. This group was painfully aware that their exile might last much longer than the first wave had anticipated. Hence most Cuban Americans refer to their status in the United States as that of "exiles" instead of "refugees." By the end of 1961 the Cuban government not only had expelled all foreign Catholic priests and closed churches, but it also had taken control of all American interests in the island as well as large Cuban businesses and private schools. Furthermore, in June 1961, one thousand Cuban students were sent to the former Soviet Union "to live in collective farms and study cultivation methods" (Conde, 1999, p. 36). The mounting concern of Cuban parents who feared the loss of their children to communist indoctrination "triggered the formation of a clandestine operation set up specifically to get children out of Cuba" (p. 47). This effort, named "Operation Pedro Pan," requested the help of American educators and volunteers so that un-accompanied Cuban children could be placed in camps and boarding schools upon arrival in Miami. Many of these children were later placed in foster homes through-out the country to await their parents. While many children were claimed by members of their extended family, hundreds waited many years to reunite with their parents. Formerly overindulged children suffered neglect and abuse while in the care of unscrupulous foster parents. The cases cited by Conde range from neglect to physical and sexual abuse.

At the age of twelve, one of my cousins was placed with a foster family in Albuquerque, New Mexico, where she was treated like a servant. She was excluded from family activities and was expected to do all the housework, including shining the family's shoes. She resolved to never again suffer exploitation, became an entrepreneur, and to this day has never worked for anyone. A close friend endured three years of sexual abuse from his foster father. Once reunited with his parents, he kept the secret from them until he began to show symptoms of severe anxiety that required psychological intervention.

This exodus was a very sad chapter in the lives of 14,048 Cuban children. Many of those who experienced the trauma of this event continue to suffer the aftereffects of the sudden separation and subsequent life with strangers or in institutions. Four hundred and forty-two individuals who arrived in the United States through Operation Pedro Pan responded to a questionnaire designed by Conde (1999), herself one of the immigrant children of the operation. Though most consider the experience as generally positive and express gratitude toward their parents for taking such a painful step, some indicate that they themselves are overprotective of their children and to this date continue to suffer separation anxiety and fear of abandonment.

CASE STUDY: MARCOS

Marcos was separated from his parents at age seven and was ten by the time he reunited with them. At that time, his parents began to overprotect him. They did not allow him to go to summer camp or to sleep over at a friend's home. Marcos felt smothered by his parents, although he had managed quite well while in one of the camps of Operation Pedro Pan. He ran away from home at the age of thirteen and was not heard from during an entire week, which he spent with a juvenile street gang. Through the mediation of a Cuban American therapist, Marcos's parents agreed to allow him more freedom, and he was returned home. The family remained in treatment for two years after that. Today, Marcos is married to a woman who also came to the United States through Operation Pedro Pan. Both say that they have struggled with their own desire to overprotect their two children and keep them close at all times, in spite of Marcos's own experience.

The early Cuban refugees were welcomed into the United States with open arms and soon became known as the "Golden Exiles" (Bernal, 1984). Though the majority of Americans had their doubts about the sudden arrival of so many Cubans, the immigrants' upper- and middle-class backgrounds convinced many Americans that the Cubans wouldn't be a burden for the social service system. This assumption proved to be true then and continues to be true for those coming from lower classes, perhaps because many Cuban communities in exile have set up networks to help new arrivals find employment and learn English. Another reason for such positive welcome is that Cubans started to flood southern Florida at a time when African American communities were beginning to flourish and the Civil Rights movement was gaining strength. Because members of the Cuban elite were white, they were given favored employee status, which further isolated Southern Florida blacks and created tensions between Latinos and African Americans that exist to the present.

Family Reunification Flights: Havana-Miami (1965)

In 1965 Cuba faced economic disaster. Seeking to "weed out" the population, Castro declared that Cuba did not need the dissidents after all, and anyone who wanted to leave the island could ask relatives or friends "up north" to come for them. The port of Camarioca, east of Havana, was opened to American boats, and soon after the news hit the airwaves, an entire flotilla of boats was bound for Cuba. Another wave of refugees ensued, and many boats, overloaded with desperate Cubans, capsized and sank in choppy seas. The tragic spectacle embarrassed the Cuban government, and the port was closed. Organized migration from Havana to Miami was again authorized through what came to be called the "Family Reunification Flights" (Olson & Olson, 1995, p. 60). But Cuban government restrictions regarding eligibility for exit visas were numerous, were subject to change without reason or warning, and had little regard for family reunification.

The Third Wave (1968)

Several changes in policy initiated by President Nixon in 1968 permitted Cubans stranded in Spain and Mexico to enter the United States as refugees (Olson & Olson, 1995, p. 70), allowing thousands to join their already-settled relatives. This wave was different from the others because the refugees had been living in a third country for years and had become reacquainted with market economies before entering the United States. This movement of Cubans from Spain to the United States lasted several years. I was among those who lived in Spain three years before coming to the United States at age twenty-one to join my younger brother, then a minor, who had left Cuba through Mexico and was living with distant relatives in Washington D.C. We were both separated from the rest of the family for eleven years and never saw our father again after leaving Cuba.

Travel Restrictions Removed in 1979

In 1979, because of the steady deterioration of the Cuban economy and the need to improve the regime's record on human rights, Castro announced that exiles would be allowed to visit their relatives in Cuba (Geldof, 1992). Many Cuban Americans took immediate advantage of the opportunity, bringing bounties of badly needed goods for their loved ones while paying grossly inflated prices for airfare and hotel accommodations. Cuban Americans thus began to help the Cuban economy while seeking to alleviate their relatives' economic hardships.

The rekindling of family ties brought about by the visits also closed many emotional gaps for Cubans both in and outside the island. A new kind of discontent arose among the Cuban people and "pressure for emigration inexorably increased" (Pérez, 1991, p. 257). Castro realized too late that with their gifts, the visitors were bringing proof of attainable well-being and prosperity from the United States.

The Mariel Exodus (1980)

Castro, responding to raising discontent, authorized another exodus through the port of Mariel. Again, Cuban Americans crossed the Florida Strait in great numbers. Although embarrassed by the overt desperation of the Cuban people, Castro sought to take advantage of the situation and thus get rid of "undesirables," including rapists, pimps, prostitutes, and thieves. When enough "undesirables" were on their way to Florida, the port of Mariel was closed. Although the criminally insane and the mentally ill account for only about 6 percent of the arrivals from Mariel (Peterson, 1982), the event altered the way many Americans viewed Cuban migration. Until 1980, most Cuban immigrants were from the middle classes, and few were Afro-Cuban. The Mariel exodus changed that. The new Cuban immigrants were considered social misfits; most were single males without relatives in Miami, and thousands were Afro-Cubans. The majority of Cuban blacks were devoted to *Santería,* a mixture of Catholic rituals and African mythology. Because these practices are often unfairly seen as primitive and pagan, religious differences alone rendered the new arrivals, now called *Marielitos,* unwelcome to the white, largely Roman Catholic Cuban Americans residing in and around Miami's Little Havana.

Despite unfair incarceration and negative propaganda, however, most *Marielitos* turned out to be as enterprising as other Cuban immigrants. Many moved to northern states, risking the nonfamiliar American brand of discrimination rather than the contempt of white Cuban exiles in Southern Florida.

The Mariel exodus of 1980 was a critical event for many Cubans, whether they were *Marielitos* themselves, relatives, or simply witnesses of the boatlift. Cuban Americans were humbled upon seeing the boats, unbelievably crowded, arriving in Southern Florida with their desperate but hopeful cargo. Perhaps the ones to suffer the most were the *children* of the Mariel exodus. Silva (1985) quoted Piedad Bucholtz, a Dade County school superintendent: "Some came without their parents and had no family in the United States, others just with their brothers and sisters to stay with relatives they had never met" (p. 14). Obviously, those parents had done what the parents of the earlier Operation Pedro Pan exodus had done. Reporting the violence of the Mariel boatlift, as evidenced by the risk at sea and the boats' crowded conditions, Silva states that "it traumatized a large number of children and left emotional scars that set many of them apart for a long time" (p. 14). But besides the drama of their odyssey, there were other marked differences between the children of Mariel and those of earlier immigrant waves. Bucholtz further remarked to Silva:

> These children had been raised in a system totally isolated from ours. Isolated from American thought, trend, habit, dress, vocabulary. . . . They had no concept of private property, nor that of authority as something to be re- spected out of admiration rather than fear. (p. 16)

After the Mariel exodus ended, Cuban migration came to a halt. In December of 1984, Cuba and the United States signed an "Immigration Accord whereby Cuba agreed to take back 2,746 Mariel 'excludables' and the US accepted an annual quota of 20,000 Cubans" (Geldof, 1992, p. xxi).

The New Refugees: Balseros

Throughout these crises, waves of *balseros* (boat people) have made it to the Florida shores. The most recent arrivals have proven difficult for Cuban Americans to accept or understand. "The people from today's Cuba are the children of a revolution that provided social guarantees but limited opportunities" (Navarro, 1999, p. A25). The new Cuban refugees appear entitled, as if assuming that those who left the island earlier owe them something. Cuban Americans find it difficult to assist their newly arrived relatives in becoming acculturated to the American work ethic. In Cuba, wages never increase, and no additional stimulus is offered in exchange for hard work. Instead, able-bodied men and women are pressured into "voluntary" labor. Thus, the repressive regime seems to have taught many of today's Cubans to avoid work and survive in other ways. As a result, many recent immigrants remain out of touch with the necessary drive to persevere and achieve in a capitalistic country, thus widening the gap between generations of Cuban refugees.

Today, the image of the well-educated, career-oriented Cuban refugees of the 1960s is but a portion of "an extraordinarily complex series of immigrant groups" (Silva, 1985, p. 5). But in general terms, Cuban Americans today remain a demo- graphically distinctive population. "Because of their urban and suburban concen- tration as well as their business success, they have exerted a powerful influence, relative to their numbers" (Green, 1999, p. 257).

SIGNIFICANT PARENTING AND FAMILY ISSUES RELATED TO CHILD REARING AMONG CUBAN AMERICANS

Economic Considerations

Cuban American families place great value in achieving and maintaining a com- fortable lifestyle. From the 1960s through the 1970s the popular belief was that Cuban workers were paid more than other immigrants because of their preferred status. However, demographic studies have since indicated that the difference was most likely because the average Cuban American family earned more than one income (Suárez, 1998). A typical case is that of the Goitía family, who arrived together in 1966. The grandmother concentrated on housework and babysitting for neighborhood families while the grandfather performed light gardening jobs that his age and skills would allow. The parents held more than one job each shortly after their arrival and quickly moved from manual labor as building janitor and elevator operator to higher positions on the occupational ladder as clerks and storekeepers. The older Goitía children eagerly accepted any available summer jobs as messengers and store helpers. Though many parents were opposed to early-morning or after-school work for their children because of concern about their schoolwork, the needs of the recently uprooted family were so great that many children were actually forced to work long hours in addition to attending school. In the case of the Goitías, they were able to buy a home only three years after their arrival in the United States.

In 1969 Cuban American families were earning only about $1,400 less annually than non-Latinos in the United States (Jaffe, Cullen, & Boswell, 1980, p. 259). The more workers within the family, the higher the income, especially for families headed by men. But it is worth noting that by 1993, Cuban Americans had the highest income among Latin American households headed by women (Shinagawa & Jang, 1998).

Although predominantly from a Catholic background, Cuban Americans have one of the lowest fertility rates in the United States and tend to delay childbearing as long as possible. Most Cuban American women work outside the home. Many have careers for which they might delay having children. Also, low fertility rates have been found to "reflect the disruptive impact of migration" (Suárez, 1998, p. 180). Studies have suggested that immigrant women tend to show much lower fertility rates than nonimmigrant women (Suárez). Fear of jeopardizing their ability to provide adequately for their children may be at the basis for Cuban Americans' hesitation to procreate. Another reason for the low fertility rate among Cuban Americans may be a natural decrease in sexual drive caused by the stress of adapting to a new environment combined with working long hours.

Education as a Priority

Cuban American children are generally expected to be successful in their studies. For the upper middle class, education means recovering the status the family had prior to the Cuban revolution, while for working-class Cuban exiles, it means a raise in status so their children don't have to struggle as they did. For most Cuban American parents no sacrifice is too much if it affords a good education for their children and the perpetuation of a comfortable lifestyle for the entire family.

Values

Cuban American children are taught to be personable. *Personalismo* refers to warm, friendly relationships, an appealing personality, and a concern for the individual person rather than for the impersonal institutions that the individual represents.

Personalismo is a concept that also permeates other Latin American cultures, but for Cuban Americans, it is as important as education. Suárez (1998, p. 184) states that for Cubans, "not being personable is a cultural sin." Cubans love to communicate with others. Because of their continuous use of nonverbal expressions and vigorous gestures during conversation, Cubans are sometimes misperceived as being emotionally "out of control." Also, their physical touching of one another may be seen as forward and intrusive by members of other cultures. The personal comfort zone of Cubans encourages close contact as an indication of acceptance, inclusion, and affection.

Generally, Cubans are very child centered and may be overindulgent with their children. Because children are considered to reflect the status of their parents, parents want children to feel and appear happy and well cared for. Young Cuban American children often wear quality clothes and may own computers and trendy toys. Parents will sacrifice their own needs, and some sink into debt, to pay for their child's ballet or piano lessons or to send their children to college.

Today's Cuban American parents—in contrast to more traditional Cubans who seemed in no hurry to see their children grow up—tend to teach their children the value of work early on, as they take "pride in a work ethic that helped many to build themselves back up in their new country" (Suárez, 1998, p. 182). But echoing the machismo of most Latin American societies, Cuban American boys are generally not expected to perform chores within the household. Mothers, however, feel their daughters must learn basic domestic chores such as cooking and cleaning. This tendency still resonates of the outdated notion that girls must marry and successfully manage a household or at least be prepared for that eventuality. Although these gender-specific traditions are slowly being replaced by more modern practices within today's Cuban American family, there is much variation and room for change.

Rites of Passage

The *quince* party is a Cuban tradition to honor a girl's fifteenth birthday. The *quince* party is traditionally seen as a "debut" into what once was considered the age of "suitor receptivity." Although Latinos recognize the importance of an education as more important than finding a husband, many Latino parents still celebrate the event with modest parties. In Cuban American families, the *quince* party resembles a very elaborate wedding celebration. Considerable debt is assumed by parents in order to introduce their daughter into society in a grand way. The party traditionally involves rehearsals, because a choreographed waltz must be performed by fourteen couples. The girls wear gowns and the boys wear matching tuxedoes. For this dance, the pairs twirl and switch partners around the birthday girl and her partner—her father in truly traditional *quinces*. A young man cuts in mid-dance, and the father bows out. After the obligatory dance, the girl and her troupe of dancers parade around the dance floor to be admired. The birthday girl, as would a bride, may then change into more comfortable clothes, as may the other girls involved in the choreography. Numerous friends and family members join in the festivities, which

are characterized by abundant food, drink, and music. If the family can afford it, the party is held in a ballroom, and the birthday girl makes an entrance amidst a fanfare punctuated by flashbulbs. She may arrive on a float designed specifically for the occasion or in a convertible, like a beauty queen. She descends, aided by a young man who escorts her into the ballroom, where she is greeted by a cloud of dry ice and showers of confetti, flashbulbs, cheers, and applause. A popular Cuban saying illustrates the importance of this rite. When a girl is homely, it is said that she was never fifteen years old, so she had no *quince* party.

There is no comparable event in the life of a Cuban boy, although college and sometimes high school graduations may be celebrated with a party or with an outing of the boy's choosing. However, up to the early 1960s a rite of passage did exist that no longer is followed because current times provide increasing opportunities for a boy to initiate himself sexually. In the past, when a boy turned eighteen, his father might arrange an encounter between his son and a prostitute. Among some Cubans this arrangement was considered an acceptable present from a father to a son on his birthday. The tradition, which brought satisfaction to the father, may have caused great anxiety to the son.

In Cuban American families, christenings are also celebrated in a grand way. Traditionally, godparenting is taken very seriously among Cubans. It is expected that the godparents will present their godchild with meaningful gifts on birthdays and Christmas and will inquire about the child's welfare with some regularity. Should one of the parents become unemployed, the godparents are expected to help with the child's needs.

OVERVIEW OF PARENT-CHILD AND EXTENDED FAMILY RELATIONSHIPS

Before the Cuban Revolution of 1959, the average middle-class family in Cuba had much in common with white American families. The ideal family was similar to that depicted on television shows such as *Father Knows Best,* a show that was also popular in Cuba. The father was boss and provider, while the mother stayed home, did the housework, and took care of the children. The only marked difference between the American and the Cuban ideal was that the Cuban family was usually extended. Often the grandparents lived under the same roof with one of their married children or at least in very close proximity to all their children. Both nuclear and extended families were enclosed within a circle of loyalty and unity that often included friends and close neighbors (Bernal, 1984).

Children were always the center of the family. Couples without children were extremely rare and hardly ever remained childless by choice. Children were included in all festivities, as I recall in a fictional account of my own childhood:

Children would be piled on the beds one by one as they dropped asleep anywhere, and the party would continue until dawn. Waking up fully dressed among cousins' arms and legs in a house filled with stale smoke and snoring adults was akin to waking as a happy frog among damp banana leaves. (Bevin, 1998, p. 94)

The extended family and the inclusion of children in most family activities has remained largely unaffected by acculturation among the Cuban American families of today. Living within a large family network may influence social and psychological well-being, and the presence of at least part of this network in the United States "facilitates the continuation of traditional and ethnic values" (Falicov, 1998, p. 158). For Cuban Americans, the fact that some of their extended family may still reside in Cuba is generally a source of concern and heartache, because the network is fragmented and largely out of touch. As quoted by Geldof (1992), Fichu Menocal stated:

We don't mind so much having to start somewhere else, having lost this or that. What we are always sad about is the loss of togetherness, the way of Cuban families. The disruption, being apart, was really most painful. (p. 15)

Cuban American families subscribe, as do all Latin American families, to the concept of *familismo,* which suggests interdependence and emphasizes collective rather than individual obligation and cooperation and affiliation rather than confrontation and competition (Falicov, 1998).

Family Rituals

Family rituals, in turn, validate and reinforce *familismo*. Cuban family tradition dictated that the extended family would get together about once a week. Generally, this custom would prompt a gathering, at the grandparent's household, of "unmarried or married offspring with spouses, children, and drop-in relatives of all ages" (Falicov, 1998, p. 162). In Cuba, when my extended family got together for the holidays, the numbers would reach up to the eighties. Today, those of us who can be reunited from time to time amount to less than twenty. Cuban Americans often attempt these gatherings at least once a year, even when it involves traveling great distances. This unity among extended families is perhaps one of the main contributors to the success of Cuban exiles. Many Cubans rely on their extended family members when they make the transition from Cuba to the United States, and these links usually remain strong in spite of distance and separations.

The Balance Between Familismo and Individualism

For Cuban Americans, the concept of *familismo* is mixed with individualism. Families remain as close as possible, but the Cuban American character needs a dose of

independence as well. This unique blend may stem from a natural affinity felt by Cubans toward Americans and their way of life, which Cubans regarded as desirable. The Cuban brand of individualism translates into "personal pride and self-confidence" (Suárez, 1998, p. 184) and involves the ability to take personal and financial risks away from family counsel. The blending of these dimensions may have some bearing on the success of Cuban immigrants.

Family "enmeshment" is rarely considered an issue in tight-knit Latin American cultures. Among educated Cuban Americans, however, it may be considered pathological, because this group may actually share more American values than any other Latino groups do. As stated by Falicov (1998), "what constitutes 'excessive' connectedness in one culture may have entirely different meanings in another" (p. 163), and there may be different levels of tolerance of enmeshment among Cuban Americans as well, depending on their degree of acculturation.

CHILD-REARING PRACTICES, VALUES, AND CHANGING FAMILY RELATIONSHIPS

Among traditional Cuban child-rearing practices, one of the most different from Anglo culture is the practice of "fattening" children. The notion was that their robust appearance was an indication that their parents were financially comfortable. A slender child was considered undernourished or even sickly, and a mother saw no option but to overfeed the child in order to preserve her reputation as a good mother. This tradition comes directly from Cuba's Spanish heritage, which focused on the quantity and quality of food as an indicator of a father's worth as a provider and a mother's ability to prepare good, nourishing foods. The Spanish practice of, literally, *cebar a un crío* (to fatten a child) thus became part of the Cuban family and has reached younger generations of Cuban Americans. Consequently, many Cuban American schoolchildren are decidedly chubby, and some are likely to overeat into adulthood. Obesity, together with high blood pressure, poor vascular functioning, and other related health complications, is as common among the Cuban American population as it is in other Latin American groups (National Coalition of Hispanic Health and Human Services Organizations, 1988). A common expectation among Cuban Americans is that as soon as a Cuban arrives in the United States after many years of lack and undernourishment, his or her weight will shoot up, perhaps even to pathological levels.

Another very important practice is that of respecting family lineage. Children are expected to respect and obey their parents and grandparents, who subscribe to the belief that *una nalgada a tiempo hace milagros* (a timely spanking can work miracles). In the traditional Cuban parenting style, even when children may be materially indulged, there is little tolerance for a child's disrespect for elders. The methods of corporal punishment vary among Cuban American parents. Usually, it is the mother who spanks, using a slipper or her bare hand on the child's behind. A father's intervention is traditionally reserved for more severe transgressions. Then the father would use a belt on the child's behind and legs, and the child could be grounded for one or two weeks. During the 1950s, it was common practice among wealthy parents to send unruly boys to private schools run by priests, where discipline was strictly enforced through confinement or corporal punishment. Difficult girls, too, would be sent to boarding schools run by nuns. These individuals now may be parents and grandparents of children who have been exposed to more lenient parent-child relationships, and this difference can cause tension.

Cultural Value Differences

Children's ability to quickly adapt to a new culture when arriving in the United States was seen by many Cuban parents as a threat to their traditional family values, especially for the upper class and upper middle class of the first large waves of refugees. Most parents continued to expect their children's absolute obedience in their new country, but teenagers began to rebel against the Cuban culture they now saw as no longer theirs. Family lineage and respect for elders, therefore, was one of the first traditional values to suffer because of exile.

Maintaining cultural conformity with their parents was especially difficult for a number of children who arrived in Florida through Operation Pedro Pan. They struggled upon reacquainting with their own parents after many months or years of separation, especially since some had forgotten most of their Spanish during their lives at camp or foster homes (Conde, 1999). Parents had sent their children away to avoid losing them to the Cuban totalitarian regime. Ironically, some parents later felt they lost their children anyway to a new culture that allowed children "too much freedom." Parental efforts to close the gap by intensifying their demands for obedience disrupted the family even more.

This struggle was not unique to those families who experienced months or years of separation, but also affected families who migrated together. Cuban children naturally associated with American peers in schools and neighborhoods, and they soon began to notice different attitudes among American parents, such as using much less corporal punishment than typical Cuban parents did. Children also learned about child protection laws in the United States and therefore felt less compelled to obey traditional parental rule (Suárez, 1998).

In today's Cuban American family, fewer intergenerational conflicts exist because parents who are in their forties lived their teenage years in the United States, endured their own difficulties with their traditional parents, and are likely to allow their children more freedom and independence. Richmond (1980) found in her study that one of the most important variables "predisposing parents to grant independence was the length of the family's residence in the United States" (p. iii), which correlates with the parents' association with American families.

Attitudes about Sexuality and Gender

Young Cuban Americans, both male and female, are still expected to live at home until they marry. Traditional intolerance of sex before marriage has created one of the most difficult intergenerational gaps to bridge. A positive by-product of this tradition is the very low rate of teenage pregnancy among Cuban American girls. Fathers, brothers, and other relatives assume the right to watch and guard the young girl's reputation by keeping close tabs on her whereabouts.

Regrettably, an overriding value that has resisted change is the traditional Cuban culture's notion of *machismo*. Girls growing up in Cuba knew that they were expected to be chaste until marriage and faithful afterward. However, they also knew that men had license to have affairs and even father illegitimate children. This aspect of the culture is still prevalent among some Cuban American men, although women today are much less likely to accept it than did their mothers and grandmothers.

Cuba, like most Latin countries, is predominantly Catholic and therefore extremely homophobic. Older Cuban Americans, especially, tend to struggle between aversion, tolerance, and acceptance of sexual ambiguity of any kind. Cuban American mothers are far more likely to accept homosexuality in their children than fathers are and will protect their child from his or her father's rejection.

CASE STUDY: THE OTERO FAMILY

The Otero family of South Miami has struggled with intolerance. The oldest son, Miguel, told his mother of his homosexual feelings when he was fourteen. His father had already suspected Miguel's homosexuality; he treated Miguel with contempt and occasionally made fun of his effeminate mannerisms. Miguel rebelled by using drugs, letting his school grades drop, and dying his hair a flamingo pink. Mrs. Otero took Miguel to a therapist to help him deal with his homosexuality, but Miguel's father refused the therapist's invitation to join them in family sessions. Miguel began to spend nights away from home, and his parents separated for a year. Eventually, with the help of his sister, a guidance counselor, Mr. Otero began to understand what his son must have endured. The family was reunited, but Miguel never truly trusted his father again.

Homosexual Cubans, especially those living within the Cuban government's repression, tend toward covert relationships that often last their entire adult life. Some have perpetuated this closeted lifestyle in exile, but the majority of Cuban American homosexuals rejoice in their sexual orientation and tend to live well-adjusted lives within gay or gay-friendly communities.

Parental Divorce and Separation

In traditional Cuba, divorce was rarely considered. When a couple had serious conflict, they were likely to endure rather than separate, sacrificing their own comfort in order to maintain the nuclear family together. The fact that the family might have been essentially dysfunctional because of estrangement between the parents was overlooked for the benefit of appearances. Marital conflict was commonly caused by the husband's infidelity, and the wife often opted for tolerance. This attitude has changed both among Cubans living on the island and for Cuban Americans. In Cuba, divorce and separation are extremely common today. Because of the lack of housing, couples are forced to live in crowded conditions with all or some of their in-laws, parents, and married siblings who may have children of their own. Among Cuban Americans holding to traditional culture, divorce is usually the last resort after all other options have failed. When divorce is inevitable, it is often a time of crisis for the extended family, whereupon they get together to discuss issues surrounding the divorcing couple's children. When the cause of divorce is infidelity, the offending spouse may be shunned by the entire family, at least temporarily. Such was the case of Alvaro, a young attorney living in southern Florida. Married to his high school sweetheart and the father of a two-year-old, Alvaro found himself falling in love with an attorney who had recently joined his firm. When he told his wife, his family as well as hers shunned and isolated him to such degree that his only refuge was his new love interest. He says that the isolation cemented the new relationship and prompted him to ask for a divorce. His own siblings stopped communicating with him for an entire year. Only his mother was approachable, though she constantly reproached him for his irresponsible behavior.

CRISIS EVENTS AND PROBLEM SITUATIONS FOR FAMILIES

The average Cuban family has seen its share of difficult crisis situations. Exile in itself is a crisis of great proportions that is likely to affect individuals over their entire life span. Nuclear families who experienced the trauma of exile together found different ways to alleviate the distress of separation from the larger family network. For some, exile was unifying rather than divisive. Parents unable to afford the quality of life they had enjoyed in Cuba learned to take advantage of free recreational facilities in the United States. Public parks and beaches brought them together at least once a week, and get-togethers with other nuclear families experiencing the upheavals of exile were a great support to many.

Dealing with Loss and Separations

As a result of exile, Cuban children became included in critical family events much earlier than had occurred previously. While still in Cuba, the first family crisis for many was the sudden loss of their property and status. Traditionally, children of the upper classes were sheltered from parental worry, bad news, funerals, and hospital visits. However, exile eliminated that, and Cuban children grew up very quickly.

Throughout the history of Cuban exile, the luckiest of families migrated together, but large numbers migrated one at a time because of exit visa restrictions. After regular flights to Miami were stopped, the transit of intact nuclear families was impossible. Additionally, the military age for men was set between the ages of fifteen and twenty-seven, rendering young males ineligible for exit visas. Hundreds of Cuban parents remained on the island with their military-aged children while entrusting their younger ones to relatives already in the United States. These separations, traumatic enough on their own, led to other complications, such as my own experience following my father's death in 1973. Like many Cuban Americans who have lost parents and siblings who remained on the island, I was unable to join my grieving family in Cuba, since reentry visas were denied by the Cuban authorities, even for funerals.

ADOLESCENCE

Intergenerational conflict has taken a toll among Cuban families. Cuban adolescents quickly embraced the American way and challenged their parents' authority. Some parents, seeking to adapt to their new country, accepted their children's new taste for independence. Others, however, tried to fight the natural evolution that comes with uprooting. They increased their demands for obedience, began to resent their children's peers, and attempted to establish unrealistic rules in an effort to maintain control over their children. Children began to rebel any way they could, and their best weapon turned out to be the English language. Youngsters, feeling smothered by parental vigilance, spoke English with their friends and siblings, leaving their parents largely out of the conversations. Parents fought hard to learn English, but this task was difficult for adults who often had to work two jobs.

Scores of Cuban children gained early maturity in the face of exile. Many had to be responsible for younger siblings or had to care for ill, feeble grandparents while their parents worked. Such was the case of singer Gloria Estefan, who as a child nursed her father, stricken with multiple sclerosis, while her mother worked to support the family. These children earned the confidence of their parents with hard work and loyalty, but a large part of their childhood was lost forever.

An example cited by Conde (1999) is that of her own brother Orlando (p. 84), who escaped his Operation Pedro Pan camp to join Mexican migrant workers in tomato fields in order to pay for his parents' visas to the United States. Other children of Operation Pedro Pan withheld from their parents, when telephone contact was possible, the realities of their lives within abusive or neglectful foster homes. A girl named María Dolores (p. 93) was separated from her older brother upon arriving in Miami through Operation Pedro Pan. She cried for a long time, but then she decided to take the matter into her own hands. She heard of a priest who could help her reunite with her brother, and tried to see him, but the priest was a very busy man. She finally crawled into his office through a window so he would find her there when he came in. And she got her wish to join her brother (p. 94).

Among Cuban Americans, the issue of parental control over teenage children largely depends on the particular family's practices prior to the exile experience. The first arrivals of the early 1960s followed traditional practices that may have changed later. Progressive waves of immigrants from middle and lower classes employed a great variety of parenting styles. On the one hand were the extremely controlling parents, usually middle class and devout Roman Catholics, and on the other, were the professionals, more in touch with the times and able to adapt to the needs of today's children.

PARENTS' TYPICAL EXPECTATIONS AND HOPES FOR THEIR CHILDREN

Typical Cuban American parents are ambitious and expect their children as well to be ambitious and to succeed. Most expect their children to study, work, prosper, find the perfect mate, and have children. They also want their children to be proud of their cultural heritage and to develop their Spanish language skills. The dating or marriages of their children with Americans is seen as a natural progression of events, and in-laws of a different cultural background are generally welcome and absorbed naturally into the extended family circle.

During the first part of the Cuban migration, parents hoped to return quickly and to educate their children Cuban-style. But most who once dreamed of returning to Cuba have long accepted that the dream has vanished. Their children are more American than Cuban and not likely to ever want to live in Cuba. Many of the children were born in the United States and never learned Spanish, while some who were born in Cuba no longer speak it. For many Cuban Americans, however, the hope of returning has survived against great odds. Some dream of retiring in Cuba, while others just want to know they can go back. Carlos García stated to Geldof (1992): "One would like to get up in the morning and find out that this thing is going away like rain. . . . Relations are re-established and we can go to Cuba" (p. 203).

Cuban Americans who return to the island to visit relatives often bring their American-born children with them. The Cuban exile community admits that this experience can be anxiety producing. Parents unrealistically hope that their children will feel as Cuban as they do. The country of their past is now under a repressive grip, but those who return still find what they are looking for, although they may not be able to put it into words. Perhaps it is the *personalismo,* that warm feeling between people who recognize each other as something more than representatives of a system or a way of life. Whatever that something may be, Cubans want their children to share it with them, and they want them to know what it is to feel Cuban. For most Cuban Americans, a return visit or a first-time encounter with the island where his or her parents were born is a humbling, sometimes life-changing experience.

> To me, Cuba had turned into much more than my homeland. It was a concept, a dimension, a place and a time that may or may not have existed. (Bevin, 1998, p. 17)

APPROACHES AND ATTITUDES TO HELP PRACTITIONERS UNDERSTAND AND WORK EFFECTIVELY WITH CUBAN AMERICAN PARENTS

Cuban Americans consider themselves the primary influence over their children and more important than teachers and counselors. They want their interactions with a practitioner to be meaningful and are willing to do their part to help their children be successful. Typical Cuban American parents would like to be treated with honesty and directness, but most of all they expect to be respected as intelligent, educated people.

Among Cubans, domestic violence has traditionally been considered dishonorable. From an early age boys learned that overpowering a weaker person, whether male or female, is unmanly, and they were taught to defend their sisters with courage. Violent behavior among women was traditionally inconceivable. When a woman hit or engaged in physical combat, with the exception of child spanking or a slap in defense of her dignity, she was shunned as "trash." In Cuba, when a man mistreated his wife, he knew that he would have to contend with her male relatives and their particular choice for revenge.

According to the reporter Pedro Juan Gutiérrez (1999), Cubans still living on the island seem to have abandoned these traditions. Mutual abuse in couples is becoming more commonplace, and new arrivals to the United States are bringing this practice with them. As a result, police intervention in domestic disputes among Cubans in southern Florida is on the increase.

An educated Cuban or Cuban American woman would probably not tolerate abuse, physical or otherwise, and would most likely seek help and protection from the appropriate agency if needed. Cuban Americans are likely to seek professional help before requesting advice from their pastor or priest, because they know the difference between words of comfort and words of guidance. In Cuban tradition and folklore, priests are revered as saintly, though sometimes unprepared for real life, while a professional commands respect based on education and experience.

When faced with a learning-disabled child, parents would typically exhaust all possible venues for improvement through special education and counselors, despite the financial sacrifice. Special educator Dania Marrero, a Cuban American and the mother of a child afflicted with Down syndrome, devoted many years of her life solely to her son's education and physical development (D. Marrero, personal interview, February 2000). During those years she met other Cuban American parents with similar problems and equal determination to help their children. The experience motivated her to return to school and make a career of special education. She states that the tendency among Cuban American parents, and especially mothers, is to spare no sacrifice in their quest to provide their learning-disabled child with every possible opportunity for stimulus and advancement. Fathers may tend to stay on the sidelines and expect the mother to do all the work, but many are just as involved with their child's education as the mothers are.

The issue of respect can never be emphasized enough with all Latin Americans. Because of the history of prejudice and discrimination toward Latinos, they tend to be extremely sensitive around the issue of respect. Many Latinos become easily hurt when they interpret a word, a look, or a gesture as disrespectful or patronizing. When such an event happens, the average Central American may simply vanish and never return for an interaction with someone they perceive as an offending practitioner. Cuban Americans, however, are unlikely to simply disappear. They have worked hard for their status, and they consider themselves equal to Americans in every respect. Their tendency would be to file a complaint or express themselves verbally without much restraint.

The Cuban American character is generally optimistic and focused on the present, on results, and on problem solving. Cuban Americans are involved, invaluable allies for practitioners when their children or their family dynamics are at stake. Today, few significant blockages based on divergent belief systems are likely between Americans and today's Cuban American young parents. Cuban Americans have adapted, or want very much to adapt, to their new country in order to join and successfully compete with those in the mainstream. When honesty and respect are at the basis of an interaction, a meaningful rapport can be established for the benefit of the family and child, and the practitioner will feel success in partnership with the Cuban American parent.

Discussion Questions and Role-Play Exercises

1. Mrs. Garza and her two children, Hilda, sixteen, and Gustavo, eleven, were the only survivors of their trip to the United States by raft. Mr. Garza and their oldest daughter, Olga, drowned near the Florida coastline. Mrs. Garza does not tolerate being separated from her children and has communicated her fears to Gustavo. Hilda, on the other hand, rebels by staying out late. How would you proceed with this family so that a balance can be reached?
2. You are a guidance counselor, and a sixth grader comes into your office crying. She is upset because her parents will not sign the permission slip for an overnight field trip. She says her Cuban parents are "paranoid" about her learning too many bad habits from Americans and about horrible things happening to her away from them. How would you proceed?
3. You are a school social worker, and a teacher refers a fifth grader to you because she stole objects from school and from other children. You find out that this child arrived from Cuba with her family in a rickety boat only last year. Why do you think she steals? What would you do? Role-play your first contact with the child and with her parents.
4. An elderly Cuban woman is taken by ambulance to a psychiatric ward. A Spanish-speaking nurse tries to help upon noticing that the woman speaks no English. He soon realizes that the woman is only complaining about a migraine headache while she cries loudly and keeps her hands on her forehead. The woman lives with her son and his family, but they were at work and could not take her to her doctor. How did she end up in a psychiatric ward? What is the next step?

References

Bernal, G. (1984). Cuban families. In M. McGoldrick, J. K. Pierce, and J. Giordano (Eds.), *Ethnicity and family therapy* (pp. 186–207). New York: Guilford Press.

Bevin, T. (1998). *Havana split*. Houston, Texas: Arte Público Press.

Brenner, P., LeoGrande, W. M., Rich, D., & Siegel, D. (1989). Chronology of major events. In P. Brenner, W. M. LeoGrande, D. Rich & D. Siegel (Eds.), *The Cuban reader: The making of a revolutionary society* (pp. 527–35). New York: Grove Press.

Conde, Y. (1999). *Operation Pedro Pan: The untold exodus of 14,048 Cuban children*. London: Routledge.

Falicov, C. J. (1998). *Latino families in therapy: A guide to multicultural practice*. New York: Guilford Press.

Geldof, L. (1992). *Cubans: Voices of change.* New York: St. Martin's Press.

Green, J. W. (1999). *Cultural awareness in the human services: A multi-ethnic approach.* Boston: Allyn & Bacon.

Gutiérrez, P. J. (1999). *Trilogía sucia de La Habana.* Barcelona: Anagrama.

Jaffe, A. J., Cullen, R. M., & Boswell, T. (1980). *The changing demography of Spanish Americans.* New York: Academic Press.

Jiménez-Vásquez, R. (1995). Hispanics: Cubans. In *Encyclopedia of social work* (19th ed.). Washington DC: NASW Press.

National Coalition of Hispanic Health and Human Services Organizations. (1988). *Delivering preventive health-care to Hispanics.* Washington DC: COSSMHO.

Navarro, M. (1999, February 11). Miami's generations of exiles. Side by side, yet worlds apart. *The New York Times,* p. A25.

Olson, J. S., & Olson, J. E. (1995). *Cuban Americans: From trauma to triumph.* New York: Twayne Publishers.

Pérez, L. A., Jr. (1991). *Cuba and the United States. Ties of singular intimacy.* Athens: University of Georgia Press.

Peterson, M. F. (1982). The flotilla entrants: Social psychological perspectives on their employment. *Cuban Studies/Estudios Cubanos, 12,* 81–86.

Richmond, M. L. (1980). *Immigrant adaptation and family structure among Cubans in Miami, Florida.* New York: Arno Press.

Rieff, D. (1993). *The exile: Cuba in the heart of Miami.* New York: Simon & Shuster.

Shinagawa, L. H., & Jang, M. (1998). *Atlas of American diversity.* Walnut Creek, CA: Altamira Press.

Silva, H. (1985). *The children of Mariel from shock to integration: Cuban refugee children in South Florida schools.* Miami: Cuban American National Foundation.

Suárez, Z. E. (1998). Cuban-American families. In R. W. Habenstein, C. H. Mindel, and R. Wright, Jr. (Eds.), *Ethnic families in America* (pp. 172–98). Upper Saddle River, NJ: Prentice Hall.

Native American Families

Parenting in Native American Families

GERI GLOVER

Although all Native Americans share a common history of oppression and discrimination, tribal beliefs and customs vary, as does individual adherence to these beliefs. Some Native Americans have become completely assimilated into the mainstream culture. Others maintain their traditional ways, which have been fairly consistent for centuries. Some families have succumbed to poverty, alcoholism, and disease, which has created dysfunctional family systems that appear to have no cultural foundation at all. As a result of the boarding school era and relocation of young adults to urban areas after World War II, a pan-Indian culture developed. The more common traditional beliefs that were shared by many of the Native American tribes were strengthened and became a unifying force for those separated from relatives and friends.

HISTORICAL OVERVIEW

To understand the Native American family, it is first necessary to look at the history that has so negatively impacted this group of people. Only recently have Native Americans, as a group, challenged the status quo and made strides in changing a situation over which they previously had no control.

In 1540, a Spanish expedition led by Hernando de Soto came to North America and found an organized society along the Mississippi River and down through the delta region. Recent estimates of the total Native American population in the present area of Canada and the United States around A.D. 1500 cluster around the 6 to 7 million figure (Edmunds, 1995). By 1640, when the British and French established their settlements, this society had been decimated by smallpox and disease, and only scattered remnants remained. The United States census of 1900 indicated the Native American population to be only 237,196.

There have been dramatic changes since those early days of devastation. According to 1990 census figures, approximately 2.3 million people now consider themselves to be members of, or closely affiliated with, one of the more than 500 different Native American tribes (Census Bureau, 1994b). Although this group is more rural than other minorities, 55 percent live in urban areas (Harrison, Wilson, Pine, Chan, & Buriel, 1990). The Native American population has doubled during the last two decades, but Native Americans continue to represent less than one percent of the total U.S. population and are the smallest of the five major culture groups.

Prior to 1800, Native Americans living in North and South America had complex functioning economies. The Native Americans of the eastern woodlands had a representative government practiced by the Iroquois Confederacy of five nations: Mohawks, Oneidas, Onondagas, Cayugas, and Senecas (Berger, 1991). A wide variety of foods was produced in both North and South America, and elaborate irrigation systems were operated in the southwest. The social organization for each tribe was internally determined and autonomous, based on the needs and values of the group. Some of the tribes had patrilineal lines of power, some matrilineal, and some unilineal, but all had some sort of clearly defined role system.

Education

Before the boarding school era that caused so much disruption to the Native American family, Puyshmataha, a leader of the Choctaw Nation, had concluded in 1817 that the most effective method of dealing with the European Americans was to send Choctaw children to schools so that they could learn the ways of their adversaries. After about a decade, the Choctaw had schools of their own, taught by Choctaw teachers in both Choctaw and English (Noley, 1992). This brief period of self-determination was terminated when the boarding schools became the preferred mode of education in the late 1800s.

Legislation to Regulate the Native Americans

In 1835, the Removal Policy displaced Native Americans to Indian territory. In 1837, the Dawes Severalty Act allotted each member of an Indian tribe, according to age, a specific portion of land. In doing so, the land base of the Indian people was reduced from approximately 140 million acres to approximately 50 million acres, with the excess land made available to settlers (Monahan, 1981). Proponents of this act assured the public that the Indian would accept individual land holdings and would be completely assimilated. During this allotment period, tribally defined membership was often not accepted by federal officials (Edmunds, 1995). A tribe, for example, may have defined membership in this way: If the Shawnees said you were Shawnee, regardless of your origin or ethnicity, you were Shawnee. With the Dawes Act, federal officials required Native Americans to state their "blood quantum," or *percentage* of Indian ancestry. During the twentieth century, many tribes adopted this government dictum as a regulatory mechanism for their own definition of tribal membership. Blood quantum measures for determining "Indianness" are a controversial issue for many tribes.

Interference with the Native American family has generally occurred through the education system. Efforts to educate focused on "civilizing" and assimilating Native Americans into white society (Reyhner, 1994). The early missionaries and politicians of the late eighteenth and early nineteenth centuries dealt with the original inhabitants as groups devoid of culture and religion. These Europeans did not consider the possibility that they were facing intact, functioning cultures; consequently, they attempted to impose their own cultures and religions on the people they called "Indians" (Noley, 1992).

Boarding Schools

Off-reservation boarding schools, which were established in the United States in the late 1800s, exhibited their greatest growth in the 1920s. The schools were highly authoritative and were run in strict military fashion (National Indian Child Abuse and Neglect Resource Center, 1980). The Canadian Indians suffered a similar fate. Although treaties that had been signed in the 1870s promised schools on the reservations, the government placed emphasis on residential institutions in order to remove the children from the "retrograde" influence of their parents (Miller, 1987).

Dr. Karl Menninger's 1977 speech to the Navajo Nation Health Symposium (as cited in Burgess, 1980) described the interference endured by the Native American family.

> The family is the most wonderful educational and character shaping institution of human life. . . . It is similar everywhere in the world because it is biologically the same. It is the unit of human social life. In most cultures, the family structure . . . is not interfered with or impaired by design; accidentally sometimes, by death or disaster or war . . . but not by human intention. In the case of the American Indians, however, it has been interfered with, purposely—with good intention, no doubt, but we psychiatrists think wrongly and harmfully, however well intentioned. (p. 71)

In the 1930s a growing attitude of tolerance and a desire to learn more about the Indian population resulted in an attempt to bring an understanding of Indian cultures to the government schools (National Indian Child Abuse and Neglect Resource Center, 1980). Federally funded boarding schools began to close. The Johnson-O'Malley Act of 1934 allocated federal funds for public school education of Native American students. Bilingual education, recognition of the importance of family, and other ideas began to find their ways into the schools operated by the

Bureau of Indian Affairs (BIA). Unfortunately the onset of World War II ended the activities that had been designed to be more culturally appropriate for Native American students. Noley (1992) surmised that the postwar conservatism of Congress was not friendly to the enhancement of diversity in America.

Post–World War II

Large numbers of Native American people participated in World War II and the Korean conflict and were exposed to life off the reservation and out of the rural areas where most had lived prior to the wars. In the 1950s, the G.I. Bill and the BIA Relocation Program for Job Training moved significant numbers of Native Americans to large urban areas, away from the support of the extended family system and the Indian community.

During the period from 1958 to 1968, the Child Welfare League of America supported the Indian Adoption Project (George, 1997). The league's philosophy was that the "forgotten child" on the reservation should be adopted and placed where there was less prejudice against Indians. The west was regarded to be the most prejudiced area, so children were often placed far from their birth homes. In determining placement, the "best interests of the child" were to be considered. Poverty was judged a factor leading to neglect and abuse, and most Native Americans were poor. Middle-class whites were often chosen as the more beneficial placement.

Other factors contributed to interstate and out-of-culture adoptions. After WWII transracial adoptions of Asian children became more acceptable (George, 1997). Adoption outside the tribes would be a solution to welfare concerns. Tribal resistance was also changing. The concept of illegitimacy was slowly taking over where it previously had not been an issue, and many Native American leaders wanted an alternative to the life of poverty their children currently faced. As a result of these new attitudes and with the support of the Child Welfare League of America, Native American children were removed in large numbers from their homes. By 1970 a nationwide survey by the Association of American Indian Affairs revealed that 25 percent to 35 percent of all Native American children had been separated from their families (Abourezk, as cited in Johnson, 1991). In Minnesota during 1971–1972, one in four Native American infants under one year of age was placed for adoption, and 90 percent of those infants were placed in non-Indian homes.

In 1978 this unprecedented removal of children from their families was halted by the Indian Child Welfare Act (ICWA). The preface to ICWA reads:

> There is no resource that is more vital to the continued existence and integrity of Indian tribes than their children . . . an alarming high percentage of Indian families were broken by the removal, often unwarranted, of their children from them by non-tribal public and private agencies . . . an alarming high percentage of such children are placed in non-Indian foster and adoptive homes and institutions; and . . . the states . . . have often failed to recognize

the essential tribal relations of Indian people and the cultural and social standards prevailing in Indian communities and families (George, 1997).

The Indian Education Act of 1972 followed the publication of a widely publicized government study, *Indian Education: A National Tragedy—A National Challenge,* popularly known as the Kennedy report (U.S. Senate, 1969). This act was intended to encourage the public schools to become more involved in the provision of activities designed to meet the unique and culturally specific educational needs of Native American children. In 1975 the U.S. Congress passed the Indian Self-Determination and Education Assistance Act that actually permitted Native American nations to control their own schools. Still, many Native American students either dropped out or were pushed out of schools that were not culturally sensitive in their approach to academic, social, cultural, and spiritual development. Significantly more Native American students were successful in schools that respected and supported the students' language and culture (Reyhner, 1994).

In the late twentieth century, changing legal interpretation of tribal sovereignty offers Indian communities new economic opportunities such as tax-free enterprise zones and gaming (Edmunds, 1995). Smaller mixed-blood communities that are relatively acculturated have clung to their Indian identity, have joined with the more established tribes, and have become a powerful economic and political force. The current trends in Native American education are fairly positive. Those who were targeted by the government and the missionaries to conform were able to master the basics of the white society and economy, although at great pain and cost. Now they have emerged as a new generation of leaders, often schooled in residential institutions but devoted to the preservation of their people as Native Americans (Miller, 1987).

Current Status

It is sad that even though beneficial changes have occurred for Native Americans, statistics continue to show a struggling population. One-half of the Native American population is under eighteen years of age, compared to 26 percent for the population in general (Census Bureau, 1994a, 1994b). The birth rate among young Native American women between the ages of fifteen and twenty-four is 1.7 times greater than the national average. Native American families are nearly three times more likely to live in poverty than American families are. Unemployment for Native Americans is twice the national average. Although the number of high school graduates has increased significantly since 1960, the dropout rate is 35.5 percent, whereas the national average is 25 percent. In urban high schools the dropout rate for Native Americans is as high as 51 percent (National Center for Educational Statistics, 1988).

Tuberculosis, pneumonia, influenza, and malnutrition are significantly more prevalent in the Native American population than in the general population. Diabetes, alcoholism, heart disease, liver disease, suicide, and accidents all contribute to a short life expectancy of forty-four years of age (Horejsi, Craig, & Pablo, 1992).

More than one-third of all deaths are of individuals under age forty-five, which is three times the rate of the general population (Campbell, 1989). The alcoholism mortality rate is 6.3 times higher than for other races (Harvey, Harjo, & Jackson, 1990; May, 1996). Cirrhosis of the liver is 3.5 times higher, homicide 1.5 times higher, and suicide 1.4 times higher than for the general population. The mortality rate in motor vehicle accidents is 2.6 times higher, and infant (age one month to one year) mortality is 29 percent higher (Snipp, 1996).

These deaths result in an endless stream of funerals and grief (Horejsi, 1987). The emotional impact is even more intense because of the bonds by blood, marriage, and long friendships that typify Native American life. These frequent losses diminish a person's coping capacity because there is no time to recover from a loss before another occurs. This situation may partially account for the population's high rate of depression (Indian Health Service, 1990). The severity of mental health problems in Native American children and adolescents is illustrated by these statistics from one state: Only 7 percent of the children are Native American, but 45 percent of the children served by the state psychiatric adolescent unit and 65 percent of the children in residential placement for mental health problems are Native Americans (Indian Health Services, 1990).

Hopes for the Future

Native Americans have the same hopes and dreams for their children and families that the general population does. Most want their children to get a good education and become productive members of society. In the more traditional families, these desires include learning about tribal values, beliefs, and customs. These families want successful children in a manner consistent with cooperative, noncompetitive tribal, community, and family values and aspirations (Burgess, 1980).

PARENTING AND FAMILY ISSUES

Like parents in other minority cultures, Native American parents often take an active role in socializing their children regarding the consequences of their ethnicity in the larger society (Harrison et al., 1990). Oppression provides the context of teaching about the assaults of mainstream culture. Parents teach their children to watch for subtle clues about whether they are welcome in a given situation (Cross, 1995).

As Native American children mature, they are more knowledgeable about differences in race, and they come to identify themselves with a particular tribe; however, they appear to prefer toys, activities, and friendships from the dominant culture (Farris, Neuhring, Terry, Bilecky, & Vickers, 1980; Spencer & Markstrom-Adams, 1990). Native parents (as cited in Dawson, 1988) emphasize the importance of self-esteem in their children: "If my children are proud, if my children have an identity, if my children know who they are and if they are proud to be who they are, they'll be able to encounter anything in life" (p. 48).

"Three Generations" by Bob Felice, 75th Gallup Intertribal
Indian Ceremonial, August 1996. Used with permission.

Positive self-esteem provides confidence, energy, and optimism to master life's tasks. This positive sense of self and confidence is important for parents as well as children. Parents who feel competent in their parenting are more able to involve themselves in their children's lives outside the home. Native American parental involvement is critical to the future educational development of their children (Dawson, 1988).

CASE STUDY: PARENTAL INVOLVEMENT

A Southern Ute adolescent female was automatically identified by her school administration as part of a group of disruptive Southern Ute teens because of her appearance. Initially, the mother of this girl verbally attacked the school administration in defense of her daughter. A counselor knew that this girl was a hardworking and responsible student and understood the mother's anger and frustration. With the support of the counselor, the initial crisis was resolved. The mother appreciated that her concerns were heard and action was taken. The counselor also encouraged the mother to become involved as a parent member of a school-based committee that brought parents, teachers, community members, and administration together to create a better environment for their children. Having Native American parents on committees in a community where there are many Native American families ensures these families a voice.

Interfacing with the Dominant Culture

Native American families believe that their children must have the opportunity to grow into adulthood with the understanding that they are worthwhile individuals who are equal to all other Americans. Native American children must believe that they are respected for their culture, as they respect the worth of others. They must believe that they are valued in American society and that they can achieve in any way they choose according to their individual talents (Noley, 1992).

Native American children view themselves more negatively than do their dominant culture counterparts, and the self-concept of Native American children is negatively correlated with chronological age and years of schooling (Lefley, 1974; Luftig, 1983). Soares and Soares (1969) found that despite living in poverty, disadvantaged children in elementary school did not necessarily suffer from lower self-esteem and a lower sense of self-worth. These findings suggest that simply being poor is not the dominant factor in the low self-esteem of Native American students. Typical methods for supporting increased self-esteem, such as increasing popularity with children from the dominant culture or learning how to give self praise, have proven to be ineffective for Native American children (Luftig). Luftig suggested that a truly pluralistic school environment would be the most effective solution to increasing the self-esteem of Native American students because it would support the culture of the student, the culture of the teacher, and the norms of the school. This environment would help the Native American student learn to interact successfully in both cultures.

All too often, the school experience teaches Native American children that the dominant society does not understand and does not value their culture and traditions (Dawson, 1988; Horejsi et al., 1992). An education system that teaches to the majority can easily alienate a student who does not quite fit in. Many reservation schools that are being controlled by the tribes are adapting curriculum and teaching methods to meet the cultural needs of their children. Increased involvement of parents and elders is encouraged. The introduction of native language, history, arts, and crafts instills a sense of pride and helps in the development of a bicultural identity. This organized educational effort is not available to students who live in the urban areas, however, where there may be only a small number of Native Americans in a school. In addition, the effects of poverty, unemployment, and dysfunctional family systems due to alcoholism are more pronounced in urban areas because of the higher cost of living and the lack of family and community support.

A college education is not necessarily the goal of all Native American children, especially those who reside on reservations in rural areas of the United States. Even among nontraditional Native Americans, the desire to remain close to family and friends in a familiar setting is very strong. For many Native Americans, art is a viable career path. Native American arts and crafts have become very popular and are an important source of income.

Keeping Young People Close to the Tribe

Many tribes have recognized the vital role of employment in the Native American community as a way of holding adolescents and young adults in the tribe (Berlin, 1987). These tribes have found ways of capitalizing on natural resources and identifying the needs of the dominant society. A degree may then become more valuable. However, leaving for college for two to eight years with the intention of returning to live and work on the reservation can be a daunting feeling for Native American youth. The high premium that is placed on achievement in typical dominant culture academic institutions can cause conflict with tribes and families (LaFromboise & Low, 1998). Being praised for success may bring estrangement from home. Some family members may actively discourage ambitions that involve leaving family and home. The failure to meet community expectations can cause dissent or guilt over noncompliance.

One solution to this problem of leaving home for higher education is to bring the higher education facility to the reservation, as they have done in northern Montana. Salish Kootenai College is centrally located on the Flathead Reservation and offers degrees in business, nursing, and Native American studies among others. Other colleges, such as Fort Lewis College in Colorado, specifically recruit Native American students. Fort Lewis provides special programs, cultural events, and support systems to meet the needs of its Native American students.

A small percentage of Native Americans do complete college and go on for advanced degrees in medicine, law, science, business, and education. Some return to the reservations and others do not. The preference of the families would be for their children to remain nearby. Overall, families support an education system that does not take their children away, yet prepares them for a world outside the Native American community.

PARENTING AND FAMILY RELATIONSHIPS

Several studies have shown that Native American parents from various tribes display parenting styles and attitudes that are similar to the dominant culture (Peterson, 1984; Strom, Griswold, & Slaughter, 1981). The difference appears to be in the degree to which these attitudes are acted on in the actual parenting of children. All parents want their children to be generous, be respectful, get along with others, and make responsible choices. Traditional Native families actively teach by modeling and storytelling from the earliest moments of a child's life that these particular values are essential and paramount to being Indian. However, the influence of the dominant culture is strong, and conflicts arise between parents and children related to differing values. Of course, Native Americans cannot go back to the world the way it was, but they continue to value many old child-rearing traditions.

Native Americans traditionally believed that children were special gifts from the creator. Tribal elders used praise and reassurance to encourage a positive loving relationship between parents and children (Northwest Indian Child Welfare Institute, 1986). Prophecies were often made about the worth of a child. The whole community recognized the child's growth and development through rites of passage ceremonies. Naming ceremonies helped the child to establish a role or identity in the tribe. Cradle boards were used to keep newborn infants close. Although cradle boards are uncommon today, infants continue to be held rather than left alone in car seats or strollers. Through storytelling, children learned about proper relationships with other people and the environment. Moral development received especially careful and constant attention. Children were taught to be good observers and to understand the meaning of nonverbal communication. Child-rearing patterns from the past continue to provide strong models for parenting today.

Levels of Acculturation

All Native Americans have become acculturated in varying degrees into the dominant culture; however, the level of acculturation depends on the strength of the family's support systems and the degree of their own conviction about maintaining their traditions. When a family enters the dominant culture, they necessarily make adjustments in their behavior to fit into their new community. M. W. Garrett (1995) describes the following four levels of acculturation.

1. At the *traditional level,* a person holds onto only traditional beliefs and values.
2. At the *transitional level,* a person holds both traditional beliefs and values and those of the dominant culture, but they may not accept *all* of either culture.
3. The third level is *bicultural.* The person is accepted by the dominant culture and also knows and practices traditional ways.
4. The fourth level of acculturation is *assimilation,* that is, embracing *only* dominant cultural beliefs and values.

Although it is true that Native Americans exhibit different levels of acculturation, Native American parents do express interest in traditional values as important in child rearing. In 1982, Kellogg, under the direction of the National American Indian Court Judges Association, conducted a survey to identify parenting and skills development programs and materials that had been implemented in Native American communities. Eighteen programs in thirteen states were evaluated to determine what Native American parents look for in parenting programs. All sites expressed a desire for more culturally relevant materials. The incorporation of tribal elders and tribal members as trainers was highly recommended, as was making comparisons between traditional and modern values.

Values

The Native American sitting in front of the practitioner may not be traditional, and even if the person is traditional, the practitioner needs to learn what "tradition" means for this particular person. An understanding of traditional Native American values is essential if practitioners wish to provide optimal services for Native American families. The traditional Native American values that are presented here include:

- generosity
- respect for elders
- respect for all creation
- harmony
- individual freedom

It is difficult to separate these values and describe each individually because they are interwoven, interconnected, and related to Native American spirituality and tribalism.

All aspects of traditional Native American life take on religious and spiritual significance (Harrison et al., 1990). Religion and culture are intimately connected, with tribal spirituality being the same as tribal life (Harrison et al.; Hungry Wolf & Hungry Wolf, 1987). All things have a spiritual nature that demands respect. This respect is extended to children as well as to the earth and creatures from the land, sea, and sky. Traditional values show the importance of honoring through harmony and balance what is believed to be a very sacred connection with the energy of life (M. T. Garrett & Wilbur, 1999).

Tribalism is a pervasive cultural attitude or interactional style that emphasizes the primacy of the extended family and kinship relations over individualism. Everything is intimately connected, biologically, spiritually, and emotionally. A person is not an isolated being, but comes attached to families, households, communities, and the group. Native American families are characterized as collective, cooperative, social networks that branch out from the mother and father to the extended family, to the community, to the tribe (Harrison et al., 1990). This kinship system combines relatives of either or both parents' families, and often nonrelated friends, in a network of responsibility and interdependency (Harrison et al.; Red Horse, 1980).

Within the context of Native American spirituality and tribalism, high value is placed on *generosity and sharing*. A person who is generous gives honor to the great spirit, to the recipient, and to self. Prestige was accorded to those who gave unreservedly (Brendtro, Brokenleg, & Van Bockern, 1990). Children were taught from an early age to share generously.

> When a young girl picked her first berries and dug her first roots, they were given away to an elder so she could share her future success. When a child carried water for the home, an elder would give compliments and pretend to taste meat in the water carried by a boy or berries in that of a girl.
> —Mourning Dove, Salish (1888–1936; as cited in Borgenicht, 1993, p. 57)

The dominant culture, which defines success by wealth and possessions, may find it difficult to accept the values of simplicity, generosity, and nonmaterialism, but these values have helped sustain the Native American people through generations of economic and personal hardship. The concept of generosity is continued today. On the Flathead Reservation, if a person tells you three times that they like something that you have, you honor yourself and that person by giving the item to the person who has made the comments. "Giveaways" are still very common at special events such as naming ceremonies. The infant, through his or her family, provides gifts to all who come to the ceremony. As a sign of both respect and generosity, when a young person completes a first piece of beadwork or leather work, it is given away, often to the person who taught the craft.

Great *respect* is shown *to the elders* of a tribe. Young children are taught that age is a gift, a badge of honor (Burgess, 1980). To have grown old indicates that a person has done the right things, pleased the creator, and lived in tune with nature and others. Elders are expected to give advice and counsel. Grandparents teach about nature and tell stories of creation and culture. They have wisdom regarding order and balance that they have learned from the mountains, rivers, trees, and wind. These structured teaching and learning experiences are supported by the parents and not interrupted. Elders are sought when things come undone. They often provide child care and financial support. They are role models and have a modulating effect when there is family strife.

Respect for others is a prominent traditional Native American value. The National Indian Child Abuse and Neglect Resource Center (1981) issued the following statement:

> Native American people have traditionally held a great respect for all peoples. We have a tradition of respect in our culture and in our spirituality. We respect the earth, elders, children, animals, all of life. We have lost some of this respect along with our languages and many of our customs. But it is not too late to maintain those which are left and to use traditional concepts of respect in raising children. (p. 6)

Harmony is valued because everything is related, and it is important that all things be in balance. Traditional Native Americans operate in a relational model that is intuitive, nontemporal, and fluid (Cross, 1997). Balance and harmony among multiple variables, including individuals, family, community, nature, and metaphysical forces, is necessary for health (Cross; Sanchez, Plawecki, & Plawecki, 1996). The weakness of this relational model is that it seeks harmony even at the expense of the individual (Cross).

The most controversial value, especially when taken out of the context of Native American spirituality and tribalism, is that of *individual freedom,* or noninterference. Any person, even a young child, is free to make choices, but the person must accept responsibility for the choice made. In the context of tribalism, the correct choice has benefits for the family, friends, or group.

One might act different from what is considered right, but such acts would bring upon the person the censure of the Nation. This censure acted as a mighty band, binding all in one social, honorable compact.

—George Copway, Ojibwa Chief (1818–1863; as cited in Borgenicht, 1993, pp. 54, 55)

Social control of children is minimal and applied subtly. In the collective, cooperative, and noncompetitive Native American society, the family, and through it the tribe, becomes the primary social and educational organization (Burgess, 1980). For Native Americans, warnings about the consequences of bad behavior are presented in community terms identifying how others might view the behavior. Rarely is a threat of physical punishment made. Shame, otherwise known as embarrassment, is a common disciplinary tool.

Discipline

Discipline may be administered in ways and in forms not noticeable to outsiders. Native American children are not punished often, nor are they in continual fear of punishment. Hoffman (1977) notes that there are only three ways of disciplining children: (1) power assertion, (2) love withdrawal, and (3) inductive discipline (e.g., learning how your behavior affects others). Native Americans have practiced inductive discipline for thousands of years. Disciplining might include disapproving words, ignoring the child, or requiring the child to give restitution for wrongdoing, such as apologizing to members of family for embarrassing them. Parents may pass information of the indiscretion on to another family member who then dispenses the punishment. This is done to protect the bonds between the parent and child and to reinforce the extended family involvement (LaFromboise & Low, 1998).

The Extended Family

Child-rearing practices among Native Americans have been closely related to the extended family concept and in that respect have depended on more than just the parents of the children in the role of parenting. Parents generally have the primary responsibility of child rearing. Uncles and aunts, one of whom may be designated as a character builder, are important teachers and mentors who share values, impart wisdom, serve as role models, and reinforce tribal teaching (LaFromboise & Low, 1998). Grandmothers and aunts often provide child care. Grandparents and elders are the safekeepers of tribal songs and stories, which they share with children through the oral tradition. For some, the extended family has become a thing of the past, and consequently some Native American parents have found it more and more difficult to be "good parents" (National Indian Child Abuse and Neglect Resource Center, 1980).

For many tribal communities, gender was socially constructed, not biologically determined (Edmunds, 1995). These communities appeared less patriarchal than those of the early Europeans. Women had more freedom and more authority and were more respected. The status of women in the tribes declined after European contact; however, women have actively, creatively, and often successfully resisted marginality. Native American women continue to exert powerful influence within their communities.

Autonomy

The dominant culture often shows concern about the relative freedom given to a Native American child and the apparent lack of parental concern about the child's behavior. What appears as excessive permissiveness or indulgence, however, may consist of allowing children to develop in a healthy way. Autonomy is highly valued, and children are allowed to make their own decisions and operate semi-independently at an early age with the freedom to experience natural consequences (LaFromboise & Low, 1998). During twelve years of working with Eskimo families in Alaska, Briggs (as cited in Sprott, 1994) found that children are not prevented from making mistakes unless the mistake might be life-threatening. Children have abundant opportunities to make choices without coercion because adults believe that making a decision for a child will make the child weak (Brendtro et al., 1990). Maslow described this process of teaching personal autonomy and responsibility by relating the following story:

> I can remember . . . a toddler trying to open a door to a cabin. He could not make it. This was a big, heavy door, and he was shoving and shoving. Well, Americans would get up and open the door for him. The Blackfoot Indians sat for half an hour while the baby struggled with that door, until he was able to get it open himself. He had to grunt and sweat, and then everyone praised him because he was able to do it himself. (as cited in Brendtro et al., 1990, p. 42)

Native American families continue to be consistently different from the dominant culture in supporting autonomy. Gfellner (1990) found that Native American parents demonstrated a more liberal child-rearing ideology than did white parents. The dominant culture often perceives this attitude as a lack of parental concern about the child's behavior. The act of disparaging child-rearing preferences of a cultural group strikes at the group's sense of esteem and indirectly challenges their right to exist, because a society perpetuates itself by the way it socializes its children (Sprott, 1994). What appears to be excessive permissiveness or indulgence, in fact, may be a healthier and more effective way to promote the development of children (Burgess, 1980). Rohner, Chaille, and Rohner (1980) found that children raised in a warm, accepting, and nurturing environment exhibited more positive social skills. Children's internal locus of control increased significantly with their perceptions of increased parental acceptance. Cox (1970) found that the self-concept of a child was highly related to parental acceptance or rejection.

DEVELOPMENTAL EXPECTATIONS

Like many aspects of traditional Native American culture, the Medicine Wheel (figure 9.1) depicts different developmental stages (BigFoot Sipes & Willis, 1993). The four directions are guides for the four stages of life. Creation starts in the east or southeast and moves clockwise until the circle is complete. The east or southeast direction is associated with birth and new learning. The south or southwest direction is associated with youth and young adulthood, when individuals begin making choices about their adult lives and learning from mistakes. The west or northwest direction presents adulthood, when individuals apply their learning and teach their families. The north or northeast direction is known for its wisdom, aging, and death. It is the end of the life and the circle.

Coyhis (1997) compares Erikson's (1963) eight stages of development and the Medicine Wheel. The baby and young child are developing trust, autonomy, and initiative. The youth and young adult are working through the stages of industry and identity. The adult is negotiating the stages of intimacy and generativity, while the eighth stage of integrity corresponds to the role of the elder in native tradition. Erikson found the parenting style of the Dakota Sioux to be supportive of positive development through at least his first three stages. He described early childhood as a rich and spontaneous existence. The child emerged from the family with relative integration, that is, with much trust, a little autonomy, and some initiative.

Givelber (1983) described the process of developing self-esteem in the context of the parent-child relationship as one in which the parent accepts the child as a separate individual at the child's current level of functioning while encouraging the child to become more mature.

ADOLESCENCE

Adolescence can be an especially difficult time for Native American youth, because at this time of their lives they are on a quest to determine who they are as individuals (identity formation). There are a number of alternatives available to most individuals, many of which are determined by the social and cultural environment. For Native American youth, values of the dominant culture, such as material wealth as a sign of achievement, have become attractive. The ways that are supported by tradition and the new ways of living and satisfying daily needs often conflict. Some adolescents in tribal communities find themselves caught between the traditional ways and the new ways, neither of which has worked for their parents (Berlin, 1987). There is often no alternative but to leave the reservation for urban areas in order to earn a living at a time when they would be better supported through Erikson's (1963) stages of development, which include forming an identity and developing intimate relationships, if they could remain with their family and friends.

The turbulent age of adolescence can result in significant problems for Native American youth. According to Horejsi (1987), low self-esteem, frequent use of alcohol, and disenchantment with school pulls teens into irresponsible sexual activity and early parenthood. Traditionally, the problems of the youth become prob-

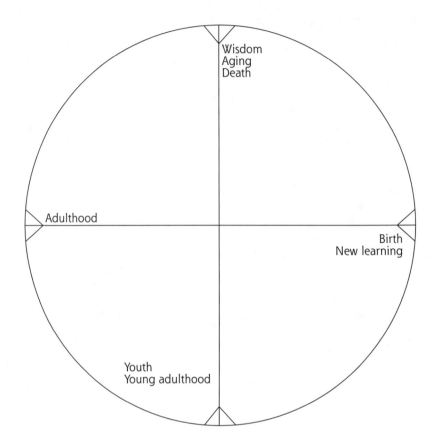

Figure 9.1. The Medicine Wheel

Adapted from Coyhis, D. (1997). The developmental cycle: Teachings on the eight stages of growth of a human being. *Winds of Change: AISES, 19th Annual National Conference Issue,* 12(4) 114–119.

lems of the community (Gibbs & Huang, 1998). Family and friends all join together to draw the young person back into activities of the group. Children who were placed in foster care or adopted by dominant-culture families often feel totally alone when they reach adolescence. They become subject to ethnic confusion and a sense of abandonment (Burgess, 1980). They are neither white nor Indian.

The high number of suicides among young Native Americans reflects the unsuccessful negotiation of Erikson's stage of identity development. Suicide rates are highest for Native Americans in their twenties and early thirties (Horejsi, 1987). These young adults find themselves insufficiently equipped for the world, especially if they attended schools that did not respect their culture. May's (1987) research, however, shows that those who come from tribes classified as traditional (maintaining the old ways) are less likely to commit suicide than are youths from transitional (neither highly traditional nor modern) or acculturated tribes.

Brendtro et al. (1990) believe that adolescents desperately need the guidance and support of their families, friends, and community. A strong foundation of self-esteem becomes the avenue to a productive and satisfying life. Coopersmith's (1967) foundations of self-esteem have been compared by Brendtro et al. to Native American empowerment values. Significance is related to belonging, competence to mastery, power to independence, and virtue to generosity. In the spirit of belonging, treating others as though they are relatives forges powerful social bonds of community and relationships of respect. In the spirit of mastery, adults must provide an environment that offers opportunities for meaningful achievement. In the spirit of independence, youth need opportunities to develop skills and the confidence to assert self-discipline. In the spirit of generosity, youth need opportunities to experience the joy that comes from helping others.

ABUSE AND NEGLECT ISSUES

A report from the Oakland Urban Indian Center (as cited in National Indian Child Abuse and Neglect Resource Center, 1980) identifies factors involved in Indian child abuse that include a special form of immaturity and associated dependency among Native American parents that precipitated from the boarding school era. This immaturity is compounded by the rising number of teenage pregnancies, tragically low self-esteem, and a sense of incompetence resulting from a feeling of racial inferiority imposed by the dominant culture over the past centuries. Additional factors include the following:

- difficulty in adjusting to the demands of the dominant culture, which is seen as being exclusive and requiring assimilation
- social isolation from the extended family or any other support community to assist in child rearing
- lack of parenting skills
- fear of spoiling the child
- belief in the value of corporal punishment
- difficulty accepting responsibility for their own lives

Those parents who spent much of their childhood in boarding schools were deprived of an opportunity to experience family life. They reached adulthood without a clear concept of appropriate parenting behavior and family functioning. The boarding school effectively destroyed the intergenerational transmission of family and parenting knowledge (George, 1997; Horejsi et al., 1992). Boarding schools also introduced new and dysfunctional behaviors, such as sexual abuse and the use of severe corporal punishment.

Poverty

In addition to the dysfunctional behaviors just described, poverty places families under great stress; shapes their behavior, attitudes, and expectations; and forces them to devote an inordinate amount of time and energy to the tasks of day-to-day survival (Horejsi et al., 1992). The hopelessness and helplessness that can stem from pervasive poverty sometimes leads an individual to alcohol as a means of escape. Coping with this hopelessness leaves little room for thoughtful parenting. Without modeling from parents, these new parents repeat what they have been taught, the authoritative and punitive style of behavior control of the boarding school. Tribal judges and attorneys have made a connection between alcoholism and depression, and child neglect and abuse (Berlin, 1987). When the children of these parents are found to be neglected and abused, they are removed from the home, and often the tribe, and placed with non-Indian families rather than sent to boarding schools. They may thrive for a time, until they come to the point in their lives at which they seek their identity. This stage is difficult because they do not belong to the dominant culture, and yet they know nothing of their native culture. They will most likely encounter identity confusion, which stalls their development and perpetuates the negative cycle of poor parenting.

In order to begin to interrupt this cycle, agencies must work hard to keep Native American children within their tribes when they must be removed from abusive or neglectful parents. If family or tribal members are not available, the child may be placed with another tribe. This placement at least keeps the child in a familiar context and with people who can support the child's development within the Native American culture.

Although directives exist for placing Native American children in foster care, the system does not always work. The following case study is not unusual.

CASE STUDY: FOSTER CARE

The Fox family was involved in the social service system because of possible medical neglect issues regarding their eight-year-old son, James. It was determined that James's condition could be treated with medication. However, the family system was disorganized, and James did not receive the prescribed medication on a regular basis. A death had occurred in the family, which disrupted things even more. The professionals involved perceived the family dysfunction to be severe and recommended removal of the child to a therapeutic foster home. Because no therapeutic foster homes were available on the reservation, James was placed with a non-Indian family in a predominantly white community off the reservation.

In order to make the transition go smoothly, the foster parents were instructed and agreed to have one of James's family members come to spiritually cleanse the foster home prior to his arrival. In addition, the foster parents were told of the great importance of hygiene and hair care. James's hair was long, in the traditional fashion. Even though it is generally expected that he would have cut his hair as a sign of mourning for the death of a relative, in this case the family had decided not to do so. Also, during this period of mourning, James would not be able to participate in any of the traditional dances; however, after the appropriate time, he could resume this activity.

Initially, the foster parents made the special arrangements for James. However, with inconsistent contact with family on the reservation, James's education in traditional values and beliefs was erratic. The foster family, not being a part of the Native American community, was not aware of tribal events, opportunities for dancing, or traditional ceremonies. An extraordinary effort would have to be made on the part of the foster family in order to keep James involved in the tribe. This effort would be difficult and disruptive. Although the family accepted the child as he was, they were unable to meet these additional needs. The opinions of the professionals were that the child's medical need outweighed his need for familial, cultural, and tribal support, and thus their only option was removal.

Because there were not enough grounds to have the parents' rights terminated and because the professionals continued to be concerned about James's medical needs, he remained in the foster care system for more than two years. During this time, he was placed with two different dominant-culture families off the reservation. James was exposed to very little about his own culture and developed a strong interest in computers and video games. He wanted to fit in with his peers at his school, so he adopted their style of dress and eventually cut his hair so that he would not draw attention to himself.

James was returned to his family at the age of eleven, when he was considered old enough to manage his own medication with monitoring from his medical doctor. James was a stranger in his own home. He did not know his younger siblings very well and seemed to have very different interests than those around him. His parents felt he had become disrespectful, and he was no longer interested in dancing or participating in any of the traditional ceremonies. James's parents felt that he was of an age that he could make many of his own decisions. They respected his individuality and did not force him to join activities for which he had no interest, although it caused them great pain. This style of noninterference left James with few, if any, boundaries, and he quickly became involved with other children who had lost respect for their parents and their culture. The outcome for James does not look good.

Had the professionals in this case been more sensitive to the repercussions of removing a child not only from his home but from his culture, they may have chosen a different alternative. Because administration of medication was the primary reason for removal, a nurse from Indian Health Services could have been given the assignment to ensure that medication was administered either at James's home or at school. If the family had been truly uncooperative and James needed to be placed in foster care because of his medical condition, a family or tribal placement with additional assistance from the Indian Health Services nurse may have alleviated the need for his removal from the reservation.

One additional abuse issue that affects many Native Americans is Fetal Alcohol Syndrome (FAS). As knowledge of the cause of FAS has grown, significant efforts have been made by tribes to enact early intervention programs to avoid this preventable condition. With education and intervention, it is hoped that there will be a steady decline in this tragic problem. Currently, children who are affected by FAS are identified and special services are offered as soon as possible.

IMPLICATIONS FOR PRACTITIONERS

In *A National Plan for Native American Mental Health Services* (1990), the Indian Health Service recognized that the incidence and prevalence of mental health problems and family disruption is high, in part because of the conflicts between traditional and Western practices. To illustrate this process, Cross (1997) contends that

> Western helping methods split the person. We give physicians the body, educators and psychologists the mind, social workers the context, and clergy the spirit. Each looks at the same person and finds different problems and different solutions. Physicians medicate them away, educators teach them away, psychologists counsel them away, social workers advocate them away, and clergy pray them away—and each is unable to communicate effectively to the other what the problems are or what to do about them. (p. 30)

In treatment, the concept of level of acculturation once again becomes an issue. There must be harmony between the treatment and the person's degree of acculturation (Williams & Ellison, 1999). In the traditional family, illness equals imbalance and is a function of the person's perception of being unable to fulfill traditional role obligations. The intervention is designed to restore physical well-being and harmony to damaged social and spiritual relationships by using ceremony, ritual, native healers, gifts, and food and by involving the family. A more assimilated, nontraditional person is likely to choose the dominant culture's lifestyle and medicine. Indicators of this preference might be a relatively high level of formal education, minimal, if any, interaction with the reservation, less dependence on the extended family, and previous experience with Western medicine personally or within the immediate family.

Weaver (1999) suggests that the practitioner preparing for work with Native Americans learn as much as possible about important issues within the Native American population. Many of the topics discussed in this chapter would assist the practitioner. In addition to general issues that affect almost *all* Native Americans, the practitioner must be alert to *individual* differences. A Navajo therapist who has worked with many Navajo families cautions that even native practitioners must always be aware of differences even within an individual tribe. This therapist has been told by several adults and children that they do not share their feelings verbally; that "it is not done in their family." The therapist honors this belief and uses other forms of expression, such as drawing and clay, as an avenue for exploring emotional issues. This approach appears to be more acceptable to the clients and has proven to be successful.

Weaver (1999) also suggests that the practitioner learn to define both the problem and the solution from a Native American perspective. If the Native American does not become invested in the intervention, it is unlikely to be of any help. For example, Joseph was assessed by a therapist as depressed and in need of medication. The educational system supported this plan and advised the family that either Joseph must be placed on the medication or he could not return to school. The family felt that certain ceremonials needed to be done; however, the grandfather was ill and could not participate at that time. In order to appease the professionals, the family accepted the medication in compliance with both the therapist's and the school's wishes, but later chose not to give it to the child. Agreeing with authority figures initially, but then not following through with recommendations, is not an unusual response for those who feel their objections will be ignored.

CASE STUDY: CULTURAL CONNECTIONS

Jennifer RedCloud Stevens was a nine-year-old girl from the Crow tribe in south-ern Montana. Both Jennifer and her mother, Michelle, were enrolled members of the tribe. Jennifer's father was half Crow and half English and was also enrolled with the Crow tribe. The family was reported to social services when Jennifer came to school with a large bruise on her upper arm. After investigating the case and verifying that this situation was probably a single incident of abuse, social services referred the family to a therapist for intervention.

Jennifer had three siblings, one of whom did not share the same father. This sibling was born when Michelle was sixteen and was being raised by Michelle's parents back on the reservation. Jennifer was the next eldest child and was born when her mother was nineteen. Jennifer's two younger siblings were ages eight and six. Jennifer's father brought his family to Spokane, Washington, to find better employment than was available on the reservation. Michelle left the chil-dren's father after continued unemployment and alcohol abuse, although they remained married and the father saw his children occasionally.

The therapist interviewed Michelle and Jennifer and talked with Jennifer's cur-rent fourth-grade teacher. The therapist learned that Jennifer disliked school, felt different from the other kids, and was arguing a lot with her mother. According to her teacher, Jennifer had been experiencing problems in school. She was dis-respectful, uncooperative, and unresponsive. In the primary grades, Jennifer had been a model student. She was reserved, but connected well with her teachers and participated in all activities. As her fourth-grade year progressed, Jennifer had become more and more withdrawn. She appeared to struggle with the academic expectations and, rather than ask for assistance, became angry. She had begun to miss school regularly and was in serious danger of being retained.

Michelle worked as a part-time cashier at a local gas station. The family lived in low-income housing and received food stamps and Medicaid assistance for the children. The therapist discovered that Michelle was raised by her parents and grandparents on the reservation. Since leaving the reservation three years prior, Michelle had not developed any type of support system and was trying to raise her three children on her own. She did not want to return to the reservation because there were no jobs and she did not want to be a failure in her parents' eyes. The therapist assessed that Michelle was overextended, lacked appropriate parenting skills, and lacked a support network. The therapist talked with Michelle about the difference between parenting in the city as opposed to on the reser-vation. Michelle felt that things moved slower on the reservation and that she did not need to worry so much about her children when she was there. She always had her parents and sisters and brother available if she needed help. In the city, she was alone and sometimes became frustrated, especially when Jennifer disagreed with her or refused to obey.

The therapist had worked with other Native American families in the past. In addition, the therapist had collected some literature on traditional Native American parenting and also knew people at the Native American Center in Spokane. She offered to call and give them, with permission, Michelle's phone number. She also encouraged Michelle to talk to her parents about how they had raised her and to learn more about the values and customs of her own tribe.

Jennifer was sent to a play therapist who was well-versed in the customs and values of several Native American tribes. The play room was equipped with toys and materials that represented many plains tribes. The play therapist was also aware that Native American children often develop difficulties in school around their fourth-grade year. During the primary grades, teachers generally use group work and kinesthetic, hands-on types of instruction. Native American children have been found to have learning styles that are group oriented and involve physical interaction. Many Native American children learn by observation and will not attempt a task until they feel confident in their abilities to be successful. Competition is avoided, and comparisons between people are embarrassing. As children progress to the higher grades, comparisons and competition increase dramatically in schools.

The play therapist was alert to any play of a cultural nature that Jennifer engaged in. The play therapist could then respond to the curiosity, confusion, or anger that this play engendered. In addition, the play therapist could talk with Jennifer's mother about helping Jennifer connect with her Indian heritage. Jennifer's teacher also needed to know the particular situations that might cause Jennifer to struggle with school. Suggestions for the teacher included providing alternatives to lectures and textbooks and involving Jennifer in more group work. The teacher was also asked to avoid making public comparisons of the students and to proactively support Jennifer's exploration of her own heritage.

Practitioners should make the effort to locate and cultivate relationships with members of the Native American community and should connect parents who are having difficulty to these community members. If a Native American community is inaccessible, practitioners can encourage the parents to discover their own roots through reconnecting with family and reading historical works about their particular tribe. Practitioners should have initial materials that they have previewed or that come recommended from a reliable source. For many Native American parents, culture can and should be an integral part of the intervention plan. "People cannot parent well when they feel powerless or bereft of their dignity and culture" (Northwest Indian Child Welfare Institute, 1996, p. 13).

Skills

In addition to proactively taking the client's perspective, practitioners can develop specific skills in working with Native Americans. These skills include patience, the ability to tolerate and respect silences, listening, and using humor and being willing to be the target of humor (Weaver, 1999; Williams & Ellison, 1999). The practitioner must practice humility and show a desire to learn about the person's culture. Respect and a nonjudgmental ability to grasp a different worldview are also valuable skills.

The practitioner must determine the importance of culture in ongoing care for the client. The interventions must be sensitive to both traditional and Western value constraints. For many Native Americans, the restoration of balance and harmony can be accomplished through ceremony and ritual, by consulting traditional healers, and by including peers, family, and community representatives in the intervention. Traditional Native Americans feel frustrated that their powerful knowledge about how to care for an illness to mind, body, or spirit is not utilized as a legitimate avenue for healing. For example, when a physical wound is treated in Western society, it is the wound that receives the treatment. A Native American might assume that the underlying cause of this physical manifestation is spiritual (Williams & Ellison, 1999). It is important to understand *why* the wound occurred. An event in a spiritual rather than physical sense may have caused a change in the body, mind, or spirit that resulted in disharmony significant enough to cause the wound. Tending the physical aspect of the wound is only a part of the treatment.

Another example is the use of the sweat lodge for the treatment of alcohol and drug abuse. Tribal leaders are well aware of the negative impact that alcohol has made on their people. Alcohol treatment and abuse prevention through education is a common project of many tribes. A traditional approach to alcohol and drug treatment incorporates "sweats" into the healing (Cross, 1997). The sweat lodge ceremony varies from tribe to tribe. The lodge itself is generally a low, hutlike structure built from willow branches and other natural materials like bark and grass. Prior to entering the lodge, participants are purified with sage or cedar smoke. In the lodge, participants place themselves around a pit that contains rocks heated from an outdoor fire. Water is sprinkled on the rocks to create steam. Traditional sweats are usually accompanied by guided prayer, chanting, and drumming. The sweat lodge provides a holistic approach that is respectful of Native American beliefs. In the sweat lodge, no person is alone. A significant relationship develops between the participants, which supports the healing process. Prayer and healing rituals are conducted that support the person's spirituality. The person may experience vivid visions and memories during the sweat. These visions and memories are often accompanied by intense emotional reactions. The teaching of belief systems supports intellectual development. And, the physical act of sweating has a cleansing effect on the body.

SUMMARY

The history of the Native American has resulted in families left highly disrupted and even disabled to such an extent that many positive traditional ways have been forgotten (Burgess, 1980; National Indian Child Abuse and Neglect Resource Center, 1980). Yet some very basic core beliefs remain common among Native American people, such as the importance of extended family relationships and support systems, nonmaterialism, health defined as being "balanced," and the concept of individual freedom within the framework of a harmonious and generous life. Traditions and practices such as rites of passage and death and mourning rituals differ greatly between tribes, and practitioners must learn these specifics with humility and an open mind.

Practitioners who have the opportunity to work with Native American families can learn ways to enhance their skills with this particular population. A person may appear to be completely assimilated into the dominant culture, but when that person is struggling with depression, identity confusion, alcoholism, or parenting, the practitioner can involve the extended family to provide a much needed means of support. In the case of a youth who exhibits identity confusion, Native American traditions provide a way of being and a value system that may feel more natural than those of the dominant culture. Traditional Native American healing ceremonies can be used to battle the disease of alcoholism that destroys many families. Parents who are struggling can be introduced to traditional Native American parenting practices that are supportive and effective.

Native Americans traditionally do not see themselves as isolated beings; they consider parent-child relationships within the context of the extended family and the tribe. Bronfenbrenner (1977) suggested that successful parenting and competent child behavior may be best achieved with the revitalization of systematic support by community, family, friendship, and neighborhood networks. Sharing responsibility for the well-being of children is a positive feature of the extended family concept (Harrison et al., 1990; Red Horse, 1980). Within the extended family environment, the traditional values of generosity, respect for elders, respect for all creation, harmony, and individual freedom can be modeled and supported.

Discussion Questions and Role-Play Exercises

1. Identify some of the historical factors that have negatively impacted Native American families, and discuss how this legacy continues to impact on children and families.
2. Describe the four levels of acculturation and how they might impact the parent-child relationship in Native American families.
3. Describe a pluralistic educational environment. How can practitioners bring about acceptance of this concept?
4. What specific interventions might be effective when working with Native American families?
5. What kind of programs, services, or activities could be offered in a middle school to involve Native American youth and possibly prevent school withdrawals?

References

Berger, E. H. (1991). *Parents as partners in education: The school and home working together* (3rd ed.). New York: Merrill.

Berlin, I. N. (1987). Effects of changing Native American cultures on child development. *Journal of Community Psychology, 15,* 299–306.

BigFoot Sipes, D. S., & Willis, D. J. (1993). *Helping Indian parents discipline their children.* South Deerfield, MA: National Committee to Prevent Child Abuse.

Borgenicht, D. (Ed.). (1993). *Native American wisdom.* Philadelphia: Running Press Book Publishers.

Brendtro, L. K., Brokenleg, M., & Van Bockern, S. (1990). *Reclaiming youth at risk: Our hope for the future.* Bloomington, IN: National Education Service.

Bronfenbrenner, U. (1977). Nobody home: The erosion of the American family. *Psychology Today, 10,* 41–47.

Burgess, B. J. (1980). Parenting in the Native-American community. In M. D. Fantini & R. Cárdenas, *Parenting in a multicultural society* (pp. 63–73). New York: Longman.

Campbell, G. (1989). The political epidemiology of infant mortality. *American Indian Culture and Research Journal, 13*(3), 1–20.

Census Bureau. (1994a). *Census of population: Social and economic characteristics, United States* (1990 CP-2-1). Washington, DC: United States Department of Commerce, Economics and Statistics Administration, and Bureau of Census.

Census Bureau. (1994b). *Census of population: Characteristics of American Indians by tribe and language* (1990 CP-3-7). Washington, DC: United States Department of Commerce, Economics and Statistics Administration, and Bureau of Census.

Coopersmith, S. (1967). *The antecedents of self-esteem.* San Francisco: W. H. Freeman.

Cox, W. H. (1970). Intrafamily comparison of loving-reject child-rearing practices. *Child Development, 91,* 437–48.

Coyhis, D. (1997). The developmental cycle: Teachings on the eight stages of growth of a human being. *Winds of Change: AISES, 19th Annual National Conference Issue, 12*(4), 114–19.

Cross, T. L. (1997). The world view of American Indian families. In Child Welfare League of America (Ed.), *Culturally competent practice: A series from Children's Voice magazine* (pp. 23–31). Washington, DC: CWLA Press.

Dawson, J. (1988). "If my children are proud": Native education and the problem of self-esteem. *Canadian Journal of Native Education, 15*(1), 43–50.

Edmunds, R. D. (1995, June). Native Americans, new voices: American Indian history, 1895–1995. *American Historical Review, 100*(3), 717–40.

Erikson, E. H. (1963). *Childhood and society.* New York: W. W. Norton.

Farris, C. E., Neuhring, E. M., Terry, J. E., Bilecky, C., & Vickers, A. (1980). Self-concept formation in Indian children. *Social Casework: The Journal of Contemporary Social Work, 61*(8), 484–89.

Garrett, M. T., & Wilbur, M. P. (1999). Does the worm live in the ground? Reflections on Native American spirituality. *Journal of Multicultural Counseling and Development, 27*(4), 193–206.

Garrett, M. W. (1995). Between two worlds: Cultural discontinuity in the dropout of Native American youth. *The School Counselor, 42*(3), 186–95.

George, L. J. (1997). Why the need for the Indian Child Welfare Act? In G. R. Anderson, A. Shea Ryan, & B. R. Leashore (Eds.), *The challenge of permanency planning in a multicultural society* (pp. 165–75). Binghamton, NY: Haworth Press.

Gfellner, B. M. (1990). Culture and consistency in ideal and actual child-rearing practices: A study of Canadian Indian and white parents. *Journal of Comparative Family Studies, 21*(3), 413–23.

Gibbs, J. T., & Huang, L. N. (with associates). (1998). *Children of color: Psychological interventions with culturally diverse youth.* San Francisco: Jossey-Bass.

Givelber, F. (1983). The parent-child relationship and the development of self-esteem. In J. E. Mack & S. L. Ablon (Eds.), *The development and sustenance of self-esteem in childhood* (pp. 163–76). New York: International Universities Press.

Harrison, A. O., Wilson, M. N., Pine, C. J., Chan, S. Q., & Buriel, R. (1990). Family ecologies of ethnic minority children. *Child Development, 61,* 347–62.

Harvey, K. D., Harjo, L. D., & Jackson, J. K. (1990). *Teaching about Native Americans* (Bulletin 84). Washington, DC: National Council for Social Studies.

Hoffman, M. (1977). Moral internalization: Current theory and research. In L. Berkowitz (Ed.), *Advances in experimental psychology.* New York: Academic Press.

Horejsi, C. (1987). *Child welfare practice and the Native American family in Montana: A handbook for social workers.* Missoula: University of Montana.

Horejsi, C., Craig, B. H. R., & Pablo, J. (1992). Reactions by Native American parents to child protection agencies: Cultural and community factors. *Child Welfare, 66*(4), 329–42.

Hungry Wolf, A., & Hungry Wolf, B. (1987). *Children of the sun.* New York: Morrow.

Indian Health Services. (1990). *National plan for Native American mental health services.* Rockville, MD: Author.

Johnson, T. (Ed.). (1991). *Indian Child Welfare Act: Indian homes for Indian children.* Los Angeles: UCLA American Indian Studies Center.

Kellogg, J. B. (1982). *Survey of existing Indian parenting programs.* Washington, DC: National American Indian Court Judges Association. (ERIC Document Reproduction Service No. ED 300 177)

LaFromboise, T. D., & Low, K. G. (1998). American Indian children and adolescents. In J. T. Gibbs, L. N. Huang, & Associates (Eds.), *Children of color: Psychological interventions with culturally diverse youth* (pp. 112–42). San Francisco: Jossey-Bass.

Lefley, H. P. (1974). Social and familial correlates of self-esteem among American Indian children. *Child Development, 45,* 829–33.

Luftig, R. L. (1983). Effects of schooling on the self-concept of Native American students. *The School Counselor, 30*(4), 251–60.

May, P. A. (1987). Suicide and self-destruction among American Indian youths. *American Indian and Alaska Native Mental Health Research, 1,* 52–69.

May, P. A. (1996). The health status of Indian children: Problems and prevention in early life. In S. M. Manson & N. G. Dinges (Eds.), *Behavioral health issues among Native American Indian and Alaska Natives: Exploration on the frontiers of the biobehavioral sciences: Vol. 1. American Indian and Alaska Native Mental Health Research.* Denver, CO: National Center.

Miller, J. R. (1987). The irony of residential schooling. *Canadian Journal of Native Education, 14*(2), 3–14.

Monahan, T. C. (1981). *An exploratory study of selected characteristics of parent committees associated with projects funded under Title IV, Public Law 92–318, The Indian Education Act, Part A.* New Brunswick, NJ: Rutgers University.

National Center for Educational Statistics. (1988). *Dropout rates in the United States.* Washington, DC: Department of Education, Office of Educational Research and Improvement.

National Indian Child Abuse and Neglect Resource Center. (1980). *Indian culture and its relationship to child abuse and neglect. Revised.* Tulsa, OK: National Indian Child Abuse and Neglect Resource Center. (ERIC Document Reproduction Service No. ED 229 193)

National Indian Child Abuse and Neglect Resource Center. (1981). *Parenting education: Discipline skills.* Tulsa, OK: National Indian Child Abuse and Neglect Resource Center. (ERIC Document Reproduction Service No. ED 229 199)

Noley, G. (1992). *Educational reform and American Indian cultures.* Tempe, AZ: Division of Educational Leadership and Policy Studies, Arizona State University. (ERIC Document Reproduction Service No. ED 362 341)

Northwest Indian Child Welfare Institute. (1986). *Positive Indian parenting: Honoring our children by honoring our traditions.* Portland, OR: Author.

Northwest Indian Child Welfare Institute. (1996). *Cross-cultural skills in Indian child welfare: A guide for the non-Indian.* Portland, OR: Author.

Peterson, M. E. (1984). Navajo Indian parent education: An experimental study. (Doctoral dissertation, University of Oregon, 1983). *Dissertation Abstracts International, 44*(11).

Red Horse, J. G. (1980). Family structure and value orientation in American Indians. *Social Casework: The Journal of Contemporary Social Work, 61*(8), 462–67.

Reyhner, J. (1994). *American Indian/Alaska Native education.* Bloomington, IN: Phi Delta Kappa Educational Foundation. (ERIC Document Reproduction Service No. ED 369 585)

Rohner, E. C., Chaille, C., & Rohner, R. P. (1980). Perceived parental acceptance-rejection and the development of children's locus of control. *The Journal of Psychology, 104,* 83–86.

Sanchez, T. R., Plawecki, J. A., & Plawecki, H. M. (1996). The delivery of culturally sensitive health care to Native Americans. *Journal of Holistic Nursing, 14*(4), 295–307.

Snipp, C. M. (1996). The size and distribution of the American Indian population: Fertility, mortality, residence, and migration. In G. D. Sandefur, R. R. Rinduss, & B. Cohen (Eds.), *Changing numbers, changing needs: American Indian demography and public health.* Washington, DC: National Academy Press.

Soares, A. T., & Soares, L. M. (1969). Self-perceptions of culturally disadvantaged children. *American Educational Research Journal, 6*(1), 31–45.

Spencer, M. B., & Markstrom-Adams, C. (1990). Identity processes among racial and ethnic minority children in America. *Child Development, 61,* 290–310.

Sprott, J. E. (1994). One person's 'spoiling' is another's freedom to become: Overcoming ethnocentric views about parental control. *Social Science Medicine, 38*(8), 1111–24.

Strom, R., Griswold, D., & Slaughter, H. (1981). Parental background: Does it matter in parent education? *Child Study Journal, 10,* 243–60.

U.S. Senate. (1969). *Indian education: A national tragedy—A national challenge.* Washington, DC: Committee on Labor and Public Welfare. (ERIC Document Reproduction Service No. ED 034 625)

Weaver, H. N. (1999). Indigenous people and the social work profession: Defining culturally competent services. *Social Work, 44*(3), 217–25.

Williams, E. E., & Ellison, F. (1999). Culturally informed social work practice with American Indian clients: Guidelines for non-Indian social workers. In P. L. Ewalt, E. M. Freeman, A. E. Fortune, D. L. Poole, & S. L. Witkin (Eds.), *Multicultural issues in social work: Practice and research* (pp. 78–84). Washington, DC: National Association of Social Workers.

Asian American Families

Parenting in Chinese American Families

SHI-JIUAN WU

The purpose of this chapter is to address issues related to Chinese American parent-child relationships with the hope of enhancing practitioners' understanding of how to work more effectively with Chinese American families. In this chapter, I examine how Chinese American parents try to reconcile their traditional cultural practices with Western cultural practices about parenting. Several topics are reviewed and discussed. First, the demographic factors and changes that reflect the diverse backgrounds of Chinese American immigrants provide a basis for understanding. Second, I present a discussion of parenting as a process of negotiation for Chinese parents living in the West. The third topic is a recognition of the need for multiple levels of negotiation not only among various family members, because of the lack of agreement among the different generations, but also between the family and the school. Finally, a summary of three focus groups of Chinese American parents is presented to explore current parenting practices and offer suggestions regarding methods of working with Chinese American parents. The following case study illustrates a typical misunderstanding between Chinese American parents and their child's teacher.

CASE STUDY: THE BAI FAMILY

Mr. and Ms. Bai came to the United States from Hong Kong because of their concerns regarding Hong Kong being returned to China. They brought their three children with them: Ken, nine years old, Lin-Lin, seven years old, and Jiun, six years old. The couple had saved all their money, and they were able to buy a small Chinese grocery store in a city in the Northeast. They had high expectations for their children and hoped that they would all do well in school and find good jobs in the future. All three children went to the same local public school. The couple worked very hard from Monday to Saturday to make a living in a new land. However, Ken started having some problems at school; he would argue and fight to the point of distracting the class. The teacher called the parents at their store, and the parents were shocked to hear this news. However, they did not speak much English, and they were uncomfortable and embarrassed about this situation. They promised they would visit the school the following week. The teacher waited but the parents never came. The teacher then began to talk to his fellow teachers about the parents as being irresponsible and uncaring. He also stated his belief that the parents should not overwork and neglect their children.

Without a thorough understanding of the culture, it is very easy to blame Chinese American parents the way Ken's teacher did.

DEMOGRAPHIC FACTORS

Chinese Americans constitute the largest group of Asian Pacific Islanders in the United States (Ong & Hee, 1993; D. Sue, 1997). The number has grown from 806,040 to 1,645,472 between 1980 and 1990 (Fong, 1992). In 1965, approximately 39 percent of Chinese Americans were foreign born (Takaki, 1989). By 1984, 63 percent were either foreign born or recent immigrants (Takaki). Furthermore, the number of Chinese Americans is expected to grow because of the relaxation of immigration quotas (D. Sue) and the opportunities existing in this country. Therefore practitioners need to understand the values and beliefs of this population in order to work successfully with them.

Chinese American communities have become more diverse and complex because of the influx of immigrants and refugees from different regions and from different socioeconomic and political backgrounds in Asia (Lee, 1996). Practitioners need to consider how this complexity might affect their understanding about Chinese American parenting. Values or generalizations that tended to apply to most Chinese American parents in the past can no longer apply to *all* Chinese Americans. This chapter, therefore, does not intend to be inclusive for all the possible dimensions of Chinese American parenting, but rather will give highlights of some key practices with some possible variations.

The literature historically has focused more on problematic aspects of Chinese families. Differences from Western culture tend be regarded as deviant or problematic. For example, Asian parents have been portrayed as wanting to control their children (Chao, 1994). However, according to Lau and Cheung (1987), Asian parental control is for the purpose of maintaining family harmony and keeping the family functioning on a stable basis. Another example of problematic portrayals of Chinese parents presents them as less warm and affectionate than Western parents (Lau, Lew, Hau, Cheung, & Berndt, 1990). Reduced affection has been labeled as "cold" and "withholding." Before making these judgments, however, it is important to understand how Chinese parents define affection and how they express affection to their children. Only when practitioners understand Chinese beliefs and practices can they begin to work with Chinese Americans without biases.

Aponte (1994), a well-known family therapist, passionately emphasized that there is no single value that all people can follow anymore in therapeutic practice; people are constantly confused and questioning the values they should have and the action they should take because of the vast changes in society and their own evolving beliefs. Chinese American parents struggle between sticking with their traditional values and subscribing to Western values. They must find a balancing point between the two. There is no formula for solving this dilemma, because new experiences create a totally different context for decision making.

PARENTING AS A PROCESS OF NEGOTIATION

Parenting is an ongoing negotiation process for Chinese parents living in the West. When encountering a new culture, the parents must decide how much to adapt to the different cultural practices and values. This figuring-out process is not fixed but is in constant negotiation among the people involved. Thus, this negotiation process occurs between the mother and the father, and between the parents' values and society's values, between what the children experience in the world and at home, and between the parents and the children in their relational negotiation (table 10.1).

These multiple levels of negotiation occur simultaneously and on an ongoing basis in the Chinese family. This negotiation is a very challenging task for the family system. When helping professionals start to recognize the complexity of these multiple levels of negotiation, they then begin to be in the same boat with Chinese parents and can understand their struggles.

These multiple levels of negotiation regarding acculturation were not considered by Ken's teacher in the case study at the beginning of the chapter; the teacher did not realize what Mr. and Ms. Bai might be facing. Bias and negative labeling can easily emerge out of lack of understanding and knowledge about the acculturation process. Practitioners must be aware of the complex negotiation regarding important values related to parenting in Chinese American families.

Table 10.1. Multiple Levels of Negotiation in a Family During the Acculturation Process

---

- Between the mother and the father and what each values from their tradition
- Between what the parents value and what society values
- Between what the children experience in the world and at home
- Between the parents and the children

THE SPECTRUM FROM TRADITIONAL TO WESTERN
PARENTING PRACTICES

This section reviews some of the pivotal values on which parenting practices rest in Chinese families. As previously stated, there is no *one* pattern that applies to all families, and even within the same family the practices may vary according to different circumstances and at different times. Despite these variations, however, it is clear that the basic values in Chinese families include certain beliefs about family interactions. These beliefs are influenced by the following factors:

- Degree of acculturation of the family
- Degree of adherence to Chinese values
- Diversity of families and evolving roles
- The degree of "fit" between parents' and teachers' values
- The children's adjustment

Degree of Acculturation of the Family

The acculturation experience of the family influences the values that families hold (D. Sue, 1997). Acculturation refers to how a person takes in and absorbs a culture that is different from his or her own. The greater the acculturation and immersion in Western culture, the more emphasis on the value of self-actualization (Leong & Tata, 1990). Obviously, acculturation affects the level of adoption of Western values in Chinese families. "It seems that as succeeding generations of Asian Americans become more acculturated, their child-rearing practices become more like those of most American families" (Uba, 1994, p. 31). This finding might be true for many Asian Americans. However, some parents continue to want to respect their cultural roots and practice their cultural traditions without wholesale adoption of Western practices. Therefore this adoption can be quite selective.

Different family members often acculturate differently. Individual differences among family members require compromise and negotiation; otherwise tension and conflict will develop. Most literature on acculturation fails to point out how family members negotiate their different acculturation levels with each other. The process of negotiation within the family and with the larger community is equally significant. A brief case study illustrates this concept.

CASE STUDY: MING

His teacher referred Ming, a twelve-year-old Chinese boy, to the school counselor because of a recent drop in his grades. Ming did not seem able to concentrate as much as he had previously. Ming was the oldest child in his family—he had two younger siblings—so he had had more opportunities to interact with peers in the mainstream society, and he began to adhere to less traditional values. Ming began to express his ideas to his parents, and he even disagreed and confronted them when he found they had made some mistakes. His parents began to feel Ming's disrespect and made verbal threats to frighten him, stating that if he continued violating the family values, he could no longer be allowed to stay in the family.

Ming loved his family and felt attacked and confused. He could no longer concentrate on his schoolwork. The school counselor, instead of accusing the parents, realized that the possible source of tension in the family was due to different acculturation levels of different family members. The school counselor invited the parents to school and, with the translator's assistance, showed empathy to the parents about the difficulty of seeing their child growing up apart from their Chinese values. The counselor also complimented the parents for teaching Ming well in many aspects so that he did bring honor to the family. The parents felt understood and began to work with the school counselor.

Ming was later invited to various meetings, and he cooperated with his parents and the counselor. The teacher subsequently reported that Ming seemed less distressed and his grades improved. The teacher contacted Ming's parents on an ongoing basis to keep them informed about how Ming was doing at school. He also encouraged Ming to learn from his parents about specific Chinese values so that his overall performance in school could be enhanced. The parents felt included and respected for having made certain contributions to their child's education. This case demonstrates a positive outcome when the professionals acknowledge and respect the parents' values.

Parental responses in a different land can shift over time. Some parents want to retain their traditional parenting practices so their children will reflect their Chinese values. Other parents prefer to adopt Western values so their children's adjustment will be smoother here. Still other parents try to teach their youngsters about their cultural identity but also try to help them absorb a new identity at the same time. Parents often shift among these three styles of parenting (traditional, new, or a blend). Sometimes the Chinese values seem to work better, sometimes Western ideas appear to be useful, and other times both approaches are needed. It is complicated for parents to figure out what position to assume. Professionals need to be aware of the complexity of acculturation in order to assist Chinese families.

Degree of Adherence to Chinese Values

Confucianism has influenced the Chinese worldview of life for more than two thousand years with regard to the concepts of filial piety, respect and obedience of children toward parents and older generations, family obligations, harmony keeping, avoiding conflict, and parental control (Chau & Landreth, 1997; Ho, 1990; J. Hsu, 1985; Lang, 1946; Lin & Fu, 1990; Wu, 1985). These values represent the "ideological basis of traditional Chinese society" (Tseng & Wu, 1985; Quoss & Zhao, 1995).

I do not intend to imply that Chinese American parents subscribe to only *one* consistent parenting practice. Instead, in this chapter I address the ongoing evolution of Chinese parents depending on how they evaluate and negotiate different American values. Chinese parenting is *always evolving* and shifting. Helping professionals need to think in terms of Chinese parents' evolving values rather than to assume that they have fixed and unchanging views.

Of course, this discussion may not be applicable to parents who immigrated several generations ago and whose values now reflect mainstream views. This chapter applies primarily to recent Chinese American immigrants who are still navigating and struggling to balance their traditional Chinese cultural practices and Western cultural practices. Several examples of Chinese values will be described in the sections that follow:

- Low-context culture versus high-context culture
- Harmony
- Conforming rather than confronting
- Filial piety
- Preferences for sons
- Emotional restraint
- Saving face
- Education as a means to social mobility
- Help-seeking patterns

Low-Context Culture Versus a High-Context Culture   Chung (1992, citing hall, 1980, 1981, 1983) presents the concept of high- and low-context culture as a means of understanding differences between Western and Chinese cultures. The term "context" refers to the various social and cultural factors that surround and influence the life of an individual, an organization, or a community. Chung concludes that traditional Chinese and Japanese cultures are "high-context" because they pay great attention to the surrounding circumstances or context of an event; thus, in interpersonal communication the elements of phrasing, tone, gestures, posture, social status, history, and social setting are all crucial to the meaning of the message. This differs from "low-context" cultures, such as Euro American, in which communication focuses more on objective facts and less on individual characteristics or circumstances.

Confucian beliefs form the cornerstone of traditional Chinese social values. These shape individual and group relationships and have resulted in an emphasis on specific expectations of behavior within the traditional Chinese family. This means that persons pay attention to each other' gender, age and birth order to guide their behavior. This protocol, based on obedience and respect dictates that women always defer to men, sons always to fathers, and younger brother to older ones. Respect flows upward from young to old and from female to male, with the elderly male the most revered.

It is challenging for a Chinese family with a high context culture to negotiate parenting within a low-context culture, as in the West. This navigating process between the two cultures must be explored and understood.

Harmony   Harmony, in the Chinese sense, refers not only to the emotional tran-
quillity of family relations but also to a balanced life guided by the teachings of
Confucius. A complete Confucian life means total social harmony.

Traditional Chinese values emphasize the importance of harmonious relationships in the family. In order to preserve family harmony, the level of conflict needs
to be minimized as much as possible (Ho, 1990). When people live in a homogeneous environment with clear values and expectations, harmony is easy to achieve.
However, when Chinese people migrate from China, Hong Kong, Malaysia, Singapore, and Taiwan to the United States, the same values and expectations may no
longer apply as strongly. Each member of the family acculturates at a different pace,
which can create conflicts and tensions within the family.

Families must redefine how much conflict their family system can sustain while
still maintaining harmony. The school and counselors need to be aware of how the
need for harmony might prevent a family from resolving its conflict in a direct and
timely fashion. Honoring the family's belief in the importance of harmony might
initially be necessary before addressing family conflicts openly.

For example, Hwa, sixteen, a female student, was afraid to tell her family that
she very much wanted to attend a youth writing camp that would cost her parents
$250. She knew that her parents worked hard in a factory and did not have extra
money. She was afraid to make the request and create stress for her parents. However, it was hard for her to miss something she wanted very much in order to
improve her writing skills. Her teacher found out about Hwa's dilemma and assisted
her in communicating with her parents in a respectful way and at the same time
explored other funding to support Hwa.

Conforming Rather Than Confronting   In Asian American communities, conforming to the group is more important than expressing one's own needs (D. Sue,
1997). This custom naturally influences how Chinese American parents teach their
children to conform to the wishes of their parents, the elderly, teachers, people of
higher status, and others. Conformity helps the society be harmonious. Following
immigration, many Chinese Americans struggle with the impact of Western values
that emphasize "being yourself" (D. Sue). Tension occurs between parental and
adolescent generations when the youngster begins to assume mainstream values
and practices.

The literature has also shown that Chinese American mothers tend to be more
protective, supervise their children more, and think their children should be independent at a later age than Euro-American mothers do (Chiu, 1987; D. Sue, Sue,
& Sue, 1983; Uba, 1994). Acculturated Chinese American mothers, on the other
hand, seem to encourage more independence from their children than do nonac-
culturated Chinese American mothers (S. Sue & Chin, 1983; Uba, 1994). Chinese
American parents constantly face the issue of whether to protect their children more
or whether to follow the Western practice of promoting independence. This decision will vary according to the particular situation, the age of the child, and the
parent's belief about whether the child can manage without adult supervision.

Filial Piety   Filial piety has been another important value in Chinese American
families (D. Sue, 1997) and has been practiced for thousands of years. Confucius

addressed the importance of practicing filial piety by not traveling far and not living far away from elderly parents. However, Chinese American families have engaged in extensive immigration for more than a century because of political, economic, and opportunistic reasons. Some elderly parents have immigrated with their adult children, and others visit their adult children for a period of time. When elderly parents remain in China, Taiwan, Hong Kong, and other areas in Asia, families are forced to redefine the meaning of filial piety. Adult children who rely on the traditional teaching as their reference point may feel guilty. They need to adapt the concept of filial piety to the reality of long distance. Thus, the expressions of filial piety evolve and change as people migrate and live in a different country.

Similarly, adult immigrants' expectations of filial piety from their children create challenges for both parties. The literature has addressed how parental obligations and expectations cause stress for Chinese students because parents want their children to follow their directions (D. Sue, 1997). This belief is different from the Western belief that children need to determine their own future. F. L. K. Hsu (1953) stated that whereas Americans emphasize what parents can do for their children, Chinese emphasize what children can do for their parents.

Preferences for Sons In traditional Chinese families a son has been valued more than a daughter. In agricultural society, the sons worked with their fathers doing the farm work, while the daughters worked with the mother at home. When the son married he would bring his wife home to join the family and to contribute to the family's work. The daughter had to leave her family to join her husband's family when she married. From a strictly economic point of view, the Chinese viewed having a daughter as a loss. Additionally the sons, particularly the eldest, were responsible for caring for the elderly parents (Yang, 1991) and the family's property.

These traditional values have changed, however, because of immigration, geographical relocation, and changes in society (such as moving from an agricultural to a more industrialized society). Some families no longer follow the traditional pattern, yet they might still value a son more than a daughter. Others might view both genders as equal, and some others might even value the daughter more than the son. Depending on who is available and the geographic location, sometimes the youngest daughter becomes the caretaker for the elderly parents today. Role expectations are no longer as strict as they used to be.

Emotional Restraint "In traditional Chinese culture, emotional expression is restrained to prevent challenges to tradition and order" (D. Sue, 1997, p. 178). These principles apply to many aspects of Chinese American life. For example, Chinese American children are less likely to be praised by their parents for their good behavior or school performance. Children may be exposed to emotional expression in their school settings, however, and they may begin to regard their parents' lack of open approval as indicative of a lack of love. Some Chinese children ask their parents why they don't show emotional expression and behavior, and many Chinese American parents consequently must consider their own views and negotiate with their children regarding the level of emotional expression they consider appropriate. Helping professionals need to assess what level of emotional expression is comfortable for Chinese American parents.

Some authors state that Chinese Americans rely on the use of physical discipline with their children (Ho, 1990), whereas others indicate less use of physical discipline (Uba, 1994). Because physical discipline tends to be viewed as abuse in the United States, many parents have decided not to use this form of discipline, but they sometimes become frustrated because they don't know how else to discipline their children. Traditional Chinese families do not typically give rewards to their children (Uba). Therefore, the degree of compatibility between the parents' and teacher's views about reward needs to be explored in order to minimize confusion for parents and children.

Overall, Asian American families emphasize self-discipline more than external controls (S. Sue & Morishima, 1982; Uba, 1994). The ideal is that behavior is based on one's *internal* morality rather than on fear of being punished (Uba) or the expectation of reward.

Saving Face "Face loss" among Chinese has also been identified as an important value related to shame (Shon & Ja, 1982). An individual's shame brings loss of face to his or her family as well as to himself or herself. Not only does a failing child experience personal shame, but the family loses face and feels shamed as well. Losing face is still a dominant concern in some Chinese families, but there are differences in how strongly each family still holds these values. When parents are very much influenced by this cultural concept, they view their children's problems as shameful and face losing, which might create barriers in discussions with professionals at school or in other related settings. This situation may explain the behavior of Ken's parents in the case study at the beginning of this chapter. For parents who are less influenced by this cultural value, talking about their children's problems might be a less shameful experience. However, it is probably true to say that most Chinese parents feel uncomfortable when their child experiences a problem, and some may be so shamed that they become immobilized.

Education as a Means to Social Mobility In ancient China, the only way for people to move into a higher class and have a better life was through success in education. Education, therefore, is viewed as an essential tool for social mobility and is emphasized by many Chinese American parents. Education is not for the individual but for the enhancement of the family as a whole (D. Sue, 1997). Children can experience a lot of stress from their parents' expectations. However, some Chinese American parents have begun to approach this issue with less pressure and to permit their children to explore their own career interests. These parents emphasize the children's self-development and redefine what is best for their children without focusing exclusively on academic performance. Helping professionals need to inquire about the educational values of Chinese American parents regarding the raising of their bicultural children.

Help-Seeking Patterns The literature has shown that Chinese Americans tend to seek help from people who are part of their own community, such as elders, physicians, and teachers, instead of consulting mental health specialists, such as counselors, psychologists, or psychiatrists (Huang & Yin, 1998). Ethnic minorities may be either underserved or inappropriately served by existing mental health services. The criteria about the usage of mental health services are often based on Western definitions of what constitutes the need for mental health services. Ethnic minorities who do not use services are regarded as disinterested, when in reality they are probably turning to help that is culturally acceptable to them. Traditional Chinese parents may be distrustful of the foreign culture.

In the Chinese community, parents are facing all kinds of challenges, and some of the challenges are new to them. When parents notice something different or something that concerns them about their children, they usually will deal with it by themselves in their own family and hope the problem can be resolved. When the problem does not improve, they might begin to talk to their extended family and good friends and hope they can be helpful. The source for support is still within their social network. During this process, parents often wonder if they have made mistakes in raising their children, even though they might not verbalize this doubt to the people surrounding them. The more the parents are uncomfortable about their own ability, the less likely they are to ask people outside their social network. When no one seems to be able to help, the parents might approach the teacher, physician, nurse, or minister/Buddhism master with growing shame and helplessness related to their continuing inability to resolve the problem.

Certain conditions that would be challenging for parents include attention deficit hyperactivity disorder, autism, mental retardation, mental illness, and their child's severe emotional and behavior disorders. In the Chinese community, psychological information about various problems may not be accessible both because of the language barrier and because psychological information is unfamiliar to the Chinese culture. Chinese parents may not know that research and treatment available in the mainstream community can help their children. The reason the parents have not sought help is not because of a lack of desire, but more likely because they have been taught to resolve family problems within the family network. Therefore, parents might place pressure and high expectations on themselves. Not being able to help their children fix the problem sometimes results in parents' self-blaming or in blaming the child for not wanting to resolve the problem.

Professionals need to be sensitive regarding these characteristics of Chinese parents' thinking. They need to understand and sympathize with the parents' wish to solve the problem within the family. At the same time, counselors can respectfully provide psychoeducation to parents about the complexities of the problem so that the parents will understand what professionals need to do to assist their children. If their child had a heart disease, parents would not be expected to treat the child themselves. The same principle applies when children have autism, attention deficit hyperactivity disorder, mental retardation, or a severe emotional or behavioral disorder. Parents cannot be expected to solve the problem themselves, but they can be instructed in how to work with professionals to solve the problem. Professionals providing treatment in these situations must show sensitivity in avoiding any suggestion of blame toward the parents for not seeking help sooner. Professionals need to be aware that this incident might be the first time that the Chinese American parents have had to seek outside mental health assistance and that they might not even be aware of the existence of a branch of medicine called "mental health." It is important to address the need to help the child without labeling the child's problem as some type of "craziness."

CASE STUDY: THE LEE FAMILY

Mr. and Ms. Lee knew something was wrong with their son, Fred, seven years old, although he looked normal. They felt their son was a good boy and was pleasant to be with. Fred seemed to be smart sometimes, but slow at other times. The parents bought more toys for Fred than for his siblings and hoped that he would advance his knowledge through playing with a variety of toys. The couple had three children and did not have this problem with the other two. The Lees never told anyone about their concerns and tried to solve this problem by themselves. They mentioned their worries briefly to their own parents a couple of times, but their parents said that they probably worried too much; Fred would grow out of it and would be fine later. No one in the extended family seemed to understand the couple's fear and concern. Ms. Lee did not know whether she did something wrong in her pregnancy or whether something happened in the process of Fred's growing that they were not aware of. When Fred was small, they thought maybe he would outgrow his immaturity. But now Fred was seven years old, and his delay seemed quite obvious.

The parents did not know what to do and began to talk to Fred's teacher. The teacher referred the child and the family to a psychologist who had worked with some Chinese American parents in the past. This psychologist, with a translator's help, complimented the parents for their concern and love and desire to help their son. He conducted some tests and discovered that Fred had a learning disability. The psychologist explained to the parents about this learning disability and about the suggested treatment. Mr. and Ms. Lee were very sad and discouraged, but they were assured by the psychologist that proper treatment would help Fred function normally. The parents wanted to do everything to help their son even if it meant long-term treatment. The psychologist agreed to talk to the teacher and principal to explore possible funding for the family.

Diversity of Families and Evolving Roles

Nontraditional Families Nontraditional Chinese American families, whose structure does not match the traditional family composition of father and mother with children, may experience a lot of stress and challenge. Very few studies have addressed Chinese American stepfamilies, divorced families, gay families, single-parent families, families with one parent living in a different country, or families with different residence patterns (Uba, 1994). Hence, practitioners need to recognize these diverse family formats and learn how to work effectively with various types of nontraditional Chinese American families.

Changing Roles Previous literature (Berndt, Cheung, Lau, Hau, & Lew, 1993; Huang & Yin, 1998) has shown that in the traditional model of the Chinese American family, the father is the breadwinner and authority in the family while the mother provides emotional nurturance and well-being. However, some families have reversed roles, and the father is the emotional nurturer while the mother is the authority. In other families, both father and mother carry both roles. The parenting role is no longer fixed by gender.

The Support System Because of possible geographic separations, the nature of the family's support system should be evaluated. Does support come primarily from the Chinese American community or from the non–Chinese American community? Or does the family rely on support from both communities? Does the family feel that this support is enough, and are they well integrated into the community? Or does the family feel isolated from the community? These perceptions can affect the parents' well-being because parental support can de-escalate stress and isolation. Do the parents have people to talk to about their parenting challenges, either within or outside their own families? The practitioner should assess these factors in order to understand the nature of each parent's experience.

Self-Image How Chinese parents evaluate their self-image in their various communities may affect their confidence as parents. They can experience their self-image either positively or negatively in various contexts, such as work, school, neighborhood, and church. Chinese parents continuously evaluate their self-image in different contexts; when the image is negative, the Chinese parent endeavors to improve and change that image in order to gain a sense of pride as a Chinese individual and parent. Schoolteachers and counselors need to be aware of how Chinese parents' self-image affects their parenting.

The school should try to become a place in which a Chinese parent can have a positive self-image. The school must be familiar with the traditional values of Chinese American parents and their parenting practices, but the counselor also must consider the family's specific style rather than make assumptions. A Chinese parent who is forced to comply with the school's requests for his or her child and is unable to negotiate with the school unavoidably develops a negative self-image. However, more traditional Chinese parents hold the school in such high esteem that they would consider it presumptuous to provide input.

Another factor to be considered is the parent's fluency in English. Parents who can speak English in their daily living do not have to rely on their children to translate. But when parents are not fluent, then their children may become their bridges to the world. When the children translate and speak for the parents, the family hierarchical structure is reversed and the roles and boundaries in the family become confused. Some children might use this power unfairly, which can become a challenge for the parents. Therefore, the use of children as translators for their parents should be discouraged because such a situation may diminish the parents' self-worth and upset the family dynamics.

The Degree of "Fit" Between Parents' and Teachers' Values

It is important that teachers work with Chinese American parents without imposing their own values on the parents. For example, the school plays a critical role in assisting Chinese parents with raising their children. However, Calabrese (1990) addressed the sense of alienation that minority parents feel in the public school system when they are viewed as "clients" rather than as customers or consumers. Minority parents may not feel welcome in the school, and they often experience the school as an unfriendly environment in which they are discriminated against because they are excluded from many decisions about their children. Schoolteachers and counselors must consciously take a different role in working with minority parents. This different role includes creating a welcoming environment so that minority parents can participate in matters related to their children.

Even when the literature refers to "parents as partners" in the school system (Casas & Furlong, 1994), rarely discussed is the process of how the Chinese American parent is perceived and invited as a partner in the school system. Many Chinese American parents are prevented from taking a more active role in the school because of their belief that the teacher knows best and that the parents' opinion is not valued. On the other hand, Asian students have been seen as the "model minority," but this label does not apply to *all* Asian students. The question that practitioners must address is how Asian parents can be supported by the school system regardless of their children's academic performance.

The school must recognize that the Chinese mother is considered responsible for her children's behavior and school performance (Shon & Ja, 1982; D. Sue, 1997). When the children misbehave or do poorly at school, Chinese Americans regard this behavior as a reflection of poor parenting (D. Sue). Helping professionals can approach the mother and work with her more closely while at the same time emphasizing that she is not failing in her duty. Some acculturated Chinese parents, on the other hand, may not perceive poor school performance as poor parenting.

Chinese American parents might expect their children to perform in certain ways, and this behavior may or may not fit into what the teacher expects. If both parties teach the children under different premises, the children often get caught in the middle and do not know what to do. Less confusion and anger is created in the children if the two sets of values fit with each other. However, when approaches are not compatible, the teacher needs to initiate contact and try to understand the parents' views and respect what is important culturally for the parents. The Ming case study presented earlier in this chapter is a good example of how children can be helped by schools who work with the parents as a team instead of an opposing force.

Different values between parents and teachers may be unavoidable. The manner in which the two parties negotiate and work together as a team, however, should avoid putting the children in the middle.

The Children's Adjustment

Many Asian youngsters seem to be more at ease when there are other Asian or students of diverse ethnicities in the school. When an Asian youngster is one of the few or the only minority student, being different can cause discomfort and may interfere with the child's social or academic adjustment. Teachers and counselors should explore how these students experience themselves in the school environment. Not every Chinese child will respond to the situation the same; differences need to be accepted. The response of the parents to the child's reaction is critical. Some parents might understand and try to work with the school. Other parents understand, but think there may not be much they can do to help. Still other parents may be totally unaware of the situation or do not believe that being a minority student will bother the child. Professionals can explore the parents' views and work with them without preconceptions.

The family's motivation for migration will have a varying impact on the children. When the incentive relates to the children's education, the focus on education will be stronger than it is among parents who immigrated for different reasons. A good school performance by the children stimulates a lot of joy and pride for parents. When children are not doing well, however, the parents are not happy, and they communicate their distress to the children. The child's age at the time of immigration, the degree of attachment to the home country, and the nature of the family's support all influence the child's subsequent adjustment.

In summary, it is essential for professionals to recognize that many Chinese American parents struggle to reconcile their traditional values with Western values. The differences must be resolved daily on a case-by-case basis. This resolution is not based on a clear model but rather on trial and error. Raising children is always difficult, but the struggles of bicultural parenting increase the complexity manyfold. The process of bicultural parenting never ends.

FOCUS GROUPS OF CHINESE AMERICAN PARENTS: A PILOT STUDY

I conducted three focus groups of Chinese American parents from three Chinese schools in the New England area in order to learn about their parenting experiences and challenges. In Chinese communities, in order for children to learn the Chinese language and culture, many parents send their children to Chinese school, usually on Sunday morning or afternoon. The age of the children in the groups under discussion ranged from three to about eighteen years old. Parents have the choice of staying in the Chinese school to serve as volunteers, or they may take some courses themselves (such as English); others prefer to talk to other parents as they wait for their children.

Methodology

There are primarily two kinds of Chinese schools, Mandarin-speaking and Cantonese-speaking. Because I could speak only Mandarin, I chose to research Mandarin-speaking Chinese schools. I consulted with the local Chinese community about locating Chinese schools and obtained the names of five schools and the principals' phone numbers. Three principals responded to the telephone request about my interest in researching Chinese American parents' experiences in bicultural parenting. These principals thought that this kind of research would be an opportunity for Chinese American parents to talk about their experiences and struggles with parenting in a new land.

The school principals announced the plan for this research interview one to two weeks ahead of time and invited parents to participate in small focus groups. Convenient sampling was used. "Convenient sampling" (Moon, Dillon, & Sprenkle, 1990) is a sampling technique used in qualitative research; the term refers to a sample that is available, convenient to access, and able to respond to the research interest of the author. The school principals addressed the issue of confidentiality with the Chinese American parents and assured them that no names would be identified in the research report. Later, when I conducted the focus group interviews, I again emphasized both the research purpose and confidentiality issues. The three groups all gave permission for their sessions to be audiotaped to allow transcription of the interviews. The format was an open group so the parents could come and go to meet children who had concluded one Chinese class and to escort them to a different program at school, such as chess, writing Chinese calligraphy, or paper cutting. Each school had different schedules, so the length of time for the focus group interviews varied from one and one-half hours to two and one-half hours.

Each Chinese school is located in a different region of the city. The first Chinese school has about 100 students and eight teachers. The second school also has approximately 100 students and ten teachers. The third school has 400 students and twenty-five teachers. Interestingly, the second school also designed Chinese classes for American families who have adopted Chinese children, so the parents and children can all learn about the Chinese language and culture together.

Composition of the Groups

1. The first focus group had about twenty parents; one-third of the parents stayed for the whole session. Five were males; fifteen were females.

2. The second focus group had six parents; most of them stayed for the whole discussion. Two were males; four were females.
3. The third focus group had twelve parents. Two were males, but they had to leave after a short period of time. Ten females stayed for the entire session.

The groups consisted of very diverse Chinese American parents. Some were recent immigrants from China, Taiwan, Malaysia, and Hong Kong. One Chinese American mother was married to a Latino. Some participants were first-generation Chinese Americans who had married either another Chinese American or a non–Chinese American.

In the focus group interview, I explained the research focus as it related to their experiences of parenting in this country and asked them to share their experiences. The themes emerging from the focus groups are discussed in the following section.

Results

Overall, Chinese American parents chose these schools based on the reputation of the school and the geographic location in terms of proximity to their home. They wanted their children to learn to speak Chinese even though the children might not learn to write Chinese characters. The parents hoped that the children, by learning the language, would keep their cultural traditions.

In the groups, parents discussed the challenge of raising their children in a different culture. Some of them felt that they had been constrained with regard to the methods of punishment they could use for fear of being reported to social services. They were confused about this topic and knew only what they had read in the newspapers. Parents were also concerned about how Western practices would affect their children, particularly when their children became adolescents.

Some parents had children with special needs, such as speech problems, and they had to fight very hard to get services from the school system. Initially, they did not know how to go about advocating for their children's needs. They did not have friends with similar experiences, and they did not know about available resources. They had talked to the school many times, but had been told that the school would not pay for the services. It was a frustrating process for these parents.

Some parents were concerned about differences between the teachers and themselves in teaching their Chinese American children. A few parents worried that the American tendency to praise children, compared to the tendency of Chinese American parents to be critical of children, would make it difficult for the children to make the transition between school and home. Some Chinese American parents also thought that their children were encouraged to play more at school than the parents thought appropriate. These parents felt they had to work very hard to structure their children's activities in order to emphasize homework rather than play at home.

One interesting theme was the parents' perspectives about their children's lives in the United States. Some parents mentioned that their children had already sensed the difficulty of being accepted in the white world. A few children asked their parents why they were brought to the United States because they found it so hard to be here. Many children were more comfortable being around American-born Chinese children than American children. Parents also stated that it was difficult for their Chinese children, who tend to be shy and introverted, to socialize with more outgoing mainstream people.

The parents in these focus groups also mentioned that living with their golden-age parents could make a difference in parenting. When both parents are working, the grandparents who spend the most time with the children and who teach them. It can be challenging for parents to negotiate with the grandparents about what to teach the children. Practitioners must consider the role of the extended family network when providing counseling or other assistance with parenting.

This focus group qualitative pilot study was conducted to understand the parenting experiences of Chinese Americans. Additional follow-up with other parents will provide a more comprehensive understanding of the challenges for Chinese American parents. I have noted the spectrum from traditional to Western parenting practices among the groups studied here. Focus groups such as these give practitioners an understanding of parents' concerns about raising their children. The next section looks at suggestions and directions for clinical practice.

CLINICAL IMPLICATIONS AND GUIDELINES FOR PROFESSIONALS

Chinese American parents face many changes in their lives and have to balance traditional Chinese cultural practices and Western cultural practices without any standard formula or guidelines. Often their efforts are invisible and silent, and professionals may not be aware of their struggle. For Chinese American parents to feel welcome, helping professionals must be willing to learn about the stresses of bicultural parenting. The following suggestions are intended to help professionals work effectively with Chinese American parents. A brief case study will be attached to each suggestion.

- Understand Chinese parents' perspectives without being judgmental.
- Show curiosity and interest in Chinese American parents' cultural practices.
- Be sympathetic about the challenge of raising children in a different country.
- Honor the parents' efforts and hard work in succeeding in a different country and in parenting.
- Help parents to look at their strengths so they do not experience failure in front of professionals.
- Learn about the complicated world in which Chinese American parents live in terms of their acculturation, their resources, their work environment, whether they have extended family living together, and other possible supports.
- Be mindful of the impact of English language fluency on a parent's self-confidence with professionals.
- Help parents understand the bicultural conflicts and struggles of their adolescent children.

- Work with parents as a team in spite of the cultural differences between helping professionals and Chinese American parents.
- Recognize the resilience of Chinese American parents.

Understanding Chinese Parents' Perspectives Without Being Judgmental

Professionals must try to understand Chinese parents' perspectives without being judgmental. Immigration and the acculturation process are very complicated and often continue long after the paperwork is finished. Fitting in to the mainstream culture while keeping one's own tradition is a major challenge. Professionals should try to listen and understand before making judgments. Child-rearing practices that are different may be based on good intentions.

> The teacher complained because twelve-year-old Hwa's parents never showed up at school. She thought that his parents did not care about how Hwa was doing. Then the teacher found out that Hwa's parents had emigrated from China eight years ago. The couple did not have much education, and they were working very long hours at minimum-wage jobs. The teacher realized that she was making quick assumptions and judgments. A translator provided by the school helped her understand the parents and communicate with them about Hwa's schoolwork.

Showing Curiosity and Interest in Chinese American Parents' Cultural Practices

Professionals need to show curiosity and interest in Chinese American parents' cultural practices. This principle may seem obvious, but it can be hard to practice because we counselors are all wearing our professional hats and want to demonstrate our expertise. The curious professional allows the parent to feel welcome and more open about sharing the reasons behind their behavior. Disinterest only closes the door and sometimes cancels the possibility for a future working relationship.

> The school counselor, Mary, was concerned that ten-year-old Kei did not go out and play very often; Kei stated that his parents preferred to have him stay at home. Instead of judging Kei's parents as restrictive, Mary asked the parents about the parenting practices in their Chinese culture in Taiwan and about their concerns for Kei here. Mary was respectful and curious. She was not interested in proving that Kei's parents were wrong. On the contrary, she was genuinely interested in understanding their cultural practice. Mary took time to listen to the parents and tried to understand their situation as much as she could. She learned that in Taiwan, children stay home doing schoolwork and rarely play independently on the street. Once the relationship was established, Mary began to invite the parents to describe their parenting practices at earlier stages of Kei's life.

Being Sympathetic About the Challenge of Raising Children in a Different Country

Counselors should be sympathetic about the challenge of raising children in a different country. People tend to view bicultural parenting as similar to regular parenting without knowing that the underlying dynamics can be extremely complicated. As I have already discussed, many Chinese American parents have to struggle with the clash of values and are conflicted about what to do. Parenting itself is already complicated; adding a bicultural factor to the process makes it even more so! Helping professionals must understand the many challenges in bicultural parenting.

> Lily was sixteen years old and dating a boy from her school. The two went out a lot; Lily's parents became uncomfortable about this behavior and accused Lily of being a "bad girl." This conflict distanced Lily's relationship with her parents. One day, Lily's parents had to drop something off for Lily at school and had a chance to talk to the teacher about their concerns. The parents both held professional jobs and spoke fluent English. The teacher listened and realized the difficulty of what Lily's parents were facing. She found out that Lily was their first child, and they did not really know what to do in this country, because in their culture children were not supposed to date at this age. The teacher appreciated the parents' openness and asked for their permission to refer them to a counselor who could help them find ways of resolving this issue. The parents accepted the referral.

Honoring the Parents' Efforts and Hard Work in Succeeding in a Different Country and in Parenting

In addition to understanding the difficulty of bicultural parenting, helping professionals should also honor the parents' efforts and hard work in succeeding in a different country and in parenting to the best of their ability by commenting on the accomplishments that parents have demonstrated in their parenting. *Honoring* people is very different from judging people. This type of transforming understanding takes training and practice.

> Ms. Ho became involved with the department of social services (DSS) because she hit her child. She was extremely upset that DSS intervened and had to visit her at her home, and she also felt ashamed. The social worker, Erin, listened to Ms. Ho's frustration and anger and learned that Ms. Ho had four children, ages twelve, ten, eight, and five. In Ms. Ho's Chinese background, disciplining the child was considered to be the parent's, particularly the mother's, responsibility. (Her husband was working and was not at the meeting.)
> Erin explained to Ms. Ho that she was there to make sure the children were safe. Erin understood Ms. Ho's hard work and good intentions and wanted to help her in any way she could. Ms. Ho was not comfortable speaking English, although she could speak some. Erin could not get a translator

but listened to Ms. Ho with respect; she even asked where Ms. Ho learned English and invited Ms. Ho to talk about the challenge of speaking English and her life in a different country. At the end of the meeting, Erin reinforced Ms. Ho's new understanding that she cannot hit her children in this country. Erin also told Ms. Ho about a parenting class in which some other Chinese American parents were enrolled. She explained that the class was confidential and that she would be willing to accompany Ms. Ho to the next meeting.

Helping Parents Look at Their Strengths so They do not Experience Failure in Front of Professionals

Counselors can help parents to look at their strengths so they do not experience failure in front of professionals. When counselors use a solution-focused approach to work with parents, it helps parents look at the solution instead of the problem (de Shazer, 1985; O'Hanlon & Weiner-Davis, 1989). Helping professionals need sensitivity to address parental issues and child issues that are considered private in Chinese culture.

> Mr. and Ms. Wang lost their daughter Lin, who committed suicide when she was thirteen years old. This loss was very traumatic for the family because suicide is viewed as taboo and shameful in their culture. The parents were not comfortable addressing this manner of death with any professionals. After Lin died, her younger sister, JeJe, ten, started doing poorly at school and became isolated. Frank, the school counselor, learned about Lin's death from the local newspaper and began paying attention to how JeJe was doing. Frank decided to call on Mr. and Ms. Wang. He knew that he had to be very thoughtful in addressing the suicide issue so the parents would not feel blamed. Frank first addressed his concern for JeJe and asked the parents whether they had noticed anything different about her. The parents said they had noticed that her grades had dropped, but they hadn't noticed anything else. Frank began to share with the family the possible impact of her sister's death on JeJe even though she has caring and responsible parents. He also tried to acknowledge the impact of the loss on the parents while at the same time emphasizing the parents' accomplishments instead of their problem. Mr. and Ms. Wang felt encouraged and supported and wanted to work with the counselor to help JeJe.

> Rung was an eight-year-old girl who had minor mental retardation. Her parents had come from Hong Kong ten years ago. Rung had good days and bad days at school; Rung's parents also had good days and bad days in parenting her. Fortunately, Rung's maternal grandmother lived with the family and could look after Rung when the couple worked. The parents often felt that they had failed as parents because of Rung's difficulty in learning. The school counselor tried to engage the couple in a strength-focused way by asking questions such as, "What are you most proud of in raising Rung?" "When

things get rough, how do you come up with solutions?" "How do you share caretaking with grandmother?" "How does your family take a break?" The parents felt supported and knew they were not blamed or considered bad parents.

Identify Families' Social Networks and Resources

It behooves counselors to learn about the complicated world in which Chinese American parents live. Helping professionals should take some time to find out about the family's acculturation, their resources, their work environment, whether they have extended family living together, and what other possible supports to which they have access.

Chin, an eleven-year-old boy, had been doing well in school but lately had begun to look worried. The teacher, Mr. Gray, asked Chin if everything was all right. Chin first said "yes," but Mr. Gray was still concerned. He then asked if everything was all right at home. Chin was silent for a moment and then shook his head. Mr. Gray did not rush Chin but just waited patiently. Chin said that his father had been fired from his job and was feeling unappreciated. His father was not in a good mood and seemed to get upset quite often. Chin mentioned that they did not have other extended family living close by. Mr. Gray knew he could not change the situation, but he told Chin that if he could do anything at school to help, Chin should let him know. Chin felt warmth and acceptance from his teacher. Mr. Gray planned to keep track of how Chin was doing, and he would decide later about whether to involve Chin's parents.

Being Mindful of the Impact of English Language Fluency on a Parent's Self-Confidence with Professionals

Professionals need to provide a respectful, open, safe, and nonintimidating environment in which parents can share information. Patience must be shown to parents who struggle to express themselves in English. Language ability affects personhood. When someone cannot master the language in a different country, his or her self-confidence becomes eroded even though the person is intelligent. The helping professional needs to be mindful of the psychological effect of competence in language and respectfully invite the person to speak.

The teacher decided to touch base with some of the families she had not talked to in the last six months. She called twelve-year-old Yin's parents, and Yin's mother, Ms. Tsang, answered the phone. Ms. Tsang spoke some English but with a heavy accent. When Ms. Tsang realized that the caller was Yin's teacher, she immediately asked if something bad happened to Yin at school. The teacher explained that nothing had happened, that she just wanted to let

Yin's family know how well Yin was doing in school. The teacher showed respect for Ms. Tsang's concern and made positive comments about Yin's attitude toward learning.

Helping Parents Understand the Bicultural Conflicts and Struggles of Their Adolescent Children

As Chinese children grow up and enter adolescence, school professionals and parents need to figure out ways to work together as a team, so the children will not be able to side with either the parent or the school against the other party. Adolescence is a period in which Chinese American parents and children struggle with many culture conflicts in their relationship because of the adolescent's acculturation experiences.

> It had become challenging for Mr. and Ms. Chou to raise their fifteen-year-old daughter, Jei. Their older two children, both sons, had not seemed to have many problems in their adolescent years. Jei was very articulate and had a strong personality. She often would confront her parents for what she considered their wrong thinking or wrongdoing. She stated that she had learned at school to be direct and could not understand why her parents were annoyed with her. Ms. Chou called the schoolteacher and shared her concern about her daughter. Instead of getting defensive, the teacher listened to Ms. Chou's concern and asked about her views on how a teenager should present himself or herself. With permission from Ms. Chou, the teacher later invited the couple to school to talk to the counselor and Jei about how to help Jei to embrace both her cultural worlds instead of negating one.

Work with Parents as a Team in Spite of the Cultural Differences Between Helping Professionals and Chinese American Parents

How can teachers and school counselors work with Chinese American parents regarding the amount of praise to be given to the children? The fact that Chinese American parents employ less praise does not mean that their parenting is inferior. Helping professionals need to understand Chinese American parents' values and try to work together as a team. Another area of difference between Chinese American parents and the school relates to their different beliefs about the desirable amount of play, both at school and home. Instead of judging the Chinese American parent for not fostering a playful environment at home, school personnel must understand the parent's values about how children should spend their time.

> Ms. Lee knew that the school was doing its best to teach her son Kai-Kai, age ten, but she was very concerned about the gap between what Kai-Kai learned at school and at home. She thought children needed to work hard and believed that praising kids might invite laziness. She did not know what to do about this problem, so she asked her friends and people in her church. Someone suggested that she call the teacher to express her concern. Ms. Lee

decided to call and make an appointment with Kai-Kai's teacher. She asked her best friend to go with her because her husband was out of the country on a business trip. At the appointment, Ms. Lee was anxious at first that the teacher might be upset about her coming, but she was relieved to find out that the teacher was thankful for Ms. Lee's visit and thought it showed a lot of commitment and care on her part. When Ms. Lee talked to the teacher about her concern, the teacher listened and was willing to work with Ms. Lee to ensure that Kai-Kai complete all his homework and even do extra work when he finished the assignments. Ms. Lee's friend was there with her the whole time, although the friend did not say much. Ms. Lee felt positive about the meeting and wanted to keep in contact with the teacher so they both could work together as a team to monitor Kai-Kai's schoolwork.

Recognizing the Resilience of Chinese American Parents

Very little research has addressed the resilience of Chinese Americans. Walsh (1998) encouraged practitioners to refrain from looking at family deficits and, instead, to recognize family resilience. In fact, it is commendable that Chinese Americans can live in a different world, juggle two cultures, and figure out ways of raising their children without guidance.

Parents should not be criticized when their views are different from those of the helping professionals. Counselors must find ways to work positively with Chinese American parents instead of viewing them as deficient. The more that parents encounter respect from professionals, the more likely they will be to work with the professionals collaboratively. Chinese parents would like to work in tandem with school professionals; the challenge is how to communicate with Chinese parents respectfully and helpfully.

Wei, an eight-year-old boy, relocated with his family from Singapore one and a half years ago to a Midwest white community. Wei's father, Mr. Yan, was doing well in his career, but the family was very aware of the strong differences between them and the community in which they lived. Wei seemed to withdraw at school, and the teacher decided to invite the parents in to discuss Wei. Mr. Yan took time off from his work and came with Ms. Yan. The teacher appreciated their coming and shared her concern. She learned the family's relocation story and asked the parents how they had raised Wei and about their life in a different country. The teacher asked the parents whether they would be interested in coming to school to talk to the class about Singapore. The couple was elated to be invited, and Wei felt good that the teacher and the school were interested in learning about the place he came from.

SUMMARY AND CONCLUSION

In this chapter, I have conceptualized the challenge for Chinese American parents in terms of navigating between their traditional values and practices and Western values and practices. Chinese Americans are constantly evolving and trying to figure out where to position themselves at different times and circumstances. Through the three focus groups that I conducted to better understand the parenting challenges of Chinese American parents, I developed guidelines for professionals who interact with Chinese American parents. These guidelines were presented in this chapter along with brief case studies that illustrated cultural issues.

We as helping professionals need to keep a few important points in mind. Our way of thinking about parenting guides our expectations about how our clients should respond. Therefore, when differences in views occur between professionals and parents, we may label parents as failures. It is important that we learn from a different culture, discover its richness, become curious about its different practices without judging, and eventually work with parents as *partners* on behalf of their children. These steps require a willingness to take the time to converse and understand another point of view. Chinese American parents do not consider themselves to be "clients." Only when we work with these parents collaboratively can we work successfully with their Chinese American children.

Discussion Questions and Role-Play Exercises

Learning about different cultures can be challenging and stimulating at the same time. The world is no longer homogenous; values and beliefs are evolving constantly. The following discussion questions and role-play exercises are designed to enhance practitioners' understanding and practice.

1. In Chinese culture, hugging is not a common practice. Imagine that you are the counselor for a ten-year-old Chinese American girl who complains that her parents never hug and kiss her. What is your response? Role-play a discussion of this issue with the parents and the child.
2. You are a school social worker, and a teacher tells you his concern that one of your Chinese American students may be using drugs. What should you do? How can you communicate with the parents and work together constructively? What cultural values do you need to consider in working with the parents? Role-play your telephone call to the parents and your first meeting with them.
3. You are a school counselor working with two Chinese American students whose parents do not speak much English. How do you meet the challenge of communicating with the parents? How will you approach them? What are the pros and cons of using the children as translators?
4. You, a counselor, disagree with your Chinese American student's parents. You feel that the parents are rigid and not open-minded to Western beliefs. What steps can you take to move away from being upset with the parents and move toward working closely with them as a team? Your ultimate goal is to help the parents create realistic goals for their child.
5. A school counselor is interviewing a Chinese American couple and their fourteen-year-old daughter. The daughter misbehaved at school, and the goal is for the parents and school counselor to figure out strategies to help the girl. Allow twenty minutes for this role-play interview. Eight people are required: One plays the school counselor, one is the mother, one is the father, and one is the daughter. The other four people are each assigned one of the four roles of counselor, father, mother, and daughter, but they spend the time listening and ob-

serving the interview. At the end of the interview, each watcher shares his or her observations with the person who played that role, and the actor will respond to the observer's comments.

References

Aponte, H. (1994). *Bread and spirit: Therapy with the new poor, diversity of race, culture, and values.* New York: W. W. Norton.

Berndt, T. J., Cheung, P. C., Lau, S., Hau, K.-T., & Lew, W. J. F. (1993). Perceptions of parenting in mainland China, Taiwan, and Hong Kong: Sex differences and societal differences. *Developmental Psychology, 29*(1), 156–64.

Calabrese, R. L. (1990). The public school: A source of alienation for minority parents. *Journal of Negro Education, 59*(2), 148–54.

Casas, J. M., & Furlong, M. J. (1994). School counselors as advocates for increased Hispanic parent participation in schools. In P. Pederson (Ed.), *Multicultural counseling in schools: A practical handbook* (pp. 121–55). Needham Heights, MA: Allyn & Bacon.

Chao, R. K. (1994). Beyond parental control and authoritarian parenting style: Understanding Chinese parenting through the cultural notion of training. *Child Development, 65,* 1111–19.

Chau, I. Y.-F., & Landreth, G. L. (1997). Filial therapy with Chinese parents: Effects on parental empathic interactions, parental acceptance of child, and parental stress. *International Journal of Play Therapy, 6*(2), 75–92.

Chiu, L.-H. (1987). Child-rearing attitudes of Chinese, Chinese American, and Anglo-American mothers. *International Journal of Psychology, 22*(4), 409–19.

Chung, D. K. (1992). Asian cultural commonalties: A comparison with mainstream American culture. In S. M. Furuto, R. Biswas, D. K. Chung, K. Murase, & F. Ross-Sheriff (Eds.), *Social work practice with Asian Americans* (pp. 27–44). Newbury Park, CA: Sage.

de Shazer, S. (1985). *Keys to solution in brief therapy.* New York: W. W. Norton.

Fong, R. (1992). A history of Asian Americans. In S. M. Furuto, R. Biswas, D. K. Chung, K. Murase, & F. Ross-Sheriff (Eds.), *Social work practice with Asian Americans* (pp. 3–26). Newbury Park, CA: Sage.

Hall, E. T. (1980). *The silent language.* Garden City, NY: Doubleday.

Hall, E. T. (1981). *Beyond culture.* Garden City, NY: Doubleday.

Hall, E. T. (1983). *The dance of life.* Garden City, NY: Doubleday.

Ho, C. K. (1990). An analysis of domestic violence in Asian American communities: A multicultural approach to counseling. *Women and Therapy, 9,* 129–50.

Hsu, F. L. K. (1953). *Americans and Chinese: Two ways of life.* New York: Abelard-Schuman.

Hsu, J. (1985). The Chinese family: Relations, problems, and therapy. In W. S. Tseng & D. Y. Wu (Eds.), *Chinese culture and mental health* (pp. 95–112). New York: Academic Press.

Huang, L. N., & Yin, Y.-W. (1998). Chinese American: Children and adolescents. In J. T. Gibbs & L. N. Huang (Eds.), *Children of color: Psychological interventions with culturally diverse youth* (pp. 33–67). San Francisco: Jossey-Bass.

Lang, O. (1946). *Chinese family and society.* London: Yale University Press.

Lau, S., & Cheung, P. C. (1987). Relations between Chinese adolescents' perception of parental control and organization and their perception of parental warmth. *Developmental Psychology, 23*(5), 726–29.

Lau, S., Lew, W. J., Hau, K. T., Cheung, P. C., & Berndt, T. J. (1990). Relations among perceived parental control, warmth, indulgence, and family harmony of Chinese in mainland China. *Developmental Psychology, 26*(4), 674–77.

Lee, E. (1996). Chinese families. In M. McGoldrick, J. Giordano, & J. K. Pearce (Eds.), *Ethnicity and family therapy* (2nd ed., pp. 249–67). New York: Guilford.

Leong, F. T. L., & Tata, S. P. (1990). Sex and acculturation differences in occupational values among Chinese American children. *Journal of Counseling Psychology, 37*, 208–12.

Lin, C. Y., & Fu, V. R. (1990). A comparison of child-rearing practices among Chinese, immigrant Chinese, and Caucasian-American parents. *Child Development, 61*, 433–39.

Moon, S. M., Dillon, D. R., & Sprenkle, D. H. (1990). Family therapy and qualitative research. *Journal of Marital and Family Therapy, 16*(4), 357–73.

O'Hanlon, W. H., & Weiner-Davis, M. (1989). *In search of solutions: A new direction in psychotherapy.* New York: W. W. Norton.

Ong, P., & Hee, S. J. (1993). The growth of the Asian Pacific population: Twenty million in 2020. In *The state of Asian Pacific America* (pp. 11–24). Los Angeles: LEAP Asian Pacific American Public Policy Institute and UCLA Asian American Studies Center.

Quoss, B., & Zhao, W. (1995). Parenting styles and children's satisfaction with parenting in China and the United States. *Journal of Comparative Family Studies, 26*(2), 265–80.

Shon, S. P., & Ja, D. Y. (1982). Asian families. In M. McGoldrick, J. K. Pearce, & J. Giordano (Eds.), *Ethnicity and family therapy* (pp. 208–28). New York: Guilford Press.

Sue, D. (1997). Counseling strategies for Chinese Americans. In C. C. Lee (Ed.), *Multicultural issues in counseling: New approaches to diversity* (2nd ed., pp. 173–87). Alexandria, VA: American Counseling Association.

Sue, D., Sue, D. W., & Sue, D. (1983). Psychological development of Chinese-American children. In G. Powell (Ed.), *The psychological development of minority group children* (pp. 159–66). New York: Brunner/Mazel.

Sue, S., & Chin, R. (1983). The mental health of Chinese-American children: Stressors and resources. In Gloria Powell (Ed.), *The psychological development of minority group children* (pp. 385–97). New York: Brunner/Mazel.

Sue, S., & Morishima, J. (1982). *The mental health of Asian Americans.* San Francisco: Jossey-Bass.

Takaki, R. (1989). *Strangers from a different shore: A history of Asian Americans.* Boston: Little, Brown.

Tseng, W. S., & Wu, D. Y. H. (1985). *Chinese culture and mental health.* London: Academic Press.

Uba, L. (1994). *Asian Americans: Personality patterns, identity, and mental health.* New York: Guilford Press.

Walsh, F. (1998). *Strengthening family resilience.* New York: Guilford Press.

Wu, D. Y. (1985). Child training in Chinese culture. In W. S. Tseng & D. Y. Wu (Eds.), *Chinese culture and mental health* (pp. 112–34). New York: Academic Press.

Yang, J. (1991). Career counseling of Chinese American women: Are they in limbo? *Career Development Quarterly, 39*(4), 350–59.

CHAPTER 11

Parent-Child Relationships in Vietnamese American Families

MONIT CHEUNG
SABRINA MY HANG NGUYEN

This chapter focuses on Vietnamese Americans' parent-child relationships with an emphasis on cultural expectations that influence parenting practices. First, it provides a brief history of Vietnamese immigration to the United States in order to identify different immigration experiences. Second, it addresses major obstacles facing Vietnamese American families in their cultural adjustments that often affect parent-child interactions. Third, it analyzes current literature to examine the traditional Vietnamese family values. Fourth, it discusses three types of Vietnamese parents and analyzes the psychocultural aspects of parenting among Vietnamese Americans. Finally, by using case studies (with fictitious names), this chapter also examines the important role of social workers, other practitioners, and educators as "multicultural connectors" helping Vietnamese Americans improve their parenting skills so that children and their parents can have more satisfying relationships.

THREE WAVES OF VIETNAMESE MIGRATION

The First Wave

When the American army left Vietnam in 1975, the first wave of refugee migration began. Approximately 135,000 South Vietnamese fled to the United States and 20,000 to France. Since then, the deteriorating living conditions in South Vietnam have forced many people to risk their lives across rough seas and dangerous mountains to escape from their war-torn country. The first wave of Vietnamese who arrived in the United States in 1975 represented a highly educated group. More than 20 percent of these immigrants were university educated, compared to the 2.5 percent of Vietnamese with higher education in Vietnam at that time (Weinberg, 1997).

The Second Wave

At the beginning of 1978, when relations between Vietnam and China deteriorated and the second wave of migration began, many Chinese people living in Vietnam resented the "Vietnamization Act" that the Communist Party enacted, which required the minority Chinese to become Vietnamese citizens and to serve in the military (Lo, 1980; St. Cartmail, 1983). During this period, many Chinese in Vietnam organized an antigovernment movement, the "Chinese Movement Division," which was directed by the Overseas Chinese Federation of Vietnam. A widespread rumor claimed that a war between Communist China and Northern Vietnam had started and that "no Chinese in Vietnam could expect to survive in such a war" (Lo, 1980, p. 9). In April of 1978, thousands of Chinese Vietnamese refugees escaped from North Vietnam to China and Thailand. Around the same time, in May 1978, a plan was implemented to crack down on private businesses in Ho Chi Minh City and Cholon. Because most of the owners of private enterprises were of Chinese descent, the hostile environment forced many Chinese Vietnamese out of Vietnam. However, instead of moving to China, many refugees fled by sea directly to first-asylum countries, that is, to members of the Association of Southeast Asian Nations such as Hong Kong and the Philippines. Many died in the journey, but many others found their way from these countries to the United States. As a result, the second wave of refugees, or the "boat people," consisted of many Chinese Vietnamese who had business experience (T. V. Tran, 1998).

The Third Wave

The third wave of Vietnamese immigrants arrived in the United States after 1979 when the United Nations High Commissioner for Refugees reached an agreement with the Vietnamese communist government that allowed families to join their immediate relatives in other countries (T. V. Tran, 1998). Because of this orderly departure policy, many new immigrants moved to the United States gradually. From 1975 to 1993, a total of 632,713 Vietnamese Americans (all three waves of refugees) migrated to the United States (T. V. Tran).

Table 11.1 presents statistics from the U.S. Immigration and Naturalization Service that illustrate the recent growth of Vietnamese Americans. Only nine refugees from Vietnam were granted legal residence status before 1971. This number quickly increased to more than 600,000 between 1971 and 1995. During the decade between 1988 and 1997, legal permanent resident status was granted to 255,684 Vietnamese refugees. Although this recent trend does not represent the entire picture about the

Table 11.1. Vietnamese Admitted to U.S. Permanent Residence

Years	Refugees Born in Vietnam and Granted Legal Permanent Resident Status
1946–50	—
1951–60	2
1961–70	7
1971–80	150,266
1981–90	324,453
1991–95	139,860
1996	29,700
1997	22,297
Total 1951–97	666,585

Sources: U.S. Immigration and Naturalization Service, 1997, 1998.

needs of this population, these statistics clearly indicate a significant increase of the Vietnamese population in the United States. The increase would be even greater if the statistics included people who were not identified as refugees and people who were not born in Vietnam but identified themselves as Vietnamese because they had been residing in Vietnam for a long time before the war and the orderly departure.

Immigration history and statistics show that many Vietnamese American parents are first- and second-generation immigrants in the United States. Inevitably, two of the major variables in examining the issues of parent-child relationships relate to cultural expectations and parenting practices. Many refugee parents have inherited their parenting style from their own parents. Their refugee children witnessed war and experienced hardship alongside their parents, but these children have a very different educational experience from that of their parents. Some of the Vietnamese refugees had children after their immigration, and these American-born children follow two sets of cultural expectations. Furthermore, some Vietnamese American parents and their children are American-born and may know more about American customs and values than about their Vietnamese cultural heritage. Of course, some parents have completely assimilated into the American culture and maintain little contact with their ethnic community and culture. However, the discussion in this chapter focuses on Vietnamese parents who associate with their ethnic community.

CASE STUDIES: TUAN AND HUY

Tuan (age seventeen) did poorly in high school. He was born in Vietnam in 1984, and his parents came to the United States in 1991, during which time he should have begun elementary school. Because he didn't know English, he started kindergarten at age 7. He appeared to adjust easily, but later discovered his ability was much below his parents' expectations. He had three brothers who were born in the United States. His father punished him for his poor grades, and he started to hate and resent his brothers because they never received the same punishment. He studied very hard and finished middle school with a B/C average. He was much older than the other kids and made only a few friends in school. After completing his first semester of the ninth grade, Tuan decided not to attend school and began skipping classes on a regular basis. Tuan told his school social worker, "I thought I could please him, but he continued to put demands on me. He punished me for no good reason. I did what I needed to do to survive but he wouldn't accept me. I just felt so tired . . . that I think . . . I gotta make my own decision. School is no use. I will be on my own feet pretty soon."

Huy was a fifteen-year-old American-born Vietnamese youth who was referred to the detention facility for assaulting his forty-five-year-old Vietnam-born stepfather. According to the stepfather, the assault occurred because the family had not moved to a new house, as the parents promised Huy two years ago. Moreover, the stepfather reported that Huy had not been attending school for more than a year because of his dislike of the high school in his district. The stepfather had tried everything to get Huy to go to school, but Huy kept refusing and threatened that he would go back to school only if the family moved. Huy's mother had come from Vietnam in 1976, married in 1983, and remarried in 1994. She allowed Huy to stay home and told him, "Since you have been working so hard in school for the past few years, I think you need to take a break this year."

This incident was not the first time Huy assaulted his stepfather. The stepfather was fearful for his life and finally decided to call the police when Huy assaulted him this time. The assault happened when the mother was not at home. Huy's eighteen-year-old sister witnessed the assault and served as translator for the stepfather. When the mother came home from work and found out what happened to Huy, she insisted that the stepfather go in front of the judge and drop the assault charge against her son. The mother threatened that if the stepfather did not drop the charge, she would move out and take Huy with her.

OBSTACLES IN PARENT-CHILD RELATIONSHIP BUILDING

Conflict occurs between parents and children as Vietnamese Americans strive for independence, identity, and integrity. As in most Asian cultures, Vietnamese parents and children do not share or discuss their thoughts and feelings. Some children are not even familiar with their parents' and grandparents' survival history as immigrants. Parents, on the other hand, do not understand the internal conflict children face because of their biculturalism. This conflict includes the differences between Western individualism and the collectivism that Southeast Asians value, as well as the multiple external pressures from parental expectations, expectations from the educational system, and misunderstandings between peers.

Many conflicts occur in Vietnamese families because of cultural differences and expectations between parents and children. Lack of communication causes tension, hurt, anger, and resentment. A study of forty-nine Vietnamese-born university students found that male children are at higher risk of having conflict with their fathers

(Dinh, Sarason, & Sarason, 1994). Children feel frustrated with their parents because of the rigidity of their parenting methods. The parents have experienced some loss of control and cultural heritage, but they want their children to succeed in their schoolwork and, later, in their career. They want their children to have ·success in America but refuse to accept the American lifestyle. They acknowledge the importance of social life for their children, but nonetheless use their parental control to limit their children's choices of activities. A typical Vietnamese parent does not agree that children should make decisions independently without parental input and supervision. Therefore, these cultural differences may result in many parent-child conflicts.

One characteristic that contributes to the problem and tension is the outward emotional reserve of Vietnamese people. They do not openly share their emotions, thoughts, and feelings of affection. Parents expect absolute obedience from their children without discussion, whereas at school, children are taught to discuss, to share varying ideas and feelings directly and openly. Parents may be totally oblivious to the acculturation struggle their children face. Children may begin to perceive their parents as negative, critical, and conservative (Cheung, 1997).

Regardless of acculturation rates, family support and informal support systems significantly impact on the lives of young people. In a study by Bankston (1997), a survey of 402 high school students found that "integration into the ethnic community is by far the most important factor in determining the scholastic performance of Vietnamese students" (p. 228). Many of the students receiving grades of As and Bs spoke and wrote Vietnamese well and usually spoke Vietnamese with their parents, siblings, and friends.

Most interpersonal barriers have been described from an individual-family perspective between children and parents. Walker-Moffat (1995) further analyzes the communication barrier from a macro perspective to explain why the "traditional" label is not preferred by Vietnamese American children in school settings. She explains that our system has unintentionally discriminated against the "traditional values" by developing English as a Second Language (ESL) programs in schools. Such programs always give the impression to immigrant students that they are less competent and their communication skills are limited because their "first language" is not English. Adjustment difficulties are self-perpetuated when new immigrants feel that they cannot communicate with their peers, teachers, or even their parents. In a study focused on the parent-child relationships among Vietnamese immigrants, potential barriers that provoked intergenerational conflict included value conflicts, challenges to parental authority, lack of respect and obedience, language barriers, gender-role discrimination, parents' unwillingness to accept changes, and children's desire for independence (Dinh et al., 1994).

TRADITIONAL VIETNAMESE FAMILY VALUES AMONG NEW IMMIGRANTS

Most literature on Vietnamese American families focuses on Vietnamese cultural values (e.g., Caplan, Whitmore, & Choy, 1989), on parental influences on academic achievement (Mau, 1997), and on the impact of the immigration history of families (Buriel & De Ment, 1997; Weinberg, 1997). Very seldom does the parent-child relationship literature address these new immigrant families in terms of value conflicts between the generations (see Dinh et al., 1994; Rosenthal, Ranieri, & Klimidis, 1996). However, a list of values can be derived from the historical, sociocultural, and family perspectives presented in the current literature related to parent-child relationship building.

Within a family, parenting values are predetermined by the culture. The instrumental values in Vietnamese parenting as presented in Caplan et al. (1989) include:

- Believing that the past is as important as the present
- Seeking new experiences
- Maintaining security and comfort
- Encouraging community respect for the family
- Labeling welfare dependence as shameful
- Sacrificing the present for the future
- Valuing work and the balance between work and play
- Emphasizing cooperation and harmony in all families
- Cherishing ancestral lineage
- Identifying morality and ethics as the foundation of life

The first three values in this list were statistically related to economic and scholastic outcome measures in studies by Caplan and associates.

Another important parental value is *obedience*. Arguments with parents are not permitted in Vietnamese American families because an egalitarian relationship does not exist between parents and children. Whatever parents tell their children to do is, traditionally, a nonnegotiable obligation, as seen in Tuan's case. A study of family values among Vietnamese youth reported that the most important family value was "to obey" (Zhou & Bankston, 1996). "Obedience to one's parents" is considered the appropriate way to prepare children for handling future life situations.

Vietnamese American parents perceive *hard work* as a very important concept to model. They believe that children should not receive material rewards for good grades because this behavior is an expectation. Accomplishments are usually acknowledged in the form of parental encouragement to do even better and strive for higher levels of achievement. In essence, "to work and study hard" is a given value in the Vietnamese family (Zhou & Bankston, 1996).

In the Vietnamese American culture, it is believed that individual behavior is either a positive or negative reflection on the entire family. Individual academic or occupational achievement is highly valued and therefore promotes family pride. Conversely, negative behaviors such as disobedience, disrespectfulness, and irresponsibility lead to collective family shame. As a result, these issues are handled within the family because Vietnamese parents prefer not to share their problems with outsiders.

THREE TYPES OF VIETNAMESE PARENTS

Immigrant families, like young children, go through various stages of development, assimilation, and psychosocial changes. Portes (1996) urges researchers to examine specific experiences of immigrant children in three distinct categories: "immigrant children, children of immigrants, and native-born children of native parentage" (p. ix). By integrating Erikson's (1968) concept of psychosocial identity development and Portes's cross-generational focus and by adding the reality of Vietnamese Americans' short immigration history, we propose to examine three types of Vietnamese American parents on a continuum of acculturation differences (Cheung, 1997). These three types are the traditional parent, the bicultural parent, and the integrated parent (see table 11.2).

Each of these three types of Vietnamese American parents can be productive and successful. However, when the relationship between parents and children comes into conflict, these parents all experience similar intergenerational stress because each separate generation represents different degrees of cross-cultural awareness and integration.

PSYCHOCULTURAL ASPECTS OF PARENTING AMONG VIETNAMESE AMERICANS

Understanding the role of the individual in Vietnamese culture is essential to developing an awareness of the basis of familial relationships in the Vietnamese community. Vietnamese individuals function not for themselves, but for the advancement of the family as a unit. The Vietnamese family has a clearly defined hierarchy, which puts the father at the pinnacle of authority and responsibility (Dinh et al., 1994; Haines, Rutherford, & Thomas, 1981; Timberlake & Cook, 1984). The mother maintains the household by providing nourishment to the family. She also supports the authority of the father by agreeing with his views (Dinh et al.; Leichty, 1963). Children are taught to be grateful for their parents' sacrifices on their behalf. They are expected to repay these sacrifices with hard work both at home and at school. They are taught to be respectful and indebted. They also must be willing to make sacrifices for the continued success of the family. These traditional Vietnamese values are modeled after traditional Chinese culture, because Vietnam was dominated by Chinese rule for 1,000 years between 111 B.C. and A.D. 939 (Montero, 1979).

The ethical and moral codes in Vietnamese culture were inspired from the teaching of Confucianism, Buddhism, and Taoism (Slote, 1998). Successful family functioning is achieved through duty, honor, debt, gratitude, and obligation. Each member of the family is considered a harmonious representative of the family as a whole. Thus, the successes and failures of an individual directly relate to all members of the family (Bankston, 1995). It is believed that children's achievement, whether economic or academic, is treasured by parents in their hearts although they may not express their pride openly. Parents believe that their children's achievements not only honor the family, but also ensure the family's continued success (Caplan

Table 11.2. Three Types of Vietnamese Parents

Type	Characteristics
The Traditional Parent	• Focuses on family expectations and honors the traditional Vietnamese values • Expects children to preserve their cultural heritage • Employs traditional parenting practices to teach children
The Bicultural Parent	• Focuses on parents' roles and understands the impact of environment on parents • Expects the children to preserve their cultural heritage while at the same time be ready for learning about the new culture • Combines both the traditional and new ways of parenting children
The Integrated Parent	• Focuses on the children's development and embraces the American values of individual learning • Expects children to integrate American learning into their Asian identity • Develops innovative ideas to involve children in the learning process

et al., 1989). Hard work, honor, and respect are the cornerstones of Vietnamese family values.

Traditional Parents

Traditional parents' attitudes toward their children reflect the cultural expectations of hard work, honor, and respect. Parents feel strongly that they must provide materially for their children while the children are young, but obedience, respect, gratitude, and repayment is expected in return. Children are a necessary part of a successful family. They represent a blessed marriage and full family life. Their good behavior is required to demonstrate fully the respectability and good repute of the family. In addition, children are taught that they should repay the parents for their sacrifices by taking care of the parents as they age. Traditional Vietnamese parents expect their children to succeed academically and to become hard workers so that they will be able to provide for the parents in later years (T. V. Tran, 1998). Therefore, the parents may view children's irresponsibility and disrespect as early signs that their own future livelihood will be jeopardized. The parents will worry further that no recovery will be possible if their children lose respect and stature and if they are not able to marry well and have successful families of their own. Disrespect and disobedience are seen as dire threats and not to be ignored.

Gender Considerations Fathers rarely communicate with their children on an emotional level. Mothers tend to communicate more emotionally to their sons than fathers do (Leichty, 1963). Sons are frequently given more opportunities, attention, and privileges than are daughters because the sons will carry on the family name.

Because of this traditional value of carrying the family name for their whole lives, sons are more closely tied to the family and are expected to be the best representative of the family (Dinh et al., 1994; Nguyen & Williams, 1989). Parents hold high expectations of success for their children and strongly communicate these expectations to instill in their children a sense of family pride, direction, and future challenge.

Leichty (1963) researched the attitude of forty-seven Vietnamese fourth graders in three areas. The first finding was in relation to their fathers: Children were strongly concerned about their fathers' health, which was considered an important contributor to the children's education and the well-being of the family. Fathers were perceived as serious, hard working and worthy of gratitude. Leichty's second observation was that these children also viewed their mothers as hard workers. The girls felt strongly about working with their mothers, and boys felt emotionally attached and indebted to caring for their mothers as they grew to an age where they could help support the family. The third observation was the awareness children had of the family's economic standing and of the sacrifices made by the family to contribute to their upbringing and schooling. Because the traditional Vietnamese view toward parents is always linked to respect, children often feel guilty if they behave in a manner that works against the good of the family. Leichty's study supports the belief that Vietnamese children absorb family values during childhood.

Obedience and Respect In Vietnamese culture, success occurs through obedience and conformity. Vietnamese parents even expect their college-age children to obey and conform. After resettlement, the adjustment is harder for older children than for the younger ones, because many youngsters learn new ways from their peers. The young people learn the language and customs faster than their parents do and soon become assets to the family's success by mediating the American language and social norms for their parents. Soon the roles are reversed. Parents must rely on their children, and the parents' ability to assert authority and power over their children becomes eroded (Nguyen & Williams, 1989; Zhou & Bankston, 1996). In addition, not only do the children learn American social norms, but they also adopt them. Tensions arise when children waver between conflicting value systems — achievement for the sake of individual glory versus achievement for the reputation of the family (Dinh et al., 1994). Traditional parents do not understand their children's new values. They may consider the behaviors of children as disrespectful and disobedient, while the children see their parents as controlling and unreasonable. Vietnamese-born children are less likely to report a positive relationship with their parents than their American-born counterparts are (Leichty, 1963). As already mentioned, male children also find it difficult to communicate with their fathers (Dinh et al.). With respect to gender differences, Vietnamese girls tend to internalize problems, while boys externalize problems (McKelvey, Davies, Sang, Pickering, & Tu, 1999; this gender difference also tends to be the case in American culture). The literature reports that parent-child conflicts occur mostly between older male children and traditionally oriented fathers. However, Q. D. Tran and Richey (1997) found that the problems for most adolescents in their sample (n = 30) were related to females, and parental support came mainly from fathers. Nevertheless, their study does not clarify how differential rates of acculturation may affect parenting styles and relationships.

CASE STUDY: MULTIGENERATIONAL ISSUES
WITH TRADITIONAL PARENTS

The Dang family came to the United States in 1975. Five years later Mr. Dang sponsored his parents to come and live with them. Now Mr. Dang is fifty years old, and his parents are seventy-five and seventy-seven. Mr. and Mrs. Dang have three high school–age children, all born in the United States.

The Dang house is not large enough to allow privacy to each of the seven persons. Conflict occurs between the high schoolers and the grandparents because the grandparents criticize the grandchildren's behaviors. Although the grandchildren do not understand their grandparents' language, they sense their negative tone. As a result, the grandchildren go to a public library after school to do their homework in order to avoid interacting with their grandparents.

Mr. Dang is the first male child in his family. He holds a strong belief that he is the one who should take care of his elderly parents. Although Mrs. Dang does not appreciate her in-laws' negativism, her traditional role is to support her husband and she does not voice her displeasure about her husband's parents. Mr. Dang does not like this conflict in his three-generation family.

Discussion and Alternative Interventions:

- Discuss with Mr. and Mrs. Dang their individual and family concerns.
- Involve the children in a separate session to allow them to voice *their* concerns without the presence of the parents.
- Identify the cultural expectations that the parents have communicated to their children. Encourage them to emphasize these expectations with the children. Praise the couple for their patience and perseverance.
- Discuss with the children some ways to accept their grandparents. Empower the children to acknowledge that acceptance does not equal agreement, and avoidance does not solve problems.
- Identify the advantages from the family and cultural perspectives about the important role of the grandparents.
- Identify alternatives to give family members a break from the multigenerational togetherness. Understand that making changes is much easier for younger generations than for the grandparents.
- Design alternatives to expand the grandparents' social circle so that they can learn from their peers about different aspects of family life. After being involved in the community, the grandparents can join short trips that are usually offered in Vietnamese community centers so that they can appreciate being with friends.
- Acknowledge the importance of maintaining the traditional values of caring for the aged and keeping a balanced family life with loved ones. Praise each family member for his or her participation in bringing the family together. Encourage family members to talk with each other in a positive manner. Ventilation of hurt feelings should not be expressed directly by family members to one another; instead, negative comments about this situation can be pre-

sented to a school counselor or social worker, who will attempt to help family members resolve the cultural expectations and family issues.
- Encourage Mr. and Mrs. Dang to use this experience to evaluate their own parenting style and identify their strengths and limitations in order to better communicate their cultural adjustment difficulties with their children.

―――

CASE STUDY: PARENTS WITH TRADITIONAL VALUES

When the Vu family came to the United States in 1979, Mr. Vu was thirty-two years old, Mrs. Vu was thirty, and their children were six and two. The children were very close to the maternal grandparents before their departure. After the family was resettled in Houston, Mr. Vu attended a community college and obtained his undergraduate degree in computer science. In 1991, they bought a new house while Mrs. Vu was starting a floral business. Their son, Minh, finished high school with honors. They expected that Minh would attend a local college and stay in this new house. They wanted Minh to study medicine. Obeying his parents, Minh pursued his studies at a college his parents chose. Unfortunately, he was not good at science and did not pass the medical school's requirements. He dropped out of the medical field and went into car sales, thinking that he could earn some quick money. His parents were very upset. Their disappointment grew worse when they later learned that he was dating. They blamed his girlfriend for his failure at the medical school. A month after the parents demanded that Minh break off from this relationship, Minh's sister ran away from home. She was later found drunk on a street.

Discussion and Alternative Interventions:
- The crisis was far from resolved, because many issues were not recognized from the outset between the parents, who maintained an authoritative parenting style, and the adult child, who expected mutual understanding and respect. Had early interventions been available when the first sign of conflict was evident, some resolution might have been possible.
- These children had to deal with family pressure and their adjustments into a new culture without the support from their extended family. Their perception about their own culture is skewed and needs to be relearned through other traditional families whose parenting style is not authoritative. (See the Trans case later in this chapter.)
- It is important to encourage the parents to foster and nurture Minh's natural aptitude and interests. If the parents reviewed Minh's high school academic record, it would reflect that physics and chemistry were not the areas in which he excelled. Therefore, insisting on a particular profession that required his excellence in science was indirectly setting him up for failure.
- The parents needed a listener. They worked very hard to achieve their economic status and expected to get a "payback" from their children. Traditionally, parents who encounter difficulties would consult with an elder within the family; they do not share their concerns with an outsider. In this case, because the parents did not have any informal support and they needed to ventilate their feelings, helping them through the school system would be the most culturally sensitive way to intervene.

―――

Bicultural Parents

Bicultural parents adopt both Vietnamese and American cultures; they expect their children to preserve their Vietnamese heritage while at the same time be ready for learning about the "American way." When Vietnamese families migrate to America, some of them come with a readiness to accept sociocultural change. In addition to setting up their family business, many bicultural parents are excited about the new opportunities afforded them and about the potential gains that their children can make. Education is accessible and higher degrees are attainable, even to lower economic classes. With high hopes, parents thrust their children forward to learn as much as they can.

Bicultural parents are aware that Vietnamese Americans can represent the image of Asian Americans as the "model minority"—hard working and adaptable (Kim, 1997). Some may even be willing to discuss with mental health professionals their family's history of political struggle, postwar issues, and related feelings of depression (Silove et al., 1997). However, when the discussion is related to family relationship problems, they are usually uncomfortable and reluctant about openly addressing their views (Cheung, 1997; Kim, 1998).

Researchers report that a majority of Vietnamese American students struggle for their own identity; endure long-term stress with adjustment, cultural differences, and language barriers; and search for understanding and sensitivity to their needs (Bankston, 1997; Kim, 1997, 1998; Romero & Roberts, 1998). Some scholars attribute the academic attainment of Vietnamese American "whiz kids" to the influence of Asian cultural values, child-rearing practices, parental socialization, and family expectations (Bankston, 1997; Zhou & Bankston, 1996). Culture is an important factor in the achievement of Vietnamese American students, but the effects of the traditional culture have been compounded by the impact of a new culture and the perceptions of others toward Vietnamese immigrants.

Bicultural parents do not follow American strategies such as reading to their children daily and encouraging their children to start their own experimental projects (Sue & Okazaki, 1990). Vietnamese parents care very much about their children's education, but they are accustomed to granting the responsibility for education to *teachers* and they view all educational issues, whether curriculum or discipline, as the province of school administrators and teachers (Caplan et al., 1989). They hold teachers in high esteem, second only to parents (Morrow, 1987). A Vietnamese proverb illustrates the importance of respecting teachers: *First you learn proper behavior, then you learn literature.* With this cultural assumption, some parents would visit the teacher only when problems exist, because they trust that children will learn what they are told to learn. Out of respect, however, they would visit the teacher when required by the school.

It is important to acknowledge the bicultural parents' role with their children at home, because their lack of parental involvement can easily be misinterpreted. Bicultural parents closely monitor their children at home, challenging them and keeping track of their academic progress. These parents adopt an authoritative demeanor in front of their children, especially when they are not doing well academically and have made no effort to rectify the situation. This approach can be deceiving because many parents actually blame *themselves* more than their children for the lack of success.

Peng and Wright (1993) indicate that in the home learning environment, Asian American parents do not communicate (i.e., discuss school plans) with their children as much as Caucasian parents do. Bicultural Vietnamese American parents are eager to learn effective communication skills to help their children with schoolwork. These parents expect and hope that success (income) will eventually parallel their children's educational attainment (Nguyen-Chawkins, 1997). They also adopt a variety of cultural practices, such as celebrating Lunar New Year and attending religious gatherings in temples, in order to maintain meaningful contact with the ethnic community. Because biculturalism is the norm in these families, bicultural parents place high value on learning opportunities and academic excellence, with the expectation that family cohesion and ethnic coherence can be promoted (Nguyen-Chawkins, 1997; Ying, Akutsu, Zhang, & Huang, 1997).

CASE STUDY: BICULTURAL PARENTS WITH THEIR TRADITIONAL PARENTS

Some Vietnamese immigrants came to this country when they were babies or young children. Their thinking and ideals are similar to those of the American-born Vietnamese because of their socialization in America. After becoming parents themselves, these immigrants' ways of doing things may be very different from those of their parents who brought them here.

> Mr. and Mrs. Pham attended elementary school through college in Houston. They are now twenty-three and twenty-five years old and have just given birth to their first child. Mrs. Pham's parents love their first granddaughter and want to rear the baby according to their beliefs about what is best for her. In one incident, the baby was not eating, and the grandmother advised the couple to purchase herbal medicine for the infant. The young mother did not take her mother's advice, but took the baby to see a medical doctor instead. The grandmother became upset when she found out, even though the daughter tried to explain her position. This incident caused conflict between them, because disobedience is considered dishonor.

Discussion and Alternative Interventions:
- In traditional families, parents expected their daughters to consult with them on child rearing. Today, child-rearing practices are rarely discussed between grandparents and their daughters because there is a mix of cultural expectations about the best practice. Younger couples do not agree that the traditional way is always the best, whereas older parents perceive the American-born parents as not capable of dealing with infants. This kind of conflict can be avoided if the parents simply acknowledge the grandparents' input. It is unwise to argue or try to persuade the grandparents to accept the new parenting ways. The defense or argument would only create problems, because traditional parents tend to view this defensive behavior as unacceptable. The focus of health care for the baby would then become shifted to a parent-grandparent conflict.

- This incident was a critical one for Mrs. Pham because she realized that her relationship with her mother had been deteriorating. She learned from this incident and identified a new coping method: listening, acknowledging, analyzing, deciding, and examining the outcome. After her child benefited from seeing a doctor, she did not need to argue the point with her mother.

▬▬▬▬

CASE STUDY: BICULTURAL PARENTS WITH PARENTAL ISSUES

Jennifer is a twelve-year-old youth who arrived in the United States from Vietnam three years ago. She was referred to the detention facility for shoplifting. According to her parents, Jennifer was a good kid until she met and started hanging out with Le, a "troubled" girl whose parents could no longer control her. Jennifer's parents reported that Jennifer's behavior began to change, she skipped school, and her grades began to drop drastically. Jennifer also stayed out very late, often until two or three o'clock in the morning. When her concerned parents confronted her, Jennifer talked back to them and told them to stay out of her business. The parents also found cigarettes, beer cans, and a lot of new and expensive clothes in Jennifer's bedroom.

Jennifer, on the other hand, stated that her parents did not allow her to do anything or go anywhere and always criticized her friends, saying that they were no good for her. Jennifer also said that her parents put too much pressure on her about school and often expected her to bring home only As. Jennifer stated that her parents were so worried about being embarrassed in front of their friends if Jennifer did not do well in school that they forgot her limitations in English. So, Jennifer stated, she had no choice but to do what she did.

Discussion and Alternative Interventions:

- Culturally sensitive questions should be used when meeting Jennifer's parents for an initial assessment. Ask, for example, "How does your culture help with children who cannot achieve because of their physical or psychological limitations?" "What would parents do if they found that their children were having difficulties in learning or socializing?"
- Identify some strategies for the parents so that they can learn different ways to make constructive comments to Jennifer. The school counselor could approach Jennifer to get her involved in the family counseling process so that Jennifer would learn about her parents' worries and concerns.
- In an individual session with Jennifer, help her distinguish some of her positive and negative attitudes (based on cultural definitions) and rehearse how she could talk with her parents to achieve harmony. In addition, use role reversal techniques in a family session to encourage the parents to understand children's needs and concerns from their daughter's perspective.
- Find ways for the parents to encourage Jennifer academically. Despite their strong feelings about Le, ask them to consider encouraging Jennifer academically by rewarding her with activities with Le. When Jennifer feels that her friend is being "accepted," she may have the motivation to work harder on her studies. As part of the reward system, the parents can set a limit on the amount of time and types of activities that Jennifer may spend with Le.
- Convince Jennifer to go along with her parents' plan. Help her identify the balance between work and play. Help Jennifer understand the advantages and disadvantages of becoming involved in problematic situations, and discuss with Jennifer the "testing" of a plan to check whether Le would isolate her because of her new study habits.

- Help the parents understand that Jennifer's academic problems may be rooted in limitations in her English proficiencies. They may need to obtain extra help for Jennifer.
- Help both Jennifer and her parents verbalize their concerns to each other.

Integrated Parents

Integrated parents focus on the child's development and embrace the values of individual learning and goal setting. They expect their children to integrate new learning into their Asian identity. Like other Vietnamese parents, integrated parents stress the importance of economic and academic successes. Integrated parents are different from bicultural parents in that they *emphasize* the interactions and inter-relationships between the two cultures, not simply adopt them.

A study of child-rearing practices of Vietnamese in Quebec found that Canadian-born mothers introduced toys and activities to their infants much earlier than did Vietnamese-born mothers (Pomerleau, Malcuit, & Sabatier, 1991). Parental beliefs that early interactions with children can enhance children's learning were found to be significantly related to healthy child development. Similarly, Schneider and Lee (1990) found a correlation between Asian students' high achievement and the values they shared with their parents, the home learning activities in which the family participated, and the expectations they shared with their teachers and peers.

Parents who adopt an attitude of openness and support of their children provide their children with learning opportunities and assistance with their cognitive and intellectual development. However, Vietnamese parents who are American-born or educated in the United States have characteristics similar to Vietnamese-born parents in three areas:

1. Academic achievement and upward mobility are not viewed by these parents as personal matters but as part of their children's *obligation* for the maintenance of the family.
2. Vietnamese American parents view their children's achievement as a family investment that is related to their own honor, pride, and happiness. Failure is difficult to accept because it represents the parents' own failure.
3. Poor grades are viewed as culturally unacceptable behaviors and therefore cannot be discussed with people outside the family.

Because of these similarities, the distinct characteristics between traditional parents and the integrated, Americanized parents have not been a focus in research. Nevertheless, Zhou and Bankston (1996) found that family values among these two types of parents can be very different. In their survey of 198 Vietnamese youth, the traditional families were perceived to have three significant values: being obedient, working and studying hard, and helping others when needed, whereas the more Americanized families were self-focused and stressed the importance of being popular.

The literature does not have data to differentiate between integrated parents and bicultural parents. Integration may mean various degrees of cultural assimilation, including complete adoption of the American culture. In this context, however, most Vietnamese parents are first-generation immigrants and they are closer to biculturalism than to complete assimilation. To Vietnamese Americans, the adoption of American culture is a means to enhance family cohesion and promote their children's well-being. Nguyen-Chawkins (1997) found that "children who perceived their parents to be bicultural or assimilated reported significantly less cultural adjustment difficulties than those who perceived their parents to be marginal types" (p. 459). Integrated parents, who have learned to use a variety of new perspectives to fulfill their achievement goals, help their children become assimilated into the American culture. They also preserve many of the traditional values for teaching and parenting purposes.

CASE STUDY: INTEGRATED PARENTS

Mr. and Mrs. Tran came to the United States in 1975. They enjoy their sense of freedom here and yet they still value the Vietnamese culture. They understand the multicultural environment in which their children live. One of their eight children married a Caucasian man with their blessing. This son-in-law is one of their favorite in-laws even though he is not Vietnamese. The Trans emphasize the importance of education, as most Asian families do, but they would not force their children to choose their preferred field. They believe that guidance and encouragement are more important than forceful suggestions.

When the Trans left Vietnam, one of their sons, Phan, had already completed his first year of college in medicine. After coming to America, Phan switched his major to music performance. Because of his talent and interest, he received his master's degree in music from a prestigious school and became a very successful musician. The Trans said that they had encouraged their son to study medicine in Vietnam because of the shortage of doctors during the war and because Phan was bright enough to pursue a career in this field. Even though he agreed to do it, they found that his main love was still classical music; he had excelled at the conservatory for many years. After coming to America, the Trans encouraged Phan to make his own choice. Music is a career that Phan thoroughly enjoys, and his performances always make the parents proud.

Mr. and Mrs. Tran also believe in independence and gender equality. When their youngest daughter started college, she wanted to move out into an apartment instead of living at home. In most cases, Vietnamese American children are not permitted to move out of their parents' household until they finish college or get married. However, the Trans knew that their daughter could manage to be independent and learn to be self-sufficient. They encouraged her to take a part-time job to pay for her expenses while going to school.

Applications of the Cases

These cases, which can be shared with other Vietnamese parents, illustrate that traditional parents can be either *authoritative* (rigid in their thinking and cultural expectations) or *authoritarian* (believing in discipline but willing to adopt new parenting methods). These cases also identify the fact that both bicultural parents and integrated parents may experience cultural identity struggles related to living in a multigenerational family system. These cases provide five major suggestions for parenting in a multicultural environment:

1. Consider the child's developmental needs
2. Assess the child's talent and interest in a culturally different environment
3. Be a good model for children by respecting their decisions while monitoring their progress
4. Identify ways to build positive relationships by sharing cultural adjustment difficulties with the family
5. Express concern and love

In summary, we want to clarify that this presentation of the three categories of Vietnamese parenting styles is not intended to be absolute. We do not maintain that traditional parents practice their actions *only* in traditional ways, or that bicultural parents *always* combine two cultures, or that integrated parents *unquestioningly* embrace a new culture. Two or three types of parenting styles can coexist because of the diverse family backgrounds and the pattern of multigenerational residence among Vietnamese. These parenting styles can be appropriately applied to encourage positive parenting. Bornstein (1991) refers to this integration as "cultural approaches to parenting" with a "developmental niche" (p. 7). Future studies can explore the opinions of Vietnamese American children regarding their views of parenting styles that most enhance positive parent-child relationships.

RECOMMENDATIONS FOR CLINICAL PRACTITIONERS AND EDUCATORS

Based on the literature and case analyses, three observations and recommendations are made. First, some Vietnamese parents and children are flexible in their style and openness to acculturation, while others are very rigid and do not accept change. In counseling and education, rapport and trust with parents are important prerequisites to good working relationships because these families may be ready and willing to take the next adjustment steps if they are asked with empathy and consideration.

Second, parents often idealize what they expect their children to accomplish, either through expressing the Vietnamese cultural beliefs or through espousal of the American value of success. Their thinking then influences their attitudes toward parenting. On the one hand, parents think that they can implicitly convey their messages to their children because they believe they have good intentions. Covert communication or hinting, on the other hand, is not sufficient.

Because Vietnamese American parents seldom bring their relationship problems to therapy, it is recommended that counselors or social workers be available in schools to help parents understand the consequences of the mismatch between their thinking and their children's behavior. These practitioners can make concrete suggestions to help parents transform their parenting ideals into constructive efforts and actions. For example, the ideal expectation is to reward children who receive good grades, and the concrete action is to increase children's motivation for learning by spending time with them while they are doing homework or asking them to report what they have learned as if they are playing the role of a teacher. If parents show patience and willingness to learn from their children, the children will be ready to show their talent.

Cross-cultural or bicultural counselors may be preferred in situations where acculturation differences are the major source of conflict in the native-speaking family. In these situations, bicultural workers need to communicate clearly with the child about their professional role and inquire about the child's interests and goals. They can become models for the child. However, empathy is necessary but not sufficient, because these children are waiting for someone to influence their parents' thinking. From the child's perspective, concrete actions to bring the family together are more helpful than are merely listening and understanding.

Third, the gender equality of children is promoted among some Vietnamese families to facilitate family harmony and ease the social adjustment process. Nevertheless, the family structure and role functions still determine how children behave and relate to their parents. Efforts should be made to help parents break down the communication barriers with their children. These efforts include not only language proficiency (both languages if bilingualism is stressed by the family) but also mutual communication with each other on a regular basis. In many families, both parents work and subscribe to a strong work ethic. It is recommended that time be divided between work and family and that the authoritative role of parents (with strict authority) be transformed into authoritarian (with clear rules and mutual agreement) to encourage the exercise of study discipline and parental involvement. The adoption of a traditional belief that parents should sacrifice their present time for the future of their children can also be advised.

It is crucial for Vietnamese American immigrants to maintain their unique cultural identity while at the same time adapting to the new cultural settings. Parenting styles are influenced by both cultures plus external factors such as the relatively new Vietnamese immigration history, bilingualism and traditional values, parental expectations, parental striving for higher education opportunities, and the ethnic community support. By contrast, internal or individual factors such as personality, childhood experience, war trauma, and psychological distress are seldom addressed as contributors to parent-child relationship problems. Teachers, school counselors, and social workers can provide outreach to children who are caught between two worlds by helping these children appreciate the two cultures and by guiding them through critical situations with patience. The provision of family counseling opportunities may help the family disclose their readiness for possible adaptation.

Discussion Questions and Role-Play Exercises

1. Considering the different parenting styles, discuss what approach or approaches would be effective with Vietnamese American parents when a school-related problem is the center of attention.

2. Identify a culturally sensitive issue that a social worker may need to consider during each problem-solving step with a Vietnamese family (i.e., contact, problem identification, assessment, goal setting, resource identification, intervention, and evaluation).

3. Select one of the cases in the chapter and discuss or role-play the following points:

   a. Your initial assessment about the relationship between the identified client's cultural background and his or her individual issue.

   b. The obstacles the client may see within his or her cultural values.

   c. The client's conflicting views between his or her own thinking and the traditional cultural value or values.

   d. How the client could help himself or herself understand the root cause of the family issue.

   e. The interventions that would help both the child and the parents.

   f. How to approach the father (or mother) to collect additional data about the parent-child relationship. How might traditional values and belief systems be utilized in the helping process? Role-play your initial telephone contact and the beginning of the first session.

   g. How to help the child in the school environment.

   h. How the parents (and siblings) could be involved in this helping process.

   i. What culturally competent intervention techniques you have learned from this case.

References

Bankston, C. L. (1995). Vietnamese ethnicity and adolescent substance abuse: Evidence for a community-level approach. *Deviant Behavior, 16*(1), 59–80.

Bankston, C. L. (1997). Education and ethnicity in an urban Vietnamese village: The role of ethnic community involvement in academic achievement. In M. Seller & L. Weis (Eds.), *Beyond black and white* (pp. 207–30). Albany: State University of New York Press.

Bornstein, M. H. (Ed.). (1991). *Cultural approaches to parenting*. Hillsdale, NJ: Lawrence Erlbaum.

Buriel, R., & De Ment, T. D. (1997). Immigration and sociocultural change in Mexican, Chinese, and Vietnamese American families. In A. Booth, A. C. Crounter, & N. Landale (Eds.), *Immigration and the family: Research and policy on U.S. immigrants* (pp. 165–200). Mahwah, NJ: Lawrence Erlbaum.

Caplan, N., Whitmore, J. K., & Choy, M. H. (1989). *The boat people and achievement in America: A study of family life, hard work, and cultural values*. Ann Arbor: University of Michigan Press.

Cheung, K. M. (1997). Cultural adjustment and differential acculturation among Chinese new immigrant families in the United States. In S. Lau (Ed.), *Growing up the Chinese way: Chinese child and adolescent development* (pp. 321–55). Hong Kong: Chinese University Press.

Dinh, K. T., Sarason, B. R., & Sarason, I. G. (1994). Parent-child relationships in Vietnamese immigrant families. *Journal of Family Psychology, 8*(4), 471–88.

Erikson, E. (1968). *Identity: Youth and crisis*. New York: W. W. Norton.

Haines, D. W., Rutherford, D., & Thomas, P. (1981). Family and community among Vietnamese refugees. *International Migration Review, 15*, 310–19.

Kim, H. (1997). *Diversity among Asian American high school students*. Princeton, NJ: Policy Information Center.

Kim, H. (1998). Asian-American students: Ethnicity, acculturation, type of problems, and their effect on willingness to seek counseling and comfort level in working with different types of counselors. *Dissertation Abstracts International (Section A: Humanities and Social Sciences), 58*(9-A), 3417.

Leichty, M. M. (1963). Family attitudes and self-concept in Vietnamese and U.S. children. *American Journal of Orthopsychiatry, 33*(1), 38–50.

Lo, S. (1980). *The reason of exodus of refugees from Vietnam and its consequences.* Republic of China: World Anti-Communist League, China Chapter, and Asian People's Anti-Communist League.

Mau, W. (1997). Parental influences on the high school students' academic achievement: A comparison of Asian immigrants, Asian Americans, and white Americans. *Psychology in the Schools, 34*(3), 267–77.

McKelvey, R. S., Davies, L. C., Sang, D. L., Pickering, K. R., & Tu, H. C. (1999). Problems and competencies reported by parents of Vietnamese children in Hanoi. *Journal of the American Academy of Child and Adolescent Psychiatry, 38*(6), 731–37.

Montero, D. (1979). *Vietnamese Americans: Patterns of resettlement and socioeconomic adaptation in the United States.* Boulder, CO: Westview Press.

Morrow, R. (1987). Cultural differences—Be aware! *Academic Therapy, 23*(2), 143–49.

Nguyen, N. A., & Williams, H. L. (1989). Transition from east to west: Vietnamese adolescents and their parents. *Journal of American Academy of Child and Adolescent Psychiatry, 28*(4), 505–15.

Nguyen-Chawkins, L. L. (1997). Vietnamese Americans embedded in multicultural contexts: Structural equation modeling of acculturation and family. *Dissertation Abstracts International (Section B: Sciences and Engineering) 58*(1-B), 0459.

Peng, S. S., & Wright, D. (1993, January). *Learning programs at home: An explanation of the high academic achievement of Asian American students.* Paper presented at the Winter Conference of the American Statistical Association, Ft. Lauderdale, FL.

Pomerleau, A., Malcuit, G., & Sabatier, C. (1991). Child-rearing practices and parental beliefs in three cultural groups of Montreal: Quebecois, Vietnamese, Haitian. In M. H. Bornstein (Ed.), *Cultural approaches to parenting* (pp. 45–68). Hillsdale, NJ: Lawrence Erlbaum.

Portes, A. (Ed.). (1996). *The new second generation.* New York: Russell Sage Foundation.

Romero, A. J., & Roberts, R. E. (1998). Perception of discrimination and ethnocultural variables in a diverse group of adolescents. *Journal of Adolescence, 21*(6), 641–56.

Rosenthal, D., Ranieri, N., & Klimidis, S. (1996). Vietnamese adolescents in Australia: Relationships between perceptions of self and parental values, intergenerational conflict, and gender dissatisfaction. *International Journal of Psychology, 31*(2), 81–91.

St. Cartmail, K. (1983). *Exodus Indochina.* Auckland, New Zealand: Heinemann.

Schneider, B., & Lee, Y. (1990). A model for academic success: The school and home environment of East Asian students. *Anthropology and Education, 21,* 358–77.

Silove, D., Manicavasagar, V., Beltran, R., Le, G., Nguyen, H., Phan, T., & Blaszczynski, A. (1997). Satisfaction of Vietnamese patients and their families with refugee and mainstream mental health services. *Psychiatric Services, 48*(8), 1064–69.

Slote, W. H. (1998). Destiny and determination: Psychocultural reinforcement in Vietnam. In W. H. Slote & G. A. De Vos (Eds.), *Confucianism and the family* (pp. 311–28). Albany: State University of New York Press.

Sue, S., & Okazaki, S. (1990). Asian American educational achievements: A phenomenon in search of an explanation. *American Psychologist, 45,* 913–20.

Timberlake, E. M., & Cook, K. O. (1984). Social work and the Vietnamese refugee. *Social Work, 29,* 109–13.

Tran, Q. D., & Richey, C. A. (1997). Family functioning and psychological well-being in Vietnamese adolescents. *Journal of Sociology and Social Welfare, 24*(1), 41–61.

Tran, T. V. (1998). The Vietnamese American family. In C. H. Mindel, R. W. Haberstein & R. Wright, Jr. (Eds.), *Ethnic families in America: Patterns and variations* (pp. 254–83). Upper Saddle River, NJ: Prentice Hall.

U.S. Immigration and Naturalization Service. (1997). *Statistical Yearbook*. Washington, DC: U.S. Department of Justice.

U.S. Immigration and Naturalization Service. (1998). *Annual Report*. Washington, DC: U.S. Department of Justice.

Walker-Moffat, W. (1995). *The other side of the Asian American success story*. San Francisco: Jossey-Bass.

Weinberg, M. (1997). Asian-American education: Historical background and current realities. Mahwah, NJ: Lawrence Erlbaum.

Ying, Y. W., Akutsu, P. D., Zhang, X., & Huang, L. N. (1997). Psychological dysfunction in Southeast Asian refugees as mediated by sense of coherence. *American Journal of Community Psychology, 25*(6), 839–59.

Zhou, M., & Bankston, C. L., III. (1996). Social capital and the adaptation of the second generation: The case of Vietnamese youth in New Orleans. In A. Portes (Ed.), *The new second generation* (pp. 197–232). New York: Russell Sage Foundation.

12

Parenting in Japanese American Families

TAZUKO SHIBUSAWA

The experiences of Japanese American families, like other immigrant families, have been shaped by the culture and values of their country of origin as well as the social, political, and economic conditions of the United States. Most Japanese American children today are fourth and fifth generation and do not speak Japanese. Furthermore, there is a growing number of Japanese American children who are biracial and multiracial because of an increase in interracial marriage. Some practitioners, on the other hand, may encounter Japanese children who are in the United States on a temporary basis as children of expatriates. Despite their differences, these children share a common thread. Researchers have found that even fourth- and fifth-generation Japanese Americans who do not speak Japanese have retained aspects of the traditional Japanese culture. This chapter provides a historical overview of the Japanese American family, discusses issues that are unique to Japanese American parenting, and finally, addresses issues specific to clinical practice with Japanese American children and their parents.

CASE STUDY: KEN

Ken is a thirteen-year-old Japanese American adolescent. He was referred to Carol, a clinical social worker who works at a child guidance clinic, by his home-

The author would like to express her appreciation to Shinhee Han, CSW, and Laura Shiozaki-Lee, LCSW, for their helpful suggestions.

room teacher. According to the homeroom teacher, Ken seemed withdrawn and kept to himself during study hall and recess. Ken was a new student at the school. He and his family moved here six months ago from another state. The homeroom teacher was also concerned because Ken had not been handing in his homework and was getting Ds on his tests. Some of his teachers wondered if Ken had a learning disability. Ken's parents were very concerned about their son's academic performance and met with the homeroom teacher. During the meeting, the homeroom teacher noted that Ken's father, David, attributed Ken's problems to the move and to lack of motivation. Ken's mother, Ann, had been aware of Ken's academic difficulties for some time because she used to help him with his homework. However, since the move, Ken had refused to let her help him. He spent most of his time in his bedroom and easily lost his temper whenever his parents mentioned his schoolwork. When the homeroom teacher suggested that the parents seek counseling and have Ken tested to rule out possible learning disabilities, Ken's father seemed shocked. He reacted by asking, "Do you think that my son is mentally ill?" Ken's mother also seemed upset and asked if there was something terribly wrong with her son. The homeroom teacher was taken aback by the parents' reactions because he had assumed that they were knowledgeable about counseling. The parents seemed well educated: The homeroom teacher knew that David was a successful engineer, and he had heard Ann say, in passing, that she was an optometrist. Although they were Asian, they spoke fluent English, and they seemed like all the other professional parents who lived in the surrounding neighborhood.

Carol was a seasoned clinician who had extensive experience working with young adolescents and their families. However, she had never worked with an Asian American family. She had guessed by their last name that Ken and his parents were Japanese. As she began the initial session with Ken and his parents, she could tell right away that Ken did not want to be there. He sat on the corner of the sofa gazing out her window. Carol sensed that David did not want to be there, either. He was polite, but seemed distant. She could sense tension between the father and the son. Ann seemed to be the only one who was eager to be there. But at the same time, Ann seemed to be overly concerned about David's reactions toward Carol. It seemed as if Ann wanted to make sure that both her son and husband were behaving themselves in front of the therapist.

As Carol sat back, she quickly went through a mental inventory of what she knew about Japanese families. While asking the parents for information about the current family situation, Carol kept wondering if she should address the fact that the family was Japanese. Fearing that she might offend the family if she asked them about their ethnicity and cultural background, she decided to hold back. Besides, she thought, culture did not seem to be relevant. Ken and Ann seemed so acculturated. Their outward appearance and mannerisms were those of well-educated professionals. Her clinical hunch was that, Ken's academic problems aside, this was a family going through a life-cycle crisis. The parents were struggling with a son who was turning into a young adolescent. Carol decided to ignore the fact that Ken and his family were racially different from her and to proceed the way she did with her Euro-American families.

By deciding to ignore culture, Carol lost the opportunity to fully understand and explore issues that were contributing to Ken's problems. In addition, she ran the risk of pathologizing Ken's family when they did not behave according to her expectations. Although most parents of Japanese American children are third or later generation, they retain certain norms and values of traditional Japanese culture. In addition, unlike their third-generation European American counterparts, they are not white, and they face the challenges that are common among other people of color in the United States. By not addressing the family's ethnic background, Carol did not have an opportunity to comprehend the anger that David often felt when he confronted subtle racism at his workplace and how this anger affected his relationship with his wife and son. She also missed the difficulties that Ken was experiencing as one of the few Asians in his new school, that he was surrounded by male and female classmates who were sexually maturing at a much faster pace than he was.

HISTORICAL BACKGROUND

The main wave of Japanese immigration to the United States occurred between the late 1800s and the early part of the 1920s. Unlike Eastern Europeans, who immigrated in family units, the first immigrants from Japan were single men who came as contract laborers (Ichioka, 1988). These men came to the United States on a temporary basis and planned to return to Japan after achieving economic success. They eventually found, however, that it was not possible to fulfill their dreams in a lifetime. At the time, antimiscegenation laws barred Japanese Americans from marrying outside their race, so some returned to Japan to find wives and then brought their spouses back with them. Others depended on family and relatives to find a suitable mate, whom they married through proxy, so that the women could immigrate as wives because immigration was restricted to family members. These women were known as picture brides because they had only seen their husband's pictures when they arrived in the United States. This arrangement continued until 1924 when the Immigration Exclusion Act banned all immigration from Japan (Ichioka). The doors for Japanese immigration did not reopen until the Immigration Act was partially revised in 1952. Because of this unique immigration history, Japanese Americans are identified by generation. The first generation is known as *Issei*, which means first generation. The second generation, those who were born in the United States, are known as *Nisei* along with a subgroup of *Nisei* known as *Kibei Nisei* who were sent back to be Japan to be educated. The children of *Nisei* are called *Sansei*, or third generation, and they fall into the same cohort as the baby boomer generation. Their offspring are *Yonsei* (fourth generation), and their grandchildren are *Gosei* (fifth generation).

Most Japanese, except for those who immigrated to Hawaii, settled on the West Coast during an era of intense anti-Asian sentiment. The anti-Japanese sentiment culminated during World War II with the internment of all persons of Japanese ancestry on the West Coast. Close to 120,000 Japanese Americans, including children who had U.S. citizenship, were suddenly classified as "enemy aliens," uprooted from their communities, and forced into camps in the hinterlands of the United States. Mental health practitioners have noted the impact that the internment had on Japanese American families (Nagata, 1993). Most families lost their homes and belongings. Some were separated into different internment camps. Others were scarred by the division in loyalties toward Japan and the United States. The second generation (*Nisei*), who were adolescents or young adults during internment, faced shame and humiliation regarding their ethnic heritage and pressure to prove their loyalty toward the United States by becoming "super American" (Mass, 1991; Nagata). The *Nisei* kept silent about the internment experience for many years, and it was not until the 1980 Redress Hearings that people began to be more open about discussing their experiences (Nagata). Nagata notes that the internment experience has left its shadows on subsequent generations of Japanese Americans in terms of distrust and fear toward the majority society.

The 1990 census indicates that the age structure among Japanese Americans was similar to that of the total U.S. population. Sixteen percent of the population were under age fifteen, and 12 percent were age sixty-five or older (Lee, 1998). The medium family income at that time was $51,550, which indicates middle- to upper-middle-class status. More than 35 percent had a bachelor's degree or higher. The poverty rate among Japanese Americans in 1989 was estimated to be somewhere between 3 percent and 7 percent, which was also similar to the poverty rate for European American families (Lee). Families tended to be very small, and the total fertility rate for Japanese American women was 1.1. The low birth rate was associated with high educational levels and high average incomes. This statistic was similar to the birth characteristics for Chinese, Koreans, and South Asians (Lee). Japanese American women, like other Asian American women, had lower rates of giving birth out of wedlock.

TRADITIONAL FAMILY RELATIONSHIPS

Japanese immigrants brought with them family norms of the Meiji era (1868–1919). During this period in Japan the household was legally organized according to an extended family system known as the *ie*. Although most immigrants were from poor rural areas, the *ie* was modeled after the *samurai* (warrior) class and implemented throughout Japan. The *ie* was headed by a male figure, who was succeeded by the eldest son. The *ie* system was reinforced by Confucian ethics of filial piety, which included:

- Obeying and respecting one's parents
- Obligation and loyalty toward the family
- Ensuring the succession of the family line
- Not bringing shame to the family (Ho, 1994)

Marriage was seen as a union of two households rather than two individuals, and wives were expected to sever ties with their own families of origin when marrying into the husband's *ie*. Family relationships were highly structured in a hierarchical order, and interactions were determined by prescribed roles. Although the *ie* system was legally abolished in Japan after World War II, family dynamics continue to center around the parent-child unit over the marital unit, and married couples identify more with their parental roles than their conjugal roles (Shibusawa, 1992).

PARENT-CHILD RELATIONSHIPS

Japanese American families have retained aspects of their culture of origin. Differences in parenting have been observed between Japanese Americans and European Americans in the areas of developmental goals (Ching, McDermott, Fukunaga, & Yanagida, 1995; Matsui, 1986), educational expectations (Schneider, Hieshima, Lee, & Plank, 1994), child rearing (Caudill & Frost, 1972, as cited in Yee, Huang, & Lew, 1998), and communication patterns (C. L. Johnson, 1977; F. A. Johnson & Marsella, 1978; F. A. Johnson, Marsella, & Johnson, 1974; Kitano, 1976).

Developmental Goals

In capturing the differences between Western and Japanese cultures, Wagatsuma and Rosett (1983) note that, "the Japanese live by the illusion of harmony while Americans live by the illusions of autonomy and self-sufficiency" (pp. 95–96). Implications of this difference for parenting are listed in table 12.1. Among European American families, individuation and autonomy are viewed as the main goals of child development. Emphasis is placed on fostering "self-determination" and "self-

Table 12.1. Cultural Differences in Parent-Child Relationships

European Americans	Japanese Americans
Conceptualization of selfhood	
Psychological self: Emphasis on individual dimension	Social self: Emphasis on collective dimension
Expectations for development	
Development of cohesive self	Development of nonegocentric self
Self-determination	Adaptability to groups
Independence	Interdependence
Self-expression	Impulse control
Leadership skills	Effective participation in groups
Emphasis on ability	Emphasis on effort
Self-enhancement	Self-effacement
Discipline	
Direct	Indirect
Authoritative	Permissive
Explicit instructional information	Passive and ambiguous instructions
Punishment	
Withdrawal of privileges	Silent treatment
Verbal scolding	Verbal humiliation

reliance" as children are expected to grow out of a dependent state of infancy into autonomous individuality. In Japanese culture, individuation and autonomy are not conceptualized as developmental goals. Rather, parents strive to instill in their children what F. A. Johnson (1993) calls a "non-egocentric conception of self," which enables children to adapt to group norms and function as social beings. While European American children are encouraged to define who they are and to shape their environment according to their own will or beliefs, Japanese children are expected to acquire skills that will enable them to understand what is expected by their social environment and to accommodate to these expectations.

Cross-national studies comparing Japanese and European American mothers show that Japanese mothers expect of their children early mastery of self-control and effective participation in groups along with emotional maturity, whereas their U.S. counterparts expect their children to be socially and verbally assertive, exert leadership, and stand up for their rights (Azuma, Kashiwagi, & Hess, 1981; Hess, Kashiwagi, Azuma, Price, & Dickson, 1980; Machida, 1996). Research among Japanese American parents also indicates that they differ from European American parents in that they emphasize "good behavior" over "self-directed behavior" (Reilly as cited in Yee et al., 1998).

Impulse control, which is viewed as a sign of emotional maturity in Japanese culture, is emphasized by parents from an early age. Children are frequently told by their parents that they have to *gaman,* which means "to endure" or "withhold ones' wishes." This term is understood even among third- and later-generation Japanese Americans who do not speak Japanese (Matsui, 1986). Children are also taught to *enryo,* which means hold back from expressing what they want.

Children are expected to behave appropriately to group norms, and this behavior is related to what Lebra terms "positional socialization" (1994, p. 265). Children are taught to act or present themselves in ways that are appropriate to their position or prescribed roles according to their gender, sibling order, and age. They become aware of the hierarchical structure of their surroundings from an early age. For example, children are often told not to act in certain ways because of their age or because of their position as an older sibling. Even third- and later-generation Japanese Americans have been found to show more concern for hierarchy and status than do their European American counterparts (F. A. Johnson et al., 1974). This behavior can place Japanese American children at a disadvantage, because they may not question the teachers' authority, leaving the impression that they do not have the ability to be assertive or think for themselves.

European American parents encourage their children to be confident and self-sufficient, in part by encouraging children to have a positive view about themselves (Heine & Lehman, 1999). Japanese children, on the other hand, are discouraged from showing off their adequacies or competence because such behavior would hinder them from blending into their groups. They put into practice the old Japanese saying that "the nail that sticks out gets hammered down." In addition, they are encouraged to dwell on their inadequacies and shortcomings (Heine & Lehman). Behaving modestly and down playing their abilities will prevent them from being threatening or offensive toward others.

As such, competition is masked with self-effacing behavior. Japanese Americans of third and later generations have been found to be more self-effacing in public and have a tendency to downplay their accomplishments compared to European Americans (Akimoto & Sanbonmatsu, 1999). This behavior can be problematic for Japanese American children and youth in that self-effacing behaviors in Western culture may be viewed as a sign of weakness. Because of their minority status, many Japanese Americans may feel that they have to fit in without creating waves. Self-abnegation may be a strategy that they use so that they can be liked and can avoid conflicts (Akimoto & Sanbonmatsu). As a result, they can end up being evaluated by their teachers and peers as less competent and less adequate. For example, Japanese American students may not speak up in situations where students are encouraged to point out their own accomplishments. As a result, they can be perceived as withdrawn, passive, and lacking in self-confidence, and they may receive poor evaluations. With a child like Ken, who is shy to begin with, school personnel must recognize the particular difficulties that Japanese American students may have in adjusting to a new school.

Education

Japanese American parents hold higher educational expectations for their children than do European American parents (Goyette & Xie, 1999; Schneider et al., 1994). These higher expectations are attributed to two factors: a cultural tradition that places value on education, and the belief that educational achievement will improve occupational opportunities and help counteract racial discrimination. Cross-cultural studies indicate that parents in Japan and the United States have different concepts regarding their children's potential for academic achievement. As a means of helping their children succeed in school, Japanese mothers emphasize *effort*, whereas European American mothers emphasize *ability* (Holloway, Kashiwagi, Hess, & Azuma, 1986). This variation in emphasis is because children in Japanese culture are viewed as having equal potential for achievement. Individual abilities are not emphasized, and in fact, in schools, all children pass from one grade to another (Lanham & Garrick, 1996). A child's success in school is assumed to be due to that child's effort rather than his or her individual ability. Because of this lack of emphasis on individual ability, Japanese parents often lack an understanding of learning disabilities. They often see academic failure as a lack of effort on the part of the child, or they may overreact and view academic difficulties as a result of a developmental disability. Another concern that can arise among school personnel is the high expectations that Japanese parents have for their children's achievement. Because scholastic excellence is not viewed in relation to ability, Japanese parents may not understand that students in European American culture are evaluated based on their abilities as well as efforts. Some teachers may reserve an A+ only for students with exceptional ability and performance, whereas Japanese parents may expect their children to get an A+ for hard work alone.

The perception that Asian Americans excel in school can be problematic. Some Japanese American children are resented and harassed by their peers for doing well in school (Schneider et al., 1994). Non-Asian parents are at times vocal about their resentment toward "the Asian kids who raise the level of test scores." Furthermore, Japanese American children who are not successful in school, like Ken, can end up feeling as if they are a *total* failure (Henkin, 1985).

Child Rearing

Very little research has been conducted on Japanese American child-rearing practices. Nevertheless, studies of child rearing in Japan enable researchers to speculate with some confidence about the cultural traits that have been retained by Japanese American families. Cross-cultural studies have found that Japanese mothers are less authoritarian and less confrontational than European American mothers are (Lanham & Garrick, 1996; Machida, 1996). In Japanese culture, emphasis is placed on the development of empathy, known as *omoiyari* (Lanham & Garrick; Lebra, 1994). European American parents expect their children to behave according to a set of values, and they communicate these values to their children directly. European American parents view themselves as the agency of authority and expect children to obey them. There is an underlying assumption that the children will obey them because they are the parents. Japanese parents also expect their children to acquire proper behavior, but emphasis is placed on teaching children to think about the ramifications of their behavior on others. Thus, in addition to being told what they can or cannot do, Japanese American children are also given messages such as, "What will others think if you do such and such" or "You will be embarrassing yourself (and consequently bringing shame on the whole family) if you do such and such."

The following is an example of the way a Japanese mother sets boundaries of acceptable and unacceptable behaviors through teaching empathy. As part of my psychoanalytic training, I conducted weekly observations over a period of twelve months of a Japanese mother and her newly born son who lived in California. The baby began to teethe at six months and started to bite his mother's nipples while he was breastfed. The mother responded by acting as if she were in pain, and she would cry out, *itai itai* meaning "ouch ouch." She would playact and place her hands on her face as if to wipe away tears. She asked me to do the same whenever the baby pulled my hair. The mother believed that her baby would stop biting her or pulling hair when he realized that he was hurting her or others. A European American mother probably would have gently pulled her nipple out of the baby's mouth and simply said "no." The Japanese mother's way of getting her baby to stop his behavior was to show how his behavior was affecting her and hurting her. It was her attempt to foster empathy in the baby, which in effect fosters concern for others. Anthropologists have in fact observed that Japanese infants are socialized from a very early stage by their mothers to be "other-oriented" (Caudill & Weinstein, 1969). Furthermore, Conroy, Hess, Azuma, and Kashiwagi (1980) found that Japanese mothers were likely to use feeling-oriented appeals to regulate children's behavior, whereas American mothers used appeals to their parental authority.

Although less authoritarian, Japanese parents do not give as much positive reinforcement as do European American parents, who place importance on praising, encouraging, and complimenting their children's positive features. Japanese parents fear that children will become too self-centered and will not be able to fit in with others if they are given too much positive reinforcement. From an early age, Japanese children are taught to be aware of their weaknesses and inadequacies and to correct them (F. A. Johnson, 1993).

Studies have found that third- and fourth-generation Japanese Americans, when compared to their European American cohorts, demonstrate a greater need for affiliation, a sensitivity toward the attitudes of others, and a tendency to put themselves down (Akimoto & Sanbonmatsu, 1999). Clinical evidence suggests that the cultural differences between Japanese and Western child-rearing approaches can be a source of conflict for Japanese Americans who have to balance both cultures.

Ken's mother, Ann, felt that her husband was too strict, authoritarian, and insensitive toward their son's psychological development. However, as Ann began to reflect on her relationship with her own mother and the way she felt as a child, she remembered how critical her mother had always been and how she had never been praised by her mother. Rather than understanding her mother's lack of positive reinforcement as a cultural trait, Ann had internalized the lack of validation from her mother as a lack of love and feared that her children would end up feeling the same way if she, as a mother, were in any way critical of them.

Although Japanese parents may be less authoritarian in interacting with their children, forms of physical punishment are at times used as methods of discipline. Traditional means of punishment include moxibustion, a Chinese remedy for body aches in which small pellets of compressed *moxa,* an herb, are burned on specific acupuncture points, such as the back (F. A. Johnson, 1993). The *moxa* pellet is very hot as it burns on the body and can leave burn marks, an act that would be considered abuse in the United States. Rates of child abuse in the Japanese American community are not available. The estimated incidence of reported child abuse in Japan is about 7 per 100,000 children, which is similar to that of the United States (Kitamura, Kimijima, Iwata, Senda, & Takahashi, 1999).

Observers of Japanese culture have noted the central role that mothers play in child rearing. Motherhood is more revered in Japan than it is in Western cultures (Lebra, 1984). The idealized image of the Japanese mother is one who is selfless and sacrifices everything for her children. Classical studies on mother-child relationships in Japan have argued that Japanese mothers see their infants as an extension of themselves, whereas European American mothers see their infants as separate beings (Caudill & Weinstein, 1969). Given the lack of physical expression of affection that has already been discussed, it is interesting to note that Japanese mothers have more physical contact with their infants than do European American mothers. The use of nonfamilial caretakers such as baby sitters is rare, and cosleeping is common until the child enters school (Caudill & Plath, 1996).

In Japanese families, discipline is usually carried out by the mother because the father spends most of his time at work. Because of the mother-child closeness, the threat of distance and separation are used as methods of punishment. Silence is used as a punishment in which the mother ignores the presence of the child (Tomita, 1998). Verbal expression of disapproval also connotes threats of abandonment. For example, "A bad child like you does not belong to us" is a typical statement used by mothers in Japan. Childhood verbal humiliation and disapproval from parents are common themes that frequently come up among Japanese American adults in psychotherapy (L. Shiozaki-Lee, interview, February 24, 2000). In traditional Japan, children were locked out of the home and not let in until they expressed regret for their actions (F. A. Johnson, 1993). This punishment is in direct contrast to the dreaded Euro-American punishment of being grounded, in which children are not able to go outside the house. Although this locking-out punishment is not practiced among Japanese American families today, it is indicative of the use of separation as a form of punishment in Japanese culture.

Japanese American mothers are more likely to work outside the home than are their cohorts in Japan (Takanishi, 1994). Most Japanese American parents make the same provisions for child care that their European American counterparts do, including the use of day care and preschool programs. Asking the grandparents to care for their children is not as common among Japanese Americans as it is in Chinese and Korean American families. Yet according to a study among Japanese American families in the Midwest, mothers along with fathers tended to spend more time with their children than did their non-Japanese counterparts (Schneider et al., 1994).

Communication Patterns

Whereas verbal communication is emphasized in Western cultures, nonverbal communication is emphasized in Japanese culture, like it is in other East Asian cultures. Children are taught to infer what others are trying to communicate from the context and the way in which something is being communicated. People are expected to use *ki* (energy) to understand and accommodate to the needs of others without explicit discussion. This approach is related to the empathy that children are expected to develop from their early years. Furthermore, Japanese place more emphasis on what is *not* said rather than what is said (Doi, 1986), partly because Japanese feel that emotions and sentiments are not something that can be captured or communicated by words. Emotions are, therefore, experienced and acknowledged but not necessarily discussed. To the Western eye, the lack of verbal communication about emotions and personal matters can appear as if direct communication is avoided in Japanese American families (Kitano, 1976; Kitano & Daniels, 1988). Avoidance, however, connotes intentionality. When people constantly use a lot of energy to try to sense what others feel or want, then direct communication is not as necessary.

Affection is not expressed physically nor demonstrated in traditional Japanese families. Parents do not display physical intimacy toward each other, nor do they demonstrate physical affection toward their children. The extent to which affection is displayed in Japanese American families differs in each family according to the extent to which they have incorporated the communication patterns of mainstream culture. For those who grew up in a traditional Japanese household while attending a Western school, the cultural differences in styles of emotional expression can be a source of conflict.

For example, Ann recalls how she used to envy her American friends whose parents seemed so affectionate and demonstrative of their affection. As a child, she wished her parents were able to be more demonstrative of their feelings.

EXTENDED FAMILIES

In traditional Japanese culture, children lived with their parents until marriage. The eldest son never left his parents: His wife joined the household upon marriage and cared for his parents when they became frail. In present-day Japan, more than 60 percent of elderly live with their adult children and grandchildren. Among Japanese Americans, 37 percent of older women who are widowed live with their adult children (Kamo & Zhou, 1994). This figure is quite high in comparison to the non-Hispanic white figure of 9.4 percent. However, unlike their Japanese counterparts, Japanese American elders do not live continuously with their adult children. Only after they become widowed do they move in with their children. As I mentioned earlier, grandparent involvement in child rearing in Japanese American families, compared to Chinese and Korean families, is not common. This lack of involvement is because more than 60 percent of Japanese American elders were born in the United States and have adapted to the values of independence and autonomy among family members once the children reach adulthood.

ADOLESCENT DEVELOPMENT

One of the issues that Ken is dealing with is low self-esteem that stems from being in a predominantly European American school. In his previous school, Ken was surrounded by other Asian Americans, and he had never thought of himself as different. In addition to the normative tasks of development, Japanese American youth, like other ethnic adolescents, must confront the stresses of being a minority. Third- and later-generation Japanese Americans, with the exception of those who live in Hawaii or the West Coast, are often asked the question, "Where were you born?" This question would not be put to a third- or fourth-generation European American. As Henkin (1985) states, Japanese Americans "may feel American, speak American, act American, and think American. But unlike their friends in the cultural mainstream, they can never look American, and as far as America is concerned, then, there is some important way in which they can never be American" (p. 502).

Researchers find that many Asian American adolescents grow up with a poorer body image and self-image than their European American cohorts do (Yee et al.,

1998). There is evidence that Japanese American youth are less satisfied with their physical characteristics than are their white counterparts (Pang, Mizokawa, Morishima, & Olstad, 1985). Kitano and Daniels (1988) note that many Japanese American youth prefer belonging to either Japanese or Asian American groups rather than to racially heterogeneous groups.

Sex is a topic that is not discussed in most Asian American families, including Japanese American families (S. Han, interview, February 23, 2000; L. Shiozaki-Lee, interview, February 24, 2000). This lack of openness can be problematic for Japanese American adolescents in the midst of developing their own sexual identity. Boys in particular are confronted with "emasculated images" of Asian American males in the media, which can affect the development of a healthy sexual self-image (Leong, 1995). David Mura, a third-generation Japanese American writer, grew up in the Midwest where there were few Asians. In his memoir, he discusses how he grew up believing that white girls would never be attracted to him because he was Japanese and how the accompanying resentment had long-lasting effects on his life (1996). Because discussion of sex in the family is effectively prohibited, adolescents who may be becoming aware of their homosexual orientation may lack an emotionally safe environment (Aoki, 1996; S. Han, interview, February 24, 2000). *Honor Thy Children* documents the story of a Japanese American family with two gay sons who died from HIV-AIDS. The father discusses the rift in the parent-child relationship because of the family's inability to discuss sex, let alone issues of sexual orientation (Fumia, 1997).

BIRACIAL AND MULTIRACIAL JAPANESE AMERICAN CHILDREN

The rate of interracial marriages among Japanese Americans has been increasing over the years. According to the 1980 census records, the out-marriage rate for Japanese American women was more than 40 percent (34 percent for whites), and more than 20 percent for men (13.7 percent for whites; Lee & Yamanaka, 1990). Furthermore, the 1990 census indicates that there were almost 40 percent more Japanese/white births than monoracial Japanese American births (1990 census as cited in Root, 1996). These statistics mean that practitioners and school personnel will come into contact with more and more Japanese Americans who are biracial or multiracial.

In recent years, biracial and multiracial Japanese American clinicians and scholars have begun to construct a framework to understand the experiences of being biracial and multiracial by incorporating analyses of the sociopolitical contexts in which identity development has taken place (Root, 1996). These researchers discuss the limitations of the current racial framework in identifying themselves as biracial or multiracial Japanese Americans (King & DaCosta, 1996; Williams & Thornton, 1998). Biracial and multiracial Japanese Americans may be forced to choose one ethnic identity and then can end up being "a minority within a minority" (Motoyoshi as cited in Root, 1998). Common themes among biracial and multiracial Japanese Americans include dissonance between the way they feel about themselves and the way they are defined by society, marginalization, the lack of role models, inability to talk with parents about their experiences, and the confusion sometimes caused by their ability to embrace multiple identities (Fukuyama, 1999; King & DaCosta; Root, 1996, 1998; Stephan & Stephan, 1989; Williams & Thornton). In addition, experiences differ between those who are part Japanese–part Asian, part Japanese–part white, and part Japanese–part other persons of color. Oriti, Bibb, and Mahboubi (1996) discuss the importance for monoracial practitioners to learn about multiple ethnic identities from their biracial and multiracial clients so that they can work from a strengths perspective.

HELP-SEEKING PATTERNS

Japanese Americans in general, like other Asian American groups, are reluctant to seek mental health services (Uomoto & Gorsuch, 1984). This reluctance has been attributed to a culturally fostered shame and stigma toward mental illness (Kitano, 1976). Traditionally, mental illness was thought to be "in the blood" and hereditary, thus leaving families with a sense of disgrace toward having a mentally ill family member. Mental illness was also attributed to "lack of will power" (Sue & Morishima, 1982). As I stated previously, impulse control is viewed as a sign of emotional maturity in Japanese culture, and people are expected to cope by enduring hardships. Japanese Americans try to resolve problems on their own before seeking help from others. Usually, help is sought from the outside only when the situation worsens. When help is sought, the preference is to seek help from family or friends or religious leaders rather than mental health professionals.

CLINICAL PRACTICE WITH JAPANESE AMERICAN FAMILIES

Western psychotherapy is based on a set of assumptions that are counter to Japanese culture. In order to work effectively with Japanese American clients, practitioners first need to be aware of the Western values that are inherent in clinical practice. This section reviews some of the assumptions that are based on Western values and some typical responses of Japanese and Japanese American clients. Practitioners must recognize, however, that some Japanese American clients may be comfortable with Western styles of therapy while others may not. The first task with Japanese American clients, as with all clinical work, is to establish good rapport so that the clinician can initiate conversations about possible cultural differences between the clinician and client.

Assumption 1. Problems Can and Should Be Solved

Japanese tend to have a fatalistic attitude toward life. The attitude of *shikataganai* (things can't be helped) is a coping method that has been used by earlier generations of Japanese Americans in coping with adversities. When clients come with a presenting problem, it is important for clinicians to offer suggestions and concrete advice. Clients want to find out what they can do, such as changing their own behavior. However, suggestions for changes that will affect others around them, such as acting in a way that will upset other family members, should not be given lightly and without discussions on anticipated consequences. Otherwise, clients may opt to live with the problem rather than provoke conflictual situations.

Assumption 2. Problems Can Be Solved by Talking About Them

Japanese do not necessarily believe that talking about problems can bring about resolutions. Clients can feel threatened if the clinician suggests a family meeting in which everyone will be asked to talk about the problem. This attitude, however, does not mean that clinicians should not initiate family meetings. In fact, given the importance of the family in Japanese culture, clinicians should include family members whenever possible. Families who are asked to attend sessions should be told that the clinician would like to meet with them *so that they can help the clinician help the client*. In family sessions, the clinician needs to take the lead in soliciting information from each family member. Giving directives to family members to talk to each other can make clients feel very awkward.

I have found Family Sculpting to be a useful tool in working with Japanese families, especially with children; although it is a silent activity, it reveals a lot of information about family dynamics. This technique was developed by family therapist Peggy Papp and colleagues (Papp, Silverstein, & Carter, 1975). The clinician asks a family member, usually the identified client, to "mold" each family member as if he or she were a piece of clay, in other words, to place that person in certain physical positions in order to create an image of the way the client experiences each family member. The clinician then asks family members to offer feedback on what it was like to be "molded" by the client. A second sculpture can also be created by asking the client to create an "ideal image" of the family, in other words, the way he or she would like the family to be.

Drawings can also be very effective in working with children and their families. There are two techniques that I have used: One is a conjoint family drawing, and the other is "animal family drawings." In the conjoint family drawing, I ask all the family members who are present to draw a picture together. This activity gives me an idea of the family dynamics while giving the family an opportunity to interact in a fun and nonthreatening atmosphere. In "family animal drawings," I ask each family member to draw the family as if each member were an animal. This activity gives me an idea of how each member views one another. I then ask each person to draw their family the way they wish it would be, again using animals to formulate an image of how each member would like the family to be. Animal family drawings can also be a useful technique for initial sessions in couples therapy with Japanese because it is a nonverbal and nonthreatening activity (Shibusawa & Ishikawa, 1987).

Assumption 3. Problems Can Be Solved by Finding the Cause to the Problem

Japanese, like other East Asians, hold a circular view toward events and do not see problems in a linear way. I have often found in my clinical practice that Westerners want to know "why" they have a problem, whereas Japanese clients want to know "what" to do about it. Psychoanalytically oriented psychodynamic therapy, in which clients explore their past family relationships, is relevant and can be conducted with Japanese clients. However, the clinician should first wait to see if exploring the past is what the client is seeking. Clients can become very uncomfortable when delving too quickly into their past. I have found the use of genogram interviews to be a nonthreatening way to begin exploring the clients' past, because genogram interviews initially begin as a fact-gathering process.

Assumption 4. Secrets Are Bad

Western psychotherapy assumes that secrets warp family relationships and prevent family members from communicating with each other in an honest way. There is a Japanese phrase that means "keeping things unquestioned." In interactions with Japanese clients, the clinician often acknowledges the existence of a secret but does not delve into details unless the situation warrants legal intervention. Secrets that clients may keep from the therapist include events from the past such as adoption, family conflicts, and alcohol addiction. The acknowledgment that there is a secret itself can, at times, be sufficient for the client to begin therapeutic work. If there is therapeutic value in exploring the secret, clinicians should first make sure that they are not viewing the client's reticence to share the secret as resistance. If they do, the client will sense it, which will create distrust in the therapeutic relationship.

Assumption 5. Emotions Should Be Expressed

As I stated earlier, Japanese experience emotions, but they do not find validity in expressing them. When asked to *express* emotions, Japanese feel as if they are being asked to *expose* their emotions. Clients who do not express feelings are conceptualized by psychodynamic therapy as being defensive or resistant. Asking Japanese clients about their emotions, however, can place them on the spot if they are not used to talking about their emotions. It is, therefore, important not to press clients to express their feelings or be too eager to elicit emotional responses. Rather, the clinician should sit back and give feedback in a tentative way, such as "while I am listening to you" or "although I am not sure, I am getting the feeling that" or "I am wondering if " or "maybe you are feeling a little." If the client has difficulty responding, then it is best to set aside the discussion on emotions for the time being.

Assumption 6. Straightforward Communication Is Therapeutic

In Western psychotherapy, clinicians try to encourage honest communication among family members. They often encourage clients to use "I Statements" to convey their feelings and wishes by taking ownership of what they say. Japanese families, as I have stated before, are socialized to act in prescribed roles. Therefore, in the beginning, clients will have trouble when they are asked to communicate differently. Adult family members often feel more at ease in sharing their private thoughts in individual sessions rather than conjoint sessions. Older fathers often feel more at ease in coming alone to talk about themselves rather than to "expose" themselves in front of the entire family. This attitude is because older Japanese men find it difficult to assume the face of a client in front of other members of the family.

Assumption 7. Process Is Therapeutic

Process is important in all therapeutic relationships. However, quite often I have found in working with Japanese clients that two contradictory processes take place simultaneously. One is the lack of process, and the other is a delayed process. First of all, clients expect clinicians to be expert authority figures. They do not expect clinicians to establish an egalitarian relationship. Thus, they seek symptom-relieving approaches that are concrete, pragmatic, and task centered. Because of the focus on providing concrete assistance, the clinician may feel that the family is not engaged in the process of establishing a therapeutic relationship. Japanese families often do not seek help unless problems become severe, because they are reluctant to seek help from outsiders until absolutely necessary. Concrete services in such cases are essential. Second, it takes longer to establish a therapeutic relationship with Japanese clients. Therefore, there is a long period in which it may appear as if the helping relationship is not jelling. The clinician has to be able to sit with his or her own doubts and anxieties during this time.

Assumption 8. Centrality of the Marital Unit Is Paramount

In Japanese families, the parent-child relationship, especially the mother-child relationship, is the strongest connection in the family. Western-trained family therapists who observe fathers blaming their wives for not "doing a proper job of raising the children" are tempted to shift their focus to the marriage. Quite often, however, the parents will drop out when focus is placed on the marriage instead of the child's problems. When the child is the identified client, it is important for the clinician to help the couple function together as a *parental* unit rather than as a marital unit.

IMPLICATIONS FOR PRACTITIONERS

Because counseling and therapy are new concepts for many Japanese American clients, clinicians need to explain the process to the families. In addition, clinicians can help diminish the family's stigma and shame by normalizing and universalizing the presenting problem with comments such as, "What we're seeing with your child is not rare for her age and the circumstances that she is in" or "This is something that many families go through." Furthermore, because of the value placed on learning in Japanese culture, support groups are better attended when they are presented as learning opportunities. For example a "parenting class" is easier for Japanese parents to attend than a "parents' support group."

The clinician also needs to respect the hierarchical structure of the family. Japanese American families tend to have stronger parent-child role differentiation. While some European American parents may feel comfortable having an egalitarian relationship with their children, Japanese American parents are not as open to sharing information about themselves with their children. Thus, clinicians need to make sure that they do not place the parents in a position where they have to "expose" themselves to their children.

Japanese, in general, avoid conflict (Tomita, 1998). Thus, they may not let the clinician know that they disagree with the clinician's opinions. This problem may be especially acute because clinicians are seen as expert authority figures. Instead of trying to work out the differences, clients may drop out of therapy. Therefore, clinicians need to address beforehand the need for clients to share differences of opinion in therapy sessions.

Because of the emphasis on politeness and observance of social protocol in Japanese culture, it can take longer to establish rapport with Japanese American clients. Clinicians, therefore, must be willing to spend more time than they do with most Euro-American clients in building a helping relationship. As Minuchin and Fishman (1981, as cited in Lappin, 1983) aptly state, "joining is the glue that holds the therapeutic system together. A 'given' in cross-cultural work is that the glue takes longer to dry" (p. 128).

Some Japanese American clients prefer to work with non–Japanese American clinicians. This preference is due to three factors. First, where there is a tight-knit Japanese American community, clients may feel uneasy discussing their problems with a Japanese American clinician because of the threat to their anonymity. Clients may not be aware that therapists are bound to the ethics of confidentiality, an issue that should be addressed with them. Second, clients may fear that a Japanese American clinician will judge them by the same standards applied by their parents. They may feel freer to express themselves to an outsider. Third, Japanese American clients may feel that European Americans are better qualified for the simple reason that they are white. This attitude, in turn, may be a reflection of internalized negative stereotypes that are perpetuated by the dominant society.

On the other hand, some Japanese American clients prefer to work with Japanese American clinicians. This preference is often the case when clients are working on family-of-origin issues. Clients feel that a Japanese American clinician will have a better understanding of parent-child relationships and will need less explanation to understand their experiences (L. Shiozaki-Lee, interview, February 24, 2000).

For Japanese American clinicians who have been trained in Western psychotherapy, working with Japanese American clients can be a challenge (Shibusawa, 1996). Japanese American clinicians may have to struggle with two conflicting thoughts. They hear the voice of the internalized supervisor telling them that they are "not being clinical enough" when they are observing the cultural protocol of being polite and nonconfrontational with their clients. At the same time there is an internalized cultural voice saying "you are not being culturally appropriate" when they go against the social protocol and establish a more egalitarian relationship in order to empower their clients. Clinicians who are faced with such conflicts will find it extremely helpful to schedule supervisory sessions with a seasoned bicultural clinician and peer consultation sessions with colleagues who have had similar experiences.

CONCLUSIONS

This chapter has presented an overview of Japanese American parent-child relationships and suggestions for clinical practice. Japanese Americans are a diverse group. Some are more acculturated into the mainstream society, whereas others retain more traditional cultural values. Clinicians, therefore, must refrain from clinging to generalizations about Japanese culture when working with Japanese American families. They need to let the clients teach them about the clients' own social and cultural realities.

The term *cultural competence* is a misnomer. A clinician cannot be truly "culturally competent," because each family has its own culture. It is when clinicians realize that they do not know their clients' culture that they become competent at learning from their clients. Once clinicians have read about the history, struggles, cultural traditions, values, and norms of a particular ethnic group, they need to rely on their clients rather than books as guides for understanding and helping them.

Discussion Questions and Role-Play Exercises

1. Role-play an initial family session.* Select volunteers to play the role of a clinician, identified client, his or her sibling, and two parents. Have the family leave the room for a few minutes while they decide on the precipitating problem and the roles they play in the family (e.g., strict father, demanding child, mother who is a mediator between child and father). Once the family has come back into the room, have family members wear masks during the initial interview.** After the interview, discuss the following questions:
   a. What was the experience like for the person who played the clinician? What types of anxieties come into play when you cannot read facial expressions?
   b. What was the experience like for the people who played the family members? How did you experience the masks? Were they comforting or hindering?
   c. How did the clinician try to engage the family and establish rapport? Where did she or he get stuck?
   d. What did the observers and the clinician notice about the family dynamics? What can clinicians do to be attuned to family dynamics when they are not able to depend on facial expressions?
2. What types of services can schools offer that would be culturally appropriate for Japanese American parents?
3. You have started to work with a Japanese American adolescent who is withdrawn and appears depressed. You have a hunch that sexual orientation may be an issue. What issues would you need to consider before introducing this topic with your client?
4. You have started to work with a multiracial child who is part Japanese American. How should you approach the issue of your client's multicultural back-

ground? What information do you need to get, and how should this information be integrated into the assessment? How are you going to explore the different cultural aspects of the family?

Notes

1. The Commission on Wartime Relocation and Internment of Civilians (CWRIC) was established in 1980 to review Executive Order 9066, which led to the internment of Japanese Americans, and to make recommendations for redress. During the testimonial hearings, Japanese Americans spoke publicly for the first time about their experiences and trauma (Nagata, 1993).
* This role-play exercise was inspired by the work of Maurizio Andolfi, M.D.
** Masks can be made out of brown grocery bags with holes cut for the eyes and mouth.

References

Akimoto, S. A., & Sanbonmatsu, D. M. (1999). Differences in self-effacing behavior between European and Japanese Americans: Effect on competence evaluations. *Journal of Cross-Cultural Psychology, 30*(2), 159–77.

Aoki, B. (1996). Gays and lesbians in psychotherapy. In E. Lee (Ed.), *Working with Asian Americans: A guide for clinicians* (pp. 411–19). New York: Guilford Press.

Azuma, H., Kashiwagi, H., & Hess, R. (1981). *The influence of maternal teaching style upon the cognitive development of children.* Tokyo: University of Tokyo Press.

Caudill, W., & Plath, D. W. (1996). Who sleeps with whom? Parent-child involvement in urban Japanese families. *Psychiatry, 29,* 344–66.

Caudill, W., & Weinstein, H. (1969). Maternal care and infant behavior in Japan and America. *Psychiatry, 32,* 12–43.

Ching, J. W. J., McDermott, J. F., Fukunaga, C., & Yanagida, E. (1995). Perception of family values and roles among Japanese Americans: Clinical considerations. *American Journal of Orthopsychiatry, 65,* 216–24.

Conroy, M., Hess, R. D., Azuma, H., & Kashiwagi, K. (1980). Maternal strategies for regulating children's behavior in Japanese and American families. *Journal of Cross-Cultural Psychology, 11*(2), 153–72.

Doi, T. (1986). *The anatomy of self: The individual versus society* (M. A. Harbison, Trans.). Tokyo: Kodansha International.

Fukuyama, M. A. (1999). Personal narrative: Growing up biracial. *Journal of Counseling and Development, 77*(1), 12–14.

Fumia, M. (1997). *Honor thy children: One family's journey to wholeness.* Berkeley, CA: Cornari Press.

Goyette, K., & Xie, Y. (1999). Educational expectations of Asian American youths: Determinants of ethnic differences. *Sociology of Education, 72*(1), 22–36.

Heine, S. J., & Lehman, D. R. (1999). Culture, self-discrepancies, and self-satisfaction. *Personality and Social Psychology Bulletin, 25*(8), 915–25.

Henkin, W. A. (1985). Toward counseling the Japanese in America: A cross-cultural primer. *Journal of Counseling and Development, 63,* 500–503.

Hess, R. D., Kashiwagi, K., Azuma, H., Price, C. C., & Dickson, W. P. (1980). Maternal expectations for mastery of developmental tasks in Japan and the United States. *International Journal of Psychology, 15,* 259–71.

Ho, Y. F. (1994). Cognitive socialization in Confucian heritage cultures. In P. M. Greenfield & R. R. Cocking (Eds.), *Cross-cultural roots of minority child development* (pp. 285–313). Hillsdale, NJ: Lawrence Erlbaum.

Holloway, S. D., Kashiwagi, K., Hess, R. D., & Azuma, H. (1986). Causal attributions by Japanese and American mothers and children about performance in mathematics. *International Journal of Psychology, 21,* 269–86.

Ichioka, Y. (1988). *The Issei: The world of the first generation Japanese immigrants: 1885–1924.* New York: Free Press.

Johnson, C. L. (1977). Interdependence, reciprocity, and indebtedness: An analysis of Japanese American kinship relations. *Journal of Marriage and the Family, 39,* 351–63.

Johnson, F. A. (1993). *Dependency and Japanese socialization.* New York: New York University Press.

Johnson, F. A., & Marsella, A. J. (1978). Differential attitudes toward verbal behavior in students of Japanese and European ancestry. *Genetic Psychology Monographs, 97,* 43–76.

Johnson, F. A., Marsella, A. J., & Johnson, C. L. (1974). Social and psychological aspects of verbal behavior in Japanese-Americans. *American Journal of Psychiatry, 131,* 580–83.

Kamo, Y., & Zhou, M. (1994). Living arrangement of elderly Chinese and Japanese in the United States. *Journal of Marriage and the Family, 56,* 544–58.

King, R. C., & DaCosta, K. M. (1996). Changing face, changing race: The remaking of race in the Japanese American and African American communities. In M. P. P. Root (Ed.), *The multiracial experience: Racial borders as the new frontier* (pp. 227–44). Thousand Oaks, CA: Sage.

Kitamura, T., Kimijima, N., Iwata, N., Senda, Y., & Takahashi, K. (1999). Frequencies of child abuse in Japan: Hidden but prevalent crime. *International Journal of Offender Therapy and Comparative Criminology, 43*(1), 21–33.

Kitano, H. H. L. (1976). *Japanese Americans: The evolution of a subculture* (2nd ed.). Englewood Cliffs, NJ: Prentice Hall.

Kitano, H. H. L., & Daniels, R. (1988). *Asian Americans: Emerging minorities.* Englewood Cliffs, NJ: Prentice Hall.

Lanham, B. B., & Garrick, R. J. (1996). Adult to child in Japan: Interactions and relations. In D. W. Shwalb & B. J. Shwalb (Eds.), *Japanese childrearing: Two generations of scholarship* (pp. 97–124). New York: Guilford Press.

Lappin, J. (1983). On becoming a culturally conscious family therapist. In C. Falicov (Ed.), *Cultural perspectives in family therapy* (pp. 122–36). Rockville, MD: Aspen.

Lebra, T. (1984). *Japanese women: Constraint and fulfillment.* Honolulu: University of Hawaii Press.

Lebra, T. (1994). Mother and child in Japanese socialization: A Japan-U.S. comparison. In P. M. Greenfield & R. R. Cocking (Eds.), *Cross-cultural roots of minority child development* (pp. 259–74). Hillsdale, NJ: Lawrence Erlbaum.

Lee, S. M. (1998). Asian Americans: Diverse and growing. *Population Bulletin, 53*(2), 2–40.

Lee, S. M., & Yamanaka, K. (1990). Patterns of Asian American intermarriage and marital assimilation. *Journal of Comparative Family Studies, 21,* 287–305.

Leong, R. (1995). Forward: Unfurling pleasure, embracing race. In G. Kudaka (Ed.), *On a bed of rice: An Asian American erotic feast.* New York: Anchor Books.

Machida, S. (1996). Maternal and cultural socialization for schooling: Lessons learned and prospects ahead. In D. W. Shwalb & B. J. Shwalb (Eds.), *Japanese childrearing: Two generations of scholarship* (pp. 241–59). New York: Guilford Press.

Mass, A. (1991). Psychological effects of the camps on the Japanese Americans. In R. Daniels, S. C. Taylor, & H. H. L. Kitano (Eds.), *Japanese Americans: From relocation to redress* (pp. 159–62). Seattle: University of Washington Press.

Matsui, W. T. (1986). Japanese families. In M. McGoldrick, J. K. Pearce, & J. Giordano (Eds.), *Ethnicity and family therapy* (2nd ed., pp. 268–80). New York: Guilford Press.

Mura, D. (1996). *Where the body meets memory: An odyssey of race, sexuality, and identity.* New York: Anchor Books.

Nagata, D. (1993). *Legacy of silence: Exploring the long-term effects of the Japanese American internment.* New York: Plenum.

Oriti, B., Bibb, A., & Mahboubi, J. (1996). Family-centered practice with racially/ethnically mixed families. *Families in Society, 77*(9), 573–82.

Pang, V. O., Mizokawa, D. T., Morishima, J. K., & Olstad, R. G. (1985). Self-concepts of Japanese American children. *Journal of Cross-Cultural Psychology, 16*(1), 99–109.

Papp, P., Silverstein, O., & Carter, E. (1975). Family sculpting in preventative work with "well families." *Family Process, 12,* 197–212.

Root, M. P. P. (1996). The multiracial experience: Racial borders as a significant frontier in race relations. In M. P. P. Root (Ed.), *The multiracial experience: Racial borders as the new frontier* (pp. xiii–xxviii). Thousand Oaks, CA: Sage.

Root, M. P. P. (1998). Multiracial Americans: Changing the face of Asian America. In L. C. Lee & N. W. S. Zane (Eds.), *Handbook of Asian American psychology* (pp. 262–87). Thousand Oaks, CA: Sage.

Schneider, B., Hieshima, J. A., Lee, S., & Plank, S. (1994). East-Asian academic success in the United States: Family, school, and community explanations. In P. M. Greenfield & R. R. Cocking (Eds.), *Cross-cultural roots of minority child development* (pp. 323–50). Hillsdale, NJ: Lawrence Erlbaum.

Shibusawa, T. (1992). Postpartum psychosis in a father: Japanese cultural dynamic. In N. Grizenko, L. Sayegh, & P. Migneault (Eds.), *Transcultural issues in child psychiatry* (pp. 119–30). Quebec: Edition Douglas.

Shibusawa, T. (1996). Espressione dei sentimenti: Prospettive dall' Orient [Expressions of emotions: Eastern perspectives]. In M. Andolfi, C. Angelo, & M. DiNichilo (Eds.), *Sentimenti e sistemi* [Feelings and Systems] (pp. 137–49). Milano: Rafaella Cortina.

Shibusawa, T., & Ishikawa, G. (1987). Use of animal drawings in marital therapy. *Rinsho Byoga Kenkyu* [Studies in Clinical Applications of Drawings], *2,* 91–108.

Stephan, C. W., & Stephan, W. G. (1989). After intermarriage: Ethnic identity among mixed-heritage Japanese-Americans and Hispanics. *Journal of Marriage and the Family, 51,* 507–19.

Sue, S., & Morishima, J. K. (1982). *The mental health of Asian Americans.* San Francisco: Jossey-Bass.

Takanishi, R. (1994). Continuities and discontinuities in the cognitive socialization of Asian-originated children: The case of Japanese Americans. In P. M. Greenfield & R. R. Cocking (Eds.), *Cross-cultural roots of minority child development* (pp. 351–62). Hillsdale, NJ: Lawrence Erlbaum.

Tomita, S. K. (1998). The consequences of belonging: Conflict management techniques among Japanese Americans. *Journal of Elder Abuse and Neglect, 9*(3), 41–68.

Uomoto, J. M., & Gorsuch, R. L. (1984). Japanese American response to psychological disorder: Referral patterns, attitudes, and subjective norms. *American Journal of Community Psychology, 12*(5), 537–50.

Wagatsuma, H., & Rosett, A. (1983). Cultural attitudes toward contract law: Japan and the United States compared. *Pacific Basin Law Journal, 2,* 76–97.

Williams, T. K., & Thornton, M. C. (1998). Social construction of ethnicity versus personal experience: The case of Afro-Amerasians. *Journal of Comparative Family Studies, 29*(2), 255–67.

Yee, B. W. K., Huang, L. N., & Lew, A. (1998). Families: Life-span socialization in a cultural context. In L. C. Lee & N. W. S. Zane (Eds.), *Handbook of Asian American psychology* (pp. 83–135). Thousand Oaks, CA: Sage.

European American Families

CHAPTER 13

Parenting in European American/ White Families

PEG MCCARTT HESS
HOWARD J. HESS

Since the census was initiated in the United States in 1791, the majority of citizens, like Betty and Janine in the case study that follows, have self-identified as "white." White Americans originated primarily from Europe; more recently, the term *European American* has been used to emphasize that whites are one of the many diverse groups that comprise the American population. Giordano and McGoldrick (1996a) report that there are fully "53 categories of European-Americans," a term that they use interchangeably with "White ethnics" (p. 427). Inherent in this change of terminology is the growing recognition that "whiteness" no longer adequately encompasses American identity. This chapter examines the dominant white culture's presumptions about parent-child and family relationships and identifies the dilemmas inherent in these presumptions for both those needing and those providing help. The following case study introduces many such dilemmas.

CASE STUDY: BETTY

Janine, an experienced practitioner, is employed in the foster family care services division of a large family services agency. She is very troubled about one of her

The authors gratefully acknowledge Cheryl Franks and Karina Walters for their helpful comments on this chapter.

cases and is preparing to meet with her supervisor. In trying to decide whether and how openly to discuss her concerns, Janine is spending a few minutes reflecting on the family. Betty, her client, is a white twenty-six-year-old single parent whose two children, Jimmy, age eight, and Tim, age six, have been placed in foster care. The boys' father, James, is African American. Since James and Betty separated four years ago, he has had erratic contact with her and with his sons.

Two months ago, Jimmy and Tim were placed with a foster family after Betty was arrested for altering several prescriptions. Betty was already known to protective services because she had often left the boys with neighbors, who had reported that she was neglecting them. Placement had previously been avoided because Betty agreed to participate in a range of services. Since the children's placement, it has become clear that they had been subjected not only to physical neglect and inadequate supervision, but to their mother's chronic, sometimes debilitating, depression. Both boys exhibited behaviors that indicated serious emotional difficulties and developmental delays.

In their meetings together, Janine and Betty had explored at length Betty's difficulties in parenting and her chronic difficulties with depression, including one brief psychiatric hospitalization following a suicide attempt. Betty had tearfully described her family's rejection of her because of her biracial children: "They are ashamed of them and of me." Betty described feeling isolated and missing her parents and two sisters terribly. When Betty recounted several very upsetting scenes with her parents and the children, Janine had wondered whether she, as a white worker, should explore Betty's family's rejection of James, of Betty, and of their children. Janine had decided not to directly explore Betty's own feelings about her children's race or about her parents' racism or to explore the possible role that these tensions might have played in the breakup of her marriage. Janine also recalled that though the boys frequently mentioned that they missed their father, Betty was reluctant to have the agency arrange for the boys' father to visit them at the home of the foster parents, who lived in a white working-class neighborhood.

A major part of Janine's responsibility is to assess each child's service needs, including each boy's reaction to the separation from his mother, and to provide supportive services to the foster family. In her most recent conversation with the children's foster mother Janine had learned that the boys' teachers called the foster parents frequently about their aggressive behavior and academic difficulties. The foster mother had raised questions with Janine about whether the boys would ever be able to "fit in" because "they really aren't like the other kids." Janine recalled feeling that she should ask whether the foster mother was referring to their status as foster children, as biracial children, or other factors, but in her discomfort, she let the opportunity pass. Janine was aware that she was unclear which factors in the boys' experience required immediate attention—their experience of neglect and abuse and of their mother's inconsistent parenting; their current separation from their mother; their wish to have a relationship with their father; their rejection by their maternal grandparents; or their identity as biracial children.

Janine wondered how her supervisor would react were she to share her ambivalence about openly exploring these issues. How would the supervisor react to Janine's questions about the role of race in the family's difficulties? Janine felt unsure about the appropriateness of the boys' placement. Should they have been placed in a different neighborhood? Should the boys' race have been more carefully considered in the placement decision? Should she, as a white social worker, directly explore with Betty the role of race in the family's and children's difficulties? Janine also questioned whether her supervisor, who is also white, would be able to understand her sense of unpreparedness to do so. Would her supervisor dismiss these issues as irrelevant? Janine wondered why it felt so risky and uncomfortable to discuss the issues in this case.

HISTORICAL BACKGROUND

The United States has rightfully been called "a nation of immigrants" (Giordano & McGoldrick, 1996a, p. 429). Even in its earliest days the country was more diverse than is often understood. At the time of European colonization, North America was inhabited by a large number of American Indian nations. Spanish settlements predated the English in Florida, New Mexico, and California, and African slaves were forcibly brought to America during the colonial period. However, the first immigration law of 1790 required European heritage as a qualification for citizenship, and by that time "the English made up 61% of the 13 colonies' three million White inhabitants" (p. 429). Currently, Americans with English ancestry constitute the second largest white ethnic group and continue to powerfully impact upon the dominant American culture. Subsequent groups have contributed to but never displaced the early English base of white American culture.

Later immigration unfolded in waves. The Germans constituted the second major wave, with the peak years for German immigration occurring between the 1830s and the 1880s. According to Lassiter (1995), the Germans "never accounted for less than one-quarter of all immigrants" during this period (p. 90). In 1992 German Americans constituted almost one-quarter (23.3 percent) of the population and currently are the largest white ethnic group.

Irish immigration can be divided into two parts. In the 1700s, Irish immigrants, designated as the "Scott-Irish," were Protestant and came from Ulster (Lassiter, 1995, p. 117). The Irish who immigrated in the nineteenth century were primarily Catholics who fled to escape poverty and famine. It is estimated that more than a million Irish immigrated in the two decades around the 1840s (McGoldrick, 1996, p. 547). Approximately 15.6 percent of the American population are of Irish descent (Lassiter, p. 117).

Immigration to the United States shifted in the late 1800s and early 1900s to include inhabitants from eastern and southern Europe. For example, in the 1880s a wave of East European Jews arrived to escape political persecution (Lassiter, 1995, p. 148). Italians began immigrating around the turn of the twentieth century, and "between 1900 and 1910, more than two million Italians, mostly peasants from southern Italy, immigrated to the United States to escape poverty and find a better life" (Giordano & McGoldrick, 1996b, p. 568). Currently, 5.9 percent of the population is Italian American. Between 1880 and 1921, other immigrant groups, such as the Poles and the Greeks, arrived as well. By the end of this period, American cities had been transformed, and the country's religious landscape was quite diverse.

Immigration patterns shifted dramatically in the twentieth century. White, European American immigration began to subside. Groups such as the Russian Jews continued to immigrate in large numbers after the breakup of the former Soviet Union. However, because of changes in U.S. immigration laws, Europeans currently constitute only 20 percent of new immigrants (Giordano & McGoldrick, 1996a, p. 431). This shift is having two major impacts on the white U.S. population. First, whites are steadily declining in proportion to other segments of the population. Second, white ethnic group identities are blurring because of increased generational distance from their original roots. Intermarriage is accelerating this trend; more than half of all Americans are thought to be "marrying out of their ethnic groups" (p. 438). Indicators suggest that such trends will continue into the future.

Socioeconomic Characteristics of European Americans

Although the findings of the 2000 census have yet to be published, the Census Bureau provides annual population estimates. In 1999, non-Hispanic whites were estimated to comprise 71.7 percent of the total U.S. population. At the time of the 1990 census, two-thirds of the children under nineteen years of age living in the United States were white (Shinagawa & Jang, 1998, p. 112). Although the actual number of whites has increased by 8.1 million since 1990, during this same period the proportion of whites in the total population decreased substantially (Population Estimates Program, 1999, pp. 2, 4). This trend reflects a rapid and pervasive change in the racial composition of the United States. In 1990, the population was 75.6 percent white, a decrease of 13 percent in the thirty years since 1960, when the U.S. population was 88.6 percent white (Brimelow, 1995, p. 67). Because of immigration, birth rates, and the aging of the white population, this trend is expected to continue (Roberts, 1993, pp. 6–7). By 2050 European Americans are projected to comprise less than 53 percent of the total U.S. population (Shinagawa & Jang, p. 111). In many cities and counties whites already constitute less than a majority (Roberts, p. 68; Shinagawa & Jang, p. 150).

Age In contrast with the total population, whites tend to be older. For example, while the mean age for the total population in 1990 was 35.2 years, the mean age for whites was 37.0. By 1999, the mean age for whites increased to 38.6. This compares with a mean age of 28.9 for Hispanics of any race, 32.3 for black Americans, 31.1 for American Indians, and 32.9 for Asian and Pacific Islanders (Population Estimates Program, 1999, p. 2).

Income and Education White Americans also tend to be more highly educated and wealthier than most other population groups. According to Shinagawa and Jang (1998), "The net worth (i.e., wages, salary, benefits and assets) of non-Hispanic White households in 1990 in the United States as a whole was more than ten times that of African-American households, and almost ten times that of Hispanic households" (pp. 113–14). The disparity in income between whites and most other groups is particularly evident in the highest fifth of income distribution. At the other end of the continuum, a much smaller percentage of whites (11.7 percent) live below the poverty level than do blacks (33 percent), Hispanics (22 percent; Shinagawa & Jang, p. 114), and American Indians (33 percent; U.S. Bureau of the Census, 1998, p. 3). However, it is important to note that in spite of lower percentages, there is a large number of poor whites. Shinagawa and Jang report that "in 1990, Whites made up more than two-thirds of the population considered poor in the United States" (p. 114). Thus, whites are among both the richest and the poorest persons in the United States.

Educational statistics mirror those of income. In 1990, 77.6 percent of the *total* population completed high school, contrasted with 79.1 percent of the white population and 80.4 percent of the Asian Pacific Americans. Similarly, 21.3 percent of the *total* population completed college in contrast to 22 percent of whites and 39.9 percent of Asian Pacific Americans. This figure compares with 11.3 percent of African Americans, 9.2 percent of Hispanics (Shinagawa & Jang, 1998, p. 151), and 9 percent of American Indians (U.S. Bureau of the Census, 1993, p. 4).

Family Composition In 1990 European American children were more likely than children of other groups to live with a father employed full-time and a mother working inside the home. This family composition has long been defined as the "traditional family" (Shinagawa & Jang, 1998, p. 112). Although in 1990 the majority (83 percent) of white households included a married couple (Roberts, 1993, p. 45), a pervasive change is taking place related to family composition. According to Pinderhughes (1995), "the nuclear family, long the norm, is now giving way to the blended family and single parent family" (p. 132). She attributes this shift to "the cultural tradition of individualism in American society, increased divorce rates, changes in values regarding the role of women, and societal attitudes toward pregnancy outside marriage" (p. 132). Increasingly, white children live with divorced or never married single parents. For example, in 1994, "one-fourth of all White families with children present were headed by a single parent" (Shinagawa & Jang, p. 115). White family composition is also shifting because of decreasing birth rates. White birth rates have decreased more sharply than those of other racial groups, contributing to the decrease in size of American families to 3.17. This contrasts to 3.76 in 1960 (Roberts, p. 58).

Geographic Location Whites continue to constitute a majority in all regions of the country. Some ethnically determined residential patterns persist among whites, but these are being blurred through relocation and intermarriage among and outside of white ethnic groups. Although American diversity is increasing dramatically, Roberts (1993) emphasizes that this "diversity is unevenly divided" (p. 62). He writes that "in 186 counties blacks, Hispanic people, Asians, and American Indians make up more than half the population. But in 24 states, these groups do not constitute a majority in a single county" (p. 62). According to the 1990 census, whites make up more than 95 percent of the population in five states (Iowa, West Virginia, Vermont, New Hampshire, and Maine) and between 85 and 95 percent in an additional twenty-one states. The ten states in which whites make up less than 75 percent of the population are New York, California, Maryland, and the bottom belt of the deep South from South Carolina to Louisiana. The highest proportion of the population in New England, the Midwest, and the West is white. German Americans tend to live in Pennsylvania, the Midwest, and the far West. Irish Americans are concentrated in Pennsylvania, Ohio, and the central Midwest. Scandinavian Americans are most frequently found in the upper Midwest.

Religious Beliefs and Practices   Although white Americans attach high value to the distinction between church and state, on the whole they are more religiously observant than their European counterparts. Religious beliefs and practices are considered a significant aspect of American culture. Giordano and McGoldrick (1996a) cite Skeler as follows: "93% of Americans said they believe in a benevolent God who hears prayers and intercedes in their daily lives" (p. 435). Throughout the history of the United States, churches and synagogues have provided continuity of association within separate white immigrant populations as well as a crucible for white ethnic mixing. Among the Protestant churches, Calvinist theology has reinforced the values of responsibility, hard work, and individual advancement. The Roman Catholic Church has eased the transition for many white immigrants while also supporting traditional family structures.

Over time, American churches are increasingly less defined along white ethnic lines. For example, by the mid-1990s in New York City, Roman Catholic mass was offered in thirty different languages (Giordano & McGoldrick, 1996a, p. 435). It is not yet clear how well America's churches and synagogues will be able to create and sustain multiracial congregations or to interact effectively with Islamic and other religious organizations. The Jewish community in particular has been challenged by the infusion of a large number of Russian Jews with distinct cultural and religious practices.

Whiteness and Racial Identity

The notion of whiteness as a source of identity is fraught with difficulty. Perhaps most troubling is our most recent collective memory of the brutal and perverse way that both race and ethnicity were used by the Nazis and other fascists to first disenfranchise and then murder millions of human beings. In addition, the concept of the white race is associated with past and present colonialism and imperialism throughout the world. For many, the term *white* inextricably signifies privilege, dominance, and oppression. One thesis of this chapter is that the concept of whiteness is essential for productive discussion about white clients and white practitioners serving families and children of any race, including their own.

Whiteness as a Concept   First we must recognize that whiteness as a concept is what Wander, Martin, and Nakayama (1999) refer to as "leaky" because "race can *only* be seen in relation to other categories, such as class, gender, sexuality, and so on, that render any category problematic" (p. 15). Helms (1995), whose theory about racial identity informs our thinking, states that "the construct of race in psychology has been used in a variety of ways . . . none of which is accurate according to basic standards of scientific practice" (p. 181). She explains: "Racial identity theory evolves out of the tradition of treating race as a sociopolitical and, to a lesser extent, a cultural construction . . . Thus racial identity themes do not suppose that racial groups in the United States are biologically distinct, but rather suppose that they have endured different conditions of domination or oppression" (p. 181). This linkage between whiteness and the awareness of racial dominance is crucial. A fascinating case in point is found in Ignatiev's (1995) consideration of how the Irish came to think of themselves as white in their struggle for social acceptance and power. Frankenberg (1997) places the term *whiteness* within a "simultaneous operation of race and racism" (p. 9), while Bowser and Hunt (1996) assert that "every white person in the United States is socialized with implicit and explicit racial messages about him- or herself and members of visible racial/ethnic groups . . . Accepting these messages results in racism becoming an integral component of each White person's ego or personality" (p. 4).

The only way for whites to counteract such distortions is to become more fully aware and therefore able to challenge the nature of their white racial identity, which is discussed later in this chapter. Such transformation has been complicated by the interaction between race and ethnicity. Multiple waves of white immigration have produced an awareness of *ethnic identity*. Many whites think of themselves, for example, as Italian Americans or Irish Americans rather than as white or European Americans. However, whites have lived in the United States for three or four generations, and the stream of new immigrants from Europe has slowed. Consequently, according to Alba (1990), "a fundamental erosion of the structural basis of ethnicity is underway among Americans with European ancestries . . . an increasing number of white Americans—perhaps even a majority have ancestry from two, three, or even four different European nations" (pp. 38–39). Alba claims that "a new ethnic group is forming—one based on ancestry from anywhere on the European continent" (p. 3). Some people, when asked about their backgrounds, respond simply, "I'm an American."

Many whites have failed to recognize the powerful presence of racism in social structures and practices. Green (1998a) writes, "I think that for members of the White majority group, it is very difficult to grasp emotionally a person of color's lifetime experiences in relation to prejudice . . . when Whites visualize racism, they tend to picture it primarily in terms of dramatic or violent instances of hatred and aggression" (p. 103).

White Racial Identity   According to Helms (1995), whites must move through a series of six statuses in a "maturation process of recognition and abandonment of White Privilege" (p. 188). These statuses revolve around the way a white person processes information related to racial stimuli. Early statuses involve denial or suppression of relevant information about race, while later statuses result from a reeducation of one's racial standards and "flexible analyses and responses to racial material" (p. 188). Helms uses the term *status* rather than *stage* in order to emphasize fluidity within her model. Her categories are "mutually interactive dynamic processes by which a person's behavior could be explained, rather than static categories into which a person could be assigned" (p. 183). Each status is characterized by an Individual Personality Structure (IPS). Helms postulates one set of statuses for whites and another for people of color. She proposes that for each person a particular status is *dominant,* others are *accessible.* The statuses for whites are listed in table 13.1.

Table 13.1. Statuses for Whites

Status	Description	Individual Personality Structure
1. Contact	Satisfaction with racial status quo, oblivious to racism	Obliviousness
2. Disintegration	Disorientation and anxiety provoked by unresolvable racial moral dilemmas that force one to choose between own-group loyalty and humanism	Suppression and ambivalence
3. Reintegration	Idealization of one's socioracial group, denigration and intolerance of other groups	Selective perception and negative out-group distortion
4. Pseudo-independence	Intellectualized commitment to one's own socioracial group and deceptive tolerance of other groups	Reshaping reality and selective perception
5. Immersion/Emersion	Search for an understanding of the personal meaning of racism and a redefinition of whiteness	Hypervigilance and reshaping
6. Autonomy	Informed positive socioracial group commitment, use of internal standards for self-definition, capacity to relinquish the privileges of racism	Flexibility and complexity

Source: Helms, 1995, p. 185.

Self-knowledge and openness to difference bring about a mature understanding of one's whiteness. Helms traces the maturational process toward the ideal of understanding white privilege and toward an identity as a white person that does not depend on the belief of white racial superiority. This understanding, in turn, is the basis for establishing a genuine high level of self-regard as a white person. In other words, one's self-esteem does not require elevation of oneself and a corresponding devaluation of others. The lifelong unexamined practice of seeing oneself and others through "white normative eyes" prevents one from easily maturing in this way.

THE EUROPEAN AMERICAN/WHITE CULTURE: NORMS AND VARIATIONS IN PARENT-CHILD AND FAMILY RELATIONSHIPS

Historically the dominant majority, European Americans have established the prescription for "normative" or "American" parent-child and family relationships. As McIntosh (1998) has pointed out, white family patterns appear "natural" within the dominant white culture, and the source of these perceptions is invisible (p. 148). Because of the privilege and power held by whites, they "take their identity as the norm and the standard by which other groups are measured, and this identity is therefore invisible, even to the extent that many Whites do not consciously think about the profound effect being White has on their everyday lives" (Martin, Krizek, Nakayama, & Bradford, 1999, p. 28). Implicitly, therefore, acculturation has required adherence to the dominant norms, benefiting those immigrants from white ethnic groups and from cultures most similar to the European American culture.

Particularly in the second half of the twentieth century, the norms regarding parent-child and family relationships have been reinforced by widely disseminated theories of child development and recommended approaches to child rearing. At least two errors have characterized these theories: first, that there could not be acceptable differences in normative patterns among white ethnic groups; and second, that white practices should take precedence over those found in other racial groups. We look more closely at the implications of these errors after our review of the dominant culture's norms regarding family relationships.

Both European Americans and Americans in other racial and ethnic groups often assume uniformity in cultural norms among all white Americans. However, differences do exist in the cultural norms of ethnic subgroups within the white population. We agree with Alba (1990) that "given the contemporary fluidity of ethnicity among whites, the degree of consensus about ethnic labels and behaviors must be taken as problematic, a subject for investigation rather than a definitional matter" (p. 24). In this section we describe European American cultural norms as well as selected variations among the four largest white ethnic subgroups: German Americans, Anglo Americans, Irish Americans, and Italian Americans. Italian Americans have generally diverged most greatly from the dominant European American norms described here (Giordano & McGoldrick 1996b, p. 568). This description of cultural norms and variations provides a context within which we can examine issues related to working with European American families and children and explore those assumptions that may undermine practitioners' capacity to be helpful.

Several norms and values have been consistently identified as characterizing the white culture (Hanson, 1998; Lassiter, 1995; McGoldrick, Giordano, & Pearce, 1996; Wehrly, 1995). Each greatly affects family relationships and parents' child-rearing behaviors. These norms and values include emphases on the following factors:

- Self-sufficiency, individualism, and independence
- Strength, self-discipline, and self-control (including control over expression of personal emotion and suffering and of interpersonal conflict)
- Work
- Privacy
- A future orientation
- Access to opportunity and equality
- Child-centeredness

Self-Sufficiency, Individualism, and Independence

The characteristics of self-sufficiency, individualism, and independence most powerfully embody European Americans' primary values. These values affect not only family relationships, but also the emphasis given to the nuclear rather than the extended family. For example, the European American family traditionally includes "immediate family members such as the mother, father, and children. Other extended family members may or may not live close by . . . (and) are usually termed *relatives* as opposed to *family*" (Hanson, 1998, pp. 107–8).

Immigrants from Britain, Wales, and Scotland formed the largest population of the colonial settlements in the 1600s and, as Anglo Americans, initially defined the European American culture. The Anglo American culture stressed that "freedom of the individual and the emphasis on psychological individualism are the values that most distinguish Anglo-American families from other American families . . . in Anglo Americans, self-determination becomes exaggerated into hyperindividualism" (McGill & Pearce, 1996, p. 451). Similarly, German and Irish American families generally expect that family members, including children, should be strong and disciplined and exert great effort to solve their own problems. Dependence on the support and resources of others is discouraged. Thus, to many white families, isolation is more acceptable than reliance on their extended families or members of their congregations or communities. For example, Irish American parents' attitudes toward their children are typically strict and restrained, and there is often a sense of "emotional isolation among siblings and extended family members" (McGoldrick, 1996, p. 550).

The white American emphasis on the individual and on self-reliance permeates the organization of a family's space, use of time, and decision-making approaches. Hanson (1998) emphasizes that from an early age, [white] Americans are taught to make decisions and to be self-reliant. Young children often have their own rooms; separation from their parents for short periods of time is acceptable even for the very young; and early self-help skills, such as independent feeding, are encouraged. Children are often given opportunities to make choices and decisions at an early age, and those decisions respected. (p. 104)

To further illustrate, "Anglo American culture historically encouraged early separation of adolescents and the development of an individualistic, self-defined adult identity" (McGill & Pearce, 1996, p. 456). This expectation, as described later in this chapter, has been incorporated into theoretical frameworks describing "healthy" developmental outcomes.

Within the white American family, however, self-sufficiency and independence traditionally have been more limited for women than for men, with family structures typically patriarchal and the husband and father explicitly designated as the family's "head." To illustrate, gender powerfully shapes Pennsylvania Germans' (Pennsylvania Dutch) family roles. In this subculture, the husband, the dominant authority figure, provides for the family by hard work, while the wife focuses on the children, the church, and the kitchen (Lassiter, 1995; Winawer & Wetzel, 1996). Similarly, in Irish American families women are viewed as "subservient to the men of the family" (Lassiter, p. 119), male needs are given priority, and favoritism is shown to sons (p. 119). In Italian American families as well, the father has been the household head who "demands ultimate respect from his wife and children" (Giordano & McGoldrick, 1996b, p. 572). Gender roles have been somewhat modified as increasing numbers of women work outside the home.

In contrast to the norms of self-sufficiency, individuation, and even isolation among extended families described in Anglo, German, and Irish American families, Italian American families, primarily families with ancestors from southern Italy, raise their children to be mutually supportive and faithful to and involved with the family. Giordano and McGoldrick (1996b) note that "there is virtually no such thing as a separate nuclear family in Italian culture . . . family comes first, and members are expected to stay physically and psychologically close, coming together in a crisis and taking care of family members who are vulnerable" (p. 571). These authors further stress that separation of children from the family is "not desired, expected, or easily accepted" and "it is not unusual for parents and grandparents to maintain daily contact" (p. 574) or for parents to care for grandparents and older family members. Consequently, Italian Americans have sometimes struggled with the differences between aspects of the European American culture and their own (p. 574).

Strength, Self-Discipline, and Self-Control

Closely related to the promotion of self-sufficiency is the European American expectation that family members exercise discipline and self-control. Children and adults are expected not only to control their behaviors but also to conceal their emotions, in other words, to "keep a stiff upper lip" or to "suffer in silence." However, with regard to communication styles, the Italian American culture once again can be contrasted with the dominant white American culture. Within the family, Italian Americans often freely express intense emotion and openly identify pain and suffering (Lassiter, 1995; Giordano & McGoldrick, 1996b).

Work

In the white American family, work is highly valued and serves both as a necessary means to achieving the goal of self-sufficiency and as a core component of one's identity. Devotion to work, often described as the Protestant work ethic, has powerfully shaped the traditional white family and has resulted in an emphasis on responsibility and gender role prescriptions. The traditional white American family's division of labor has seen the father as the breadwinner and the mother's work centered on the home and child rearing. Children have also been expected to "work," with chores matched to age and to gender.

White Americans' definition of self and measure of success frequently revolves around work. McGill and Pearce (1996) emphasize that

> above all, Anglo Americans value work . . . an Anglo American's identity, relationships, self-esteem, and sense of adequacy and well-being may all be tied to work. Indeed, Anglo Americans have a tendency to transform many aspects of life into work. Men and women "work" at making a living, and "work" at raising the children. Anglo Americans may talk of "working" on relationships, love, sex, fulfillment, and identity. (p. 454)

Thus, to be described as lazy, to be unemployed, or to fail at work-related endeavors, including education, is to risk loss of self-esteem and mutual esteem by family members.

Privacy

Consistent with the principles on which America was founded, white Americans not only highly value privacy, but have defined privacy as a right. Thus, there is an expectation that boundaries (e.g., personal and private space in one's home or workplace, personal information regarding age or family history) will be respected. This concept extends to a range of topics often viewed as "taboo" both within and outside the white American family, including income, sexual practices, and areas of disagreement among family members.

A Future Orientation

Perhaps America's history as a nation primarily of immigrants with hopes and dreams for a better future has shaped the dominant culture's emphasis on the future. As Hanson (1998) states, "change, newness, and progress are all highly valued . . .

the belief that individuals and groups are in control of their destinies is a powerful influence on the lives of most dominant-culture Americans" (p. 105). This future orientation is often associated with the expectation of *access to opportunity* for achievement. Thus, family resources are often invested in "the future" of the next generation, such as saving to buy a home in a "better neighborhood" with "better schools" that will lead to preparation for college or for other opportunities supportive to future success.

Child-Centeredness

Hanson (1998) characterizes American family culture as "very 'child-centered' " and prone to afford children "a great deal of say in events and in the practices of the family" (p. 105). This emphasis is reflected in choices made by parents to enhance their children's education, social status, and opportunity, often at great expense or sacrifice. Hanson notes the degree to which white American parents seek their children's opinions and involve them in decisions about purchases such as toys, clothing, and food.

CHILD DEVELOPMENT FRAMEWORKS AND GUIDES THAT REFLECT DOMINANT EUROPEAN AMERICAN CULTURAL NORMS

The study of the psychology of child development and of the influence of parent-child relationships on adult mental health expanded in the late nineteenth and twentieth centuries. Many European and European American authors became very well known to the American public—among these were Sigmund Freud, Erik Erikson, and Benjamin Spock. Their work became influential within the mainstream of American thinking and illustrates the ways in which "experts" have reinforced the dominant European American culture. Frameworks have been developed and widely applied that have privileged white American developmental and family interaction patterns.

Freud, an Austrian, introduced numerous concepts into mainstream American culture, including the mechanisms of defense, the conscious and unconscious, the ego, the id, and the superego (Freud, 1940/1949). His work presented human beings as neurotic and conflicted (White, 1974, p. 68) and stressed the powerful effects of parental relationships on human development and mental health. Freud asserted that the indicators of a healthy personality are the ability to love and to work. His experience drew on middle-class European norms of individual respectability and sexual repression. In postulating his theory of psychosexual development, Freud normalized an anxiety-ridden nineteenth-century Victorian white culture.

Erik Erikson, an immigrant from Vienna, Austria, proposed a psychosocial theory of development that expands on Freud's theory. Erikson's phase-specific developmental tasks have defined children's "healthy" and desirable developmental outcomes for generations of parents, teachers, and helping professionals. Erikson's work further emphasizes the ways in which "the society into which the individual is born makes him its member by influencing the manner in which he solves the tasks posed by each phase of his epigenetic development" (Rappaport in Erikson, 1959, p. 15). The reciprocal influence between individuals and their social development permits discussion of Erikson's theories through a "cultural lens," as in chapter 1 in this book. Several of Erikson's desired stage outcomes—autonomy (stage 2), initiative (stage 3), and industry (stage 4)—are particularly consistent with the dominant European American cultural norms described earlier in this chapter. In addition, Erikson's emphasis on the sense of identity as the desirable outcome of stage 5, coinciding with adolescence, strongly emphasizes independence and individuation: "[young Americans'] whole upbringing, and therefore the development of a healthy personality, depends upon a certain degree of *choice,* a certain hope for an individual *chance,* and a certain conviction in freedom of *self-determination*" (Erikson, 1959, p. 93, emphasis in the original).

The pediatrician Dr. Benjamin Spock, perhaps the best known American expert on parenting, drew heavily on both Freud's and Erikson's theories in his advice to American parents. Trained in both pediatrics and psychiatry, Spock underwent two psychoanalyses, examining the impact of his Anglo-American parents' child-rearing practices on his own development (Maier, 1998). According to biographer Thomas Maier, Spock's high motivation to understand and provide a range of options for child rearing was in part based on his own childhood experiences (p. 100).

An Alternative View of Parent-Child Relationships

Compared to Erikson and Spock, the authors Julian, McKenry, and McKelvy (1994) offer a broader construct of how families socialize their children. These authors indicate that major differences are present among whites, African Americans, Hispanics, and Asian Americans in terms of "adaptive strategies including extended families, role flexibility, biculturalism, and collectivism versus individualism" (p. 30). After controlling for social class, these authors found that parents of some ethnic groups emphasized their children's self-control and school performance more than others did (p. 36). Hines, Garcia-Preto, McGoldrick, Almedia, and Weltman (1992) concluded that significant patterns of variation relating to intergenerational dependence, responsibility to one's ethnic group, and resolving conflict also existed among families. Unless a practitioner understands, respects, and knows how to work with these patterns, his or her intervention efforts are inevitably compromised.

IMPLICATIONS FOR PRACTITIONERS

The racial identity of white clients and the dominant white cultural norms inevitably figure prominently into the efficacy of the helping process. Practitioners must understand the powerful impact white cultural values have had on all aspects of the dominant North American culture, including the helping professions. This impact is evident, for example, in the emphasis on confidentiality and self-determination incorporated in the NASW Code of Ethics (National Association of Social Workers, 1996). These values draw attention to the worth of each individual human being and therefore justify humane social welfare and social work practice principles. However, the practitioner needs to be aware of the way that white values may not apply in their work with culturally diverse clients. White cultural values have been internalized by many human service professionals, including social workers, and these values and beliefs about "human nature" and "the way things work" create biases and blind spots in one's professional practice. For this reason, we have emphasized the critical importance of self-awareness in practice with white families and by white practitioners.

Potential Effects of White Cultural Norms

In the extreme, each cultural norm discussed in the previous section can become a source of stress and psychosocial difficulties for both white clients and white practitioners.

Self-Sufficiency, Individualism, and Independence At their best, the norms of self-sufficiency, individualism, and independence encourage children and youth to develop realistic goals and, through goal achievement, to build self-esteem. Families who are able to modulate achievement expectations with support and encouragement help their children enjoy success as well as learn from failure without damage to the child's developing sense of self. Balance between support and self-sufficiency in the life of the family is critical. The norm of self-sufficiency in the extreme promotes a myth that the individual can pull herself or himself up into success by effort alone. This rugged individualism belies the amount of interpersonal and economic support on which a child's success is always built. White American cultural expectations related to children's performance and achievement can sometimes negatively affect family relationships. Isolation and disappointment can become interactional family themes, as the following case study illustrates.

CASE STUDY: KEVIN

Kevin is an eleven-year-old white child who lives with his two parents and one younger sister in an affluent suburb of a large Midwestern city. Recently Kevin's school referred him to the local mental health center because of disruptive behavior in the classroom. He is also difficult to manage during lunch periods, in gym class, and at other less structured times. While conducting a biopsychosocial assessment, the social worker at the mental health center learned that Kevin's family is at a complete loss to explain his behaviors. Sometimes they attribute Kevin's difficulties to poor management by school staff. At the same time, they have also experienced problems with Kevin at home. He increasingly refuses to complete his homework and often sits staring off into space when he is supposed to be reading. This behavior is particularly frustrating to Kevin's parents, who have believed him to be an extremely bright child. They report that Kevin was always precocious. He learned to speak very early and began reading in preschool. Kevin's parents, particularly his father, expect Kevin to be at the top of his class.

Kevin's parents have now concluded that he is an underachiever. They have talked with him at great length about the importance of his doing well academically. As a part of these talks they have stressed the value of good study habits and emphasized that if he works hard enough he could get into an excellent college. Kevin's father would like him to attend the Ivy League university where he graduated from law school. His parents are angry at Kevin for his refusal to apply himself. In fact, this past year Kevin almost didn't pass English and history, ironically his father's favorite subjects. In contrast, Kevin's father grew up in a family where hard work and sacrifice had resulted in considerable success. Kevin's paternal grandparents had immigrated from Ireland in the 1920s with no more than the clothes on their backs. They had worked long hours and multiple jobs in order to send their children to college. Kevin's father had always been earmarked as the brightest child in the family. He was awarded a substantial scholarship that enabled him to attend law school. While in law school, Kevin's father met his wife, who was also attending an Ivy League school. She came from a family of professional people. Kevin's father has always thought that Kevin would follow in his footsteps, or perhaps become a doctor. Now he is worried. How could Kevin succeed if he doesn't understand the importance of hard work? Ironically, the more worried Kevin's parents have become and the harder they've pushed Kevin, the more serious his problems have become. Kevin's parents are very confused about what to do next.

Upwardly mobile white families often rely on two incomes and long work days. Children and adolescents participate actively in many competitive activities. Academic grades are emphasized, admission to college is sought, and time is divided between multiple extracurricular activities. Increasingly, few families share meals together, and parents must constantly choose between competing worthwhile activities. Practitioners working with such white families must often recognize and draw attention to the isolation that can result. Individuals can be isolated within families, and families can become isolated from their extended family members. A variety of psychosocial difficulties can grow out of and become intensified by a depletion of family resources. Practitioners must identify and attend to these patterns in the lives of the families with whom they work.

The Expectation of Strength, Self-Discipline, and Self-Control The notion of keeping a stiff upper lip is very familiar to white families. It is based on the assumption that excessive emotion is suspect. Practitioners working with white families will often encounter unexpressed emotions, unnamed fears, and pains and feelings that are acted out or suppressed rather than discussed. Underlying these behaviors is a European American cultural belief that the expression of such feelings is a sign of weakness and could undercut competent coping. In many white families, parents even hide their strong emotions from each other and from their children. Thus children may have no role model for expressing and sharing their intense emotions. The practitioner's task is to guide families into and through the inner and interpersonal world of feelings and thus to demonstrate that strength results not only from self-discipline, but *also* from concomitant self-expression.

Many white families need to learn how to communicate the full range of emotions in ways that do not undermine family balance. For example, the failure to express differences often results in outbursts of anger. Excessive self-control can undermine family problem solving. In the case just presented, Kevin's father is becoming estranged from Kevin because of his own feelings of fear and disappointment. The practitioner will need to skillfully elicit an open discussion of these feelings without greatly increasing family members' isolation from one another or overwhelming the family with emotion.

The Value of Work

White families are often at risk for excessive preoccupation with work and work achievement. Investment in one's work is, of course, not itself dysfunctional. Only when this investment is the major or only source of self-esteem do families suffer. Practitioners often need to help white families make changes in the priority afforded to work-related activities. When work leads to the persistent absence of a parent or both parents from family life, family members can become distant from one another. Many white families need assistance in investing in family leisure or recreational activities or in protecting family rituals from the intrusion of work demands. Some economically successful white families can be impoverished in terms of family relationships.

White Concerns About Privacy White families are often concerned about the extent to which others know about their problems. Underlying this concern can be an excessive sense of shame about not being able to sort out one's own difficulties and not being strong and self-sufficient. The more emphasis an individual places on self-sufficiency, the more pronounced this shame is likely to be. The practitioner will need to help families credit themselves for seeking help and for sharing family information in the problem-solving process. When information about the family needs to be sought and discussed, the practitioner must acknowledge the discomfort this openness may cause. In some instances, help must be sought from extended families and the community, which could compromise the family's privacy. The practitioner should be sensitive to a white family's concerns about privacy and guide the family through this process.

The European American Future Orientation The dominant white culture tends to emphasize the deferral of gratification for future gain. This characteristic can combine with the norm of self-sufficiency to result in inadequate attention to family members' current needs. Like in the other areas being discussed here, the practitioner's role in this area may appropriately consist of assisting the family to identify and establish a functional equilibrium. The multiple demands on family life related to future success may make it difficult to maintain a balance that takes into account the family members' current needs. The practitioner can teach families how to assess their current needs and how to shift their functioning before family problems result.

The White Expectation of Access to Opportunity and Equality   White families often believe that they have a "right" to opportunities, more so than other ethnic and racial groups do. Psychological health depends on a person's ability to move beyond a white-centric belief system; this assertion is consistent with Helms's (1993, 1995) work on white racial identity. The practitioner must be able to identify and challenge assumptions of white privilege that become apparent in working with white families when these assumptions distort relationships within white families and between white families and their social environment. As we discuss later in this chapter, this work is only possible if the practitioner has confronted his or her own racial assumptions and prejudices.

White Families' Child-Centeredness   Children are highly valued in many white families. However, children may be given too much central importance and power. Practitioners will need to help some white families reinforce generational bound-aries, support parental decision making, and maintain the integrity of the parental subsystem.

PRACTITIONER PERSPECTIVES, CAPACITIES, AND ABILITIES FOR PRACTICE WITH WHITE PERSONS

Whether practitioners themselves are white or are from other racial groups, their ability to be helpful to white families and children depends on the degree to which they understand and can work with the dominant white cultural norms and as-sumptions about parent-child and family relationships. As a means to challenge practitioners to understand their diverse clients and themselves more accurately, Pinderhughes (1995) presents six "perspectives, capacities, and abilities [which con-stitute] cultural competence." These are:

- The ability to respect and appreciate the values, beliefs and practices of all clients . . . and to perceive [clients] through their own cultural lens . . .
- Knowledge of specific [client] values, beliefs, and cultural practices
- The ability to be comfortable with difference in others . . .
- The ability to change false beliefs, assumptions, and stereotypes
- The ability to think flexibly and to recognize that one's own way of thinking and behaving is not the only way to think and behave
- The ability to behave flexibly (p. 133)

Thus, as we have already discussed, practice with white American families and children requires not only knowledge about cultural norms, but also knowledge regarding the variations within the white population associated with ethnic group identity. In this regard, white practitioners and practitioners of color face similar challenges.

In addition, practitioners must develop awareness around their own racial iden-tity and around assumptions clients may hold based on the practitioner's race. As Pinderhughes (1989, 1995) points out, such self-awareness results in the capacity to appreciate difference and to think and behave flexibly. This flexibility allows white families and the practitioners who serve them to understand their own cultural patterns and make necessary adaptations. When cultural norms are not challenged, they are not open to understanding and, when indicated, revision.

As we have discussed elsewhere in this chapter, many typologies utilized by practitioners are threaded with assumptions about the equivalency of white cultural norms and psychological health. Practitioners of all races typically have been trained to understand and assess child development and parent-child relationships through the dominant white cultural lens. Practitioners must critically examine the theories and practice models from which they draw. In addition, Giordano and Carini-Giordano (1995) emphasize, "Therapists are vigilant about not allowing their own emotional issues to become an impediment in treatment. For more analytically oriented clinicians, this issue usually is identified as countertransference. However, this heightened awareness usually has not included the impact of the therapist's own ethnic identity" (p. 352). A practitioner's difficulties in achieving positive outcomes may in some instances be interpreted either as the practitioner's countertransference or as the client's resistance rather than as a consequence of the practitioner's cultural incompetence.

Challenges for White Practitioners in Serving White Families

European American social workers, who comprise the largest group of social work professionals (Frecknall, 1996; Gibelman & Schervish, 1997), have often defined cultural competence as being prepared to work with clients different from themselves. Thus, preparation for multi- or cross-cultural practice has focused on learning about "others." Increasingly, however, learning about "self" has been recognized as a critical first step to developing cultural competence (Wheeler, Walters, Hess, Franks, & Sheiman, 1999). Cross-cultural competence requires *intentional* effort to change race-related attitudes, knowledge, and behaviors. Franks (1999) writes, "self-awareness implies more than just an awareness of one's values, attitudes, and worldview. It implies understanding self in relation to within and between-group differences, identity development, power and privilege statuses and the experience of multiple statuses" (p. 1). Franks emphasizes that exploration of one's whiteness is often painful, it uncovers anxieties about one's security, and it is associated with grief over losing one's privileged racial status (pp. 3, 7, 26). Thus, white practitioners attempting to achieve the "perspectives, capacities, and abilities" described by Pinderhughes (1995, p. 133) must be willing and able to examine their own racial and ethnic identities and to acknowledge the privilege and power associated with their whiteness. Self-assessment and self-awareness are at the center of initial and ongoing efforts by practitioners to develop competency.

As we emphasized earlier, this process can be particularly challenging for white practitioners who tend to take their racial identity as "the norm and the standard by which other groups are measured" (Martin et al., 1999, p. 28). Making the invisible visible to oneself is essential if European Americans are to be helpful either to other whites or to persons of color. Furthermore, there is no reason to conclude that racism is any less present in white helping professionals than it is in the general white population or that racism in white helping professionals is less likely to be denied. For practitioners, insufficient objectivity about their own whiteness can interfere with accurate assessments of white children and their families. Several of the case studies in this chapter illustrate dilemmas that predictably occur when white helping professionals have not examined their own identity and privilege, when they assume that they and their white clients share the same values about child rearing and family life, or when they attempt to engage families as if their own whiteness and its associated privilege and power are invisible. For example, Janine, described in the case study at the beginning of this chapter, cannot act in the face of what she sees as "unresolvable racial moral dilemmas" (Helms, 1995, p. 183). Characterized by Helms's *disintegration status* (see table 13.1), Janine has a beginning recognition that race and racism are factors that contribute to the difficulties experienced by Betty, James, and their children. However, because Janine's white racial identity is largely unexamined and quite powerful, she is too uncomfortable to openly discuss race with her clients or her supervisor. Further, she does not recognize that her discomfort about doing so, given the power associated with both her professional status and her race, reinforces others' discomfort with exploring these issues and creates a lack of trust in the helping relationship. Janine's sense of risk in discussing race and racism can ironically be a consequence for whites of their power and privilege. Unlike persons of color, who have not had the privilege of experiencing their race as invisible, European American practitioners more easily avoid discussions with colleagues and clients about the uncomfortable issues of race and thus develop neither full awareness of their identity nor the skills to explore racial issues. As McIntosh (1998) emphasizes, "As a white person, I realized I had been taught about racism as something which puts others as a disadvantage, but had been taught not to see one of its corollary aspects, white privilege, which puts me at an advantage" (pp. 147–48). Accepting and addressing this aspect of race can be very uncomfortable, but is essential. Janine cannot help her clients address the complicated issues of whiteness and racism in their family's relationships until she examines and changes her own white racial identity and develops skills in communicating about race.

Janine's lack of clarity regarding her supervisor's ability to help her sort out case issues related to race strongly suggests that her white supervisor also has neglected this part of her own professional development. It would appear that Janine's supervisor may not be fully prepared to serve as a role model and resource for her staff. We want to emphasize that social work supervisors, mentors, and educators carry a particular burden to demonstrate through their words and actions that they are engaged in an ongoing examination of not only their racial identity but also their multiple statuses and identities (Walters, 1998). In addition, they must explore the potential effects of these statuses and identities on their understanding of others' experiences and needs and on their own personal and professional development. For whites, the task is to tolerate and manage the anxiety and guilt that inevitably emerge.

The following case study describes a situation in which a white practitioner is inhibited in her ability to serve an Italian American adolescent and her family because of an underlying fear of persons of color on the part of both the practitioner and the white family members and because of the practitioner's unquestioning adherence to her own Irish American values and norms.

CASE STUDY: CATHERINE

Catherine is a forty-seven-year-old Irish American counselor recently hired by a youth services agency in a racially mixed large city. One case assigned to her is a fifteen-year-old Italian American female, Maria, who is experiencing intense family conflict. Maria and her parents describe themselves as fighting all the time. When Catherine met with the family, they were unable to be together without screaming at one other. Soon after the case was referred, the family's situation further deteriorated, and Maria ran away from home. The parents strongly suspected that Maria was dating a young Mexican American man, Javier, and was sneaking out to see him after curfew. The parents believe that Hispanics are "beneath them" and had made arrangements to move Maria to a parochial school that was primarily attended by white youth.

In working with this family, Catherine concludes that Maria's interest in Javier is a result of her acting out against parental authority and a reflection of her need as an adolescent to individuate and to establish her independence. Catherine believes, however, that parental authority should be respected and that Maria should comply with her parents' plans for her schooling. She emphasizes to Maria that she herself had attended parochial school and had received a fine education. Catherine is also frightened by the "escapades" Maria describes and tries to convince her that she should adhere to her parents' expectations. Catherine is very uncomfortable with the "loud and aggressive manner" of young Hispanic men who live near the agency and agrees with many of the concerns that Maria's parents have expressed.

Catherine does not fully explore Maria's feelings about her parents, her own hopes for her life, or her feelings about Javier. Maria refuses to continue meeting with Catherine. No observable reduction in family conflict has occurred; in fact, the conflict appears to be escalating.

Catherine is ineffective in her work largely because of her inability to empathize with Maria's struggles. Catherine unwittingly but solidly aligns herself with the parents' stereotypes regarding Javier and supports the parents' view that this relationship might be harmful to Maria. Catherine appears incapable of comprehending the racial complexity in this case, including the presence of deep racism both in Maria's family and in her own reactions. Catherine appears to be operating on Helms's first level, that of *Contact Status* (see table 13.1). She appears not to be offended by or willing to question the racial dynamics of this case and thus is *oblivious* to key aspects of Maria's problem. Viewing her own racist reactions as normative, Catherine operates out of an unexamined European American value base. She fails to identify the negative effects of the parents' racism on their relationship with Maria. In contrast to Janine, Catherine shows no likelihood to develop such awareness without interventions, such as supervision or continuing education, that challenge her to assess her racial identity, address her racism, and enhance her knowledge about herself and her white clients.

Catherine is also unaware of the influence of her own Irish American values on her reactions to Maria and her family. Catherine herself seems to be overly deferential to the parents' authority. Maria's family is having difficulty around the issue of separation and independence, a challenge to many Italian American families because of the premium set on closeness. Although it is likely that Catherine and her clients share some values shaped by their European American heritage, Catherine's assumption of similarities between her Italian American clients' values and her own Irish American values may, in fact, be quite faulty. In acting on these assumptions, she has no awareness of the limits in her own personal and professional development. When a practitioner's identity with the dominant European American culture has not yet been examined, he or she cannot perceive those who are different "through their own cultural lens" (Pinderhughes, 1995, p. 133).

Pinderhughes's (1995) and Helms's (1995) schemes require a European American practitioner to become free of the need to equate white practices with desirable normative practices. Only then can the white person fully explore racial difference without reverting to stereotypic thinking and the assumption of and preference for "white standards of excellence." Flexible and accurate assessment of a client's problems and needs requires the white social worker to critically examine his or her own assumptions and live with the ambiguity and discomfort that might result from not assuming expert power in the helping relationship.

To this end, Franks (1999) recommends consistent didactic attention to issues of white racism in educational programs, including at least one experiential course focused on expanding self-awareness (p. 32). Others emphasize the importance of socializing students in multicultural and multiracial universities and training programs (Green, 1998b) and of incorporating that focus in supervision and consultation (Cook & Hargrove, 1997). Successful strategies include enhancing the ability to empathize with others from outside one's racial group (Akamatsu, 1998), setting a climate for racial identity work within a supportive relationship (Thompson, 1997), and using group and family interventions to facilitate white racial identity development (Gushue & Sicalides, 1997; Regan & Huber, 1997).

Issues for Practitioners of Color Working with White Families

Practitioners of any race or ethnicity may not be mindful of the variations within the white American population, particularly those differences associated with white ethnic group identity. Assumptions of "sameness" among the various white ethnic groups present an important obstacle to competent service provision. Although ethnic cultural norms have become blurred, a family's ethnic ancestry may continue to powerfully influence family interactions and relationships.

Knowledge of *both* the dominant white cultural norms and the traditional white ethnic groups' cultural norms serves as an important background for individualized assessment of children and families. Both sets of norms interact differently within the lives of individual families. The practitioner must be able to transcend his or her own values, which might reflect yet another and often very different cultural lens. In this way, as Pinderhughes (1995) emphasizes, flexibility is required to "perceive the specific ways in which such knowledge applies or does not apply to a given client" (p. 133).

In the following case study, Marsha, an African American practitioner, assumes that the white German American family she is serving shares her values about the extended family as a major resource for family problem solving.

CASE STUDY: MARSHA

Marsha, an African American practitioner in a suburban mental health center, has been assigned to work with the Hoffmans, an upper-middle-class white German American family experiencing both marital and parent-child difficulties. Mrs. Hoffman has recently been diagnosed as having breast cancer, and Mr. Hoffman has been spending longer and longer days at the office. Both of the children, Roger, age eleven, and Allison, age sixteen, have begun exhibiting mild adjustment difficulties in school. It is clear to Marsha that the members of this family are isolating from one another because of fear about Mrs. Hoffman's health. Marsha, herself a member of a large and close extended family network, has concluded that extended family therapy is indicated in this case. Both Mr. and Mrs. Hoffman's parents live nearby, although they are described as not "being particularly close or involved with our family." The Hoffmans have not been enthusiastic about including the extended family in counseling sessions. They fear that family members will be judgmental about how they are handling the children as well as their decisions about Mrs. Hoffman's health care. Marsha also has the sense that there may be some family secrets that have not yet been expressed. Marsha and the family have a serious disagreement about how to proceed. Both children have refused to come to additional sessions, and Mr. Hoffman has suggested a change in practitioner. It would appear that the family does not see their extended family as a genuine resource in this situation. Marsha has concluded that they are being resistant to breaking out of their self-imposed isolation.

Marsha's insufficient understanding of the Hoffmans' cultural norms and values, particularly their emphasis on self-sufficiency and privacy, creates an impasse in her work with this family. Her intervention might have been more acceptable to an Italian American family, whose assumptions about the closeness of family members is more similar to her own. Again, this case study illustrates the critical importance of being able to comprehend a family's crisis through the family's own cultural lens. Without such understanding, practitioners of color may view impasses such as the one with the Hoffmans as caused by their white clients' resistance, low motivation, or racism rather than normative family patterns.

Practitioners of color must also be vigilant to the effects of the dominant white culture on their own understanding of and assumptions about "normal" child development and family functioning. A lack of skepticism about the relevance of frameworks grounded in white cultural assumptions about normalcy, family functioning, and effective intervention models can contribute to inaccurate assessment and ineffective treatment of white families as well as of families of other racial and ethnic groups.

An understanding of the varying statuses of white racial identity and the ways in which these statuses inevitably affect the practitioner-client relationship is also critical for practitioners of color. Such practitioners need to examine their own reactions to white clients who deny their racism and white privilege and who are unaware of the ways in which their understandings of themselves and the world are grounded in their white dominant cultural expectations. Persons of color may well find practice with white families personally challenging because of their clients' beliefs and assumptions. It is therefore important that practitioners of color seek supervisory or consultative resources if necessary in working with white clients.

CONCLUSION

In this chapter, we have presented principles for practice with European American/ white children and their families. Cultural norms that are based on historical patterns of European American cultural dominance have emerged and gained considerable currency. These norms privilege western and northern European family patterns that emphasize individual achievement and responsibility. Cultural norms of other racial and ethnic groups have been ignored, misunderstood, and sometimes depreciated by many white social workers. In addition, white cultural norms have been embedded in many professional training programs and professional standards of practice. In contrast, we urge an approach to practice that acknowledges, respects, and is skillful in working with racial and ethnic differences. This approach emphasizes cognitive flexibility and comfort with ambiguity when approaching racial differences (Pinderhughes, 1995; Walters, 1998). It is crucial for white practitioners to examine and alter their own white racial identity and for all practitioners to acquire and flexibly apply knowledge about both the dominant patterns *and* the great variations within the European American culture.

Discussion Questions and Role-Play Exercises

1. Conduct a role-play in which Janine raises with her supervisor the questions she has about the role of race in Betty's family difficulties. What responses would be helpful to Janine?
2. In your view, is it appropriate for Janine to explore with Betty the role of race in Betty's family difficulties? If she decides to do so, what might Janine expect from this interaction? Conduct a role-play of this discussion.
3. This chapter outlines the primary values and norms associated with the dominant white culture in the United States. Can you identify other values and norms? What other variations in cultural norms that affect child development and family relationships can you identify among white ethnic groups?
4. In what ways has your own family experience and professional training been influenced by the dominant white American culture? What implications does this influence have for your future training and ongoing professional development?

5. In the case of Kevin, difficulties emerged when white cultural norms became exaggerated. Discuss how an overemphasis on self-sufficiency and achievement can undermine parent-child relationships and a family's sense of cohesion. For discussion, provide other examples, either from your own family experiences or from families with whom you have worked, in which white cultural norms and values have contributed to the difficulties of a family with children.

6. Using Helms's framework, identify either your own racial identity status or the racial identity status of a white client that you serve. How may this status affect practitioner-client relationships?

7. In the Hoffman case, Marsha has failed to appreciate the full importance of privacy and self-sufficiency in the family. First, role-play how Marsha might obtain assistance from her supervisor about her impasse with the family. Then role-play a different intervention approach that Marsha might employ with the Hoffman family.

References

Akamatsu, N. (1998). The talking oppression blues. In M. McGoldrick (Ed.), *Revisioning family therapy* (pp. 129–43). New York: Guilford Press.

Alba, R. (1990). *Ethnic identity.* New Haven: Yale University Press.

Bowser, B., & Hunt, R. (1996). *Impacts of racism on white Americans* (2nd ed.). Thousand Oaks, CA: Sage.

Brimelow, P. (1995). *Alien nation.* New York: Random House.

Cook, D., & Hargrove, L. (1997). The supervisory experience. In C. Thompson & R. Carter (Eds.), *Racial identity theory* (pp. 83–96). Mahwah, NJ: Lawrence Erlbaum.

Erikson, E. (1959). *Identity and the life cycle.* New York: International Universities Press.

Frankenberg, R. (1997). Introduction: Local whitenesses, localizing whiteness. In R. Frankenberg (Ed.), *Displacing whiteness.* Durham, NC: Duke University Press.

Franks, C. (1999). *Helms' theory of white racial identity development and the relevance for the social work profession.* Unpublished paper.

Frecknall, P. (1996). Big Brothers/Big Sisters of New York City: Cultural matching/parental satisfaction follow-up survey. Unpublished report. August 27, 1996.

Freud, S. (1940/1949). *An outline of psychoanalysis.* New York: Norton.

Gibelman, N., & Schervish, P. (1997). *Who we are.* Washington, DC: National Association of Social Workers.

Giordano, J., & Carini-Giordano, M. A. (1995). Ethnic dimensions in family treatment. In R. Mikesell, D. Lusterman, & S. McDaniel (Eds.), *Integrating family therapy* (pp. 347–56). Washington, DC: American Psychological Association.

Giordano, J., & McGoldrick, M. (1996a). European families: An overview. In M. McGoldrick, J. Giordano, & J. Pearce (Eds.), *Ethnicity and family therapy* (2nd ed., pp. 427–41). New York: Guilford Press.

Giordano, J., & McGoldrick, M. (1996b). Italian Americans. In M. McGoldrick, J. Giordano, & J. Pearce (Eds.), *Ethnicity and family therapy* (2nd ed., pp. 567–82). New York: Guilford Press.

Green, R. (1998a). Race and the field of family therapy. In M. McGoldrick (Ed.), *Revisioning family therapy* (pp. 93–110). New York: Guilford Press.

Green, R. (1998b). Training programs: Guidelines for multicultural transformation. In M. McGoldrick (Ed.), *Revisioning family therapy* (pp. 111–17). New York: Guilford Press.

Gushue, G., & Sicalides, E. (1997). Helms' Racial Identity Theory and Bowen's Family Systems Model: A case study. In C. Thompson & R. Carter (Eds.), *Racial identity theory* (pp. 127–46). Mahwah, NJ: Lawrence Erlbaum.

Hanson, M. (1998). Families with Anglo-European roots. In E. Lynch & M. Hanson (Eds.), *Developing cross-cultural competence: A guide for working with children and their families* (2nd ed., pp. 93–120). Baltimore: Brooks Publishing.

Helms, J. (1993). *Black and white racial identity.* Westport, CT: Praeger.

Helms, J. (1995). An update of Helms' White and People of Color racial identity models. In J. Ponterotto, J. Casas, L. Suzuki, & C. Alexander (Eds.), *Handbook of multicultural counseling* (pp. 181–98). Thousand Oaks, CA: Sage.

Hines, P., Garcia-Preto, N., McGoldrick, M., Almedia, R., & Weltman, S. (1992). Intergeneration relationships across cultures. *Families in Society, 73,* 323–38.

Ignatiev, N. (1995). *How the Irish became white.* New York: Routledge.

Julian, E., McKenry, P., & McKelvy, M. (1994). Cultural variations in parenting. *Family Relations, 43,* 30–37.

Lassiter, S. (1995). *Multicultural clients.* Westport, CT: Greenwood Press.

Maier, T. (1998). *Dr. Spock: An American life.* New York: Harcourt Brace.

Martin, J., Krizek, R., Nakayama, T., & Bradford, L. (1999). What do white people want to be called? In T. Nakayama & J. Martin (Eds.), *Whiteness: The communication of social identity* (pp. 27–50). Thousand Oaks, CA: Sage.

McGill, D., & Pearce, J. (1996). American families with English ancestors from the colonial era: Anglo Americans. In M. McGoldrick, J. Giordano, & J. Pearce (Eds.), *Ethnicity and family therapy* (2nd ed., pp. 451–66). New York: Guilford Press.

McGoldrick, M. (1996). Irish families. In M. McGoldrick, J. Giordano, & J. Pearce (Eds.), *Ethnicity and family therapy* (2nd ed., pp. 544–66). New York: Guilford Press.

McGoldrick, M., Giordano, J., & Pearce, J. (Eds.). (1996). *Ethnicity and family therapy* (2nd ed.). New York: Guilford Press.

McIntosh, P. (1998). White privilege: Unpacking the invisible knapsack. In M. McGoldrick (Ed.), *Revisioning family therapy* (pp. 147–52). New York: Guilford Press.

National Association of Social Workers. (1996). *Code of ethics.* Washington, DC: NASW Press.

Pinderhughes, E. (1989). *Understanding race, ethnicity, and power.* New York: Free Press.

Pinderhughes, E. (1995). Empowering diverse populations: Family practice in the twenty-first century. *Families in Society, 76,* 131–40.

Population Estimates Program. (1999). Resident population estimates of the United States by sex, race, and Hispanic origin: April 1, 1990 to November 1, 1999. U.S. Census Bureau. Available: http://www.census.gov/population/estimates/nation/intfile3–1.txt

Regan, A., & Huber, J. (1997). Facilitating white identity development: A therapeutic group intervention. In C. Thompson & R. Carter (Eds.), *Racial identity theory* (pp. 113–26). Mahwah, NJ: Lawrence Erlbaum.

Roberts, S. (1993). *Who we are.* New York: Times Books.

Shinagawa, L., & Jang, M. (1998). *Atlas of American diversity.* Walnut Creek, CA: AltaMira Press.

Thompson, C. (1997). Facilitating racial identity development in the professional context. In C. Thompson & R. Carter (Eds.), *Racial identity theory* (pp. 33–48). Mahwah, NJ: Lawrence Erlbaum.

U.S. Bureau of the Census. (1993). *We the . . . first Americans.* Washington, DC: U.S. Department of Commerce.

U.S. Bureau of the Census. (1998). *Census Bureau facts for features.* Department of Commerce. Available: http://www.census.gov/Press-Release/cb98ff13.html

Walters, K. (1998). Negotiating conflicts in allegiances among lesbians and gays of color: Reconciling divided selves and communities. In G. Mallon (Ed.), *Foundations of social work practice with lesbians and gay persons* (pp. 47–75). New York: Harrington Park Press.

Wander, P., Martin, J., & Nakayama, T. (1999). Whiteness and beyond: Sociohistorical foundations of whiteness and contemporary challenges. In T. Nakayama & J. Martin (Eds.), *Whiteness: The communication of social identity* (pp. 13–26). Thousand Oaks, CA: Sage.

Wehrly, B. (1995). *Pathways to multicultural counseling competence: A developmental journey.* Pacific Grove, CA: Brooks/Cole.

Wheeler, D., Walters, K., Hess, P., Franks, C., & Sheiman, E. (1999). *Self-awareness for practice in a multicultural world: A training curriculum.* Unpublished paper.

White, R. (1974). Strategies of adaptation. In G. Coelho, D. Hamburg, & J. Adams (Eds.), *Coping and adaptation* (pp. 47–68). New York: Basic Books.

Winawer, H., & Wetzel, N. (1996). German families. In M. McGoldrick, J. Giordano, & J. Pearce (Eds.), *Ethnicity and family therapy* (2nd ed., pp. 496–516). New York: Guilford Press.

Challenges and Guidelines in Working with Culturally Diverse Families

CHAPTER 14

Strains and Challenges of Culturally Diverse Practice

A Review with Suggestions
to Avoid Culturally Based Impasses

NANCY BOYD WEBB

The process of working on this book has been one of my most challenging experiences in more than thirty years as a professional social work practitioner and educator. I have learned a great deal from the chapter authors, and I believe that my understanding about culturally sensitive and responsive practice has increased significantly as a result. However, because of my growing awareness of the many issues embedded in culturally diverse practice, I realize that the suggestions made in this chapter must be formulated in very tentative terms.

My own path to understanding has been emotional as well as cognitive as I have become painfully aware of the concept of white privilege (McIntosh, 1998) and the unspoken barrier it represents within counseling situations. I now feel awed by the chapter outline I proposed more than a year ago that promised concluding guidelines to help practitioners avoid culturally based impasses. I hope that my greater awareness of the potential obstacles in multicultural practice, together with the contributions of the chapter authors, will result in some helpful suggestions to assist practitioners toward more culturally sensitive responses and interventions. However, this topic requires *ongoing* attention and continuous evaluation and input from *all* thoughtful practitioners.

In rereading the ten chapters devoted to specific culture groups, I have identified several recurring themes that emerged as obstacles to practice with culturally diverse families. These potential obstacles can be converted and reframed into suggestions for more effective practice. I believe that examination and discussion of some of the strains in working with diverse families can help practitioners enhance their understanding and comfort about using alternative approaches to engagement and collaborative intervention. At the same time, however, I fear overgeneralization, and I have asked myself if the risk of possible stereotyping outweighs the potential benefits of presenting some selected practice guidelines, even when these guidelines are enveloped in numerous warnings. My quandary reminds me of a story from my husband's childhood: He was asked by his father (a junior high school principal) prior to entering first grade if he was happy to be starting school; the little five-year-old slumped in his kitchen chair, shook his head, and mumbled, "No, 'cause I don't know nuttin'!"

I am very aware of my own ignorance regarding this topic, and I do not want to offend anyone by suggesting that the essence of any culture can be summed up with a few pointers. I do believe, however, that we know *something* about culturally sensitive practice, based on the growing literature on this topic over the past ten years (Congress, 1997; Devore & Schlesinger, 1996; Gibbs & Huang, 1989/1998; Green, 1999; Ho, 1987, 1992; Lee, 1999; Lum, 1996, 1999; Lynch & Hanson, 1998; McAdoo, 1997; McGoldrick, 1996; McGoldrick, Pearce, & Giordano, 1982; Paniagua, 1998; Pinderhughes, 1989, 1995; Ponterotto, Casas, Suzuki, & Alexander, 1995; D. Sue & Sue, 1990; Vargas & Koss-Chioino, 1992).

This book, with its specific focus on parent-child and family relationships, provides the opportunity to learn from the experience and suggestions of its culturally diverse chapter authors as well as from the growing literature on this topic. My task in this chapter is to summarize and present selected commonalties, differences, and guidelines for practice with culturally diverse groups. Although this task feels daunting, I believe that the goal is worthwhile as long as practitioners understand that they must never apply any guideline without tailoring it to the reality of the *individual* client within her or his cultural context. Practitioners always must actively ask, listen, and pay attention to each client's *unique* situation.

Few, if any, of us would want to be considered the template for the beliefs of our own entire ethnic group, even though we recognize that we do share some commonalties with other members of our group. We are aware of how much variation there is among our family members, friends, and neighbors despite our shared race and ethnicity. As a white Anglo-American woman, I very much value my individuality, and I would not want anyone to use her or his understanding about *my* attitudes and behavior as a model for understanding *all* middle-class white Anglo-American women. Nonetheless, I acknowledge that an Asian or Hispanic practitioner who spent an hour interviewing me about my views and experience as a parent and grandparent would probably learn something about *my* values related to parent-child relationships that might apply, with caution, to other white Anglo parents and grandparents. Even though there is great variation in the degree to which people of similar cultural backgrounds share the same beliefs and practices about child rearing, a counselor from a totally different background could certainly enlarge her or his own understanding by listening carefully to one person. The experience of that one client could be considered a starting point from which the practitioner could then explore the extent to which other members of the same group share or differ in their values and beliefs. As long as the counselor realizes that there will be many variations among views within the same cultural group, the experience of one client can be useful, as can *general* guidelines about the attitudes and behaviors of group members. Individual differences in values are inevitable in all groups. Schriver's (2001) expression "diversity in diversity" conveys this important concept of intragroup variation.

The purpose of this chapter is to identify and discuss some of the strains and challenges that pervade practice with culturally diverse families. The intent is to emphasize the practice implications flowing from cultural differences and to offer some suggestions for responding in a manner that avoids culturally based impasses.

Although the focus of the chapter is on *direct practice* with individuals, families, and small groups, an important challenge also exists on the larger social scale to advocate for fairness and equal opportunity for culturally diverse persons. Schools, hospitals, workplaces, and recreational environments can impact either positively or negatively on everyone and especially on culturally diverse people, who may have numerous problems. Racism and oppression affect many people of color, and the helping professions have an obligation to exert political, economic, and psychological pressure on institutions and communities to encourage them to become more culturally inclusive and accepting. The education of practitioners in the twenty-first century must include content on macrolevel advocacy and methods of community organization and intervention in addition to methods of direct practice. This topic is discussed further in chapter 15.

CULTURALLY FRIENDLY DIRECT PRACTICE

Some recurring themes related to strains in multicultural work have surfaced in the ten preceding chapters. These themes appear to apply to cultures that are quite different from one another. When the themes emerge in practice situations, they often contribute to difficulties and misunderstandings between counselors and clients who are from different cultural backgrounds. In the following sections, I identify several of these themes and consider how they may create obstacles that interfere with the helping process. I then present suggestions for avoiding the obstacles through more culturally sensitive responses and interventions.

The themes that create strains in practice with members of different cultures, as discussed in this book, appear in table 14.1. I examine these themes by analyzing

Table 14.1. Themes Related to Strains and Obstacles in Culturally Diverse Practice

- The practitioner's lack of understanding about the multidimensional reality and stresses of the client's individual situation in the context of the client's specific cultural and family environment
- Difficulty in engaging, communicating, and agreeing about the problem
- Different ideas about seeking help and dealing with the problem situation
- The different values and worldviews of the practitioner and the client

instances in the helping process in which lack of agreement between practitioner and client leads to divergent understandings about the problem situation and contribute to the client's subsequent decision to discontinue in counseling (Boyd-Franklin, 1989; Tsui & Schultz, 1985).

The Initial Telephone Contact

A typical contact between a counselor and a parent occurs because of some concerns about a child's behavior or difficulty in school. When this contact is made by telephone or by letter, there is little or no opportunity for the practitioner to gauge the parent's response nor to answer the parent's questions. The parent is at a distinct disadvantage and may feel confused or angry about the nature and implications of the child's problem. When the parent is not fluent in English and the practitioner cannot communicate in the parent's language, the initial discomfort becomes magnified.

Often the counselor wants to make an appointment with the parent to discuss the matter more fully. However, the time and place of the proposed meeting may disregard the realities of the parent's life and work schedule. Few school-based practitioners offer late day, evening, or Saturday appointments, and parents simply may not be in a position to take time off from their work. This obstacle ignores the client's individual situation. Some clients may have no transportation or method to get to the school. All too often these overworked parents are labeled as "resistant" or "uncaring." In a previous publication (Webb, 1996), I referred to the practitioner's responsibility "to reach out and make the extra effort to connect with parents" (p. 119), sometimes by making a home visit or by scheduling an appointment at a restaurant near a parent's workplace during her or his lunch hour. Such home-based and community interventions have been discussed as "reaching out family therapy" (Boyd-Franklin & Bry, 2000).

In making the appointment to see a parent, a culturally sensitive practitioner will invite the parent to bring other family or kin members if the parent wants to do so. This invitation conveys the worker's understanding that the parent may, during the consultation with the professional, want support and advice from one or more family members regarding the child's difficulty.

The Engagement Process in the First Session

Many factors influence the building of a helping relationship during the beginning phase. These factors include:

- The practitioner's level of self-awareness
- The practitioner's degree of knowledge about the client's culture
- Adherence to culturally expected interactions ("relationship protocol")
- Open acknowledgment of cultural differences
- Language similarity or difference (use of a translator)
- Confidentiality considerations

- Inclusion of members of the client's support network
- Reframing the child's "problem" into an obstacle or challenge
- Treating the parent and the helping network as collaborators

It is the responsibility of the culturally sensitive practitioner to be aware of the possible significance of these factors in work with different parents. The therapist, in preparing for the first meeting with a parent, should think about the possible meaning of the child's difficulty in the context of a particular family's culture. The practitioner who has no background for making such speculations could review some information about the culture and talk to colleagues who might be knowledgeable. Lynch and Hanson (1998) refer to using a "cultural guide" in their work with families of diverse backgrounds.

In addition to seeking general information, thoughtful practitioners will analyze their feelings about working with clients from a cultural background different from their own. Even with this type of preparation—self-awareness and obtaining general information—the counselor must remember that a child's problem can mean different things, within the context of each family's unique history. The practitioner should listen carefully and ask tactfully about the parents' views of the problem prior to going into detail about the concerns that precipitated the referral.

Adherence to Culturally Expected Interactions At the beginning of the session it is important for the practitioner to try to put the multicultural parent at ease. Lum (1999, p. 116) uses the term *relationship protocol* to refer to the recommended methods the practitioner may use to help persons of color feel comfortable and respected. Other writers refer to "basic etiquette" (Caple, Salcido, & diCecco, 1995), which might include, for example, casual conversation about the weather or recent news or sports events that are not related to the purpose of the meeting. To help the worker develop empathy with the client, Green (1999, citing Squire, 1990) refers to the dual processes of "perspective taking and affective responsiveness" (p. 105). For example, during the beginning phase of contact, the worker might state her or his appreciation about the parent's taking the time to meet.

The practitioner also should ask clients how they prefer to be addressed (first or last name) and, in turn, state her or his own name as well as any title that describes her or his position and role in the agency. Some cultures associate formality in address with respect, so it is important to ask and observe the client's customs. Business cards help clients learn and remember the counselor's name, and diplomas on the wall convey professional legitimization that may reassure some culturally diverse clients. The worker should acknowledge with interest the fact that the client may be from a different culture or may be a recent immigrant. If the family has recently moved to the area, it is appropriate to refer to the stress that *any* family would undergo during the transition and the tasks of becoming familiar with a new community, job, and school.

During this early phase of developing the relationship, some multicultural therapists (Lum, 1999; see also Zayas, Canino, & Suárez, chapter 6 of this text) recommend the use of selected relevant personal disclosure by the professional to help put the client at ease. Some Asian clients might consider the sharing of personal information to be unprofessional, so the practitioner should proceed with caution. This initial phase should not be rushed, because it actually serves to give the client a chance to begin to know the practitioner and to come to some tentative opinion about the counselor's personal and professional credibility and trustworthiness.

Therapists want to begin to develop a relationship by acknowledging and respecting cultural differences, by identifying the family's strengths in making the necessary adaptations to a new culture (when relevant), and by expressing interest in and respect for the client. During this beginning phase the practitioner should speak as clearly and as simply as possible, especially when the client's native language is not English. The considerate worker will watch the client carefully to try to determine whether the client understands and will pause periodically to ask the client if she or he needs further clarification or has questions. Communication is both spoken and unspoken, and the worker must attend to the client's bodily cues as well as verbalizations. However, body language is not universal among different cultures, so all observations must be considered tentative at the beginning.

Trying to learn and communicate in a foreign language can be very frustrating and embarrassing. I still remember my own struggles to speak French in France and Portuguese in Brazil; learning a new language takes constant concentration and energy, and it does not help when the natives speak in loud voices! Practitioners need to think about the difficult process of learning another language and acknowledge with praise the efforts of clients for whom English is a challenging second language.

Practitioners must not assume that the clients' different views about the seriousness of the child's difficulty and its management indicate a lack of concern about the child. Different cultures may not share mainstream views about behaviors that are considered "problematic," and their differing views bring complexity to multicultural work.

Using Translators   When the client and worker speak different languages, a translator can provide essential help in communication, although using a translator may retard and even interfere with the development of a relationship between the parent and the counselor. Using children to translate for their parents should be avoided at all costs, because this situation creates role reversal and puts a child in a position of power over her or his parents. *The New York Times* (Hedges, 2000) discussed the inappropriate stresses created for a twelve-year-old girl who served as translator for her immigrant parents who did not speak English. Ideally, schools should have professional staff available to translate the languages spoken by their pupils. When translators are not available, the parent can be invited to bring a trusted bilingual relative or friend to the meeting. Again, this request places demands of time on family or friends, which may be unrealistic or impossible to fulfill. In addition, family members or friends may not be objective about the situation and might even emphasize certain points in the translation because of their own knowledge or opinions about the problem situation.

The concept of confidentiality must be explained to all clients, and it may be totally unfamiliar to clients from some cultures. Many families feel shamed by the fact that one of their children is having a problem that has been identified by strangers in the mainstream culture (Canino & Spurlock, 1994; see also Crawford-Brown & Rattray, chapter 5 of this text). Furthermore, revealing personal difficulties to persons outside the family network may be a taboo (see Wu, chapter 10, and Shibusawa, chapter 12, of this text). A survey about the help-seeking behavior of nearly five hundred culturally diverse parents reported that parents were concerned that their problems would not be held confidential by professionals. They also were concerned that "professionals would be unable to understand the reality of their lives [and] their beliefs and values about family life; [furthermore, they feared] that the values of the dominant culture would be imposed upon them" (Keller & McDade, 1997, p. 76).

Parents must be reassured that conferences with school personnel are confidential and that the content and recommendations of the meetings will be shared only with people who are in a position to help their child, such as the teacher, principal, and guidance staff. Although the child's record will be available to school personnel for years to come, parents need to know that these people will not talk about their family and child to nonprofessional people *outside* the school.

The principle of confidentiality applies to the translator as well. Because the parents may fear exposure of the problem within their cultural community, the counselor should pay particular attention to be certain that the translator explains and promises the parents that she or he will respect their confidentiality.

Inclusion of Members of Client's Support Network Whether or not the practitioner invites the client to bring someone to the session, many culturally diverse clients will bring a trusted family member or friend. Paniagua (1998) advises the therapist to expect the client to bring both biological and nonbiological members of the extended family. Hispanic clients may include the *compadre* (godfather) and the *comadre* (godmother), whereas African Americans who are involved in the church may want to bring a church member or the minister.

When multiple family members attend together, the practitioner is given a wonderful opportunity to see firsthand some of the significant people in the child's family and cultural network. The practitioner may also be able to see which family members hold authority positions in the family. In a Native American family, for example, the grandmother may be the primary caretaker of the children and probably would accompany a child's mother to a school conference, as also might one of the elders in the tribe. This action reflects the cultural view of a child's problem as something that affects the entire family and community (Weaver, 1999; see also Glover, chapter 9 of this text). By contrast, a parent who comes alone may be indicating that she or he is assuming sole and full responsibility for handling the child's difficulties. Certainly the practitioner would want to find out about the extent of available support in any family. However, if a parent is ashamed about the child's problems, she or he may be reluctant to share this information with relatives and friends. This reluctance might be found in some white families (see Hess & Hess, chapter 13 of this text). Depending on the specific situation, it might be appropriate and helpful for the practitioner to indicate that the child is by no means the *only one* experiencing similar difficulties and that the school knows appropriate ways to help such children.

When the Practitioner Is from the Same or Different Ethnic Group

The issue of similarity or difference in the ethnicity of the client and practitioner has been studied by different researchers (Paniagua, 1998; S. Sue, 1988; S. Sue, Fujino, Hu, Takeuchi, & Zane, 1991) and the findings are mixed. Clearly, this issue is complicated by other factors such as education, class, and level of biculturalism.

Sometimes the awareness of cultural difference can lead to distancing behavior by either the practitioner or the client, who feels uncomfortable or anxious about the other person's ethnicity (Pinderhughes, 1989). Gil (1999) points out that even within the same culture (e.g., Hispanic/Ecuadorian), distancing can occur based on skin color, which may connote class. Practitioners must remind themselves that the same language is no guarantee of similar background in education, opportunity, or values and beliefs. Practitioners who think they understand a client based solely on ethnic similarity may, in fact, have blind spots because they miss the uniqueness of the individual's particular experience (Pinderhughes, 1989). An argument could even be made that practitioners who share the same ethnicity with the client must pay *even greater* attention to avoid assumptions of similarity regarding the client's values and their own.

When the practitioner and client are from different cultural backgrounds, the practitioner must address the issue of difference in the first session and ask if the clients would prefer to speak with someone from their own ethnic group. Canino and Spurlock (1994) point out that "prejudice and stereotyping can be bi-directional" (p. 130). If language difference is a factor, the clients' wish to work with a practitioner who speaks the same language is understandable. In many instances, however, it is not possible to match potential clients with a practitioner from the same cultural group, which makes it even more critical to address the clients' feelings regarding differences between themselves and the practitioner. For example, the practitioner might state that she or he has some or only limited knowledge about the clients' culture and that she or he hopes that the clients will be willing to answer questions and explain relevant matters to the practitioner as the counseling proceeds. Approaching the parents as collaborators rather than as clients may be an effective way to engage Asian parents, for example, who tend to feel excessive shame related to their child's problem and do not comfortably assume the role of "client" (see Wu, chapter 10, and Shibusawa, chapter 12, of this text).

Some researchers have found that racial matching between client and practitioner led to more positive treatment outcomes for Mexican Americans but not for Asian Americans, African Americans, or whites (S. Sue et al., 1991). *For most of these clients, the practitioner's personal qualities of sensitivity and competence were more important than was similarity of ethnicity and race.* This finding highlights the importance for all practitioners to develop their own qualities of cultural sensitivity and competence through ongoing self-scrutiny and openness to learning about and appreciating the validity of other cultural practices.

Communicating About the Child's Problem   During the first session, after the initial formalities have been observed and after a degree of comfort has been achieved, the purpose of the meeting must be addressed. Almost all parents feel uncomfortable when others make critical statements about their children. When these statements come from a professional who is concerned about the child's behavior or performance in school, many parents will feel devastated. Therefore, the skillful practitioner finds ways to present her or his concerns so that the parents can absorb the information gradually.

Although the child's problems led to the meeting, it is not wise to overwhelm the parents with a description of the child's disturbing behavior. Instead, the practitioner can move toward this discussion by inviting the parents to talk about the child's strong points and areas in which the parents may feel some concern. This approach of letting the parents begin permits the practitioner to make a tentative assessment about whether the child exhibits the same disturbing behaviors at home and also about the parents' overall level of concern regarding the child.

Sometimes parents who are very anxious will prefer to have the practitioner speak first about the child's difficulties. In these situations, the counselor should state that the school has noticed some behaviors or reactions that are of concern and that the purpose of the meeting is to see if the parents can help the school understand the child better in order to help more effectively.

Data Collection   Many practitioners are trained to use the first session with parents as an opportunity to collect data about the child and the family, obtain a history of the problem, and survey the parents' views about the reason for the child's difficulty. Sometimes this process includes the construction of a genogram and the signing of releases to request information from other persons who are knowledgeable about the problem. This process needs to be modified in work with culturally diverse families.

Paniagua (1998) suggests that extensive data collection is not appropriate for multicultural families; he recommends, instead, that the process of obtaining information be extended gradually across several sessions. Williams-Gray (chapter 3 of this text) points out that some African American families are composed of different fathers, and the mothers may utilize patterns of child care that involve both the extended family members and close friends (fictive kin). The family structure and the network of helpers may be complicated and difficult to describe. Therefore, a modification in the usual process of data collection and assessment tools should be considered. Modified approaches might include the construction of an extended family tree or a diagram of "Circles of Kin" that would include all people who provide support to the family. However, Asians might be very uncomfortable about questions regarding various extended family members. Practitioners must respect the limits of disclosure that are culturally acceptable rather than expect all clients to reveal their personal family histories to a stranger.

In the first session with a minority client, the practitioner is probably on more secure ground to focus on forming the relationship and establishing some understanding about the problem. Information about relevant family and kin and the support network will come up naturally during the discussion of the child's situation.

The role of the practitioner implicitly creates a power differential between the parent and the worker, which creates some discomfort, because judgment is implicit in assessing the problem and making recommendations about how to improve the situation. It is possible, however, for a culturally sensitive practitioner to complete an assessment in a manner that respects and even empowers the parents. The use of a strengths perspective emphasizes a family's strengths, protective factors, and sources of resiliency. The practitioner who starts with the assumption that there are strengths in the child-rearing practices of *any* culture will immediately counter any tendency to consider unfamiliar child-rearing patterns as deficits. When the worker can identify the family's sources of strength and can work to augment them, the clients will feel respected by the worker and intervention is more likely to be successful (Davies, 2000).

Contracting and Planning Future Contacts   Many culturally diverse parents look upon professionals as "experts" and expect to be directed to follow certain procedures to relieve the problem. They do not anticipate being involved in a counseling process that extends over several weeks or months. It is therefore essential for the practitioner to orient the parent about the expectations for ongoing contact. Because the culturally diverse clients will have a desire to deal with the problem in as timely a manner as possible, the practitioner should present a plan that is behaviorally oriented and directive and that emphasizes outcome objectives. Paniagua (1998, citing Sue and Sue, 1990) states that

> in general, African Americans, American Indians, Hispanics, and Asians prefer a therapy process that encompasses a directive approach (what is the problem and what to do to solve the problem), an active approach, and a structured approach (the therapist's recommendations). (p. 17)

Canino and Spurlock (1994) agree that short-term therapy focused on the presenting problem and the immediate future is the appropriate modality for many culturally diverse clients. They recommend that the counselor assume an active and supportive stance that emphasizes measurable goals. If the worker avoids associating the problem with pathological overtones and instead reframes the difficulty as an obstacle or a challenge that can be overcome, the parents may agree to collaborate with the counselor on finding a solution. This collaborative approach emphasizes the clients' strengths and thereby empowers the family to work together on behalf of the child.

A successful engagement process between the practitioner and the family that follows this low-key but structured approach leads naturally to an agreement about how to proceed. After summarizing the problem situation as viewed by the school and the family, the worker attempts to find areas of agreement. Through partializing and prioritizing, the counselor can engage the parents in deciding how best to proceed, giving the family the opportunity to state their suggestions first. Depending on the age of the child and the nature of the problem, the next step might be to have a conjoint meeting in order to help the child realize that the family, the school, and others are concerned and want to work together to help him or her.

Many cultures do not share the mainstream European white notion of the child as an independent and autonomous individual, and therefore the inclusion of the child may be considered unwarranted and even inappropriate by some families. Some clients may not initially agree with the counselor's views about the importance of the child's participation and taking ownership and responsibility for changing her or his behavior. If the practitioner has engaged the parents with a mutual and collaborative problem-solving approach, however, most families will feel respected and more likely to consider the practitioner's recommendations for involving the child in the behavior plan. The culturally responsive practitioner tries to help families create treatment plans that conform to their values and therefore are culturally friendly and more likely to succeed.

In this section I have emphasized the importance of the first session because of the many potential pitfalls in establishing relationships when the worker and clients are from different cultures. Subsequent sessions with the child and families should follow the same guidelines I have recommended for the first session, that is, allow the family to set the pace and recognize progress toward their goals.

DIFFERENT WORLDVIEWS AND HELP-SEEKING PATTERNS

The concept of worldview refers to "how a person perceives his/her relationship to the world (nature, institutions, other people)" (D. Sue & Sue, 1990, p. 137) and to "the collective thought process of a people or cultural group" (Cross, 1995, p. 143). There is a danger of oversimpifying and overgeneralizing when discussing worldviews, but it is important for practitioners to recognize that mainstream European white cultural beliefs are very different from those of many other cultures. Cross distinguishes between the *linear worldviews* of mainstream Americans and the *relational worldview* that is typical of American Indians and many other cultures.

The Linear View

Proponents of the linear worldview believe that problems are based in the individual and that if practitioners understand all the multiple factors that contribute to the problem, they will know how to help. This view depends on cause-and-effect thinking, which leads to specific helping interventions. People and their symptoms become the objects of treatment, and success is measured by changes in individual symptoms (Cross, 1995).

The Relational View

Subscribers to the relational worldview emphasize helping the individual restore balance and harmony among the various cognitive, emotional, physical, and spiritual components of the person's life. The emphasis is on balance and harmony between the four forces of mind, body, spirit, and context (environment). It includes the person's thoughts, memories, and emotions as well as physical conditions and spiritual teachings. The person who stays in balance is considered healthy.

Differing Patterns of Seeking Help

An individual who is experiencing stress and difficulty in life will rely on her or his culture's worldview to determine the nature of help that will be sought. Glover (chapter 9 of this text) describes the use of sweat lodges as an acceptable method for the treatment of alcoholism in a Native American adolescent. This method (according to native beliefs) helps adolescents restore their sense of balance and harmony through engaging their physical, emotional, spiritual, and cognitive faculties in the experience of sweating with others who understand and encourage them. Alcoholics Anonymous utilizes some of the same treatment elements (group support, spirituality, teaching, and emotional expression). However, AA's requirement that the alcoholic state her or his name at the beginning of every meeting and self-identify as an alcoholic emphasizes the illness as an intrinsic part of the person's identity.

Furthermore, the linear model tends to split a person, because physical problems are dealt with by physicians, emotional problems by mental health practitioners, educational difficulties by education specialists, and spiritual problems by the clergy. In contrast, natural healers who use the relational model combine intellectual, physical, and spiritual methods in their treatment.

Practitioners must realize that many multicultural families seek or accept help from social agencies and institutions *only as a last resort*. McAdoo (1997) states that African Americans often mistrust help from institutions other than churches, and Siegel (1994) maintains that this group uses social services only when all else fails. Overall, most African Americans have indicated that they would seek help through print and video materials (94 percent) or through family members (88 percent), according to Keller & McDade's (1997) survey of help seeking.

Several authors in this book (McAdoo, chapter 4; Shibusawa, chapter 12; Wu, chapter 10; Zayas, Canino, & Suárez, chapter 6) confirm the preference among different cultures to seek help from family, friends, or religious leaders rather than from mental health or social service practitioners. Furthermore, the use of indigenous healers is prevalent among many cultures, and sometimes practitioners openly recognize and sanction their clients' reliance on special healing methods that fall outside the range of typical counseling practice. These methods might include, for example, the use of herbal teas, meditation, and tribal dances and ceremonies. Canino and Spurlock (1994) state that "clinicians . . . must be aware of both the strengths and the limitations of indigenous assessment and treatment approaches and must be willing to respect and integrate these cultural beliefs into their theoretical framework" (p. 136). Clearly the centrality of spirituality in the lives of many clients needs to be viewed and appreciated as a potential source of comfort and strength.

Because parents in many diverse cultures rely on their families to provide emotional and physical support, the culturally responsive practitioner should include extended kin whenever the parents indicate a desire to do so. The child's difficulties may be viewed more from a family rather than an individual perspective by some culturally diverse parents, so it is logical to enlist the family system in working together for the child's benefit.

In conclusion, I believe that when practitioners use creativity and commitment in their work with multicultural clients, there are rewards for both the clients and the counselors. Potential obstacles can be recast into challenges that will help practitioners increase their understanding of themselves and their own culture in addition to the various cultures of the diverse children and families with which they work. "The lifelong task of becoming a competent, multicultural counselor is filled with profoundly fulfilling opportunities, such as clarifying one's own values, confronting one's fears and biases regarding the culturally different, developing new counseling skills, and experiencing the beauty of other cultures. Counselors who view multiculturalism in this manner are likely to embrace the experience as one of personal and professional enrichment" (Kiselica, Changizi, Cureton, & Gridley, 1995, p. 530, quoting Kiselica, 1991).

References

Boyd-Franklin, N. (1989). *Black families in therapy. A multisystems approach*. New York: Guilford Press.

Boyd-Franklin, N., & Bry, B. H. (2000). *Reaching out in family therapy: Home-based, school, and community interventions*. New York: Guilford Press.

Canino, I. A., & Spurlock, J. (1994). *Culturally diverse children and adolescents: Assessment, diagnosis, and treatment*. New York: Guilford Press.

Caple, F., Salcido, R. M., & diCecco, J. (1995). Engaging effectively with culturally diverse families and children. *Social Work in Education, 17*(3), 159–70.

Congress, E. P. (Ed.). (1997). *Multicultural perspectives in working with families*. New York: Springer.

Cross, T. L. (1995). The worldview of American Indian families. In H. I. McCubbin, E. A. Thompson, A. I. Thompson, & J. E. Fromer (Eds.), *Ethnic minority families: Native and immigrant American families* (Vol. 1, pp. 143–58). Boston: Sage.

Davies, D. (2000). *Child development: A practitioner's guide*. New York: Guilford Press.

Devore, W., & Schlesinger, E. G. (1996). *Ethnic-sensitive social work practice*. New York: Allyn & Bacon.

Gibbs, J. T., & Huang, L. N. (Eds.). (1989/1998). *Children of color: Psychological interventions with minority youth*. San Francisco: Jossey-Bass.

Gil, E. (1999, October). *Culturally sensitive play therapy*. Paper presented at the annual meeting of the Association of Play Therapy, Baltimore, MD.

Green, J. W. (1999). *Cultural awareness in the human services: A multi-ethnic approach*. Boston: Allyn & Bacon.

Hedges, C. (2000, June 19). Translating America for parents and family: Children of immigrants assume difficult roles. *The New York Times*, B1.

Ho, M. K. (1987). *Family therapy with ethnic minorities*. Newbury Park, CA: Sage.

Ho, M. K. (1992). *Minority children and adolescents in therapy*. Newbury Park, CA: Sage.

Keller, J. D., & McDade, K. (1997). Cultural diversity and help-seeking behavior: Sources of help and obstacles to support for parents. *Journal of Multicultural Social Work, 5*(1/2), 63–78.

Kiselica, M. S., Changizi, J. C., Cureton, V. L. L., & Gridley, B. E. (1995). Counseling children and adolescents in schools: Salient multicultural issues. In J. C. Ponterotto, J. M.

Casas, L. A. Suzuki, & C. M. Alexander (Eds.), *Handbook of multicultural counseling* (pp. 516–32). Thousand Oaks, CA: Sage.

Lee, W. M. (1999). *An introduction to multicultural counseling*. Philadelphia, PA: Accelerated Development.

Lum, D. (1996). *Social work practice and people of color: A process-stage approach* (3rd ed.). Pacific Grove, CA: Brooks/Cole.

Lum, D. (1999). *Culturally competent practice: A framework for growth and action*. Pacific Grove, CA: Brooks Cole.

Lynch, E., & Hanson, M. (Eds.). (1998). *Developing cross-cultural competence: A guide for working with children and their families* (2nd ed., pp. 93–120). Baltimore: Brooks.

McAdoo, H. (1997). *Black families* (3rd ed.). Thousand Oaks, CA: Sage.

McGoldrick, M. (Ed.). (1996). *Ethnicity and family therapy*. New York: Guilford Press.

McGoldrick, M., Pearce, J. K., & Giordano, J. (Eds.). (1982). *Ethnicity and family therapy*. New York: Guilford Press.

McIntosh, P. (1998). White privilege: Unpacking the invisible knapsack. In M. McGoldrick (Ed.), *Revisioning family therapy: Race, culture, and gender in clinical practice* (pp. 147–75). New York: Guilford Press.

Paniagua, F. A. (1998). *Assessing and treating culturally diverse clients: A practical guide* (2nd ed.). Thousand Oaks, CA: Sage.

Pinderhughes, E. (1989). *Understanding race, ethnicity, and power*. New York: Free Press.

Pinderhughes, E. (1995). Empowering diverse populations: Family practice in the twenty-first century. *Families in Society, 76,* 131–40.

Ponterotto, J. C., Casas, J. M., Suzuki, L. A., & Alexander, C. M. (Eds.). (1995). *Handbook of multicultural counseling*. Thousand Oaks, CA: Sage.

Schriver, J. M. (2001). *Human behavior and the social environment: Shifting paradigms in essential knowledge for social work practice* (3rd ed.). Boston: Allyn & Bacon.

Siegel, L. (1994). Cultural differences and their impact on practice in child welfare. *Journal of Multicultural Social Work, 3*(3), 87–95.

Sue, D., & Sue, D. (1990). *Counseling the culturally different*. New York: John Wiley.

Sue, S. (1988). Psychotherapeutic services to ethnic minorities: Two decades of research findings. *American Psychologist, 43,* 301–8.

Sue, S., Fujino, D. C., Hu, L., Takeuchi, D. J., & Zane, N. W. S. (1991). Community mental health services for ethnic minority groups: A test of cultural responsiveness hypothesis. *Journal of Consulting and Clinical Psychology, 59*(4), 533–40.

Tsui, P., & Schultz, G. L. (1985). Failure of rapport: Why psychotherapeutic engagement fails in the treatment of Asian clients. *American Journal of Psychotherapy, 55,* 561–69.

Vargas, L. A., & Koss-Chioino, J. D. (Eds.). (1992). *Working with culture: Psychotherapeutic interventions with ethnic minority children and adolescents*. San Francisco: Jossey-Bass.

Weaver, H. N. (1999). Indigenous people and the social work profession. *Social Work, 44*(3), 217–25.

Webb, N. B. (1996). *Social work practice with children*. New York: Guilford Press.

CHAPTER 15

Educating Students and Practitioners for Culturally Responsive Practice

NANCY BOYD WEBB

People who enter the helping professions usually do so because of their desire to understand and help other people. Most think that they are compassionate, open, empathic, and willing to interact with people of all ages and from various backgrounds. Few practitioners are aware, or would admit, that they might have difficulty or blind spots in engaging with persons of different races, ethnicities, or cultures. Furthermore, any such admission might give the impression that they are prejudiced or biased, which in turn might suggest that they are unsuited for their chosen career. Most human service trainees and professionals have very high personal standards for themselves, deplore discrimination, and may be totally oblivious regarding any personal attitudes about other people that could interfere with their effectiveness in carrying out their helping role. Although the majority of practitioners are white, the concept of white privilege may be unknown to them. Students and practitioners of color also have views about persons of different cultural backgrounds that can help or hinder them in their counseling. Cultural attitudes and beliefs are like the air that people breathe; they don't pay attention until something goes wrong, such as air pollution or when a client fails to return for a second interview.

This chapter focuses on educating students and counselors to practice in a culturally responsive way. Three areas are emphasized: (1) the development of self-awareness; (2) the acquisition of a body of knowledge that enhances culturally diverse counseling, including recognition of the social and historical contexts of racism and discrimination; and (3) the teaching and learning of skills necessary for culturally competent practice. Practitioners working with culturally diverse children and families will be expected to become knowledgeable about culturally specific child-rearing practices. As I emphasize in this chapter, however, the expectations for self-awareness and skills for culturally competent practice are as applicable and necessary in work with other clients as they are with children and families.

CULTURALLY COMPETENT AND RESPONSIVE PRACTICE

Since the 1970s the helping professions have tried to update their educational programs to meet the needs of the increasingly diverse population in this country. Consequently, the terms *culturally sensitive, culturally responsive,* and *culturally competent* have been used almost interchangeably to describe the ideals of practice with multicultural clients.

Definitions

According to Vargas and Koss-Chioino (1992), the terms *culturally sensitive* and *culturally responsive* are somewhat synonymous; however, they prefer the more active stance conveyed by the expression *culturally responsive.* Lum (1999) uses the term *cultural competency* and defines it as "the set of knowledge and skills that [the practitioner] must develop in order to be effective with multicultural clients. The culturally competent person has the task of bringing together elements from his or her culture of origin and the dominant culture to accomplish bicultural integration and competency . . . *cultural competency involves the areas of cultural awareness, knowledge acquisition, skill development, and continuous inductive learning*" (p. 3, my emphasis). Lum's book specifies desired competencies at both the generalist and advanced levels related to cultural awareness, knowledge acquisition, skill development and inductive learning. It contains a number of self-assessment inventories to allow the student (or practitioner) to assess his or her own cultural competency at two points in time (first, before any instruction on this topic, and later, as a posttest at the completion of the course or training). I recommend Lum's book for detailed information on the various components considered essential for competent practice as well as for use of the self-assessment inventories.

Curriculum Policies of Various Professional Programs Regarding Multicultural Content

The major demographic changes in the racial, ethnic and cultural composition of the United States, as was cited in the first chapter, have influenced many instructors in the helping professions to revise their curricula to ensure that it includes content that will be useful to practitioners working with culturally diverse clients.

Social Work In more than twenty years as a social work educator, I have witnessed a growing recognition of the need to incorporate content about diversity into the curriculum for educating social workers at both the baccalaureate and master's degree levels. During the 1990s, this emphasis increased.

Since 1994 the Council on Social Work Education (CSWE) Commission on Accreditation (1994, M6.8) has required the inclusion of content related to women and *people of color*, and also content regarding populations-at-risk, such as groups distinguished by *age, ethnicity, culture*, class, religion, and physical or mental ability. The inclusion of this content clearly indicates a focus on culturally diverse children, on ethnic minorities of color, on cultural differences, and on the special needs of young people.

Psychology The American Psychological Association (APA) developed guidelines for providers of psychological service to ethnic, linguistic, and culturally diverse populations in 1991, and in the following year the APA, in their code of ethics called for appropriate training (APA, 1992).

Marriage and Family Therapy and Other Counselors The American Association of the Marriage and Family Therapy (AAMFT) Committee on Accreditation requires all marriage and family therapy programs to offer multicultural studies, although the particular content is not specified. By contrast, there is no general requirement that school or counseling psychology students receive training in multicultural counseling before becoming licensed or certified (Lee, 1999). Nonetheless, 90 percent of counselor education programs do include specific coursework on multicultural counseling (Das, 1995).

DIVERSITY MODELS FOR PROFESSIONAL EDUCATION

Once there has been agreement about the necessity for including certain content in the curriculum, decisions have to be made about where and how to insert it. There are at least three basic alternatives, and studies have shown no conclusive research to support the choice of one design over another (Le-Doux & Montalvo, 1999). The three options are:

- A separate course on cultural diversity
- The infusion of content on cultural diversity into *all* courses
- A combination of the first two options, or other methods

A Separate Course on Cultural Diversity

Different instructors use different approaches to teaching a cultural diversity course. Some instructors emphasize content on racism, white privilege, and social justice (Hyde, 2000), while others (Preli & Bernard, 1993) focus on increasing the white majority students' awareness regarding their own ethnic heritage as a way to help them develop appreciation of how their own cultural background impacts on their current lives. The hope is that the students' increased understanding about the diversity within white cultures will lead to a greater recognition of the diversity of *other* groups. Through in-class sharing of experiences, the white majority students become aware of the tremendous intragroup differences within their majority culture, which they can then apply and transfer to their understanding about the diversity of minority clients. Lee (1999) points out that focus on within-group differences can help counter the stereotyping that sometimes occurs when a single group is discussed as if it were homogeneous and when "diversity within diversity" is not recognized.

Many courses on cultural diversity employ a strong emphasis on experiential learning. This learning may include the use of games, small group discussions, role plays, and other methods intended to raise students' consciousness about racism and white privilege (Singelis, 1998). Students sometimes become quite anxious and uncomfortable in these courses because of the emotional hot-button topics and because of their perception that they will be exposed as prejudiced and then be expected to adopt a culturally neutral or totally open attitude. Hyde (2000) recognizes this anxiety and states that "multiculturalism is not a 'safe' topic in contemporary America where discussions of race . . . are often fraught with anxiety and misunderstandings. . . . *We need to help our students understand that multicultural learning and practice are not easy endeavors*" (Introduction, my emphasis).

The Infusion Model

Another approach to including the required content on diversity into the curriculum involves infusing this content vertically and horizontally throughout all courses (Hyde, 2000; Le-Doux & Montalvo, 1999). Hyde states that "multiculturalism isn't just a fad or a 'special topic' to be addressed once or twice in a course and then forgotten. *It needs to be woven into the very fabric of social work theory, education and practice*" (Introduction, my emphasis). This statement could also apply to other counseling professionals. The expectations obviously exact great demands for teaching and learning that include the anticipation for ongoing personal growth in addition to content learning and skill development (Lee, 1999; Lum, 1999).

Combined Approaches

The combined approach uses different methods of teaching students about cultural diversity. One possibility involves the use of both a designated course and the infusion model, which requires some content about diversity in *all* courses. This approach is considered most likely to produce competent practitioners (Haynes & Singh, 1992).

Other methods for multicultural training include professional workshops and study groups as well as actual experience counseling diverse clients. The use of the fieldwork training component for this purpose is discussed separately in a later section on the field practicum.

A systematic study of the success of the various models currently used to comply with the CSWE diversity mandate is needed in order to inform the profession regarding the advantages and disadvantages of the different approaches. Currently, different schools use methods according to faculty preferences regarding curriculum.

Culturally Responsive Course Content

Lum (1999) and Lee (1999) each have tackled the question of what body of knowledge and theory is especially relevant and essential in educating students to become culturally competent practitioners. Both these authors acknowledge the earlier work on this topic by the Association for Multicultural Counseling and Development, which prepared a position paper in 1992 recommending thirty-one multicultural competencies for its accreditation criteria (Sue, Arredondo, & McDavis, 1992). Lum (1999) presents his recommendations specifically for social work education, whereas Lee (1999) focuses on counselor education programs. Both authors divide the competencies into sections related to (1) cultural awareness, (2) knowledge acquisition, and (3) skill development, with Lum adding a fourth dimension, that of inductive learning: "the life-long process of continuous discovery about the changing nature of multicultural individual, family, and community dynamics" (p. 146).

With regard to the acquisition of knowledge, Lum (1999) identifies the following six specific competencies *at the generalist level*:

- Understanding of terms related to culturally diverse work
- Knowledge about demographic profiles of culturally diverse populations
- A critical thinking perspective on cultural diversity
- Understanding of the history of oppression of multicultural groups
- Knowledge about the strengths of people of color
- Knowledge about culturally diverse values

Three additional competencies *at the advanced level* include:

- Application of systems and psychosocial theory to multicultural practice
- Knowledge of theories on ethnicity, culture, minority identity, and social class
- Drawing on a range of social science theory

Each of these competencies is discussed more fully in Lum's text (pp. 35–37).

The training curriculum proposed by Lee (1999, pp. 194–95) lists some knowledge components for a model training curriculum that also merit consideration, including the following:

- Cultural and racial bias in testing
- Cultural identity development models
- Acculturation issues
- Cultural variations in family makeup, developmental patterns, client expectations, and views of health and illness

- Second language fluency
- Indigenous healing practices
- Immigration regulations
- Laws regarding harassment, hate crimes, and housing or employment discrimination

Clearly there is a large body of knowledge for practitioners to master, which must be combined with continuous focus on the development of the student's cultural awareness and skills for multicultural practice. Some educators are concerned that if they pack more content into the already full curriculum, they will be sacrificing breadth for depth. However, Huang and Gibbs (1998) maintain that "if ethnic content is distributed across all or most courses, students will accept it as valued, relevant academic material rather than viewing it as a token session on minority mental health or a perfunctory lesson on social awareness" (p. 379). The challenge of how to best educate students for culturally competent practice requires clear thinking and the ability to transform these worthy goals into a manageable, practical format. It is a work in progress that deserves educators' best efforts.

Development of Skills Through the Field Practicum

Lee (1999) states that "the greatest challenge in multicultural counselor training is in the area of *skills*" (p. 193, my emphasis). Because the field work component is an integral part of social work education and because this component involves direct practice, the practicum offers the ideal setting for supervisors to teach students how to work with culturally diverse clients. Family counseling trainees often participate in laboratory training to enable them to practice skills through role playing, the use of videotape feedback, and constructive responses from the supervisor and other trainees (Preli & Bernard, 1993).

A supervisor, however, cannot teach what he or she does not know, and many supervisors completed their master's level training prior to the 1992 CSWE or APA mandates for inclusion of content related to cultural diversity. Therefore, it is quite possible for a well-qualified, experienced supervisor to have received little or no specific course content on the topic of cultural diversity. Sometimes field instructors have obtained this knowledge through workshops, staff training, or other personal experiences. However, many supervisors need training about culturally competent practice in order to prepare them to educate students to work with diverse clients. Again, educators need information about supervisors' actual experiences in trying to guide their students' practice with culturally diverse clients. A survey of supervisors from different programs around the country could give educators some specific information about the challenges implicit in helping students develop competence in multicultural counseling.

Lee (1999) identifies twelve skills for multicultural competence, and Lum (1999) specifies fifteen at the generalist level and an additional eight at the advanced level. Supervisors may or may not be knowledgeable about these skills. Again, the profession needs to confirm through empirical research the particular skills that are essential and appropriate for culturally competent practice. Clearly, the practicum could serve as a safe place for students to learn to identify value differences between their clients and themselves. The supervisor can help students explore these value differences in a sensitive and helpful way. The field practicum is a wonderful opportunity for training culturally competent practitioners, but educators must help supervisors use this opportunity effectively.

EDUCATING PRACTITIONERS FOR CULTURALLY DIVERSE PRACTICE

The topic of *practitioner* education about cultural diversity has received some attention in the literature (Beckett & Dungee-Anderson, 1996; R. J. Green, 1998; Huang & Gibbs, 1998; Miranda & Kitano, 1986; Stevenson, Cheung, & Leung, 1992), but not nearly enough in comparison with the importance of the subject. Because practitioners trained prior to 1991 probably have not received course content related to cultural diversity, it is essential for staff training and programs of continuing education to provide information and skills training related to this topic.

Stevenson et al. (1992) outline a model for training child protective workers for ethnically sensitive practice that uses cases to avoid reinforcing ethnic stereotypes. This approach trains workers to use an ongoing self-evaluation approach to monitor their own practice. It incorporates three training and evaluation components—attitudes, knowledge, and skills, with a strong emphasis on attitudes. Because so many child protective services workers' clients are nonvoluntary and are culturally diverse, they are particularly vulnerable to being misunderstood and regarded in a negative way by the majority culture. This potential for misunderstanding argues strongly for ongoing staff training focused on helping practitioners learn to help their clients counteract these negative influences and identify their areas of strength.

Beckett and Dungee-Anderson (1996, p. 37) present an eight-step process model to help social workers become more effective multicultural practitioners:

- Acknowledge cultural differences
- Know yourself
- Know other cultures
- Identify and value differences
- Identify and avoid stereotypes
- Empathize with persons from other cultures
- Adapt rather than adopt
- Acquire recovery skills

Training exercises accompany these steps, with the guiding philosophy that it is the social worker's responsibility to "meet the client where the client is," rather than to expect the client to adapt to the practitioner.

Other approaches to staff training include national conferences and certificate programs in multicultural family therapy. The National Multicultural Institute sponsored a four-day conference in 1999 on the topic of "building personal and professional competence in a multicultural society." The goals of the conference—

targeted for professionals in the fields of human resources, mental health, and social services—included in-depth training and skill building in multiculturalism through focus on some of the issues that professionals face in working with culturally diverse populations. A different training approach, offered at Fordham University, featured Monica McGoldrick and other faculty, who gave two four-day summer seminars in 2000 to train practitioners in multicultural family therapy. Many professions require continuing education credits to maintain licensing. These requirements offer an opportunity for schools of social work and other educational disciplines to address the educational gap and fulfill the need for more practitioners who are trained to be culturally competent.

Resources

A number of useful references provide very helpful guidance for curricula enhancement and content related to educating students and practitioners about cultural diversity. I have listed these references here, along with brief annotations:

Council on Social Work Education. (1997). Human diversity content in social work education. A collection of course outlines with content on racial, ethnic, and cultural diversity. Alexandria, VA: Author.

> This reference includes twelve peer-reviewed course outlines from three undergraduate and nine graduate courses. The 129 pages provides specialized bibliographies, definitions of terms, assignments, and detailed outlines of topics and specific readings. In addition to syllabi on Human Behavior and the Social Environment, other outlines include special populations, such as the aged, African American families, American Indian families, and women.

Council on Social Work Education. (2000). Teaching racial, ethnic, and cultural diversity in social work: A collection of model course outlines. Alexandria, VA: Author.

> This reference contains thirteen outlines to assist instructors in incorporating content on human diversity in social work courses. The 148 pages include innovative assignments and extensive reading lists.

Hyde, C. (2000). Teaching multicultural content: Challenges and solutions. Baltimore: University of Maryland.

> This handbook, prepared for a Faculty Development Institute at the 2000 annual meeting of the Council on Social Work Education, contains a veritable wealth of teaching materials that were developed for courses that specifically focus on multicultural content as well as for more general courses such as Human Behavior and the Social Environment. The materials have been used in both bachelor's and master's courses. It is divided into four sections: Introduction, Handouts, In-Class Exercises, and Assignments.

Green, J. W. (1999). Cultural awareness in the human services: A multi-ethnic approach (3rd ed.). Boston: Allyn & Bacon.

> As a cultural anthropologist who has applied ethnographic interviewing principles to social work practice, Green has set forth a model for enhancing cultural awareness that is very useful to mental health practitioners. A special feature of his book includes thought-provoking ideas, exercises, and questions at the end of every chapter.

Lum, D. (1999). Culturally competent practice: A framework for growth and action. Pacific Grove, CA: Brooks/Cole.

> Lum's self-assessment inventories represent a major contribution to the profession. Although many practitioners may profess allegiance to the values of culturally sensitive

practice, Lum gives them a way to assess themselves. These self-assessment inventories provide a necessary tool for the development of competent practitioners.

Singelis, T. (1998). Teaching about culture, ethnicity, and diversity: Exercises and planned activities. Thousand Oaks, CA: Sage.

This book—consisting of twenty-eight exercises and planned activities that can be used to teach about culture, ethnicity and diversity—is a useful handbook for instructors and trainers who want new ideas about involving participants on a meaningful level.

This list of resources is not comprehensive, but it can serve as a reference to guide faculty and practitioners. Content tends to be general, but it can be adapted to various groups and levels of expertise.

References

American Psychological Association. (1991). *Guidelines for providers of psychological services to ethnic, linguistic, and culturally diverse populations.* Washington, DC: Author.

American Psychological Association. (1992). *Ethical principles of psychologists and code of conduct.* Washington, DC: Author.

Beckett, J. O., & Dungee-Anderson, D. (1996). A framework for agency-based multicultural training and supervision. *Journal of Multicultural Social Work, 4*(4), 27–48.

Council on Social Work Education. (1997). *Human diversity content in social work education: A collection of course outlines with content on racial, ethnic, and cultural diversity.* Alexandria, VA: Author.

Council on Social Work Education Commission on Accreditation. (1994). *Handbook of accreditation standards and procedures* (4th ed.). Alexandria, VA: Author.

Das, A. K. (1995). Re-thinking multicultural counseling: Implications for counselor education. *Journal of Counseling and Development, 15*, 25–36.

Green, J. W. (1999). *Cultural awareness in the human services: A multi-ethnic approach* (3rd ed.). Boston: Allyn & Bacon.

Green, R. J. (1998). Training programs. Guidelines for multicultural transformations. In M. McGoldrick (Ed.), *Re-visioning family therapy: Race, culture, and gender in clinical practice* (pp. 111–17). New York: Guilford Press.

Haynes, A. W., & Singh, R. H. (1992). Ethnic-sensitive social work practice: An integrated, ecological, and psychodynamic approach. *Journal of Multicultural Social Work, 2*, 43–51.

Huang, L. N., & Gibbs, J. T. (1998). Future directions: Implications for research, training, and practice. In J. T. Gibbs, N. H. Huang, & Associates (Eds.), *Children of color: Psychological interventions with culturally diverse youth* (pp. 356–87). San Francisco: Jossey-Bass.

Hyde, C. (2000). *Teaching multicultural content: Challenges and solutions* [Handbook of materials]. Mimeo. Baltimore: University of Maryland.

Le-Doux, C. L., & Montalvo, F. F. (1999). Multicultural content in social work graduate programs: A national survey. *Journal of Multicultural Social Work, 7*(1–2), 37–55.

Lee, W. M. (1999). *An introduction to multicultural counseling.* Philadelphia, PA: Accelerated Development.

Lum, D. (1999). *Culturally competent practice: A framework for growth and action.* Pacific Grove, CA: Sage.

Miranda, M. R., & Kitano, H. H. L. (Eds.). (1986). *Mental health research and practice in minority communities: Development of culturally sensitive training programs.* Rockville, MD: U.S. Department of Health and Human Services.

Preli, R., & Bernard, J. M. (1993). Making multiculturalism relevant for majority culture graduate students. *Journal of Marital and Family Therapy, 19*(1), 5–16.

Singelis, T. (1998). *Teaching about culture, ethnicity, and diversity: Exercises and planned activities.* Thousand Oaks, CA: Sage.

Stevenson, K. A., Cheung, K. F. M., & Leung, P. (1992). A new approach to training child protective services workers for ethnically sensitive practice. *Child Welfare, 71*(4), 291–305.

Sue, D. W., Arredondo, P., & McDavis, R. J. (1992). Multicultural counseling competencies and standards: A call to the profession. *Journal of Counseling and Development, 70,* 477–86.

Vargas, L. L. A., & Koss-Chioino, J. D. (Eds.). (1992). *Working with culture: Psychotherapeutic interventions with ethnic minority children and adolescents.* San Francisco: Jossey-Bass.